A Garland Series

THE
RENAISSANCE
AND THE
GODS

A Comprehensive Collection of
Renaissance Mythographies, Iconol-
ogies, & Iconographies, with a
Selection of Works from
The Enlightenment

*Fifty-three Titles in Fifty-five Volumes Including
over 2,900 Illustrations, Edited with
Introductions by*
STEPHEN ORGEL
The Johns Hopkins University

LETTERS CONCERNING MYTHOLOGY
London 1748

Thomas Blackwell

Garland Publishing, Inc., New York & London

1976

Library of Congress Cataloging in Publication Data

Blackwell, Thomas, 1701-1759.
  Letters concerning mythology, London, 1748.

  (The Renaissance and the gods ; 42)
  Reprint of the 1748 ed. printed in London.
  1. Mythology. I. Title. II. Series.
BL305.B55   1976   291.1'3   75-27887
ISBN 0-8240-2091-X

Notes

Blackwell, Scottish classical scholar, Professor of Greek and later Principal at Marischal College, Aberdeen, was probably the only writer of his age with a real feeling for the Renaissance mythographic tradition. The *Letters Concerning Mythology* is a remarkable work, genuinely learned, anti-rationalist and anti-simplistic. It was, not surprisingly, generally ignored. Blackwell presents the case for the allegorical, the mysterious and symbolic, with all the resources of 18th-century clarity and good sense; and read in context, he provides a powerful counter-argument to writers like Addison and Spence. Our copy is from the Bodleian, shelfmark 8°.P.194 Linc.

S.O.

LETTERS

CONCERNING

MYTHOLOGY.

O Voi! c'havete gl' Intelletti fani,
Mirate la Dottrina, che s'afconde
Sott'il Velame de gli Verfi ftrani.

DANTE.

LONDON:

Printed in the Year M. DCC. XLVIII.

PREFACE.

AS IT IS *of more Importance that a Book be worth reading, than to know by whom it is writ,* there would have been no Neceſſity of acquainting the *Public,* that *ſome* of the firſt of the following LETTERS *paſſed* in Correſpondence, *if the lamented Death of the worthy Man who wrote them, had not prevented his proſecuting a Plan, which the Reader without ſuch Notice might be juſtly ſurpriz'd to find abruptly relinquiſhed.*

A 2 *The*

The ADDITIONS *to the se-venth and eighth, and all the rest, were written by the Author of the* ENQUIRY into the Life and Writings of HOMER. *They take, it is true, a quite different Road; yet all tend to one and the same End of promoting Learning and Virtue, and do-ing Justice to the first Instructors of* MEN.

Part

PART of a

LETTER

TO

SIR EVERARD FAWKENER.

****BUT is it *possible the Hurry of a Court, and the Duty of* of two *such Places, should leave you a Moment's Leisure to bestow upon Literature*---? *If they do, may this come to your Hands at the lucky Hour, when, disengaged and easy, you can afford to listen to the old Story I am just going to tell you.* 'That FABLE *was the* first ' Form *in which* Religion, Law, *and* ' Philosophy (*united originally*) *ap-* ' *peared in the* World; *that the an-* ' *cient Fables, as we* now *read and un-*

A 3 *derstand*

Part of a LETTER to

' derſtand them, convey no ſuch Know-
' ledge : that conſequently they are not
' underſtood : that therefore learned
' Men have had Recourſe to ſeveral
' ingenious but claſhing Schemes to ex-
' plain them ; while ſome will have all
' the GODS of Antiquity to be deified
' Heroes ; ſome, to be Jewiſh Patriarchs ;
' others, to be the firſt Egyptian Kings ;
' others, to be emblematical Figures,
' like Sign-Poſts, in the ſame Country ;
' and a late well-meaning Writer has
' even diſcovered them to be Types of
' our modern Divinity.'

To decypher then theſe obſcure Remains, and trace this loſt Stream of
ancient Wiſdom to its real Source, is
the Aim of the following LETTERS.
Some of them having been writ to a
young Gentleman of great Parts, but
in a wrong Purſuit of Happineſs, has
ſpread an Air of Pleaſantry thro' the
Whole ; which I am apt to think will
be

Sir EVERARD FAWKENER.

be no Disadvantage. The unnatural Separation of Learning *from* Life, *has done infinite* Harm *to both.* 'Twere *indeed pity a Treatise should be less instructive that it* smile; *or less entertaining that it lay open ancient* Wisdom, *canvass solemn* Rites, *and explore the Recesses of the mysterious* EAST. *Several familiar humorous Terms have escaped in the Revisal of the first six Letters, which tho' very pardonable in* private *Correspondence, will yet require some Grains of Allowance from the* Public: *Nor ought we to lose Sight of the* original Design *of these Letters, which is,* ' To explain the religious ' Opinions of the ANCIENTS, and ' their consequent Practice:' *If that be accomplished, no matter whether these Opinions were* true, *or such as a purer Religion, and improved Science have since shewn us to be without Foundation. The Fable, for Instance, of the Death of* ADONIS, *proceeds upon a*

A 4 *Mistake;*

Part of a LETTER, &c

Miſtake ; that of the Birth of SATURN
upon Truth : And ſo Men of your Can-
dour will judge of the reſt.

FROM ſuch, *the Difficulty of this
Attempt will procure an eaſy Pardon
of Errors ſcarcely to be avoided in
ſo various and abſtruſe a Reſearch :
And both the Difficulty and* Dignity *of
ſuch a Subject as the firſt* RELIGION
and PHILOSOPHY *of the Lords and
Lawgivers of the World, will be my
beſt Apology for making this Work
a Proof of my Diſcernment in Men,
while I publiſh the particular Affection,
and unfeigned Attachment taken to*
SIr EVERARD FAWKENER, *by*

IT's AUTHOR.

THE

CONTENTS.

CONTENTS.

* * * * * * * * * *

CONTENTS.

CONTENTS.

TRAN-

TRANSLATIONS.

Sive

TRANSLATIONS.

Pag. Line

98. 4. *Sive bunc*—Whether of Seed divine he firſt was made
By the ſupreme Creator, Source of Worlds;
Or if the recent *Earth*, ſever'd ſo late
From *Ether*, ſtill retain'd ſome Kindred-Seeds,
Which fly PROMETHEUS moiſt'ning with the Stream,
Fram'd in the Likeneſs of th' all-ruling *Gods*.

110. 19. *Jupiter*—JOVE firſt cut ſhort the Term of ancient SPRING.

140. 11. *Jupiter*—Almighty JOVE, Father and Mother both
Of Gods, and Men, and Things.—

146. 16. *It Ver & Venus*—VENUS and *vernal* Gales go hand in
hand,
And balmy-pinnion'd *Zephyr* tends their Steps,
Sweet Harbinger of *Venus* and the *Spring*.

153. 6. *Bagatelle*—Trifling and Senſuality.

154. 4. *Fœlix qui*—Happy the Man, who vers'd in Nature's Laws,
Can each Effect aſcribe to it's own Cauſe;
Trample on Terrors and relentleſs Fate,
And bear the Din of *Acheron*, ſedate!

Ibid. 23. *Quis enim*—Who e'er unanxious lov'd?—

157. 10. *Virtutem Verba*—Meer *Words* make Virtue, juſt as *Trees*
a Grove.

236. 14. *Quantum Relligio*—What diſmal Deeds RELIGION cou'd
adviſe.

282. 29. *Naturam*—Drive NATURE out, war't with a naked
Sword,
She'll ſtill return.—.

301. 22. *Qui ſui*—Whoſe high Deſerts acquir'd a deathleſs Name.

Mutavit

TRANSLATIONS.

E R R A T A.

PAGE 7. Line 25. Ben. *read* Brown. p. 9. l. 2. r. barefooted. p. 50. l. 20. r. behold'ft. p. 176. l. 12. Father, r. Grandfather's. p. 55. l. 11. fprung, r. fprang. p. 87. l. 26. Note *, r. p. 58. p. 143. Note (n) ὑγκϱαῖς, r. ὑγϱαῖς. p. 198. Note (z) fimilia, r. fimilis. *Ibid.* & facrilegas, r. facrilegas, &c. p. 272. Note (e) ﺟ ﺮ ﺟﺮ. p. 282. L. 12. Bofom, r. Womb. *Ibid.* l. 25. there hear, r. there let you hear. p. 327. l. 18. Difdain, r. Difdain of. p. 335. Note (c) κιιϛ, r. κιϕ. p. 341. l. 4. *after* Goldfword, r. or rather *Fire-Artift*; from אוּר — חָרַשׁ Cha-rêfh-oûr. Πυϱιτιχνίης. p. 352. Note (s) r. *Stillingfleet* in Note (t). p. 383. Note, l. 2. is always, r. is almoft always. p. 391. Note (g) αἰτιλογία, r. αἰτιολογία.

LETTER FIRST.

'TIS ſtrange, my Friend! 'tis wond'rous ſtrange!—Whence this new Curioſity? *New* indeed to you; to enquire about ancient Opinions; or about modern Books that entertain us with ſuch obſolete Stuff. Are you really become a Convert? Have you renounced the State of Infidelity in which you formerly lived, and begin to believe, ſincerely believe in the Knowledge and Capacity of the Ages long preceeding our own? Not a great while, ſince you wou'd hardly allow the credulous Ancients a moderate Share of Common Senſe; or if they had been forced into any Acquaintance with the Arts of Life, you ſtill preſumed that all the World agreed with a great Prelate [*], in

A 2   thinking

---

[*] *Des Fables* plus *ridicules que celles que l'on conte aux Enfans, ont fait la Religion des Payens.* M. Bſſuet Diſc. ſur l'Hiſt. Univer.

Lett. 1. thinking their *Fables* ridiculous, beyond the Folly of Children; and laughed at me, you may remember, fomewhat immoderately, for taking it into my head, *That fome of them had a Meaning.*

MAY I now laugh a little in my Turn? Are you indeed come to think that their Authors were Men? Juft fuch Men as You or I? *That*, you will fay, I never doubted: Perhaps not; but only of its Confequences: An Ancient might have the fame human Figure, and walk about upon two Legs as We do: But that they had the fame Underftanding, the fame Views in Life, and purfued them after the fame Manner, *that* was *a hard Saying*: And ftill a harder, That it wou'd have been as difficult to have perfuaded a Gentleman in *Athens* or *Rome* of the Legend of *Venus* and *Adonis* literally underftood, as to make a *Briton* fwallow a Tale of the Virgin *Mary* and her Spoufe St. *Dominic*; or an ingenious *Parifian* of the *Abbé's* miraculous Tomb. "But " now Dr. *M*** has fent you a Book, to which " when once fet down, you cou'd not rife; and " when quite thro' it, the ftrange Fancies it put " into your Head, obliged you juft to begin again. " They call it an *Enquiry into the Life and* " *Writings of* Homer; tho' you think it fhou'd " rather have bore the Title of the *Rife of Arts* " and *Progrefs of Languages and Learning*; and " is full of *Plates*, whofe Meaning above all " things you wifh to have explained."

GIVE

GIVE you Joy, my Friend, of this new Turn Lett. 1. of Mind, which puts you upon enquiring into the Meaning of thefe mythological Enigma's ; thefe extravagant Tales, and apparent Inconfiftencies; which yet our learned Lord *Verulam* cou'd call the *Wifdom of the Ancients,* and a conftant Source of Pleafure to a fpeculative Man, as they reprefent fome of the grandeft Ideas in Nature and Art. Thus you will be more of a piece with yourfelf; and will not defpife any Species of Knowledge, or Form of conveying it, until you are well affured of its Emptinefs and Infignificancy. For 'tis, methinks, but modeft to fuppofe that what imployed the Heads of the Philofophers, the Tongues of the Poets, and Hands of the Priefts for fo many Ages, fhould be able to afford *Us* fome *Amufement.* Tho', to fay the Truth, yours is a common Cafe ; and there are few greater Inftances of the unequal Judgements Men make of Things, than the current Prejudices concerning the Ancients, and particularly their *Mythology*. How elfe fhou'd it come to pafs, that in an Age which in moft refpects has done them Juftice, and in fome refpects *more* than Juftice; when their Title not only to a Superiority in the Arts of Life ftands fairly recognized, but even to Reach and Invention in moft of the Sciences, that ftill they fhould be reckoned Children or Changelings in their Mythology?

I am not therefore furprized at this Revolution in *your* Tafte, who wifh to *think*, as well as *act*

A 3 con-

Lett. i.confiftently; nor much at the Occafion of it. The Enquiry into the Life and Writings of *Homer* is not ill calculated to deftroy either a blind Zeal for the Ancients, of which you ufed to impeach *me*, or a blind Prejudice againft them, with which I ufed to return *your* Compliment; and a Glimpfe of Truth, fuch is her Beauty, tho' but a fide-long Glance, naturally produces Defire of more.

NEED I warn a Man of your Pleafantry againft taking this Way of fpeaking, ferioufly? — No: I would not, you well know, altogether follow the old Sages in their Philofophy, how much foever I may admire their Morals; much lefs would I theologize (forgive me that hard word) with thofe whofe Schemes were irreconcilable to Reafon and themfelves. Thefe Things, when fet about in earneft, muft be taken in other Lights. All the Ufe I wou'd have you to make of them, is *a little innocent Speculation,* whofe fole Effect, as *Jack Anvil* fays of all the fine things you can write, is *to make you fimper a little, fhake your Head, fay it is a pretty, ingenious kind of a Thing, and fo have done.*

I am,

My dear Friend

Yours &c.

LETTER

LETTER SECOND.

" **H**EAVEN profper all good Purpofes, " and give Virtue to put them in exe- " cution ! "—Be not offended at my well-meant Wifh : One of your former Favourites [a], whofe Fellow all Antiquity, you were fure, had never produced, fays a plain thing prettily;

Chi ben commincia, hà la Metá de l'Opra:
Nè fi commincia ben, fe non dal Cielo.[b]

Believe me, my Friend, to pafs from a Life of Gayety and Pleafure to *Study*——and that kind of Application which *real* Learning requires, is no eafy Tranfition. I know you make great E-lopements; and have at times paffed a whole long Week without feeing * * * *. And who knows but thefe ftudious Fits may return ftill more frequently, and at laft fix the Habit on the other fide ? Mean time give me leave to cherifh the good Difpofition, and to feed the tender Babe with Aliment not too oppofite to its wonted Diet.

D o you remember the laft time you did me the Pleafure to fpend fome Days at *B* * * *, the Wit you threw away upon the uncouth Figure of the old mufty Book, in Boards and Ben-Lea-

A 4 ther,

[a] Sigre *Battifta Guarini.*
[b] He who begins aright has near half done;
Nor can we well begin, if not with Heaven.

Lett. 2. ther, hafped with Brafs, that lay upon my Table ? Out of that fame aukward Utenfil, as you
called it, will I give you a Specimen of the
harmlefs Entertainment to be had from an old Story, which I read this Morning. Your Experience
in the Subject will render it very intelligible.

    ‘ A t the Birth of *VENUS*, or *Beauty*, the
‘ Gods held a grand Feaft ; to which among the
‘ other Deities came *Plenty*, the Son of *Forefight* ;
‘ and, as is ufual on fuch Occafions, *Poverty*
‘ came likewife a begging, and hung on about
‘ the Door. Tow’rds the End of the Entertain-
‘ ment, *Plenty* being intoxicated with Nectar,
‘ (for there was as yet no Wine) went into the
‘ Garden of *Jove*, and oppreffed with the cele-
‘ ftial Liquor funk down in Sleep. *Poverty*
‘ fpied him in this plight ; and as fhe had long
‘ wifhed for a Child by him to fupply her
‘ Wants, fhe flipt fecretly into the Garden, laid
‘ herfelf gently down by his Side, and was made
‘ the Mother of *Cupid*, or *Defire*. For this rea-
‘ fon the Child became a Vaffal to *Venus*, both
‘ as being begot on the Feftival of her Birth,
‘ and being likewife naturally addicted to Beau-
‘ ty, which fhe poffeffed in the higheft Degree.
‘ *CUPID* therefore, as the Ofspring of *Plenty*
‘ and *Poverty*, takes after either Parent, and in-
‘ herits a mixed kind of Fate.

    ‘ I n the firft place, like his Mother, he is
‘ perpetually *in want :* and far from being beau-
‘ tiful or blooming, as moft People imagine,

                    ‘ he

' he is eager, ravenous and rough ; wandering a-Lett. 2.
' bout barefoot, without Houfe or Habitation ;
' fleeping before Doors, or by the Way-fide
' under the open Sky, and conftantly accompa-
' nied with Craving and Indigence. But at the
' fame time, like his Father, he is ever forming
' Defigns upon all that is *beautiful* and *good :* is
' courageous, forward, indefatigable and cunning ;
' ftill contriving fome Fetch, and fond and fruit-
' ful of new Tricks. He is plodding all his Life
' long ; is artful, perfuafive, plaufible and be-
' witching : Neither mortal nor immortal in his
' Conftitution ; but at times, in one and the fame
' Day, he lives and blooms in Affluence ; then
' languifhes and dies ; and in a little time revives
' again, in virtue of his *Father's* Nature. What-
' ever he receives is immediately fpent and gone :
' So that *Love* can never be truly called rich ;
' nor is he ever wholly deftitute ; but confifting
' of Contraries, is at once covetous and profufe,
' bafhful and brave ; has a Defire to domineer,
' and a Difpofition to Servitude ; the Elevation
' and Port of a Prince, and Fawning and Mean-
' nefs of a Slave. '

N o w you have read this little Tale ; be ingenuous and tell me, cou'd any pretty Fellow about
Town have better painted the blind mifchievous
Boy ? Say, you who are a *Connoiffeur,* I am afraid
to your coft, is he truly reprefented ? Did the Painter, think you, underftand Life ? For if he was a
Mafter in this delicate Part of it, you will doubt-

Lett. 2. lefs admit he might excel in the whole. Think upon your former Ways, my Friend! of the Contempt you ufed to exprefs for the ignorant impolite Ancients, and, as you are in a fair Road, repent throughly of your Infidelity. But I have another Queftion, a little different, to afk.

Cou'd any body, do you imagine, take it into his Head after reading this Allufion, ' That ' the Author of it actually believed the little flut- ' tering Thing he has fo exquifitely defcribed, to ' be a real divine Perfon, and wou'd worfhip ' him accordingly as *a God?*' One fhou'd think *not :* Efpecially as this very Parable has been taken for an Argument of his Unbelief of the whole Train of his national Divinities, whom he reverenced in Obedience to the Laws of his Country, and profeffed himfelf incapable of explaining their Natures and myftical Generation. Or, on the other hand, wou'd it not be as abfurd to fay, that it had *no Meaning at all?* It muft be a ftrange Turn of Mind that cou'd lead to either: " For to believe it literally, or to " condemn it for Want of Ingenuity, are equally " prepofterous." I fhall certainly expect you on *Wednefday,* with Mr. *V* * * * *, and always am,

Yours &c.

LETTER

LETTER THIRD.

WERE you not afhamed to confefs fo much
Lazinefs in good Company? Not to endure the Labour of making out the Plan of a
Work you fo much wifh to comprehend! Was
it a long Letter from *B* * * ** in bad Writing
and beau-fpelling, you cou'd plod till Midnight;
and be at abundance of Pains to decipher the
crooked Scrawl, in order to come at all the pretty Sentiments it contained. Well——, I will indulge you for once; and try to intangle you in
Study, by laying Baits in your Way, and fending
you *the* Plan, you fo confiftently long to fee, and
will not take the Pains to make out.

THE ENQUIRY into the *Life* and *Writings* of *HOMER* promifes little by its Title-
page: It bears no Name of Author, or Printer,
nor of the Lord to whom it is addreffed; neither is there a Dedication; but after the manner
of the *Ancients* it has a refpect to this noble and
learned Perfon from Beginning to End. The
Head of *Homer*, which you fee prefixed, is taken from the Buft of a fine Statue, probably
that mentioned by *Cedrenus*, as formerly one of
the chief Ornaments of *Conftantinople*, and now
in the rich Cabinet of that great and good Man,
the celebrated Dr. *Mead*. In viewing his beautiful Collection of fome of the fineft Remains

of

Lett. 3. of Antiquity, I took particular Notice of this
Buft, and well remember to have been ftruck
with a *plain ruftick Look*, fomething *niais*——
but *ingenious* and *thoughtful*, fuch as they fay *Voi-
ture*'s was, which I don't think truly reprefented
in the Plate prefixed to the E N Q U I R Y; but
the Original gave me a jufter, more natural Idea
of a *ftroling fanciful Bard*, than the Head of
the noble *Farncfe* Statue in the Great Duke's
Gallery.

T H I S is one of thofe Perceptions or Prejudices, if you pleafe, one cannot fo eafily give account of: We feel it; but for the moft part are
not able to tell, *Why it is fo.* Muft there not
be fome Connexion in Nature between a fruitful
teeming Fancy, and *this* Part of Phyfiognomy?
You, my Friend, who are a fecond *Cherea*, and
have fo nicely viewed *one* fort of Faces, try your
fkill now upon the other Sex, and tell me why
many of the greateft Poets have had a *fimple
country Look?* The immortal *Mantuan* is recorded by *Donatus* to have been *rufticanâ Facie*;
the peaceful *Hefiod*, ἀγϱοίκῳ ωϱοσώπῳ; *The-
ocritus* ποιμενικόν τι ϰ̀ βλέπων, with even a *paftoral* Look; (not meaning, I fuppofe, a Bifhop's.)
The celebrated *Vida* was thought by his Cotemporaries [a] to refemble *Virgil* for the fame very
reafon: *Facie prope rufticanâ, adeo ut noftro* Vidæ
*non abfimilis fuiffe videri poffit. Dante Ali-
geri*, the Parent of *Italian Poetry*, is faid to have
been

a *Lil. Greg.* G I R A L D I.

been *di fincero e grato Afpetto :* His Succeffor
the divine *Petrarcha, Di Color tra bianco e bru-*
no con Ifguardo e Fatezze che ben moftravan la
Schiettezza del Cuor : And the two Rivals, in
one kind of Poetry, *Taffo* and *Guarini,* (if an O-
riginal and Copy may be properly fo called) had
both *una certa Ciera di ingenua femplicitá, In-*
dizio di rado fallace di bei Coftumi : Even the
fhrewd witty *La Fontaine,* (for fuch you know
he appears in his Writings) was in his old Houfe-
keeper's Opinion, *plus bête que malin :* and had
fo much the Appearance of that fame *Bêtife,* that
the Countefs of *C* * * * *, with whom he lived,
faid to a Lady who afked if fhe was got into
her new Houfe? That fhe had now only three
domeftic Animals to fetch home, her *Cat,* her
Parrot, and *La Fontaine.* [b]

WHAT fhall we fay of this ftrange Correfpondence of Features? A Correfpondence
which extended not only to Poets in general,
but to Poets of the fame Turn and Temper?
The polite amorous Cardinal *Bembo,* before he
obtained that Dignity, was complimented by
his learned Friends with refembling the elegant Mafter of Love, the fweet-tongued *Ovid,*
not only in his Face, but his flender fprightly
Perfon[c]; and a Life of *Petrarcha,* the Author of
many a delicate Strain, wrote by another Hand,
makes

[b] *Notes fur Boileau.*
[c] *Ovidius omni vitâ atque victu excultus atque expolitus, tum
tenui & vefco Corpore, Nervifque compacto ; qualis fcilicet eft PE-
TRUS BEMBUS Vir unus omnium elegantiffimus.*
L. G. GYRALDI Dial. de Vitis Poet.

Lett. 3. makes him to have been *juft fuch another: di commune Statura, non di molto gran Forze, mà di mirabil Deftrezza* [a]. Had the Decency of the Cardinal's Character permitted, what Leffons in the *belle Paffion* might you not have expected from the Pen that produced the inimitable *Azolains* [b]; and had *Ovid* been under any happy Neceffity of a like Decorum, what Refinements, what Gallantry wou'd have fhone in his *Art of Love?* A Satirift, 'tis true, may well be thought to wear a different Afpect; his Converfe with the World, treading the beaten Road, fearching out and expofing Vice in all its little Difguifes, may fharpen his Looks, and imbitter his Face : But let us remember, his Province is the moft unpoetical of *Parnaffus* ; and ftill, that one of the moft approved among the Ancients was remarkable for his *Verecundia virginalis,* the *Modefty of a Maid* in his Countenance and Manners; which at the fame time I can by no means affirm to appear in his Writings.

N o w, for a Wager, are you running over all the Poets by Profeffion, and all the poetically difpofed of your Acquaintance, and claffing their Vifages in your Imagination. This one, fay you, has a *comic,* that a *tragic,* t'other a *tragicomical* Look. Here is an *epic,* there a *fatiric,* yonder a *pindaric* Phyfiognomy. Mr. *X * * * *looks juft like—

But

---

[a] Of a middle Stature, not very ftrong, but wonderful Agility.

[b] They are Dialogues upon *Love,* wrote with great Delicacy and Deccncy.

But what am I doing? and whither has this Lett. 3.
Idea of Simplicity in the Head of the great Poet ◠◠◠
led me? Quick let us return, *my Friend*, and
quit the *Genus irritabile Vatum*, the tefty rhim-
ing Race, without difcompofing a Hair in the
Toupée of the meaneft Servant of the Mufes;
and rather enquire, what Foundation there can
be in Nature for this unqueftionable Refemblance
in the Afpects and Manners of Men?

SHALL we liften to the ingenious *Phyfiognomift?*
who tells us, "That the chief Indications of Mens
" Difpofitions are to be found in their Countenan-
" ces, and center particularly in their *Looks*, their
" very Souls appearing thro' their Eyes to an
" intelligent Spectator, as thro' the Gates and
" Avenues of the Mind [a]: That a fet, fimple
' Look, for example, little moift Eyes, moving
' Eye-brows, foftened Features, are Signs of a
' Man's being *contemplative, thoughtful, given*
' *to learning*, and particularly the *Belles Lettres* [b].'
Again, ' That a dark humid Eye, open, and
' frequently fixed, is a Sign of *Thought* and *Per-*
' *ception*; but if it likewife look *mild*, and *be-*
' *nign*, it further betokens *Worth* and *Ingenuity*;
' for fuch, fays he, was the Eye and Looks of
' the wife and worthy *SOCRATES*.'

PER-

[a] Τὰ δὲ πολλὰ τῶν ζημείων κỳ τὰ ζύνολα τοῖς 'Οφθαλ-
μοῖς ἐνίδρυται· κỳ ὥσπερ διὰ Πυλῶν τότων ἡ Ψυχὴ διαφαί-
νεται.   ΑΔΑΜΑΝΤΙΟΥ Φυσιογνωμιχ. A.
[b] 'Οφθαλμοὶ ἰς-ῶτες, μιχροὶ, ὑσοὶ. μέτωπον ἀνειμένον,
βλέθρα κι κ̇ινα δεῖνν 'ητνν ἀνδρα ΦΡΟΝΤΙΣΤΗΝ, ΦΙΛΟ-
ΛΟΓΟΝ, ΦΙΛΟΜΑΘΗ.   Ibid. Περὶ 'Οφθαλ ἐς-ηκ.

Lett. 3. PERHAPS you will hold yourſelf a better Judge of the following Aſpects, which he deſcribes much to the ſame purpoſe : ' Eyes, ſays ' he, ſtanding frequently open, without winking, ' looking gentle and humane, ſwimming in a ' tranſparent Fluid, ſhew the Perſon to be ' *contemplative, a Lover of Knowledge, of a* ' *ſweet Diſpoſition,* and addicted to *Love :* ' And ſtill ſtronger, ' That ſuffuſed Eyes, fluctuating, ' and as 'twere *beaming* in themſelves, beſpeak a ' ſtrong Inclination to Pleaſure and the Delights ' of *Venus* ; and that Perſons with ſuch a Look ' are generally *ſtraight, beneficent,* of a *noble* ' *Nature,* and addicted to *Poetry* and *Verſe.*' [a]

WHATEVER the Caſe may be, or how ſlippery ſoever the Judgement, when we deſcend to Particulars, the *Opinion* we cannot help forming of every Man at firſt ſight to his Advantage or Prejudice, according as his Aſpect and Appearance pleaſe or diſguſt us, ſeems to ſay, That it is not without reaſon we ſuppoſe a *Connexion* between a certain Set of Features, and ſuch and ſuch Manners which uſually attend them. *Yours* did not deceive me, who am affectionately,

Your &c.

---

[a] 'Οφθαλμοὶ κλυζόμενοι, κυμαίνοντες ἐν αὐτοῖς, εἰς ἀφροδίσια ϗ εὐπάθειαν ἐπίοπιται· ὄυτε δὲ ἄδιχοι, ὔτε κακѫργοι, ὔτε Φύσεως Φαύλης, ὔτε ΑΜΟΤΣΟΙ.
Ibid. Περὶ 'Οφθαλ. κινѫμεν.

LETTER

LETTER FOURTH.

WHAT a Flow of Spirits muſt you have
had, my gay Friend! when you re-
ceived my laſt Letter ? I will forfeit a good deal,
or you had been juſt come home from ϒ****,
or perhaps were to go thither next Morning. In
either Caſe the Infection wou'd work : Our Mind
not only retains Impreſſions of the Companies we
leave, but moulds itſelf beforehand to the Humour and Manners of thoſe with whom we are
about to aſſociate, ſo it be done with our good
Liking, and Hopes of Pleaſure. I am ſure you
have been in high Humour by the ſprightly
Debût [a] of your Anſwer. " *Wonderful Science,*
" ſay you, *profound ſagacious* Phyſiognomy !
" *highly befitting a grave contemplative Man !*
" ——You therefore *expect that I will ſhortly ſend*
" *you a* Treatiſe of Palmeſtry, *or revive old* Par-
" tridge, *and write an* Almanack."

'Tɪs very well, Sir, and not much out of
Character :——But after ſo ſaying, may I venture to put you in mind of a certain Perſon, the
quickeſt at catching Faces, and odd Miens, of
all the Circle of my Acquaintance. Can you remember, dear Sir, this young Gentleman, who
after he had, like *Leonardo da Vinci,* been ſtro-
ling, if not from Street to Street, at leaſt from
Company to Company, and obſerved all the

B ſtrange

[a] Beginning ; Firſt Stroke.

Lett. 4. ſtrange Setts of Features, uncouth Airs, and con-
ſtrained Poſtures he had met with, uſed to come
full fraught to me, " Who ſhou'd I meet with in
ſuch a Place but Mr. * * *? I proteſt I can't a-
bide that Man's Look. He's double and kna-
viſh for certain. If you obſerve, he never looks
you ſteadily in the Face ; a Half-grin upon one
ſide of his, betrays ſome crooked Sentiment
within.

" P R A Y, have you ever ſeen the plump Mr.
" *Papillon ?* How ſmooth his blooming vacant
" Face! Thought and Wrinkles wiped clean out
" of it! But happily ſupplied by the two pret-
" tieſt unmeaning Dimples in his Cheeks, and
" the two perteſt pinking Eyes that ever charmed
" a fair Lady. Mr. *B* * * * came in, and ſat
" juſt by him, with his ſedate Aſpeét, and
" compoſed Countenance, that commanded Re-
" ſpeét whenever he appear'd, and drew At-
" tention whenever he ſpoke. Bleſs me, how
" intent and piercing he looks! But for the
" *Spirit* that every now and then flaſhes from his
" Eyes, and the gentle Smile that o'erſpreads his
" Features, I ſhould take him for a meer plod-
" ding Wight, not without a Daſh of the *Mi-*
" *ſanthrope.*[a] His Friend Mr. *M* * * * looks *open*
" like Heaven : You wou'd think you ſaw into
" his Heart : Truth and Generoſity ſeem painted
" in every Lineament.——I am ſure he is a good
" Man. But oh! the painful Piéture of Chagrin !

The

[a] Man-hater.

" The imbittered excoriate Look of *** *Efqr.! Lett. 4.*
" An old exhaufted fickly Rake! Difmal! A
" moft forbidding Phiz. I wou'd have thee
" drawn and fet up a *Memento mori* in St. *J.****
" *C * * *l,* where thou'd reform more young
" Fellows, than all the laboured and lab'ring
" Sermons ever preached in the Place. But *à*
" *propos* to Sermons.——Of all the living Bufts I
" ever faw, no one comes up to the *gloomy*
" *buck'ram Vifage* of the *Vicar.* How is every
" better Sentiment effaced from his whole Coun-
" tenance! Not a Spark of Goodnefs or Veftige
" of Humanity in any one Feature: Dark, un-
" focial and fullen, with cloudy Brow, lightlefs
" Eyes, pendant Cheeks, and double Chin, he fits
" recollected in gruff Silence: But upon the
" leaft Emotion, the *Bear* and the *Clown* appear
" tumbling in all his Geftures, begrim his un-
" gainly Looks, ftrain his Mufcles, diftort his
" Motions, and briftle his whole Behaviour."

OF whofe drawing, my good Friend, are
thefe Characters? Upon what are fuch quick
Feelings of Men and Manners founded? *Wonderful Science!* fay I in my turn, *profound fagacious* Phyfiognomy! *there's but a fhort Step,*
'twou'd feem, *between thee and thy Sifter-Science*
Palmeftry, *and from thence to* Aftrology, *predict-
ing the Weather, and telling Fortunes.*

YET don't be too much out of Countenance
at being catched exercifing that perceptive Fa-

culty

Lett. 4. culty with which Nature has endowed you, of discovering Mens Conditions from their Air and Aspect: You have some good People for Patterns, who practised the same Art. What tho' Fortune-tellers, Quack-Doctors and Gypsies abuse it; you need not go a stroling with them, except you please. Because there are *Empirics*, wou'd you have no *Physicians?* Because there are *rhyming Dunces*, wou'd you have no *Poets?* Or because there are *wicked Heretics*, would you have no *orthodox Divines?* But you have better Company than Sir *Sidrophel*, tho' not yet of your Acquaintance: I will venture to introduce you to one or two of them in my next Letter. Till then,

My dear Friend,

Adieu.

LETTER

LETTER FIFTH.

YOU are a very hard Craver. Is your Impatience owing to a Defire of knowing
your Fellow-Phyfiognomifts, now you have
found out your felf to be one of the number ;
or to an Inclination incident to young People, for
which a Royal Miftrefs (if fhe was one) was remarkable in the laft Century, a Liking to hear
old Stories? Which of them foever it be, in performance of my Promife, hear the Sentiments
of——I will not yet tell you who.

" THAT the *Difpofitions* of Mens Minds
" are connected with their *Bodies,* and influ-
" enced by the Changes that happen to *them,* is
" very evident both in People intoxicated with
" Liquors, and under Diftempers : In both Cafes
" the Temper and Sentiments appear extremely
" different ; and are plainly made fo by the dif-
" ferent Temper and Difpofition of the Body.
" On the other hand, the Body is frequently
" affected by the Paffions of the Mind, as ap-
" pears in languifhing Lovers, in Perfons who
" have been violently frighted, who are funk
" with Grief, or ecftatic with Pleafure. And
" not only fo, but in things that happen *natu-*
" *rally,* without any Shock or Violence, it is
" eafy to perceive that the Soul and Body are
" linked together in fo intimate an Union, that

B 3 " they

a *Memoires de la Vie du Comte de* GRAMMONT. Chap. VII. XL.

Lett. 5. " they are generally speaking the reciprocal Caufes
" of the Alterations happening in each other. For
" never was there fuch a Creature produced or
" feen, as had the Body and Shape of an Animal
" of *one* Species, and the Inftinct and Difpofitions
" of an Animal of *another* Species : But always
' along with the Body, it muft have the Man-
" ners too, of one and the fame Animal.　It
" follows therefore that of *fuch a Caft* of Bo-
" dy, *fuch a Mind* muft be the neceffary Con-
" fequence.　Among the Irrationals, we fee the
" fkilful in the feveral kinds, forming their
" Judgements of them by their *Make :* By this
" Jockeys judge of Horfes, and Sportfmen of
" Dogs : But if *their* Method of judging be
" well founded, as the fame Caufes muft needs
" produce the fame Effects, it muft be likewife
" poffible to difcern *Mens* Conditions and Cha-
" racters by their Perfons and Afpects." [a]

T H E N the Author ventures to lay down the
general Principles upon which you are to reafon,
and proceeds to put them himfelf in Practice,
not only by going over the principal Parts of the
human Body, and affigning the various Difpofitions of the Mind, which ufually accompany their
various Make and different Structure ; but, *vice
verfâ*, runs over the chief Characters in Life,
and accurately defcribes the Perfon and Appearance of a *brave* Man, of a *Coward* ; of an *in-*
genious

[a] ΑΡΙΣΤΟΤ. Φυσιογνωμονικά.

genious Man, of a *Blockhead*; of an *impudent* Lett. 5.
Man, of a *modeſt* one, and ſo on throughout the
great Variety of Charaċters in the World, both
good and bad. After which, being led back as
it were naturally, by an Induċtion of Effeċts to
their Cauſe, he reſumes the Conſideration of
this ſtrange Connexion.

   " I AM perſuaded, ſays he, that the *Soul* and
" *Body* ſympathize with one another, for many
" Reaſons. The Temper and Diſpoſition of
" the Mind being any way altered, makes the
" Form and Habit of the Body to alter with
" it ; as on the other hand, the Form and Make
" of the Body being changed, produces a ſimi-
" lar Change in the Diſpoſition of the Mind.
" Grief and Joy are Affeċtions properly belong-
" in to the *Mind:* Yet every body can perceive
" Grief in the heavy Look of an afflicted Man,
" and Joy in the chearful Countenance of a hap-
" py one. When the *Soul* is affeċted, and its
" Temper varied, were it poſſible that the *Body*
" ſhou'd retain, unmoved, its former State, there
" might, it is true, be ſtill ſome ſort of ſympa-
" thetic Intercourſe between them, but not ſo
" thorough and mutually affeċting as it is at pre-
" ſent. For now it is very evident, that the one
" follows and participates with the other ; and
" from no Conſideration more than from the
" Effeċts of *Madneſs*. This Diſtemper likewiſe
" ſeems properly to affeċt the thinking Faculty,

         B 4   " the

Lett. 5. " the *Soul.* Yet Phyſicians by cleanſing the
" *Body* by Medicines, and by making the Pa-
" tient obſerve Rules of Diet preſcribed for the
" ſame Purpoſe, rid the Soul of that terrible
" Diſorder: So that by one and the ſame Re-
" medy, applied to the *Body*, both its own State
" and Appearance is changed from what it was
" under a diſordered Mind, and the *Mind* it-
" ſelf is delivered from Madneſs. But ſince they
" both change *by one and the ſame Means* ap-
" plied to *one* of them, and change *both together*,
" it is evident that they throughly depend upon
" and mutually affect one another." [a]

Now wou'd I give ſomething to know,
whoſe Opinions you imagine you have been
reading? Some fanciful viſionaire Doctor's, I ſuppoſe, like the Spaniſh *Huarte*, or French *Deſ-
marêts :* ſome *Mumpſimus*, who ſat in his Cloſet,
and built chimerical Schemes, a Stranger to the
World, and to ſtrict Reaſoning. Juſt the contrary : They are the Opinions of no leſs Man
than *Plato*'s Rival, and *Alexander*'s Maſter—the
ſevere, abſtract, diſcerning *ARISTOTLE*; who
was ſo fully convinced of their Juſtneſs and
Truth, that in his moſt elaborate Work, his favourite new-invented *Organon*, upon which he ſeems
willing to reſt his Reputation [b], he concludes
the

[a] ΑΡΙΣΤΟΤ. Φυσιογνωμονικά.

[b] Δεῖ δὲ ἡμᾶς μὴ λεληθέναι τὸ συμβεβηκὸς περὶ ταύτην
τὴν πραἰματείαν.——Ταύτης γὰρ, ἢ τὸ μὲν ἦν, τὸ δ᾽ ἐκ ἦν
προε-

the fecond Book of the firft *Analytics* with an Lett. 5.
Abridgement of the *Principles* of Phyfiognomy.
Thefe the Philofopher lays down as Foundations
upon which you may *reafon*, and from which,
according to the Conditions there prefcribed, you
may form certain Conclufions.

IN the Progrefs of Philofophy *Speufippus* taught
after *Plato*, and *Xenocrates* fucceeded *Speufippus*. *Xenocrates* was a perfect Pattern of Virtue
in his Life and Manners. He began his Lectures
early in the Morning, and his Gate ftood open
to all Lovers of Wifdom and Knowledge. A
young *Athenian*, *Polemo* by Name, very wild
and abandoned to Pleafure, in his Return from
a Night Ramble, happened to be paffing drunk
that way about Sun-rifing. To go in and bam-
boozle the old ftarched Philofopher was too
tempting a Frolic to be refifted by a Youth in
that Condition. Fluftered therefore as he was,
and in his gaudy revelling Drefs, flowing with
Perfumes, and crowned with Flowers, in he
bounced among the learned Band who were
liftening to their ftay'd Teacher ; He fat down
too, with a mimical Gravity, that he might
watch

προεξειργασμένον· ἀλλ' ἐδὲν παντελῶς ὑπῆρχε.——Περὶ τῶν
Ῥητορικῶν μὲν, ὑπῆρχεν ἴσως πολλὰ καὶ παλαιὰ τὰ λε-
γόμενα· περὶ δὲ τῦ ΣΥΛΛΟΓΙΖΕΣΘΑΙ, παντελῶς ἐδὲν
εἴχομεν πρότερον ἄλλο λέγειν· ἀλλὰ ΤΡΙΒΗ'Ν ζητῦντες πολὺν
χρόνον ἐπονῦμεν.——Διὸ λοιπὸν ἂν εἴη πάντων ὑμῶν, ἢ τῶν
ἀκροωμένων ἔργον, τοῖς μὲν παραλελειμμένοις τῆς μεθόδε συſ-
γνώμην, τοῖς δ' εὑρημένοις πολλὴν χάριν ἔχειν.
ΑΡΙΣΤΟΤ. Περὶ Σοφιſ. Ελεſχ. βιϐ. Β.

Lett. 5. watch a witty Opportunity to confound the mufty Moralift, and march off. At his firft Appearance fome Marks of Indignation broke from
the Audience that threatned him with a fudden
Exit: But *Xenocrates,* without altering his
Countenance, made a Sign to let him alone; and
changing the Subject of his Difcourfe, he began
to reafon of *Modefty,*—of *Temperance,*—of governing the *Paffions,*—and *Self-command.* P O-
L E M O was not fo far gone, as to be incapable
of underftanding what he heard; but looking
fomething amazed and foolifh, he began to *liften*
to the eloquent Philofopher; and liftened fo long,
until he was ftruck with the Gravity of the
Man, and the Truth of his Doctrine. He then
firft ftole up his Hand, and taking the Garland
from his own Head, he threw it upon the
Ground; then he pulled in his Arm under his
Robe; by and by he gathered in the flowing
jaunty Skirts of it; by degrees his Looks changed;
the *impertinent apifh Fleer* of a fine Fuddle-cap
fettled into Senfe and Compofure: He forgot the
intended Frolic, was afhamed of his Debauch,
and went home fo ftung with a Senfe of his Folly, and fo convinced of the Amiablenefs of Virtue, that he became a conftant Hearer of *Xe-*
nocrates, eminent for the Regularity of his Life,
and fuch a Proficient in Learning, that at his
Mafter's Death he fucceeded in the Direction of
the *Platonic School.*

THIS

T H I S celebrated Convert from Intemperance to Wifdom excelled likewife in *Phyfiognomy.* Among his other Writings, as if *the great Philofopher* had not fufficiently exhaufted the Matter, he new-modelled and confiderably augmented the Treatife written by *Ariftotle* upon that Subject. The Introduction is remarkable. ' If any ' Branch of Science, fays he, be ufeful, thofe ' who ftudy the Knowledge of the Natures and ' Difpofitions of Men from their Appearance and ' Afpect, may reap many and great Advantages ' from their Art : For no body wou'd chufe to ' commit his Wife or Child, or entruft a Sum ' of Money, or any valuable *Depofitum* ; or in- ' deed wifh to contract any kind of Friendfhip ' with a Man who has a Mark of Perfidy, In- ' temperance, or other wicked Difpofition writ- ' ten in his Face. But to fum up the Matter ' in a Sentence, all Mankind, as it were by an ' immediate, infallible, Heaven-fent *Divination,* ' demonftrate in their Looks and Motions, their ' peculiar Caft of Mind, and Manner of Life [a] : ' So that the fkilful Phyfiognomift may cul- ' tivate Friendfhip with the *Good,* and avoid all ' Commerce with the *Evil* ' [a]

How

[a] Πάντων γὰρ, ὡς ἔπΘ εἰπεῖν, ἀνθρώπων, ὥσπερ-εἴ τινΘ ἁπλαῖς-ε ἢ θεοπετάς-ε ἡ ὀξυτάτης μαντείας, συʃγνωρι- ζομένων ἔθΘ τε ἡ βίε πρόθεσιν, διὰ τύτων ὁ Φυσιογνώμων μαθήσεται, τὰς μὲν τῶν χρηςῶν φιλίας αἱρεῖᾰαι, τὰς δὲ τῶμ πονηρῶν κακίας Φυλάτ]εᾰαι.

ΠΟΛΕΜΩΝ. Φ.σ.ογνωμικόν.

Lett. 5. H o w happy wou'd that Man be, who cou'd exercife this rare Art with certainty ? Who cou'd put in practice the repeated Advice of one of the beft and greateft Men the World ever faw ; ' to ' look within — to let the particular Quality and ' Worth of no Perfon or Thing efcape us ; ¹—— ' to be accurate Enquirers into the Manners and ' Actions of Men ; ²— to accuftom our felves ' to enter attentively into the Sentiments of thofe ' we converfe with ; and as far as is poffible to ' get into the *very Soul* of the Perfon who fpeaks ' to us.³ One of the moft remarkable and fur-prizing Inftances of this Sagacity I have met with, is the celebrated *P L O T I N U S.*

T H E Ancients held fuch of their *Philofo-phers,* as lived in a manner becoming their Pro-feffion, in the higheft Efteem. Their Schools they looked upon as the *Sources of Virtue,* and their Houfes as *Sanctuaries,* which nothing bafe or difhonourable durft approach : The greateft Perfons not only recommended their Children to their Care in their own Life-time ; but fre-quently left them, with their whole Eftate and Concerns, under their Tuition at their Death. The Family of *Plotinus,* the holy pure *Platonic,*

con-

---

¹ Ἔσω βλέπε· μηδενὸς πράγματος μήτε ἡ ἰδία ποιότης, μήτε ἡ ἀξία παρατρεχέτω σέ. ² Ἀκριβὴς ἐξεταστὴς ἠθῶν κ̀ πράξεων. ³ Ἔθισον σεαυτὸν πρὸς τῷ ὑφ' ἑτέρυ λεγομέ-νῳ γίνεσθαι ἀπαρενθυμήτως, κ̀ ὡς οἷόν τε ἐν τῇ ΨΥΧΗΙ τῷ λέγοντ@ γίνυ.

M. ANTONIN. ΑΥΤΟΚΡ. τῶν εἰς ἑαυτὸν βιϐ. ϛ.

I

confifted but of a Servant or two for himfelf; but his Houfe was full of the Youth of either Sex of the prime Nobility, entrufted to *him* with all that they had, as to a facred and divine Guardian. With the moft incorruptible Integrity he was mild and affable, and ready to ferve every body, who had the fmalleft Acquaintance of him, or Connexion with his Friends; and at the fame time of fuch Candour and Difcretion, that having lived fix and twenty Years in *Rome,* and been chofen Umpire in numberlefs Differences between private Perfons, he demeaned himfelf fo as that he had not one Citizen his Enemy: So impartial and prudent was his Humanity.

O N E of this extraordinary Man's Talents was a true and juft Perception of the Tempers and Manners of the Perfons who lived with him; whofe Deeds and Defigns he quickly difcovered in their Looks, and often foretold what wou'd happen to them in the after-part of their Lives. " This Youth, (faid he of a young Nobleman left to his Management) " will prove exceffively " amorous, and intangle himfelf miferably in " Intrigues.——I fufpect he will not be long- " lived: " which in every point came exactly to pafs. A Widow Lady in high Reputation of Virtue, *Chione* by Name, who lived in his Houfe with her Children, had loft a Diamond Necklace of very great Value. *Plotinus* ordered his own, and the Servants belonging to all the

Lodgers

Lodgers in the Family, to be brought together into his Prefence: When they were met, he caft his Eye upon them, and immediately pointing to one of them, *This Perfon*, faid he, *has ftole the Necklace.* The Fellow ftoutly denied it, at firft; but being led off to be whipt, he confeffed the Theft, and went and fetched the Necklace from whence he had hid it.

But the chief Proof of the Juftnefs of his Penetration, was his difcovering the fecret difmal Intention of his favourite Scholar *P O R-PHYRY,* whom this great Judge of Men loved not more upon account of his Learning, than his Virtue and Sweetnefs of Manners. Hear how the Youth ingenuoufly tells the Story of himfelf. 'I had once, fays the *young Platonic,* through
' fome Diftafte or Contempt of Life, taken a
' Refolution to put an End to my Days; and
' had fhut my felf up in my Lodgings for that
' purpofe; when my loved *Mafter* came unex-
' pectedly, and broke in upon my Retirement.
' He told me without hefitation, That my pre-
' fent Intention was far from being the Refult
' of Reafon, or the Dictates of an *intellectual*
' *Principle:* That the Gloom in my Mind was
' occafioned by fome bodily Diforder I laboured
' under, fome Diftemper of Melancholy, for which
' he directed me to go and *travel* for a Cure. I
' believed and obeyed him in this, as in every thing
' elfe, and paffed over to *Sicily,* where I heard the
' Lectures

‘ Lectures of the Philofopher *Probus*, a Man in Lett. 5.
‘ good Reputation, with whom I ftayed in the
‘ pleafant wholefom Town of *Lilybeum.* Here
‘ I quitted my pernicious Purpofe of dying, and
‘ at the fame time, was by this Accident pre-
‘ vented from attending my Mafter *P L O T I-*
‘ *N U S* until his death. ’

But to what purpofe need we range Antiquity for Inftances of an £ t, which you are your
felf practifing every day? not only upon Perfons and Companies, but upon Paper in your
Clofet. You who *defign* and *draw* fo prettily,
and have gone thro’ the *academic Faces*, if not
the *Figures*; who know the Play of a Mufcle,
at leaft on the Outfide, from the fmalleft Simper
to the higheft Diftortion of Features; who diftinguifh fo nicely the Characteriftics of the bor-
dering Paffions, *Grief, Fear, Dejection, Melancholy*; ——*Emulation, Averfion, Envy* and *Hatred*, can *you* with any Confiftency ridicule Phyfiognomy, even in *our narrow* fenfe of the
Word? We underftand it to be nothing more
than judging of Men by their *Faces*: But the
Authors of the Term, and firft Inventers of the
Art meant nothing lefs than “ a Judgement of a
“ Man’s whole Nature and Inclinations from an
“ attentive View not of his *Face* only, but of
“ his entire Perfon; and that not motionlefs and
“ unemployed, but in Action and Agitation,
“ engaged

ΠΟΡΦΥΡΙΟΥ περὶ Πλωτίνε βίε ᾗ βιβλ.

Lett. 5. " engaged in the Affairs of Life; the Eyes fpark-
" ling, the Tongue fpeaking, the Heart beating,
" and the whole Man in Motion and guard-
" lefs." Purfue now this Thought a little further,
and confider what are your *Dutch* Drolls, your
Harlequins, your Pantomimes, your *Rich's* and
Francifques——nay what were (alas! they *were*)
your *Booths, Bracegirdles* and *Oldfields,* but fo
many fhining Proofs of the Power and Reality
of *Phyfiognomy?* What has eftablifhed the unvaried Idea's of the Heads of the *hiftoric Characters* among the Painters, (whofe Originals
they never had, and fome of them never exifted)
but the unvaried Connexion between the fuppofed Character of the *Saint* or *Hero,* and *fuch*
a Set of Features as beft mark it? Even the
great, the fupreme Effort of the Art, the inftructing Mankind by Dumb-fhew and Example, *Hiftory-Painting* it felf, and the Produce
of *Sculpture,*

Fair genuine Forms of Beauty's eldeft-born,
A living Race by plaftic *Virtue markt,*
What are they but *Human Figures* reprefented
in Action, in fuch Attitudes, Poftures and Movements, and with fuch *Looks* and *Features,* as
Nature has adapted to the inward Difpofition of
the Heart? And ftill, the moft exalted and ex-
tenfive of all the Ways of Painting, I mean *real*
Poetry and its nobleft Branch, Mythology, how
largely does it borrow from this inexhaufted
                                    Source?

Source ?   Reprefentations of things *natural* and Lett. 5.
divine by proper *Perfons* ; and thefe Perfons
properly accoutred, their Enfigns, their Faces,
their Mien and Actions being all *of a piece*, and
all *in Character*, muft be the refult of the moft
natural of all Sciences, *Phyfiognomy :* I fay the
moft *natural* ; an Infant looks you full in
the Face to find out your Temper *,— and your
Dog keeps a ftrict Eye upon your Features, and
behaves himfelf accordingly ;

Unde nifi intùs,—monftratum ?

But whither have I wandered from my Sub-
ject?—It is your wanton Wit and craving Curiofity
that lead me aftray, and make me forget the chief
Point of the Queftion, Whether that Head of
Homer, which adorns one of the moft elegant
Libraries in *Britain*, has been well *imagined* by the
Statuary, and has a Look becoming the *poetical
Patriarch?* The Queftion I fay is, Whether the
Artift has done well? who drew not from the Life ;
but from his own *Idea*. For I much queftion whe-
ther the Likenefs of *Homer's* real Face was pre-
ferved.   It is not altogether impoffible that it
might ; but more probably it was among the
C   number

---

* C'eft au Mouvement du Vifage, et fur tout *des Yeux* que
l'on fait le plus d'Attention——— pareeque ces Mouvemens font
les Indices de ce qui fe paffe au dédaus de nous : Ils meritent
donc qu'on les approuve à proportion de ce qu'il y a de louable
dans les Sentimens intérieurs dont ils font les Indices.
Traité du Beau, Cap. IV. § 10.

Lett. 5. number of thofe mention'd by *Pliny*, as the greateft Pitch of Happinefs that can happen to a Mortal: A Likenefs contrived for him by Pofterity, when the real is wanting, in order to fatisfy the general Defire of Mankind *To know what fort of a Man He was* [a]. Thus, at the firft acting a new Play, fays a Man of Wit, the Ladies feldom fail to afk,——

What like *a Man's the Poet?*

And I believe the fame Queftion is as natural to a Gentleman upon reading a fine Piece of old Poetry. To indulge this natural Curiofity, to give you a truly *poetic* Face, which of the two Artifts have beft judged?——Whether he who has imagined his infpired Bard with a fimple, rural, contemplative Look—or he who has given him a grander Air, and filled his Countenance with Elevation and Majefty—?

I am, &c.

P. S.

I HAVE thought of a way of procuring a Plan of the ENQUIRY, &c. without much Trouble: Expect it therefore in my next. But now the Vifit at *Y* * * * is over, what if you fhould fit down to read and think a little, and try to *make out* one to yourfelf: You would be better able to judge of another's when it comes.

---

[a] Quô majus, ut equidem arbitror, nullum eft felicitatis Specimen, quam femper omnes fcire cupere, *Qualis fuerit aliquis?*
                       PLIN. Lib. xxxv. § 2.

LETTER

LETTER SIXTH.

SOME time before the ENQUIRY *into
the Life and Writings of* HOMER was pub-
lished, a detached Advertisement appeared in
several public Places, containing, besides the
Title of the Book, the *Subjects* of the twelve Sections of which it consists, and likewise some
short Account of their Contents. One of these
Advertisements I procured, after the Piece came
from the Press, and found it assisted me not a
little to comprehend the Design and original Plan
of the Whole. It runs thus :

'*AN ENQUIRY* into the Life and
' Writings of *Homer.* In Twelve Sections.
' THE Book is properly an Answer to this Que-
' stion : "By what Fate, or Disposition of Things
" it has happened, that no Poet has equalled him
" for upwards of two thousand seven hundred
" Years ; nor any, that we know, ever surpassed
" him before."
' Sect. I. An Enquiry into *Homer's* Country ;
' and the Climate of that Country.
' II. Into the public Manners of his Nation.
' III. Into his Language : Origin of Lan-
' guages ; their Progress, and its Causes.
' IV. Into his Religion : Origin of the *Grecian*
' Rites.

Lett. 6.   ' V. Into the Manners of the Times: ancient
    ' and modern Manners compared.

    ' VI. Into the Influence of such a Conjuncture.

    ' VII. Into *Homer*'s Education and Learn-
' ing: History of Learning, and preceeding
' Writers.

    ' VIII. Into his Character, Employment,
' and Manner of Life.

    ' IX. His Journey to *Egypt* : His Allegories.

    ' X. His visiting *Delphi* : Rise of Oracles
' and Theology.

    ' XI. His Converse with the *Phenicians:*
' His Miracles.

    ' XII. His Subject: The *Trojan* War, and
' Wanderings of *Ulysses*.

    ' With a new Head of *Homer*, and sixteen
' Copper-Plates done by the greatest Masters:
' As also a new Map of *Greece*, and of the
' Countries known to the Ancient *Greeks* about
' the Time of the *Trojan* War; their ancient
' Names, and first Inhabitants, with a Draught
' of the Voyages of *Menelaus* and *Ulysses*.'

THE whole Book therefore is an Attempt
to resolve this Single Question, " *By what*
" *means did* Homer *become a greater Poet, than*
" *either any one, known to us, ever was before him,*
" *or than any who has appeared since his Time* ?"
" Or in other Words, *Why no Poem ei-*
" *ther formerly heard of, or now extant, was or*
" *is comparable to the* ILIAD *and* ODYSSEY ?"

I N

I N order to refolve it, you muft either afcribe his Superiority to a fupernatural divine Afiiftance, which many of the Ancients
firmly believed, tho' *We* do not; or, allowing
him to have been an ordinary Man, you muft
enquire into every *Caufe*, natural or accidental,
that can poffibly have Influence upon the human
Mind, towards forming it to Poetry and Verfe.
You muft confider the Influence of Education,
of Example, of Fortune public and private upon
the Soul of Man, and as you go along you muft
always compare their different Kinds, and apply
them to the various correfponding Branches of
Poetry. You muft trace that Art from its earlieft Beginnings; feparate its conftituent Parts,
Language, *Manners*, *Religion*, *Fable*, *Hiftory*,
Characters, *Rythmus*, *Meafure*, and proper
Mythology. You muft view and afcertain the
abftract Nature of each of thefe Parts, then
trace its Progrefs, and compare that again with
the Age of *Homer*, and enquire How *He* came to
excel in it, and in what refpects he does fo.
To bring all thefe together, and make them
bear upon a *fingle Point*, was a Tafk infeparable
from the *Anfwer* of the Queftion. A Queftion
which you fee muft neceffarily include a fur-
prizing number of different Refearches into the
Nature and Origin of *Fiction*, and its Connexion with the various, indeed almoft infinite
Turns of Life and Learning.

C 3

Now,

Lett. 6.   Now, my lively Friend! you have the Clew
of the Book in your Power; give me leave to
infinuate, that it will prove ufeful only in proportion to the Care and Attention with which
you ufe it. If you confider it meerly as an
amufing, curious Speculation, it will juft ferve
to amufe you a little, for the prefent, and then
evanifh : But if after fully comprehending the
Plan you will fit down and compare it attentively with the feveral Sections of the ENQUIRY,
and ftrictly examine whether each Section makes
out the particular Point it was meant to prove,
and how that Point ftands connected with the
general Defign, in that cafe the Plan will effectually rid you of that *fleeting Notion* of the Subject of which you formerly complained. I ex-
perienced the fame thing the firft time I perufed
the Book. While Impatience and Curiofity
hurried me on thro' the various Scenes of Antiquity from the firft barbarous State of wretched
Mortals, to their gradual Improvement by Arts
and Laws and Learning, I quickly loft the Idea
of the preceeding Section, and would have found
it very difficult to have recollected the Thread of
the Subjects when I had done. But after I had
read the Book over and over, and had confidered the Order and Strictnefs of the Inveftiga-
tion, I began to attribute that flippery elufive
Quality to two Caufes. Firft I fufpected the
Author had been at pains to *cover* the Regularity of his Model, and purpofely effaced every
                                    Appearance

Appearance of Form ; avoiding thofe Divifions,
Subdivifions and Repetitions which afford artificial Helps to the Memory, but ftiffen a Treatife like
an old Sermon. This Method leaves the Work
to your own Judgement, and depends folely upon
the Senfe and Capacity of the Reader. The
other is the carelefs familiar manner in which
thefe abftrufe Subjects are treated. You find
nothing to ftop you, if you do not ftop yourfelf;
no uncouth Terms or fcholaftic Phrafes: A
Succeffion. of new Ideas is ever paffing before
you, and fome of the moft rugged Materials in
Learning are handled with that familiar Eafe
and Plainnefs of Speech, as makes you forget
their Nature, and glide over thefe thorny Fields,
where the Critics have fo often tore themfelves,
with unfufpected Security. But, as I faid, in
proportion to our Negligence and Hafte, muft
of neceffity be the Slipperinefs of our Retention.
The folideft Bodies, as they take the fineft Polifh, are likewife the moft ticklifh to handle:
You muft poife well and grafp firm, ere you
have a fure Hold, and be careful how you fhift
hands, left they flip from between them. Moft
People read Books as Children vifit a Flower-
Garden : They amufe themfelves with this or
t'other gaudy Knot ; the Colour calls their Eye
from one Border to another ; the Sight of the
prefent banifhes the laft. It is the Man of real
Tafte, who takes in the Flower- and other Gardens at one View, who confiders the Caft of the

Lett. 6. Grounds, the croſſing Lines, the Diſpoſition of
the Walks, the Arrangement of the Trees, and
the Conveniency of the Shades and Arbours,
the Propriety of the Statues, and perceives
the Symmetry reſulting from the Whole.   But
here's Company coming up ; I muſt leave
you : Adieu, my Friend! May you be happy
as your reaſonable Wiſhes can make you, or, if
you can truſt them, thoſe of

Yours, &c.

LETTER

LETTER SEVENTH.

SAY you fo, Sir! Never ftirred from your Clofet for two whole Days——No, not to make an Excurfion crofs the Meadow to *I——y C——h!* Well, Heaven grant the Charm may not foon lofe its Virtue, but continue to operate, until you have truly tafted the delightful Entertainment of well-directed Study, and be throughly convinced, that it is a manly thing to facrifice a little fleeting Pleafure in the Purfuit of genuine Knowledge. Moft willingly would I fatisfy your growing Curiofity: But as for an Explication of thefe fame Plates, prefixed to the feveral Sections of the ENQUIRY, I muft ingenuoufly plead Ignorance; and will venture to fay, that few People can give a juft one, but the firft Inventor of the original Drawings, who can alone afcertain his own Ideas on fo vague a Subject as *Mythólogy.* But you fhall be very welcome to my Conjectures about fome of them; on which I have beftowed fome Time and Attention, with that pleafing Curiofity you now begin to feel in your turn, in fearching for the Meaning of an Allegory. Some of thefe Conjectures may perhaps be right——and others, I make not the leaft doubt, very wide of the real Intention of the firft Defign. For all Compofitions in Painting——and emblematical Pieces more

than

Lett. 7. than any, give unbounded Scope to the Fancy.
Don't you remember how long a Company of
Sages, and some of them truly learned, stared
upon that beautiful Cartoon of *Julio Romano*'s
Marriage of *Psyche*, in the Duke of *M*——'s
great Gallery? And the extravagant Guesses
Mr. *H*—— made at *Julian*'s Feast of the Gods,
painted by honest VARRIO, in the Stair-case of
Hampton-Court? I found my Conjectures chiefly
upon the Connection of the Story represented in
the Plate, with the Subject of the Section whose
Front it adorns; for the *Inscriptions of* the
Plates at the End of the Book only puzzled and
led me astray. For instance, the fourth Plate
bears for its Inscription, *A* SACRIFICE, *The*
OATH—Now with the strictest Attention, I
cannot find the Vestige of an Oath throughout
the whole Section. I conceive therefore that the
Representations in the Plates are either taken from
the general Design of the Sections to which they
are prefixed; or from some principal Part; some
remarkable Fact related, or some Principle advanced, upon which the Subject possibly turns.
The Design of the first Section is plainly to prove
the various Influence which *Soil* and *Climate*
have upon their several Productions;—and particularly, as the Curious love to speak of late, upon
animal-Plants, I mean their Natives of the human Species.

THE Point of View therefore of the first Plate
directs your Eye to a stately Temple, the Inscription

fcription of whofe Portal bears, that it was facred
to CERES and the SEASONS: or, in other
words, to EARTH the univerfal Mother, and
to the various Influences of Spring, Summer,
Autumn and Winter, in its various Climes. Four
beautiful female Figures follow one another into
the Temple. The Chaplet on the Head and
Feftoon in the Hands of the firft befpeak the
Spring, by which the Ancients began their
Year: The Sheaf and Sickle, and a faintifh
Look difcover the fultry *Summer*: Harveft is
known by her Garland of Grapes and Horn of
Plenty: and fhivering Winter by her Coverings
and Pan of Coals. A Section of the Zodiac
cuts the Sky behind them, intended, I judge, to
fhew upon what the Succeffion of the Seafons
depends. But the Figure in this Plate that gave
me moft pleafure, is the fine venerable old Man
who fits in the Corner, fo ftudious and full of
Attention in forming a human Creature, which
he has almoft finifhed, and obferving thoughtful, whether it wants not yet another Touch of
his all-framing Hand. PROMETHEUS it muft
be; both from the Subject of his Story, and
from the Torch lying at his Feet—but which,
by the by, ought to have been the Reed in
which he ftole celeftial Fire from the Wheel
of the Sun's Chariot, and thievifhly conveyed
it from Heaven to animate his new-made terreftrial Creature, for which he was punifhed as
you now know.

HOWEVER

Lett. 7.   However ingenious this Part of the Design
may seem, I am of opinion, that it erss against
the known Law of Composition, *That all the
Figures, especially in little Pieces, should be employed in one Action:* Unless you say that the Formation of Man is the Action in which both the
Earth, the Seasons, and *Prometheus* are all engaged; which may indeed be understood, but
is by no means the *apparent* Attitude of the
Seasons in the Draught.   Be that as it will, the
Idea so clearly conveyed by the Representation of
this Man-moulder, makes me easily pardon a
moderate Trespass upon a Rule of Design.   In a
Play, I can bear with the Scene's shifting, (contrary to one of the sacred *Unities*) from an Anti-
chamber to a Garden, or from *Pall-Mall* to the
Park, tho' my Fancy turns resty, and refuses to
follow our admired dramatic Poet over Seas
from *Venice* to *Cyprus*, or from *Spain* to *Constantinople*.   These are too unconscionable Strides
for my prosaic Imagination: But a Licence mo-
destly used may be tolerated, if it makes
amends by its Instruction or Entertainment.
The Design of this first Section, is to shew the
Power of Soil and Climate; and that Power exerted in the Formation of Man, who is to be
inspired with a celestial Flame; for which we
have a Temple sacred to Earth and the
Seasons; and behind them a human Creature
forming, to be enlivened with Fire stole from
Heaven.

Now,

Now, methinks, I fee a fignificant Smile
forming upon every Feature of my Friend's
Face: Umph! fays he, And fo this is the way
your ancient Sages, your *Mythologifts*, d'ye call
'em, contrived to account for the making of
MAN? Another Man already made took fome
fresh Clay, newly fubfided in the *Chaos*, and
impregnated it with etherial Seed [a] : Of this he
formed a lifelefs Lump in the Shape of a human
Creature; then had a folar Beam, fome how,
blown into its Breaft, which proved a vivifying
Spirit, and made it inftantly ftart up a Man,
like the *unborn* Doctor ——— !

FAIR and foftly, *Good Sir!* and before you
finally judge of the Fiction, or conclude it to
be ridiculous, hear the ancient poetic Tale. ‘ In
‘ the Beginning of the Reign of *Jove*, when
‘ the happy golden Age was paffed and gone,
‘ the wretched Remains of the human Race
‘ were in a miferable Plight, and in hazard of
‘ utterly perifhing from the Face of the Earth.
‘ Naked, needy, and ignorant they paffed their
‘ dreary Days, living in Woods, and lurking in
‘ Dens like wild Beafts, without Laws, without
‘ Arts, without Humanity; fcarcely fuftaining
‘ their helplefs Lives by the harfh Diet of Her-
‘ bage and Acorns, and making Rocks and
‘ hollow

---

[a] Sive recens Tellus, feductaque nuper ab alto
Æthere, cognati retincbat Semina Cœli ;
Quam fatus Iapeto miftam fluvialibus undis
Finxit in effigiem moderantum cuncta Deorum.

Ovid. Metam.

Lett. 7.‘ hollow Trunks of Trees their fole Shelter from
‘ the Injuries of the Weather. In this haplefs
‘ Condition they perifhed unheeded and un-
‘ known, torn by the Tyger of the Mountain,
‘ and the Bear of the Foreft, famifhed for want
‘ of Food, and froze to Death, or overwhelmed
‘ with Snow. Thus they piteous lived and
‘ unlamented died,—until *Prometheus,* the Son
‘ of *Iapetus* and *Themis,* (that is FORESIGHT,
‘ the Child of *Defire* and *Deftiny*) came to
‘ their Relief. To retrieve wretched Mortals
‘ from Mifery, he called *Pallas* the Goddefs of
‘ Wifdom, (the Power of *Mechanifm,* and
‘ Source of *Invention*) to his Aid : By her means
‘ he mounted to Heaven, where he flily held
‘ the Reed he carried in his Hand to the Wheel
‘ of the Chariot of the Sun : It’s Pith prefently
‘ catched and kept the celeftial Fire, which
‘ he fecretly conveyed to Earth, and made a
‘ Prefent of to *Men.* Inftantly enfued an a-
‘ mazing Turn : It entirely changed the Face
‘ of the World, and made the grand Revolution
‘ in *Human Life.* For along with the Ufe of
‘ Fire, the inventive *Prometheus* difcovered the
‘ latent Treafures that lay concealed in the Bow-
‘ els of the Earth : He brought the till then
‘ unknown *Metals* to Light ; thofe ineftimable
‘ Aids and Ornaments of Life ; thofe Materials
‘ of our Tools, and Propagators of our Power !
‘ By *their* means he firft taught the ftroling
‘ Tribes the Art of building in Timber, Brick

3   ‘ and

' and Stone. He shewed them how to alleviate
' their Toils and supply their Wants, by joining
' Oxen to a Plow and Horses to a Chariot.
' He observed the rising and setting of the Stars,
' the Motions of the Sun and Moon, and by
' them distinguished the *Seasons*, and planned
' out the revolving *Year*. He instructed them
' in the various Virtues of Herbs, Fruits and
' Fossils, and made known their Efficacy in dif-
' pelling Diseases, and allaying the Pains incident
' to Mortals: He even opened a Path thro' the
' Deep, and made them cross the untrod Ocean
' in Vessels compacted of Wood, with Sails ex-
' panded to catch the gliding Gale. In a word,
' no useful Art or rare Invention in Life; no in-
' genious Method of supplying its Wants or
' fulfilling its Wishes, that is not the Gift and
' Product of *Prometheus* [b]: And to crown all,
' he likewise taught them the wondrous, tho'
' now common Contrivance, of painting Sound,
' and speaking to the Eyes; he taught them the
' use of LETTERS, those Guardians of Arts,
' Parents of Memory, and ready Ministers to
' every Muse.

' WHAT wonder then, if the great Friend of
' Men, the Author of their Happiness, their De-
' liverer from Cold, Hunger and Death, their
' Instructor in every thing valuable or pleasant,
'   should

---

[b] Βραχεῖ δε μύθῳ πάντα συλλήβδην μάθε·
Πᾶσαι Τέχναι βροτοῖσιν ἐκ ΠΡΟΜΗΘΕΏΣ.

                                    ΑΙΣΚΥΛ.

' fhould be faid to have *new-formed* the Creature,
' whofe *Life* and *Lot* he had wholly changed ;
' transformed from a Brute to a Man, refcued
' from endlefs Woe, and retrieved from Blood-
' fhed and Barbarity ?'

So far is very well,——and may pafs in the
loofe figurative Language of the Poets: But
is not *Prometheus* plainly and literally faid to
have *made Man*, as well as inftructed him in the
Arts of Life ? The Queftion is fair ; but how
will you relifh it if the Anfwer lead us into a
Labyrinth of Mythology? Have you Spirits
and Patience to remount to the Rife of Things,
and fcan the various Principles, which, in the
Opinion of the Ancients, produced the *World*
and *Man ?*

IMAGINE then the Metropolitan of *Mem-*
phis, or other folemn Myftagogue of *Egypt*,
about to initiate a young Prieft (duly prepared
by Faftings, Purifications and Chaftity) in their
traditional Myftery of *Creation.* " My Son,
" would he fay, LISTEN with Attention and
" Reverence, while I deliver the awful Doc-
" trine of the Birth and Progeny of the ever-
" living Gods—the Doctrine we carefully con-
" ceal from the vulgar and profane, and only
" unfold to the Favourites of Heaven, and Mi-
" nifters of its myfterious Will.

' *WHEN*

' *W H E N* the primeval Parent, CHAOS,
' hoary with unnumbered Ages, was firſt moved
' by the Breath of *Erebus*, ſhe brought forth her
' enormous Firſt-born *Hyle*; and at the ſame
' portentous Birth the amiable almighty *Eros*
' Chief of the Immortals: They were no ſooner
' come to Light than they produced an infinite
' Offspring; various and jarring at firſt, but
' afterwards the Fountains of Being (*a*), the ter-
' rible TITANS. Five and forty of their Names
' have been revealed to Men; among whom
' the chief are *Cæus, Creion, Hyperion*, and
' *Iapetus*, Males; and *Thea, Rhea, Themis,*
' *Mnemoſyne*, and the lovely *Tethys*, Females;
' after whom was born of the ſame Parents,
' their youngeſt Son, the mighty *Saturn*. *Ia-*
' *petus* and *Themis* joining, had the divine *Pro-*
' *metheus*; after whoſe auſpicious Birth, and no
' wonder, they had Eight and twenty Children
' more; or, according to a more authentic Tra-
' dition thirty Sons, and as many Daughters,
' Authors of the various *Orders* of living Things,
' while *Prometheus* with the Aſſiſtance of his
' Spouſe *Celeno* the Daughter of *Atlas*, the

D   ' mighty

(*a*) Ἀϱχαὶ ϰ̀ Πηγαὶ ϖάντων Θνητῶν ϖολυμόχθων,
Ειναλίων, ϖ]ηνῶν τε ϰ̀ ὅι χθόνα ναιετάɤσιν·
Ἐξ ὑμέων γὰϱ ϖᾶσα ϖέλει γενεὰ ϰα]ὰ ϰόσμɤν.

ΟΡΦ. Υμν. ΤΙΤΗΝΕΣ.

Lett. 7. ' mighty Prop of Heaven, created their Lord
' and Lawgiver, mortal Man.'

WITH profound Submiffion, we may fuppofe,
and entire Refignation of his Intellects, would
the young Candidate of the Priefthood receive
the Doctrine he did not underftand : and in re-
ward of his Docility, or upon fome other weighty
Confideration, his reverend Teacher might
perhaps condefcend to remove a Corner of the
Veil, and give him a Glimpfe of the latent
Truth.

" To Thee, my Son, who may one day prove
" a ftately Pillar in the Temple of *Noph*, and a
" Support of our facred Order, the Glory of
" *Egypt*, will I difcover a Part of the divine
" Tradition, denied to vulgar Ears, and uttered
" by the pure High-prieft on folemn Days, not
" without Trembling and Amazement." Know
then, confecrated Youth! ' That ere this fair
' Univerfe which thou beholds, appeared ; ere
' the Sun mounted on high, or the Moon gave
' her paler Light ; ere the Vales were ftretched
' out below, or the Mountains reared their
' towering Heads—ere the Winds began to
' blow, or the Rivers to flow, or Plant or Tree
' had fprung from the Earth—while the Hea-
' vens yet lay hid in the mighty Mafs, nor e'er
' a Star had ftarted to its Orb, for Ages infinite,
' the various Parts of which this wondrous
' Frame confifts, lay jumbled and inform,—
' brooding

‘ brooding o’erwhelmed in the Abyſs of
‘ Being (*):
 ‘ THERE they had lain for ever and for ever,
‘ if the Breath of the tremendous *Erebus* (*a*),
‘ the Spirit that dwells in eternal Darkneſs had
‘ not gone forth and put the liſtleſs Maſs (*b*) in
‘ vital Agitation. ’Twas then the congenial
‘ Parts began to fever from their heterogeneous
‘ Aſſociates, and to feek a mutual intimate Em-
‘ brace—*Matter* (*c*) appeared, and inſeparable
‘ from it *Attraction* (*d*) inſtantly began to ope-
‘ rate: And O! Who can unfold, or ſufficient-
‘ ly declare the Strife ineffable, th’ unutterable
‘ War that attended their Operation. *Quali-*
‘ *ties* (*e*) their firſt-born oppoſite and jarring,
‘ never before exiſting ſprung into Being, and
‘ fwift began the univerſal Shock. *Powers* (*f*)
‘ till then unknown, and *ſuperior* (*g*) Degrees
‘ of theſe Powers, all active Principles, continued
‘ and increaſed it. *Order* (*h*), *Succeſſion* (*i*),
‘ *Retention* (*k*), and *Figurability* (*l*) were paſſive

    D 2   ‘ in

(*) Ἦν ὁμῦ πάνlα δυνάμει, ἐνεργείᾳ δ᾽ ὄυ.

       Ἀρις. Τὰ μεταὰ τὰ Φυζ. Λ.

 (*a*) *Erebus* is plainly the Power of DARKNESS, or Dimneſs ;
being a Greek Termination put to an Eaſtern Word ערב *Eréb*,
the Evening, *Mixture* of Darkneſs and Light. See the *Phenician*
Coſmogony below. (*b*) The CHAOS. (*c*) HYLE. (*d*) *Eros*,
or *Love*. (*e*) *Cæus*. ΚΟΙΟΣ is the ancient *Ionic* for ποιΘ.
(*f*) *Creion*, Κρειων, powerful. (*g*) *Hyperion*, Ῠπερειων, tran-
ſcendant. (*h*) *Thea*, from the old Verb ΘΕΩ, whence Θηwι.
(*i*) *Rhea*, from Ῥέω, the Flux of Time. (*k*) *Mnemoſyne*, Μνμω-
ſυνη, Memory. (*l*) *Tethys* from the old שט which the *Chal-*
deans pronounce תשא *Tetha*, liquidâ perfundere, whence *Tethys*,
               Fuſion,

Lett. 7.' in the genial Conteſt. But *Deſire* (*m*) and
   ' *Poſſibility* (*n*) (or *Intention* and *Aptitude*) mild-
   ' ly interpoſed, and begot *Providence* or *Fore-*
   ' *ſight* (*o*), who being joined with his Bride (*p*)
   ' ᴗMeaſure (*q*) or Perfection (the Daughter of
   ' Contemplation (*r*,) preſided over the forming
   ' World, directed the Births of the lab'ring
                  ' Parts,

Fuſion, Moiſture. (*m*) *Japhet* פָתֵה in Kal, to allure, raiſe, deſire, ſeduce ; whence πειθ.. *Japhet* is elder than *Saturn*, who
was the youngeſt of the *Titans* ; that is to ſay, *Time* did not begin
till the World was made ; ſee the *Platonic* Account of Time below. (*n*) *Themis* the moſt ancient and venerable of the Goddeſſes ;
whoſe Oracles were from the Beginning, and ſo infallible, that
ſhe taught *Apollo* himſelf to propheſy ; firſt married to *Iapetus*,
the *Titan*, and then to the all-governing Nature, *Jupiter* himſelf.
(*o*) *Prometheus*. The *Athenians*, diſtinguiſhed among all the
Greeks by their Ingenuity and Devotion, had an Altar in the *Aca-*
demy (the Reſort of the moſt ingenious of *Athens*) on which they
ſacrificed the Day of the Lamp-Solemnity. It was dedicated to
Prometheus, Pallas, and *Vulcan*. In their opinion theſe were
συμβώμοι Θεοὶ, conjunct Gods to be worſhipped on the ſame
Altar, for the ſame obvious Reaſon that *Venus* is ſometimes
joined with *Bacchus* and *Ceres*, and at others with *Cupid, Hebe*,
and the *Graces*. But the moſt Orthodox of the Mythologiſts,
Orpheus, ſolemnly addreſſes *Prometheus* as the ſame with *Saturn* ;
and joined with the ancient Rʜᴇᴀ, that Flow of Durationin the
Fulneſs of which all Things were formed by *Providence*,

    ῬΕΑΣ ΠΟΣΙ΄! ΣΕΜΝΕ΄ ΠΡΟΜΗΘΕΥ̃ *.

The former took him, 'twould ſeem, for a *moral*, or *human* Principle ; and the latter for a *natural* or *divine* one.
    (*p*) כלא *Calai* in *Syriac* ſignifies a Bride.
    (*q*) כילי Menſuræ : from כל menſus eſt. But כליל Perfec-
tiones from כלל, conſummavit, perfecit.   (*r*) *Atlas.* طلب

Talab, Conſideravit, animum advertit, intentus fuit.   طكع

et طكاع *Talao* et *Atthalao* qui res perſpicit, cognitione ſuperior ; *inde Virgil*.—Docuit quæ maximus *Atlas*. The *Greeks* put
frequently their Σ for the Aſpirates of the Eaſterns, and particularly for the moſt unutterable of them to a Weſtern Throat the
ع Ain, which they entirely omitted in the Beginning of Words,
contenting themſelves with the bare Vowel.

    * Ὕμνῷ εἰς ΚΡΟΝΟΝ.

‘ Parts, called to Light the vegetable and animal Lett. 7.
‘ Race, and then crowned his wondrous Work
‘ with the Formation of Man.'

BUT bleſs me ! How have I been led into the Receſs of the *Egyptian* Sanctuary ? Quick let us retire : and you, my Friend, forgive me, both for having been betrayed into ſuch a Sally of the abſtract metaphyſical Mythology, and for preſuming to join you with ſuch bad Company, as at once to bid you and the Metropolitan of *Memphis Adieu.*

I am, &c.

D 3   LETTER

LETTER EIGHTH.

THE Subject of the second Section of the
ENQUIRY, &c. is said to be *Ancient
Manners*; by which, I suppose, is meant the
rude unhappy Life which Mankind lived in the
early Ages of the World, and what is with great
Impropriety called their *natural State*; when
the Earth was not adorned with Towns, nor inhabited by civilized Nations governed by Laws,
or polished by Arts, but was peopled with vagrant independent Tribes, lawless among themselves and often at war with their Neighbours;
unawed by any but present Dangers, and therefore satisfying their present Passions whenever it
was in their power. This View of the Subject
of the Section gave me some notion of a very
compounded Representation in the Plate prefixed
to it, but which belongs all to the same Subject
when put together, and has a strict Unity in
Sense, if not in Shew.

PAN, as the Word signifies, is the ancient
Emblem of the WHOLE *of Things:* He represents the *Universe*; and with the most learned
and thoughtful of the Ancients, passed for the
first and oldest of their Divinities. His Figure
is a Delineation of *Nature*, and that rough Face
which first it wore as mentioned above. His
spotted Robe of a Leopard's Skin expressed the

spangled

spangled Heavens; his Person is composed of various and opposite Parts, rational and irrational, a Man and a Goat, as is the World of an all-governing Mind and of butting prolific Elements Fire and Water, Earth and Air. He loves to chace the flying Nymphs; few Productions being brought to maturity without *Moisture*; and like the *alma Parens*, has a strong Propensity to Generation. According to the *Egyptians*, and the very ancientest of the *Grecian* Sages, he had neither Father nor Mother, but sprung of DE-MOGORGON at the same instant with the fatal Sisters the *Parcæ*: A beautiful Way of saying, that the Universe sprung from an unknown Power (to them) and was formed according to the unalterable Relations and eternal Aptitudes of Things; the Daughters of *Necessity*. But his most significant Symbol, and most elegantly expressive of his divine harmonious Constitution, is the wondrous R E E D on which he incessant plays, composed of *seven* Pipes unequal among themselves; but fitted together in so just proportion, as to produce the most perfect and unerring Harmony. The Orbits in which the *seven* Planets of our solar System move around their Center are all of different Diameters, and are described in different Times, by Bodies of different Magnitudes; yet from the Order of that solemn Movement results that celestial Music of the Spheres, not perceptible indeed by our material Organs,

D 4

but

Lett. 8. but delicious and ravifhing to the Ear of the Mind.

OTHERS however went ftill deeper, and applied it to the *Pythagoric*, that is the *Egyptian* Account, not only of the Creation, but of its *Caufes.* Their abftrufe enigmatical Method of explaining or more properly concealing their Doctrines from every body but their own Difciples, I will not trouble you with at prefent; farther than to put you in mind, that they defigned every Species of Things by certain *Numbers.* Your happy Turn for thefe Kinds of Studies, muft have long fince taught you, that Numbers are capable of reprefenting geometrical Figures, Triangles, Squares, Cones and Polygons of all Sorts. All thefe Numbers reprefentative of material Things when compounded, made the Sum of *twenty-eight*, of which *feven* is the Root, and therefore the ΕΠΤΑΣ, *SEVEN* and its Powers, was the Reprefentative of all the *material* Creation. The various Degrees of Spirits and Genii were expreffed by Numbers amounting to *Sixteen*—of which *four* is the Root, and therefore the ΤΕΤΡΑΚΤΥΣ, FOUR and its Powers, was the Reprefentative of the *immaterial creating Principle*, and all the intellectual Beings united to it; and for that reafon conftituted the folemn *Pythagoric* Oath,

NAI

ΝΑΙ ΜΑ ΤΗΝ ΗΜΕΤΕΡΑΝ ΨΥΧΗΝ ΓΕΝΝΗ-
ΣΑΝΤΑ ΤΕΤΡΑΚΤΥΝ,
ΠΑΓΑΝ ΑΕΝΝΑΟΥ ΦΥΣΕΩΣ!

Yes, by the Soul-begetting *F O U R* I fwear,
Nature's eternal, ever-flowing Spring.

THE ΕΠΤΑΣ therefore, or material Creation,
confifting of the various Combinations, Divifions
and Multiplications of the Number *Seven*, is the
wondrous Inftrument of PAN, from the Concord
and Harmony of whofe unerring Notes refults
the ECHO, the Object of his Love. So that of
this divine harmonious Reed, the Symbol of our
Solar-Syftem, one may fay with the pious Poet,

> What tho' in folemn Silence all
> Move round our dark terreftrial Ball,
> What tho' nor real Voice nor Sound
> Amid their radiant Orbs be found,
> In *Reafon's Ear* they all rejoice,
> And utter ftill their glorious Voice ;
> For ever finging, as they fhine,
> *The Hand that moves us is divine.*

Or as it is painted by a great Mathematician,

En tibi Norma Poli—! en divæ Libramina
　　Molis!
Computus en Jovis! Et quas dum primordia
　　rerum
Conderet, omnipotens fibi Leges ipfe Creator
Dixerit, & Operis quæ Fundamenta locârit.

　　　　　　　　　　　　　　BUT

Lett. 8. But I do not suppose that *Pan* appears in this Plate, either in his physical or philosophical Capacity, but sits piping upon the jutting Point of a Rock, as the honest rural God of *Arcadia*, Protector of the Shepherds, and expressive of that rude pastoral Life led by the early incivilized Inhabitants of *Greece.* On one hand, an humble Supplicant prostrates himself before the ancient *Vesta*; and on the other, a military Man is running off with an unhappy Female he has seized as his Prey.

Vesta, among the contemplative Priests of the East, passed for the latent Power of Fire; or that internal Texture and Disposition of some sorts of Matter that renders it combustible, while others are little affected with Heat. As such she was the Wife of *Cælus*, and Mother of *Saturn*,—the sacred eternal Fire, worshipped with the greatest Reverence, and most pompous Ceremonies by all the Eastern Nations (*a*) : But among the less speculative *Europeans*, who received the Knowledge of this Goddess at second hand, she was confidered only as *Saturn*'s Daughter, a national tutelary Divinity; as for instance, by *Numa* the pious *Sabine* Priest and King, who made her the *Poliuchos* or Guardian of the Infant-State; tho' generally speaking over all *Italy*, and long before in *Greece*, she was worshipped as a domestic-Deity, and Protectress of the

(*a*) The common Word in *Chaldee* signifying Fire is אֵשׁ Fſh:tt. ʹΕΣΤΙʹΑ, Vefta.

the Family-Seat. ' *Vesta*, says the knowing *Po-*
' *sidonius*, the Daughter of *Saturn*, first invented
' a human Habitation, whose Image for that rea-
' son they constantly place within the House,
' that she may preserve the Edifice and protect
' the Inhabitants.' (*b*)   An Invention indeed of
the highest Beneficence to miserable Mortals
ranging the Woods or creeping into Caves, which
History attributes to *Phoroneus* the Son of *Inachus*,
at least of building Houses wrought with Brick(*c*),
and which cannot be done without the Assistance
of *Vesta*.

WHEN *Homer*, who had plain undisguised
Nature ever in his eye, is describing the Mind of
a Man intent upon Building, he says he squares
one Stone, and lays it carefully and exactly upon
the top of another ——ANEMOIO EIN' ΑΛΕΩΡΗΝ
to be a Defence against the Wind.   The same
Poet addresses this Goddess in one of his Hymns,

Vesta to whom in every lofty Pile
Of Gods immortal or Earth-faring Men
A Seat eternal's doom'd: to thee, old Queen!
The first best Honours piously be paid.

THIS hoary recluse Goddess (*d*) then, the
pure eternal *Vesta* (*e*) appears in a double Capacity;

(*b*) The same Word, in another Form שׁוֹשִׁ signifies the
Foundation and Strength of a Building,
   (*c*) πλινθυφεῖς δόμυς.   ΑΙΣΧΥΛΑ.
   (*d*) ——Canæ Penetralia Vestæ. Virgil.
   (*e*) Anciliorum nominis et togæ,
        Oblitus, æternæque Vestæ.
                                    Horat.

Lett. 8. city; either as the grand enlivening Genius of the terreſtrial Globe, worſhipped with ſolemn Ceremonies, and honoured by annual Proceſſions under the Name of *Oroſmades* (*f*) by the *Per-ſians*, and under that of *Serapis* (*g*) by the *E-gyptians*; or as the permanent immoveable Seat of Gods and Men, the EARTH itſelf, and by an eaſy Tranſition the native Soil of a Nation, or the fixed Habitation of a Family: *Ovid*, in his *Faſti*, the moſt learned and uſeful of all his Works, hints at them both:

> *Veſta* eadem eſt et *Terra*; ſubeſt vigil Ignis utrique;
> Significant *Sedem, Terra Focuſque* ſuam.

But *Plato* confines her to the latter; when de-ſcribing in his ſublime manner the Movement of the Univerſe, he ſays, ' That the ſupreme ' God, the beneficent *Jupiter*, driving a winged ' Chariot thro' the Heaven, marches firſt, direct-' ing and inſpecting all Things; after whom the ' whole Hoſt of Deities and Demons, ranged into ' twelve Bands follow in order: But that *Veſta* ' alone remains at home (*h*).

IN

(*f*) אירים חסדי *Orim-haſde*, The bleſſed Fire: it imports originally in the Chaldee, the *beneficent Lights*, that do good without Compenſation.

(*g*) Some derive *Serapis* from שׂרָף Seraph, to burn. I believe it to be a Compound from סָר אַפִּי Sar Api, the Lord Apis.

(*h*) In TIMAEO.

In the same way then, as *Pan* is the plain rural God, *Vesta* in this Reprefentation feems likewife to be taken in the tritest Acceptation for a Hearth and a Home: A Blessing whose Importance our naked Forefathers when driven from Wood to Wood by civil Wars, or harassed by *Danish* and *Saxon* Incursions, could much better conceive than We, whom Liberty and Property, those inestimable Possessions, distinguish from all the Inhabitants of the Earth. A *House*, besides being a Shelter from the Inclemencies of the Weather, and a Repository for all the various Conveniences of Life, is a kind of *Sanctuary* to its Possessor, and a Protection from Insult and Violence, especially to the weaker Sex, who in the lawless Days when Force alone bore sway, were seldom safe but when they kept at home. It was a noble Boast, and worthy of a Conqueror, that *William* the First made concerning the Effects of his Policy, That a fair Maiden might now travel all over *England* with a Purse of Gold in her hand without Fear or Molestation.

As it was by the Assistance of Vesta, the enlivening igneous Principle, that *Jupiter* obtained the supreme Government of the Universe, he allowed her in return to chuse what Privilege or Honour she thought fit. *Vesta* made choice of perpetual Virginity, being incapable of being associated with any other Element, and of the *first Share* (a) of every Offering made to all the other Gods.

(a) Ἀπαρχαὶ, Primitiæ,

Lett. 8. Gods. Her Prieſteſſes muſt therefore be pure, unſpotted Virgins, and have the precedency at every Feaſt or Sacrifice where they happened to be preſent: Her Temple is a Sanctuary from Violence, and eſpecially from Violence offered to the Honour of a Maid. Accordingly, in this Plate, we are preſented with Nature's rudeſt Draught. Firſt the ſhaggy God, frequenting the Rocks and Wilds; that is, uncultivated Lands, and a ſolitary paſtoral Life, obnoxious to Rapine and Inſult: then, its firſt Protection, the Power of *Veſta*, human Habitations juſt beginning to form and become fixed before the Birth of Laws, in the Infancy of Arts, amidſt Ignorance and Barbarity. That Barbarity firſt makes way for military Improvements, which naturally produce Incurſions, Plunder, and ſuch Inſtances of Inhumanity, as you have repreſented in Perſpective on t'other ſide the Plate.

HERE I intended to conclude my Letter: The Emblems are explained. What more is to be done? To moralize—and draw Inferences from the Explication—? No—but only to obſerve a ſtrange ſort of Likeneſs between ancient and modern Superſtition.—A Paſſion diffuſed thro' all Ages and Generations, and acting uniformly, however its Objects may be varied. The Circumſtance of the preceding Allegories that makes me ſay ſo is this: The Gods of the Ancients, you ſee, appear in a double Light; as the Parts and Powers of Nature to the Philoſophers, as real Perſons to the Vulgar; the former underſtood and admired

them

them with a decent Veneration ; the latter Lett. 8.
dreaded and adored them with a blind Devotion.
Has not the fame thing happened in modern religious Matters? Are there not many Parables and
Prophecies well underſtood and juſtly explained
by the wiſe and knowing, that are groſsly ſhock-
ing, in their literal Signification, and yet greedily
ſo ſwallowed by the unthinking Vulgar? Are there
not many Images, Relicks, Wafers, Agnus-Dei's,
and other ſacred Utenſils among the Appendages
of Devotion, that were never worſhipped by a
Beſſarion nor a *Bembo*, by a *Borromeo* nor a
Sarpi; but which the far greater Part of thoſe
who arrogate to themſelves the Name of *Catho-
lics* abſurdly adore? Some worſhipping them as
real preſent *Divinities* (*a*), and others reverencing
them as ſomething *divine!* And yet theſe very
People would be apt to laugh at an *Egyptian,*
we may ſuppoſe, for worſhipping, or worſhipping
before an emblematical Figure of a Deity with
a Dog's Head, or a Hawk's, or a Wolf's; deſervedly, to be ſure, but at the ſame time moſt inconſiſtently with themſelves: And even the better
ſort of them as inconſiſtently imagine that the
learned and thinking Part of the *Egyptians* believed their Gods to have in reality theſe diſſi-
milar monſtrous Shapes: That the *Mendeſian*
Sages, for inſtance, really believed their God *Pan*
to have the Limbs of a Goat, or that they indeed
worſhipped

(*a*) Sic Homines novêre *Deos*, quos arduus Æther
Occulit, et colitur pro Jove *FORMA* Jovis.
Ovid de Ponto, Epiſt. VIII.

Lett. 8. worſhipped that Animal as a Deity. That the
Bulk of the People did ſo, I make not the leaſt
doubt: But I will give you one convincing Argument, that the better inſtructed Prieſts and the
more knowing of the Rulers did not ; an Argument which will for ever baniſh your Doubts, if
you had any, and perſuade you of the Truth of
this ſeeming Paradox, ' That the wiſe and learned
' of the Ancients did not believe their Gods to be
' Perſons, nor underſtood literally their perſonal
' Qualities and Adventures.' For this purpoſe,
lend, my Friend, an attentive Ear to a pious
Prayer, and accompany with ſerious Thought a
ſolemn Invocation: But firſt, on the Wings of
Fancy, again waft your ſelf to the ancient holy
Land, the Mother of Myſteries, and native Soil
of moſt Religions that have prevailed on the
Earth. Imagine you are ſailing up the *Mendeſian*
Branch of the *Nile* in the Opening of the Spring,
when the vernal Gales firſt begin to invite Vegetation. What Crouds are haſting joyous along the
Banks? What a multitude of Boats full of Men
and Women in their beſt Attire cover the whole
River! It is the grand Feſtival of the ancient
PAN. See! his auguſt Temple thrown open;
its Dome, orbicular like the Vault of Heaven,
re-echoes to the ſeven-fold Reed—the Shrine is
adorned—and the Goat-limbed God ſtands diſcovered in Majeſty. The Altar begins to blaze—
the naked Prieſt approaches—he fills his Hands
with ſacred Incenſe, and lifts them reverent towards

wards the holy Place. The Muſic ſtops. The Lett. 8.
attending Crouds fall proſtrate on the ground:
He bows—he burns Incenſe—Hark—he prays!

H Y M N.

PAN! *I invoke: the mighty God,—the univerſal Nature—the Heavens—the Sea—the all-nouriſhing Earth, and the eternal Fire; For theſe are thy Members, O mighty* PAN!

COME, *thou happy Source of ever-wheeling Motion— revolving with the circling Seaſons— Author of Generation— divine Enthuſiaſm, and Soul-warming Tranſport!— Thou liv'ſt among the Stars, and lead'ſt in the Symphony of the Univerſe by thy all-chearing Song :— Thou ſcattereſt Viſions and ſudden Terrors among Mortals— delight'ſt in the tow'ring Goat-fed Rock, the Springs alſo and Paſtures of the Earth! of Sight unerring— Searcher of all Things— Lover of the* ECHO *of thy own eternal Harmony! Allbegotten and all-begetting God! invoked under a thouſand Names— Supreme Governour of the World—! Growth-giving— fruitful— lightbringing Power! co-operating with Moiſture— inhabiting the Receſſes of Caves—dreadful in Wrath, true two-horned* Jove!

E   *By*

Lett. **8.**

> By *Thee* Earth's *endlefs Plain was firmly*
> *fixt :*
> *To Thee the* Sea's *deep-heaving Surge gives way :*
> *And ancient* Ocean's *Waves thy Voice obey,*
> *Who in his briny Bofom laps the Globe.*
> *Nor lefs the fleeting Air ; the vital Draught*
> *That fans the Food of every living Thing :*
> *And even the high-enthron'd all-fparkling Eye*
> *Of ever-mounting* Fire : *Thefe all divine,*
> *Tho' various, run the Courfe, which* Thou *or-*
>   *dain'ft ;*
> *And by* thy *wond'rous Providence exchange*
> *Their feveral jarring Natures, to provide*
> *Food for Mankind all o'er the boundlefs Earth.*
>
> *But O bright Source of Ecftafy divine*
> *And Dance enthufiaftic, with our Vows*
> *Inhale thefe facred Odours, and vouchfafe*
> *To us an happy Exit of our Lives,*
> *Scatt'ring thy Panics to the World's End*.*

I am,

Yours, *&c.*

ᵃ ΠΑΝΟ῀Σ ΘΥΜΙΆΜΑ, ποικίλα.

ΠᾶΝΑ καλῶ κρατερὸν *, κόσμοιο τὸ σύμπαν,
᾽Ουρανὸν, ἠδὲ θάλασσαν, ἰδὲ χθόνα παμβασίλειαν,
Καὶ πῦρ ἀθάνατον · τάδε γὰρ μέλη ἐςὶ τὰ Πανός·
᾽Ελθὲ μάκαρ σκιρτητὰ, περίδρομε, σύνθρονε ῞Ωραις·
᾽Αιγομελὲς, βακχευτὰ, φιλένθεε, ἀςροδίαιτε·
῾Αρμονίαν κόσμοιο κρέκων φιλοπαίζμονι μολπῇ.
Φαντασιῶν ἐπαρωγὲ, φόβων ἔκπαγλε βροτείων.
᾽Αιγονόμοις χαίρων ἀνὰ πίδακας ἠδέ τε βήταις,
῎Ευσκοπε, θηρητὴρ ἠχῦς φίλε, σύγχορε νυμφῶν.
Παντοφυὴς, γενέτωρ πάντων, πολυώνυμε δαῖμον.
Κοσμοκράτωρ αὐξητὰ φαεσφόρε, κάρπιμε παιάν·
᾽Αντροχαρὲς, βαρύμηνις, ἀληθὴς Ζεὺς ὁ κεράςης.
Σοὶ γὰρ ἀπειρέσιον γαίης πέδον ἐςήρικλαι,
῎Εικει δ᾽ ἀκαμάτκ πόντκ τὸ βαθύσωορον ὕδωρ,
᾽Ωκεανός τε πέριξ ἐν ὕδασι γαῖαν ἑλίσσων.
῎Αεριόν τε μέρισμα, τροφῆς ζωοῖσιν ἔναισμα,
Καὶ κορυφῆς ἐφύπερθεν ἐλαφροτάτκ πυρὸς ὄμμα.
Βαίνει γὰρ τάδε θεῖα πολύκριλα σαισὶν ἐφετμαῖς.
᾽Αλλάσσεις δὲ φύσεις πάντων ταῖς σαῖσι προνοίαις,
Βόσκων ἀνθρώπων γενεὴν κατ᾽ ἀπείρονα κόσμον.
᾽Αλλὰ μάκαρ βακχευτὰ φιλένθεε βαῖν᾽ ἐπὶ λοιβαῖς
῾Ευιέροις ἀγαθὴν δ᾽ ὄπασον βιότοιο τελευτὴν,
Πανικὸν ἐκπέμπων οἶςρον ἐπὶ τέρμαλα γαίης.

ΟΡΦΕΩΣ ΥΜΝΟΣ ἐις ΠΑΝΑ.

* There is a Gap in this Verſe : I believe the Word σῶμα,
or πλέςμα, has been loſt.

LETTER NINTH.

" **Y**OU begin to have fome *Lueurs* *, you
" fay, of what this fame Mythology
" wou'd be at : But are apprehenfive, if you
" purfue it, that it will lead you aftray, and
" like *Will-with-the-Wifp* land you in a Quag-
" mire."——Fear not, my Friend ! It is a harmlefs *Medium* thro' which many beautiful Objects
that will not bear a near Look, or vanifh quite
if narrowly canvaffed, may be fafely viewed at
a proper diftance : For in a fkilful Hand, it
magnifies or diminifhes at pleafure, while

> *Ten thoufand Colours wafted thro' the Air*
> *In magic Glances play upon the Eye,*
> *Combining in their endlefs fairy Forms*
> *A wild Creation* †.

Indeed, when one has been well accuftomed to
it ; and been often entertained with its animated
Scenes, it is not eafy to lay it afide.   A good
Bifhop, who inftead of his Bible, fpent moft of
his Time in making large Commentaries on
Homer's Poems, ingenuoufly confeffes in the Introduction to his Work,

THAT

---

* Gleams of Light.
† From *The Pleafures of the Imagination :* a noble genuine
Poem : the Production of real Genius, and full of important
Inftruction.

THAT it had perhaps been better, to have avoided liftening to thofe Syrens at the Beginning ; to have ftopped his Ears with Wax, or turned off another Road, to efcape the bewitching Charm : But, adds the poetical Prelate, if any one has not abftained at firft, but ventured to liften to their alluring Voice, I cannot believe that he will afterwards eafily pafs——, no not tho' he be bound with many a Chain: nor if he cou'd, do I think it would be wife or grateful fo to do. For if as they commonly reckon up feven Wonders in the World worthy *to be feen*, we could likewife afcertain the Number of Things moft worthy *to be heard*, the prime of them would undoubtedly be *Homer's* Iliad and Odyffey.

BUT you, my Friend, are in no hazard ; you are too much in the Gayety of Life to be deeply ftruck with the Contemplation of any other than living Objects of your own Species; or if perchance you fhould be feized, as lately, with a thoughtful Fit, Quadrille, or a Vifit to Υ**** will cure you at any time. However, to banifh your Apprehenfions entirely, and upon more reafonable Grounds, I comply with your Defire, and fend you a fhort Account of the Nature and different Kinds of Mythology: and becaufe to a Mind not much accuftomed to abftract Reafoning, bare Definitions are but dry Entertainment, an Example or two will beft delineate each Species of this mimical Art.

Lett. 9. MYTHOLOGY in general, is *Inſtruction con-veyed in a Tale.* A Fable or meer Legend without a Moral, or if you pleaſe without a Meaning, can with little Propriety deſerve the Name. But it is not ſtrictly confined to *Narration:* Signs and Symbols are ſometimes brought in play, and Inſtruction is conveyed by ſignificant Ceremonies, and even by material Repreſentations.

THE firſt and ſimpleſt flows from pure untaught Nature; a *Similitude,* a *Metaphor,* is an Allegory in Embryo, which extended and animated will become a perfect Piece of full-grown Mythology. Take for an Example a vulgar Saying, *The World's a Stage:* How ſimple in itſelf; and yet how eaſily enlarged ? ' On this great Theater, ' would a Mythologiſt ſay, a new Piece is play'd ' every Day; and he who yeſterday was only a ' Spectator, ſhall to-morrow become himſelf the ' Subject of the Play : while Fortune ſits abſo- ' lute Miſtreſs of the Drama, diſpoſes of the ' Parts at her Pleaſure, and aſſigns the Charac- ' ters of Kings or Coblers ; Stateſmen or Moun- ' tebanks, Buffoons or Biſhops as her Caprice ' dictates : Then ſhifting the Scene, he who ' lately appeared a ridiculous Mummer comes ' on a Monarch, a baniſh'd Tyrant ſtrolls about ' a Beggar, and a Swine-herd turns Cardinal and ' ſupreme Pontiff: Happy the Man, who, be it ' high or low, acts with Decency his allotted
' Part,

' Part, and retires applauded by the real Judges
' in the Audience.'

Now *Metaphor* is the Produce of all Nations— especially of the Eastern *; People given to Taciturnity, of strong Paffions, fiery Fancies, and therefore seldom opening their Mouth, but in dark Sayings and myftic Parables. For Metaphor is the Language of *Paffion*; as Simile is the Effect of a *warm Imagination*, which when *cooled* and *regulated* explains itself in diffuse Fable and elaborate Allegory.

The second fort, and more properly deferving the Name of Mythology, are the admirable *Esopic Tales*, retaining the ancient Simplicity, but so exquifitely adapted to the peculiar Inftincts of the Birds and Beafts he employs, and so juftly applied to Life and Manners, that the natural *La Fontaine*'s, the polite *La Motte*'s, and even our ingenious *Gay*'s Imitations, tho' highly entertaining, only ferve to fhew the *Phrygian* to be inimitable. All their Wit, and various Refinings can not compenfate his *elegant Simplicity*. It is in effect the happieft way of Inftruction. The Mind eafily perceives the Moral; and retains it with the fame Pleafure as the Memory preferves uneffaced the Imagery in which it was conveyed; and their joint Impreffion is so lafting and perfuafive, and finds fuch ready accefs to the the raweft

E 4   Fancies,

---

* Thus with the *Syrian* Patriarch, *Reuben* is unftable as Water, *Judah* a Lion's Whelp, *Iffachar* a bony Afs, *Dan* a Serpent by the Way, *Naphthali* a Hind let loofe, *Joseph* a fruitful Branch, and *Benjamin* a rending Wolf.

Lett. 9. Fancies, that it is propofed by the *grand Con-noiffeur* * in human Nature, as the propereft Method to form the Minds of Children, that little moral Tales fhould be told them by their Mothers and Nurfes as foon as they can fpeak. But as thefe enticing Tales, if of a bad Tendency, might lead young Minds to Vice; he is at great pains to give fome remarkable Reftrictions concerning the Species of Tales he would alone have told. As firft, that no authorized Tale muft bear That ever there was War in Heaven, or any Difcord or unbecoming Paffion incident to the divine Nature: Then, that as the fupreme Being is always juft, good, and beneficent; no God muft ever be faid to be the caufe of any real Ill to Men: And laftly, fince the Deity is abfolutely one fimple Effence, always true in Word and Deed, he neither transforms himfelf into various Shapes to appear to Men, nor does impofe upon our Senfes by empty Phantoms, much lefs deceive us by falfe Speeches or by fending delufive Signs to Men whether afleep or awake. Wherefore the Gods muft never in any Tale, be reprefented as transforming themfelves like Jugglers, or leading People aftray with any fort of Sophiftry in Words or Deeds (a).

THESE

* Great Judge.

(a) Δεῖ περὶ ΘΕΩΝ κỳ λέγειν κỳ ποιεῖν, ὡς μήτε αὐτὸς ΓΟΗΤΑΣ τῷ μεῖαϐάλλειν ἑαυῖὺς, μήτε ἡμᾶς ψεύδεσι παράγειν ἐν λόγῳ ἢ ἔργῳ.

ΠΛΑΤΩΝ. Πολιτ. B.

THESE Cautions were chiefly intended againſt *Heſiod, Homer,* and *Eſchylus,* out of whoſe Poems he produces Inſtances of Tales unworthy of the divine Nature; and of whoſe bewitching Imagery the Philoſopher is ſo apprehenſive, that he will not allow ſuch Stories to be told to young Perſons neither *with* an Allegory nor *without* one. 'For, ' ſays he, a young Creature is not capable of diſ-' cerning what Parts of the Tale may be allego-' rical, and what not; while in the mean time ' the Impreſſions made at theſe Years on the ' Imagination are ſcarcely to be afterwards ' wiped out; but for the moſt part remain inde-' lible during Life.'

BUT tho' theſe larger Fables being generally detached Parts of the ancient Theology, were diſagreeable to the ſevere Model of Education contrived by this moral Stateſman, he wou'd have found no fault with his eloquent Country-man's (a) waving his keen Rhetoric for once, and telling the *Athenians* in *Æſop's* humble Strain, when *Philip's* Son, the hereditary Enemy of their Liberty, demanded Eight of their leading Men to be delivered up to him, as the great Impedi-ments of mutual Amity. ' On a time, ſaid the ' Orator to his Fellow-Citizens, an Embaſſy ' came from the Wolves to the Sheep, aſſuring ' them that the Dogs attending them, were the ' ſole Occaſion of the War: Wherefore if they ' would

(a) DEMOSTHENES.

Lett. 9.' would give *them* up, all would be well, and
' land in lasting Peace. The Sheep were persuad-
' ed, gave up their Dogs, and thenceforth the
' Wolves devoured them at pleasure.'

Of the same kind was the honest Apologue related by *Menenius Agrippa*, (Ambassador from the *Roman* Senate to the mutinous Commons,) of the Dissension that arose among the Members of the human Body, when the *Feet* and *Hands* refused longer to toil for the idle *Belly*, until they were almost starved themselves. May I acknowledge that I admire the Beauty of that simple Tale beyond the most elaborate Oration, recorded or rather framed by the excellent *Livy* ; who seems to me to have spoke like a meer modern Wit, when he says that *Agrippa*, *intromissus in Castra, prisco illo dicendi et horrido modo, nihil aliud quam hoc narrasse fertur*, being admitted into the Camp, to which the Commons had retired, is reported *in the old rude way of talking to have only told them*— the Story above-mentioned. Could the new-fashioned polite one have contrived any thing patter, or more convincing ? Or, in the former Instance, was it because *Demosthenes* found himself at a loss,—because his wonted Flow of Eloquence failed him ; that he must have recourse to a Fable of *Æsop's* ? Were those glowing Images and striking Terms, that with his Voice and Gesture seemed Thunders rather than Sounds, and Portents

rather

rather than Pleadings, quite exhausted? Or did
he imagine the little instructive Tale less obnoxious
to Envy, and more likely to persuade the People of
Athens than the most pathetic Declamation he
could have made? But one of the most beautiful and
lively Specimens of this same kind of Mythology
is recorded in that great Treasure of Antiquity,
as well as Religion, *our sacred Scripture.*

THE *Jewish* Patriarchs, like the Eastern Mo-
narchs, kept Seraglio's, and had great Numbers
of Children; and these Children when they grew
up, sometimes like the Sons of the *Porte*, murdered one another for the Succession. The brave
Gideon had threescore-and-eleven Sons; besides
one by a fav'rite Mistress, he kept at *Shechem*.
This aspiring Youth, soon after his Father's
Death, found means to hire a Band of Ruffians,
with whom he broke into his Father's House,
seized his Brethren and killed them, threescore-
and-ten Persons upon one Stone. But *Jotham*
the youngest escaped, and went and stood on the
Top of a neighbouring Hill; whence he called
to the Men that had made his Bastard-Brother
a King. ' On a time, said he, the Trees went
' forth to anoint a King; and they said unto
' the *Olive-Tree*, Reign thou over us. But the
' Olive-Tree said unto them, Shall I leave my
' Fatness, wherewith by me they honour God
' and Man, and go to be promoted over the
' Trees? And they said to the *Fig-Tree*, Come
' thou

Lett. 9.' thou and reign over us.   But the Fig-Tree
'   ' said unto them, Shall I forsake my Sweetnefs,
' and my good Fruit, and go to be promoted
' over the Trees ? Then said the Trees unto the
' *Vine*, Come thou and reign over us.   And the
' Vine said unto them, Shall I leave my Wine,
' which cheereth God and Man, and go to be
' promoted over the Trees ? Then said all the
' Trees unto the *Bramble*, Come thou and reign
' over us.   And the Bramble said unto the Trees,
' If in truth you anoint me King over you, then
' come and put your truft in my Shadow ; and
' if not, let Fire come out of the *Bramble* and
' devour the *Cedars of* Lebanon.'

I NAMED a third Sort of Mythology that
would perhaps furprize you at firft hearing, and
which will not, as was obferved, fall under the
Definition ; it confifts in *material Reprefenta-*
tions of Virtue and Vice, or Inftruction conveyed
by *Wood* and *Stone*, inftead of a *Tale*.   Such, in
fome refpect, are all the Badges or Enfigns of the
Gods, when carved, or caft in Metal ; and fuch
the *fecret Symbols* delivered to the initiated in
their feveral Myfteries, which they carefully
kept from vulgar Eyes, and only fhewed upon
certain Signs, like Free-Mafons, to their Fellow-
Adepts (*a*).   But the Example that beft illuftrates
this *material* Species of Mythology, contains at
the fame time a beautiful Moral.   It was the
Temple of HONOUR, which had no Entry of its
own—

(*a*) See *Apuleius's* Apology.

own— But the fole Paffage to it was thro' the Lett. 9. Temple of VIRTUE. Happy the Man who truly worfhips in the *firft*, whether the Ignorance or Envy of his Cotemporaries permit him to reach the *fecond* or not; where yet he will fooner or later certainly poffefs the Station due to his real Merit.

EQUALLY filent, and equally fignificant, was what We may properly call *ritual Mythology*; which tho' fometimes accompanied with confecrated Forms of Speech, and efficacious unintelligible Sounds, as the *Eleufinian* Myfteries (*a*), yet the principal Part confifted in *Action*, that is in the Practice of certain Ceremonies in commemoration of a God or Hero; or even pointing out the moral Duties of Life. Moft of the religious Practice of the Ancients, I mean the facred Rites performed at Sacrifices, and annual Solemnities, were of the firft fort; and many of the precife *Egyptian* Inftitutions, the *Cretan* Cuftoms, and *Lycurgus*' Laws, were of the fecond. Examples of all thefe, tho' they might entertain you, would lead us too far from our purpofe: The fhort *Pythagoric* Precepts of *Egyptian* Original, and thoughtful Stamp, will at once fhew you the Spirit and Purpofe of this practical Mythology. *Stir not the Fire with a Sword*, faid the folemn Philofopher; *Step not over the Beam of a Balance,*

(*a*) The Initiated, having firft been fufficiently terrified, were inftructed out of the ΠΕΤΡΩΜΑ (two Stone-Tablets) and then difmiffed with thofe two wonderful Words ΚΟΓΞ, ΟΜΠΑΞ.

Lett. 9. *lance*, nor *fit down upon a Bufhel.* That is,
' Touch no deadly Weapon while you are in
' Paffion ; reverence Juftice in all your Conduct ;
' and remember there is a Day after To-morrow.'
Abftain from Beans, continued the Sage, *Eat not
the Heart* ; and *touch not a Lyre with unwafh'd
Hands.* That is, ' Sin not againft Humanity in
' any Shape [a] ; Rack not your Mind with anxi-
' ous Care ; nor attempt any thing rudely, that
' requires Meafure and Confideration.'

H A D you feen one of the filent Fraternity
fhrinking from the Touch of a Bean, or going as
religioufly to wafh his Hands before he took
down his Lyre, as a *Pharifee* before he eat, his
Circumfpection muft have furprized you, and
fet you a thinking what the Reafon of fuch Rites
might be ; as, no doubt, the obferving them attentively was a daily Leffon to a thoughtful *Pythagorean.*   *Stand not upon a Threfhold ; but
falute your Gates as you go out and come in ; and
when arrived on the Borders of a Country never
turn back, for the F U R I E S are in the way ;*
appear fimple, not to fay filly Prefcriptions of the
fame great Mafter : But to his enlightened Followers they were hourly Admonitions of the
Mifchiefs of Idlenefs and Irrefolution, of the
Sweets of Retirement and Independency, and of

ftill

---

[a] The Ground of this Explication may be feen in *Lucian*'s
ΒΙΩΝ ΠΡΑΣΙΣ ; in *Ariftoxenus,* as quoted by *Gellius* ; in *Ariftotle*'s Treatife *O F B E A N S,* as quoted by *Diogenes Laertius* ;
but moft evidently in *Origen*'s Philofophic Mifcellanies, where he
relates the Opinion of Zaretas the *Chaldean.*

ftill a more important Duty, to be contented
with their Life and Lot; nor vainly attempt to
return after they had run their Courfe; or foolifh-
ly wifh for Things contrary to the Order of Nature and all-wife Deftination of Providence.

THESE, *my Friend*, are fome of the mimic
Shapes which this grand Inftructrefs formerly
took to form the Minds and model the Manners
of the human Race, in order to fit them for
Society, that is for public and private Happinefs:
But her brighteft Attire, the Garb in which fhe
fhone, and at once commanded Love and Veneration, remains yet undefcribed.

IT was a various enchanted Robe of triple
Texture, with Heaven and Earth, Air and Sea,
and all they contain, reprefented in every poffible
Attitude, varying as it changed Lights, and according to the different Pofitions in which you
held it to your Eye. The Hiftory of the *Creation*, or *Rife of the Univerfe*, what we call *natural Philofophy*, and the Ancients called *Theogony*, was the Ground-work of the Garment.
The *Powers* that govern the World, for which
We have no feparate Name, framed the Figures and planned the Defign; while the *Paffions
of Men*, the Harmony of the human Breaft
(moral Philofophy) gave the Glofs and Colouring,
and as they languifh or glow, it is tarnifhed and
fades or blooms with Life, and by a fecret Magic
feems

Lett. 9. feems at times to take fire, and mount into a
Blaze.

This was the wondrous Robe long wore by
the Power that enchanted Mankind, that tranf-
formed them from Brutes and Savages into civilized Creatures ; and of Lions and Wolves made
focial Men. It was She who led the Woods in
a Dance, whofe Melody ftopt the Courfe of Rivers,
and drew after her the Rocks obedient to her
Song. Her Robe refplendent for upwards of a
thoufand Years began to fade twice that time ago,
and fince then has been fo mangled, patched and
fpoil'd, that it has greatly loft its Virtue, and of
late is fcarcely to be known. Wou'd you wifh
to fee the Goddefs herfelf, who under its Cover
performed fuch Wonders ? Her Power is re-
trenched fince its Figures were effaced ; but her
infpiring Spirit remains the fame.

" Look yonder, then, as the Mythologift
" points ; Observe that noble Appearance,
" that fine Figure of a Woman, fitting majeftic in
" her moving Chariot ! What a dazzling Splen-
" dour furrounds her ! a Mixture of Gayety and
" Sweetnefs o'erfpreads her whole Perfon. Her
" Face is for ever covered with a thin flowing
" Veil, thro' whofe tranfparent Texture you
" can perceive an Ecftafy in her Looks, which
" at times increafes, and enflamed by degrees,
" draws to a divine Fury ; then in a little, fub-
" fides to a milder Joy, and contemplative Plea-
" fure. But fee ! How fhe changes ! Blefs me !

I　　　　　　　　　　　　　　" Her

" Her Features alter: her Poſture varies: her Lett. 9.
" Eyes dart Amazement and Rapture: her
" whole Perſon is in commotion: What is
" *ſhe* about? Her Looks are eagerly fixed
" upon a ſtrange Repreſentation, *a ſpangled*
" *kind of Sphere* ſhe holds in her hand, with
" an Inſcription ΦΥΣΙΣ (NATURE.) She
" is perpetually turning it on all ſides; viewing
" it, now near, now at a diſtance; ſometimes
" held direct, ſometimes oblique, ſometimes
" ſteady, ſometimes paſſing. As ſhe turns it,
" new Figures appear; and as they appear,
" Cameleon-like, the Goddeſs changes Colour,
" Attitude and Mien. What is it ſhe caſts a
" ſquint Eye upon in her other hand, ſtealing
" a Side-Glance of it in the midſt of her Ecſtaſy?
" *A myſterious Tablet*, bearing ſome harmonic
" Reſemblance to the other Repreſentation; but
" variouſly traced with equal and unequal Num-
" bers, *ſix, five, three, eleven,* and ΡΥΘΜΟΣ
" in the middle ª. See! ſhe lifts her Eyes from
" it, and ſeems attentive to a muttered Sound.
" She liſtens, ſhe looks at the Tablet, and
" by turns, ecſtatic views her Ideal-Orb. A
" ſtill Voice behind her utters ΝΟΜΟΣ and
" ΑΡΜΟΝΙΑ, (MEASURE and HARMONY)
" and ſhe ſtarts, and changes Poſture at the
F   " Name.

ª Neither *Engliſh* nor *Latin* afford a Term equivalent to this. It expreſſes the Likeneſs which the *Numbers* of a Verſe ought to bear to the Paſſion it paints: A Similitude between Senſe and Sound.

Lett. 9. " Name. Garlands of Laurel, Myrtle and
" Ivy hang all around her reſtleſs Car ; which
" the Multitude of her Followers greedily
" ſnatch at, but frequently in vain : For her
" inſeparable Attendant Π Ε Ι Θ Ω (PERSUA-
" SION) muſt firſt be won, ere a Twig of
" them will detach from the inchanted Cha-
" riot ; which is beſides guarded by a Chorus
" of coy Virgins, * inacceſſible without a Re-
" commendation from *Apollo, Cytherea,* or *Se-*
" *mele*'s Son."

VIEW here, my Friend, at your leiſure,
the Picture of the *Parent* of real Mythology.
She was aſſociated by Philoſophy in the great
Work of civilizing the rude Tribes of unin-
ſtructed Men. Her Robe of triple Tiſſue, you
will find to be, A Tale, monſtrous, yet moving, of feigned allegorical Perſonages engaged
in Action, and ſpeaking and performing ſo
much in Character, as at once to repreſent
Cauſes, narrate *Tranſactions,* and irreſiſtibly
convey *Inſtruction* to the Mind, by ſtriking the
Fancy, and winning the Heart. *I am,*

* The Muſes.

Yours, &c.

LETTER

LETTER TENTH.

D O you never remember, my dearFriend!
to have read with Wonder the *Mantuan*
Bard's Account of the Source of Life, and the
Origin of Men?

Principio Cælum ac Terras, Campofque liquenteis
Lucentemque Globum Lunæ, Titaniaque Aſtra
Spiritus *intùs alit.*

Your laſt Letter brought the concluſive Stroke
of this Deſcription freſh to my Mind. ' Now,
' ſaid I, Mr. * * * * is certainly not only
' quite recovered, but his Genius blooms;
' here he is *in Spirit*, if not in Perſon *:
' The noble Sentiment and elegant Fancy
' paint the Gentleman; Kindneſs and Candour
' characterize the Friend in every Sentence.
' His Letter breathes a refined Goodneſs, and
' ſhews every lovely Feature of his Mind: He
' has wrote it with Pleaſure, and I find it in-
' fects me: What a bewitching thing is *a real*
' *Friend!* How attractive, when his Worth is
' poliſhed; render'd amiable by Good-nature,

F 2   ' humane

* Quid mirum noſcere Mundum
Si poſſunt Homines, quibus eſt & Mundus in ipſis;
Exemplumque Dei quiſque eſt in Imagine parvâ.
                                    MANILIUS.

Lett.10.' humane by Condefcenfion, and exalted by a
'comprehenfive View of Ages paft, with all
'the various fhifting Scenes of the unchangeable
'Theater of Nature?'

THE *Egyptian* Doctrine concerning *Prome-*
theus, which I formerly tranfcribed, might well
ferve for an Example of the Power of Fiction
and Allegory.   But fince you wifh for another,
with great Pleafure will I contribute to your
Entertainment, and give it from one of the Fathers of the *Grecian* Poetry [a].

HE firft invokes the Mufes, who inhabit the
heavenly Manfions, and whofe wonderful Generation and Birth he had formerly fung.   He
calls them the divine Daughters of *Jove*, that
bring Oblivion of Ill, and Refpite from Care.
' Happy the Man whom they love ! for a Strain
' fo fweetly-foothing flows from his Lips, that
' if any one be oppreffed with Grief, his Heart
' pierced with fharp Affliction; and a Bard,
' the Minifter of the Mufes, fit by him and fing
' the glorious Deeds of the ancient Heroes, or
' celebrate the bleffed Gods the Lords of Hea-
' ven; immediately he forgets his Woe, his Sor-
' rows evanifh; for the Gifts of the Mufes drive
' them all away.
' TELL, ye celeftial Powers! continues the
' Poet, How firft the GODS, and WORLD was
' made? The *Rivers* and boundlefs *Sea*, with
' its raging Surge? How the bright-fhining Stars,
'   ' and

[a] HESIOD in his THEOGONY.

' and wide-ftretched Heaven above, and all
' the *Gods* that fprung from them, Givers of
' good Things ?

The Anfwer of the Mufes.

" FIRST OF ALL EXISTED *CHAOS*: Next
" in order the broad-bofomed EARTH, (Mat-
" ter;) and then LOVE appeared, the moft
" beautiful of the Immortals.   Of CHAOS
" fprung EREBUS and dufky NIGHT, and of
" *Night* and *Erebus* came ETHER and fmi-
" ling DAY.   But firft the *Earth* produced
" the ftarry HEAVEN commenfurate to her-
" felf, and the barren SEA, without mutual
" Love; then conjoined with *Celus* (the Hea-
" ven) fhe bore the tremendous TITANS;
" after whom TIME, crooked in Counfel,
" was produced, the youngeft and moft dread-
" ful of her Children."   The CYCLOPS were
" next engendered, BRONTES (*Thunder*) STE-
" ROPES, (*Lightening*) and ARGES, the can-
" dent *Bolt*."   Befides thefe, three other rue-
ful Sons were born to Heaven and Earth,
Cotus [a], *Briareus* [b], and *Gyges* [c], with fifty Heads and an hundred Hands, haughty,
hateful, at enmity with their Parent from the
F 3   moment

---

[a] The *Breaker*, the *Deftroyer*; it is the Participle in Cal of
נכה fregit, comminuit, contudit. [b] *Impetuous Violence*; it
is from ΒΡΙΑΩ and ΡΕΩ. [c] *Hid in the Earth*, fpringing from
the *Ground*; from ΓΑΩ and ΓΗ. We would tranflate the three
Brothers, ERUPTION, HURRICANE, and EARTHQUAKE.

Lett.10. moment of their Birth : for which Caufe, as
foon as they appeared he hid them in the Grottoes
of the Earth, and never permitted them to fee
the Light. But SATURN, (*Time*) with his adamantine Scythe, having bereaved his Father, the
HEAVEN, of the Power of further Generation,
monftrous Births fprung of the Remains of his
Vigour, half formed, unnatural Productions,
the *Furies* and the *Giants*. Mean while O-
cean[a], married to *Tethys*[b], the eldeft of the
Titans, produced the Rivers and Fountains,
with three thoufand Daughters, the *Oceanides*,
Properties and Productions of Moifture ; and
Heaven's ufurping Son *Time* marrying the fecond Sifter *Rhea*, had three female Children,
Vefta, *Ceres*, and *Juno*, and as many Males,
Pluto, *Neptune*, and defigning JOVE, Father
of the Gods and Men[c].

No fooner was this fovereign Source of Life
brought forth, that is, difembaraffed of heterogeneous Parts, than he feized the Reins of the
Univerfe, which under him affumed at laft a
ftable, everlafting Form. For affociating with
METIS[d], by her fupreme Direction, he re-
called his inhuman Parent's Progeny to light,
and

---

[a] *Fluidity*, or the Source of Moifture.   [b] *Fermentation* ;
Loam ; the Ἰλὺς πρωτογένης ; from טיט, *Titb*, Slime.

[c] ΖΗΝΑ ΤΕ ΜΗΤΙΟΕΝΤΑ, ΘΕΩΝ ΠΑΤΗΡ ΗΔΕ
ΚΑΙ ΑΝΔΡΩΝ.

[d] ΜΗΤΙΣ, Counfel, Contrivance, Thought.

and fettled his congenial Powers each in their
refpective Dignity : *Ceres* to fructify the Earth;
Juno to impregnate the Air ; *Neptune* to rule
the Sea ; and *Pluto* to reign in the Regions
below ; while *Saturn's* firft-born *Vefta* remain'd
unmoved, the coercive Band of the immenfe
Machine *. But in this Settlement he met with
cruel Oppofition : The *Titan-Gods* ᵃ combined againft him, and in a long and furious
War endeavoured to drive him from the
Throne of Heaven, and reverfe thefe recent
Dignities of the upftart *Saturnian* Race. And
now the mighty Frame with horrid Crafh had
again fallen into its priftine Chaos, if prompted
by his all-wife Affociate he had not firft made
his kindred-Gods Partakers with himfelf of
Nectar and Ambrofia ᵇ ; and then releafed
from darkfome Durance the predominant igneous Powers, Sons of Heaven and Earth,
Cotus, *Briareus* and *Gyges*, whom he called
up to Light, and made his Allies in the War.
By their irrefiftible Strength he at laft van-
quifhed the Titan-Gods, and confined them
faft bound to a Prifon wafte and wild, as far

F 4 under

---

* See above, page .
ᵃ It is their proper Epithet, Τιτῆνες Θεοὶ· The *Clay-Gods*,
Properties of Matter. Hence,
    Quêis meliore *Luto* finxit Præcordia TITAN.
ᵇ INCENSE and IMMORTALITY. קטר *Chald.* to burn Incenfe has in Hiph. אקטר EKTAR; thence the Noun, with
the fervile נ. NECTAR. ΑΜΒΡΟΣΙΑ, IMMORTALITY, is
a trite *Greek* Word of eafy Derivation.

Lett.10. under the Earth, as the Heaven is above it. A Bulwark of Brafs, with three-fold Night brooding on its top, runs round it ; and its Gates of Adamant are guarded by the fame three enormous Brothers, faithful Jaylors of all-mighty *Jove.* Here are the Seeds of all things ; the Roots of the opaque Earth, of the barren Sea, and the Beginnings and Bounds of the various Orders of BEING, all now fhut up by the Will of *Jove* in this bottomlefs Chafin, where Darknefs reigns, and Tempefts rowl, tremendous to the Gods themfelves [a].

BUT JOVE, now Lord of all, joined with THEMIS [b], and begot firft the three eternal FATES, *Clotho, Lachefis,* and *Atropos* ; then the amiable Guides and Guardians of Life, *Irene, Eunomia,* and *Dice* [c] : Afterwards, married to *Juno,* he had two fair Daughters, *Hebe* and *Ilithya* [d] ; and two furious Sons, *Mars* [e]

and

---

[a] Ενθάδε γῆς δυοφερῆς, κỳ ταρτάρȣ ἠερόευἾος,
Πόντȣ τ' ἀἹρυγέτοιο, κỳ ȣρανȣ̃ ἀϛ-ερόενἾος,
Ἐξείης πάνἾων ΠΗΓΑΙ κỳ ΠΕΙΡΑΤ' ἕασσιν,
Ἀρ[α]λέα, ἐυρώενἾα· τά τε ϛυἹέϰσι θεοίπερ,
ΧΑΣΜΑ μέγ'.   ΗΣΙΟΔ. ΘΕΟΓΟΝ.

[b] It fignifies *that Poffibility or Aptitude* arifing from the Nature of Things, which neceffarily conneƈts them with the *End* of their Exiftence. In Aƈtions *Themis* is the Source of Law ; ἥτ' ανδρων αγορὰς ἤ μέν λύει, ἠ-δε καθίζει. and in Prediƈtions of Truth. Her Oracles were the moft ancient in the World.   [c] PEACE, GOOD ORDER, and JUSTICE.
[d] YOUTH, and TEEMING.

[e] MARS, ΑΡΗΣ, the PLUNDERER, the SPOILER by Violence. It is plainly from עריץ Prædo fortis, truculentus, Tyrannus. To a Weftern Throat this is juft AREZ. Plunder was the Origin of War.

and *Vulcan* ª, the Gods of War and Fire. Lett. 10.
Of LATONA ᵇ famed for fable Locks, he ⌒
                             had

ª VUL-KAN, I conjecture to have come from a Transposi-
tion of the Vowels of בַּעַל כִּיּוּן BAL-KIUN, the *Lord Kiun*;
the Eastern Idol mentioned by one of the *Jewish* Prophets, and
joined with *Moloch*, whom the Rabbins, with good reason, take
to be *Saturn:* It was customary among the Easterns to add
Baal, or LORD, to the proper Name of their Gods, as the *Latins* added *Pater*, in *Jupiter, Marspiter, Diespiter, Liber-pater,
Jane-pater* * ! &c. The Repetition of it was so frequent before their numerous Deities, that our Sacred Writers generally
mention them in the plural Number בְּעָלִים the *Baalim*, or
LORDS †. Another Prophet (1) reproaches the *Jewish* Women
with making *Keavans*, which the Targum explains to be Tarts
or Cakes offered to the Host of Heaven; and to this Day the
Arabs and *Persians* call *Saturn* كَيْوَان *Kajwan*, from a
Word that signifies the Source of BEING and EXISTENCE. Now
VULCAN, says *Herodotus*, was among the oldest and most honoured of the *Egyptian* Gods; and by their Neighbours the *Assy-
rians* and *Phenicians*, was identified with *Saturn* and the *Sun*,
because of their similar Nature. *Lingua Punica* BAL *Deus
dicitur: apud Assyrios autem* BEL *dicitur quâdam sacrorum ratione, &* SATURNUS & SOL, says *Servius*, on occasion of *Belus*'s
Cup, mentioned by *Virgil*. This *quâdam ratione sacrorum*, in
ancient Theology, is as wide as *Reason of State* in modern Politics, and therefore as hard to be ascertained. The Fact is
however certain, that several Gods were denominated from one
and the same Subject. Thus *Luna, Hecate* and *Diana* were
three different Goddesses all representing one Planet, the Moon;
and *Orus, Apollo, Phœbus, Hyperion*, with many more were
denominated from the Sun; in whom a very learned and ingenious Man has lately attempted to shew that all the Gods of
Antiquity center (2). The Author of the *Alexandrian* Chronicle
writes that *Jupiter* had a Son by *Juno*, ὃν ὠνόμαξε Βῆλον,
whom he named BELUS; (certainly one of the בְּעָלִים) And
                                Homer

* Ut nemo sit nostrûm, quin Pater optimu' Divûm,
  Ut Neptunu' Pater, Liber, Saturnu' Pater, Mars,
  Janu', Quirinu' Pater, omnes dicamur ad unum.
      LUCILIUS apud Lactant. Div. Inst. Lib. IV. ſ. 2:
† See the excellent *Selden* de Dis Syris, Syntag. II.
(1) JEREMIAH.   (2) Gisb. Cuperi HARPOCRATES.

Lett.10. had the brighteſt of the Immortals, *Apollo* and *Diana*; and by the blooming DIONE, the youngeſt

Homer makes *Vulcan* himſelf tell how he was toſſed from Heaven by his angry Father, ἀπο Βηλῦ Θισπεσίοιο, which the Commentators explain τὴν περίοδον τῦ ἀιθίρ᾽ καὶ τῶν ἀςρῶν, *The Circumference of the Heaven and Stars.* All this I take to be Traces of the *Aſſyrian* Doctrine concerning the oldeſt of the Gods, which we have from *Eupolemus,* in theſe remarkable Words, Βαβυλωνίας λέξειν πρῶτον γενέσθαι ΒΗΛΟΝ, ὅν ἶιναι Κρόνον. ἐκ τύτν δὶ γενέσθαι ΒΗΛΟΝ καὶ Χανάαν (1). Here are two Gods, Father and Son, both BAALS, (LORDS) the eldeſt *Saturn* and the *Sun,* and the youngeſt his Offspring *Fire* (2.) BAL-KIUN therefore, or BUL-KAN, is the LORD FIRE, the Child of the Sun ; juſt as he is in *Greek,* or rather *Syriac,* ΗΦΑΙΣΤΟΣ, אֵבִּן אֵשָׁתָא, Father-Fire. The Ancients ſuppoſed he was tranſmitted to Earth in a Shot-Star, which ſhould have kindled the Vulcano's in *Lemnos,* upon which they built the Fable put in his Mouth by *Homer.* The Orphic Initiations appointing a God, or the Attribute of a God to every Sphere, give *Pericyonius* to the Sphere of *Saturn,* which the learned *Bochart* derives from KIUN, his Eaſtern Name : The real wandering *Jew,* BENJAMIN, one of the greateſt Travellers of the Eaſt, has this curious Deſcription of the Solar Worſhip in his Itinerary. ' There is a People, ſays he, of the Poſterity of *Chus,* addicted to ' the Contemplation of the Stars ; they worſhip the Sun as a ' God, and the whole Country for half a Mile round their ' Town, is filled with great Altars dedicated to him. By the ' Dawn of Morn they get up, and run out of Town to wait the ' riſing Sun, to whom on every Altar there is a conſecrated ' Image, not in Likeneſs of a Man, but of the *Solar Orb,* ' framed by magic Art. Theſe Orbs, as ſoon as the Sun riſes, ' take fire, and reſound with a great Noiſe, while every body ' there, Men and Women, hold Cenſers in their Hands, and all ' burn Incenſe to the Sun.' One would ſuſpect theſe Orbs to have been filled with ſome nitrous Compoſition, and kindled by a Collection of the Rays. It nicely explains, not the Shrine of *Molech,* which is eaſily underſtood to be a portable Tabernacle, ſuch as was uſed by the *Egyptians* ; but *the Image of* KIUN, *the* STAR

(1) Apud Euſeb. Præparat. Evang. Lib. IX.
(2) Hyperionem alii *Patrem* Solis, alii *ipſum,* quòd eat ſuper Terras ita appellatum putabant.
                     FESTUS.

youngeſt of the Titan-Siſters ᶜ, was laſt of all made Father of *Venus* ᵈ, the Goddeſs of Beauty,

STAR *of your Gods, which you have made to yourſelves.* (1) This Piece of Idolatry committed by the *Jews* in the Wilderneſs, ſoon after they had come out of *Egypt*, and on the Borders of the Sun's Votaries, the Poſterity of *Chus*, is not, as I remember, recorded in the Pentateuch.

ᵇ The common Opinion derives *Latona* very juſtly from ΛΗΘΗ, Oblivion or Night: the obſolete *Greek* Verb λήθω, the *Latin lateo*, have the ſame Original לָאט *Laat, Latuit,* whence, as *Dido* is formed from דוד *dilectus*, being the Feminine of *David*, ſo ΛΗΤΩ *Lato*, (Obſcurity) the *Greek* Name of *Latona*, is formed of רום.

ᶜ DIONE is a formal Participle of the *Syriac* דָּנַח *denah, ortus eſt, eluxit,* ἐξέλαμψε. Thence דָּכִיח *illuſtris*, and דָּכִיחָא *Doniahe* DIONE. And hence, I judge, not from ونٮ *appropinquavit*, (with which it has no Connexion) the *Arabs*, who ſpeak a Dialect of the ſame Language, and have borrowed the *Syrian* Characters, call the World itſelf ونيا *Dunia, Mundus.*

ᵈ VENUS: beſides the numberleſs *local* Divinities of this Name, and beſides the celeſtial and vulgar *Venus*, denominated from human Paſſions, there were two original Powers acknowledged by the firſt Mythologiſts; the eldeſt the Child of CELUS, or laſt Production of the Heaven, when caſtrated by TIME, and therefore of the *Titan*-Race, who bore her Part in the Production of the Univerſe; the youngeſt the Daughter of *Jupiter* and *Dione*; the Power ariſing from the vivifying ethereal Spirit, acting upon the Plenitude of Matter. The former brought forth the World, and all it contains according to *Orpheus*. "All "Things, ſays he, are of Thee: Thou cemented'ſt the Uni- "verſe: Thou ſway'ſt the threefold Fates: Thou generates "whatever is in the Heaven above, on the teeming Earth below, "or in the Depths of th' unfathomed Sea." This is ſhe whom *Epimenides*, the *Cretan* Sage, makes the Daughter of *Saturn* and *Eunomia* (2), that is of TIME and GOOD-ORDER. The Latter, ariſing

(1) Amos V. ℣. 26. On which ſee the moſt learned and literal of the *Jewiſh* Commentators, *R. Selemo Ben Melech*, in his מכלל יופי.

(2) Γήματο δʼΕΥΝΟΜΙΗΝ θαλερὰν ΚΡΟΝΟΣ ἀγκυλομήτις,

Ἐκ τῦ καλλίκομ⌐ γένετο χρυσῆ ΑΦΡΟΔΙΤΗ.

Lett.10. Beauty, the Perfection of the Creation, the genial Power prefiding over the Propagation of every Species of Being. And now, every Power being confined to its proper Province, Harmony henceforth enfued in Heaven, and good Order prevailed upon Earth, while all-mighty *Jove* holds the Reins of the Univerfe in his unerring Hand, Parent of Gods and Ruler of Men e.

SUCH was the portentous Tale told by the primitive Sages for the Inftruction and Reftraint of ignorant barbarous Mortals; rude like them
in

arifing immediately from *faline Fermentation*, is wafted to Shore by the *Zephyrs* ; nourifhed by the ΩΡΑΙ or *Seafons*; lands at *Cyprus*, the moft benign, delicious Spot on the Globe; and courted by all the Gods, is married to the Lord of FIRE. As for her *latin* Name, I can fcarce conceive it fhould come *à veniendo*, quia Venus omnibus *venit* (1), or from the *Siccoth Benoth*, the Tents of the Women about the Temple of *Mylitta* at *Babylon* (2). But it is probably one of the Names of the Gods carried over to *Italy* by the firft *Grecian* Colonies: The *Bœotians* called a Woman BANNA. So fays *Hefychius* the Lexicographer. βᾶννα, γυνὴ ὑπὸ Βοιωῖῶν. VENUS therefore will fignify the Deity of *Woman*, or FEMALE NATURE: which indeed may very well have been formed from the *Phenician* בנות *Benoth* Daughters : Since it is certain that many of the *Roman* Names of the Gods, whether brought over by the *Lydians*, or by the early *Grecian* Colonies, are of *Phrygian* or *Phenician* Extraction, not in the leaft refembling their *Grecian* Appellations. *Saturn, Ceres, Vulcan, Neptune, Diana, Venus*, are all evident Proofs of this ; and even the *Greek* Name of the laft-mentioned Goddefs, ΑΦΡΟΔΙΤΗ, tho' purely, one fhould think, of Weftern Compofition, yet one of the greateft Men *Europe* ever produced, takes it to be the *Syriac* Feminine of פְּעוֹר PEOR, אֲפֵעוֹרְתָא APHEO-RETHA (3).

˙ ΗΣΙΟΔ. ΘΕΟΓΟΝΙΑ. Απολλοδορ. βιβλιοϑ. βιβ. α.

(1) CICERO de Natura Deorum.
(2) SELDEN de Diis Syris.
(3) HUG. GROTIUS ad Deuteron.

in its Structure, and uncouth and cruel in its
Circumstances. How well it was otherwise
fitted to serve that noble End of civilizing Nations, and bringing them to a Belief and Reverence of an invisible Power or Powers above
them, who protect the pious and the just, and
irremissibly punish the oppressive and impious,
I will not even enquire: nor will I take upon
me to give you my particular Sense of its Meaning. Persons of warm Fancies are apt to measure others by themselves, and to suspect that
an Attachment to any one Subject will tempt
its Admirer to assist its natural Imperfections,
and enable him to call up a *fairy* kind of Creation out of the most unmeaning Materials. To
obviate any such Surmise, I beg leave to tranf-
scribe the Opinions of two great Men, not so
much to be regarded in the present case for their
Learning and Genius, tho' eminent in both, as
that each of them having struck out a new
Track in Philosophy, their Attempts to efta-
blish their favourite Notions, at the same time
illustrate the Doctrine of the Ancients without
Partiality, and one of them indeed without
Design. They will shew you that I am neither singular nor fanciful in supposing, ' *That*
' the old Sages imposed no particular Person or
' Character upon their primary Gods, nor in-
' terwove those Characters in a Tale, without a
' MEANING.'

THE

Lett.10.　THE firſt of theſe eminent Men, after having given an ingenious Account of the Creation
of the World, (whether ſtrictly true, or intermixed with Illuſions, is not to our purpoſe)
ſeems upon a Review of his own Theory to
have diſcovered its Affinity with the myſterious
mythological Traditions of the Poets. ‘ In re-
‘ trieving, ſays he, the Notion of the primæval
‘ Earth, and the Doctrine depending upon it,
‘ we have, methinks, unexpectedly caſt a Light
‘ upon all Antiquity.’ To begin with their
ancient CHAOS :——“ They tell us of *moral*
“ Principles in the confuſed Maſs, inſtead of
“ natural ones ; of *Strife*, and *Diſcord*, and
“ *Diviſion*, on the one hand ; and *Love, Friend-*
“ *ſhip*, and *Venus*, on the other ; and after a
“ long Struggle, LOVE got the better of *Diſ-*
“ *cord*, and united the diſagreeing Principles.
“ Then they proceeded to explain the Forma-
“ tion of the World in a kind of *Genealogy* or
“ Pedigree. CHAOS was the common Parent
“ of all ; and from *Chaos* ſprung firſt *Night*
“ and *Tartarus*, or *Oceanus* : NIGHT was a
“ teeming Mother, and of her were born
“ *Ether* and the *Earth* ; the Earth conceived
“ by the Influences of the Ether, and brought
“ forth MAN, and all *Animals*.”

　‘ THO’ this ſeem to be a poetical Fiction
‘ rather than Philoſophy ; yet, when ſet in a
‘ true Light, and compared with *our* Theory
‘ of the *Chaos*, it appears to be *a pretty regular*
‘ *Account,*

‘ *Account*, How the World was formed
‘ at firſt ; or How the Chaos divided itſelf ſuc-
‘ ceſſively into ſeveral *Regions*, riſing one after
‘ another, and propagated one from another, as
‘ Children and Poſterity from a common Pa-
‘ rent.　We ſhewed how the *Chaos* from an
‘ uniform Maſs wrought itſelf into ſeveral Re-
‘ gions or Elements, the groſſeſt Part ſinking
‘ to the Center; upon this lay the Maſs of
‘ Water, and over the Water was a Region of
‘ dark, impure, caliginous Air; this impure
‘ caliginous Air, is that which the Ancients call
‘ Night; and the Maſs of Water, *Oceanus*
‘ or *Tartarus :* for theſe two Terms with them,
‘ are often of the like Force, *Tartarus* being
‘ *Oceanus* encloſed and lock’d up: Thus we
‘ have the firſt Offspring of the *Chaos*, or its
‘ firſt-born Twins *Nox* and *Oceanus*.’

‘ Now this turbid Air purifying itſelf by
‘ degrees, as the more ſubtile Parts flew up-
‘ wards, and compoſed the *Ether*, ſo the
‘ earthly Parts that were mixed with it, dropped
‘ down upon the Surface of the Water, or the
‘ liquid Maſs; and that Maſs on the other
‘ hand, ſending up its lighter, or more oily
‘ Parts towards its Surface, theſe two incorpo-
‘ rate there, and by their Union and Mixture,
‘ compoſe a Body of *Earth* quite round the
‘ Maſs of Waters, and this was the firſt habi-
‘ table Earth; which as it was, you ſee, the
‘ Daughter of *Nox* and *Oceanus*, ſo it was the
‘ Mother

Lett.10. ' Mother of all other things, and of all living
' Creatures, which at the Beginning of the
' World fprung out of its fruitful Womb.'

' THIS Doctrine of the *Chaos* the Ancients
' called their THEOGONIA, or *the Genealogy*
' *of the Gods:* For they gave their Gods, at
' leaft their terreftrial Gods, an Original and
' Beginning, and all the *Elements*, and greater
' Portions of *Nature*, they made Gods and God-
' deffes ; or their *Deities* prefided over them
' in fuch a manner, that the Names were ufed
' promifcuoufly for one another. We alfo men-
' tioned before, fome *moral* Principles which
' they placed in the Chaos, *Eris*, and *Eros*,
' Strife, Difcord and Difaffection, which pre-
' vailed at firft ; but afterwards *Love, Kindnefs*
' and *Union* got the upper hand ; and in fpite
' of thofe factious and dividing Principles, ga-
' thered together the feparated Elements, and
' united them into an habitable World. This
' is all eafily underftood, if you will but look
' upon the annexed Schemes of the rifing
' World, being Draughts reprefenting the va-
' rious States thro' which the Earth paffed
' from ancient *Chaos* to the *Deluge*. For in the
' firft univerfal Commotion, after an inteftine
' Struggle of all the Parts, the *Elements* fepa-
' rated from one another into fo many diftinct
' Bodies or Maffes : and in this State and Pofture
' Things continued a good while, which the
' Ancients,

Place this before Page. 96.

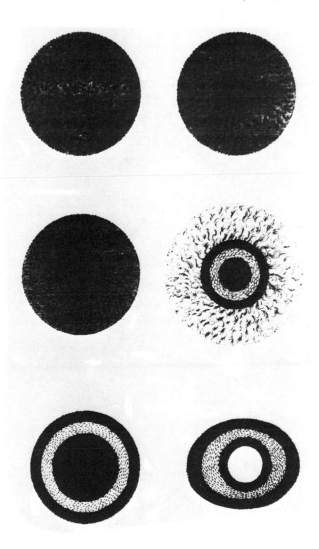

' Ancients, after their poetic or moral way, call Lett.10.
' the *Reign of Eris or Contention*, of Hatred,
' Slight, and Difaffection; and if Things had
' always continued in that Syftem, we fhou'd
' never have had an habitable World. But
' *Love* and *Good-nature* conquered at length;
' VENUS rofe out of the SEA, and received
' into her Bofom and entangled into her Em-
' braces the falling *Ether*, that is the Parts of
' lighter Earth, which were mixed with the
' Air in that firft Separation, and gave it the
' Name of *Night*: Thefe, I fay, fell down
' upon the oily Parts of the Sea-Mafs, which
' lay floating upon the Surface of it, and by
' that Union and Conjunction, a new Body and
' a new World was produced, which was the
' firft *habitable Earth*.

' THIS is the Interpretation of their myftical
' Philofophy of the *Chaos*, and the Refolution
' of it into the plain natural Hiftory of the
' Creation.' But after the great Bodies, or primary Parts of the Univerfe were thus called out
of the mighty Mafs, and ranged according to
their feveral Natures, Inhabitants adapted to
thefe Natures were to be produced, and proper Provifion made for their Propagation. It
was therefore the common Opinion of the Ancients, that the new-formed Earth lately fe-
vered from the *Ether*, and pregnant with celeftial Seed, no fooner felt the genial Ray of
the recent Sun, than fhe teemed with every

G   various

Lett.10. various Species of living Creatures, and affifted by PROMETHEUS or *Providence*, brought forth their Prince and Ruler mortal *Man*;

> *Sive hunc divino Semine fecit*
> *Ille Opifex rerum, mundi melioris origo:*
> *Sive recens Tellus, feduĉtaque nuper ab alto*
> *Æthere, cognati retinebat Semina Cæli;*
> *Quam fatus* Iapeto, *miftam fluvialibus Undis,*
> *Finxit in effigiem, moderantum cunĉta Deorum**.

THIS was the poetic Account of the Pro-
duĉtion of Animals, which was followed by the
fevereft Seĉt of the Philofophers, with this Precaution, that they would enter into no Detail, nor
defcribe particularly the manner of their immedi_
ate Generation; as indeed they declined med-
dling with the Caufes of the greater Part of the
Produĉtions and Appearances of Nature becaufe
of their Obfcurity ᵇ. But in general they held,
' That the Operations of NATURE and PRO-
' VIDENCE were direĉted to one and the fame
' End. That by *Nature* all Things tended and
' inclined to the Center of the Univerfe, and
' were conglobated around it: wherefore the
' thickeft and heavieft Body is the middlemoft,
to

---

* OVID. Metamorph. Lib. I.
ᵇ Πολὺ γὰρ ἐς-ὶν τὸ ἀἰἸιολογικὸν ϖαρ' αὐτῶ (τῷ
ΠΟΣΕΙΔΩΝΙΩ) ἢ τὸ ἀριϛοτελίζον· ὅπερ ἐκκλίϗϗσιν μ
ἡμεῖέροι διὰ τὴν ἐπίκρυψιν τῶν ἀιτιῶν·
ΣΤΡΑΒΩΝ. ΓΕΩΓΡΑΦ. ΒΙΒ. Α.

‘ to wit the *Earth*, and the next heavieſt and Lett. 10.
‘ neareſt to it, *Water*; being each a Globe,
‘ the one ſolid, and the other concave, having the
‘ Earth within it. But that *Providence* by
‘ it’s diverſifying Power under a thouſand Forms,
‘ and productive of ten thouſand various Ef-
‘ fects, in the firſt place intended Animals to
‘ be formed as far more excellent than the other
‘ Parts of the Creation ; and the prime of theſe
‘ Animals to be *Gods* and *Men*, for whoſe ſake
‘ all the reſt of the World was to be ſet in
‘ order. That to the Gods it had aſſigned
‘ the Heaven as their Seat, and to Men the
‘ Earth, the extreme Parts of the Uni-
‘ verſe ; the Extremities of a Globe being the
‘ Center and Circumference. But ſince the
‘ Water ſurrounded the Earth, and that Man
‘ is not a Water but a Land-Animal, ſtanding
‘ in need of Air and much Light, *Providence*
‘ contrived Eminences, and Depreſſions in the
‘ *Earth*, the latter capable of receiving the
‘ whole or greater part of the Water formerly
‘ covering it’s Surface, and the former fit for the
‘ Habitation of the Human Race, and to hide
‘ under it the Water, except what is neceſ-
‘ ſary for the Plants and Animals deſigned for
‘ the Uſe of Men.’ So far the learned and
cautious Stoïc [a].

But

---

[a] STRABO, Lib. XVII. Ægyptus.

Lett.10. But the great Parent of Medicine, one of the moſt ſagacious Minds that ever ſurveyed the Works of Nature, goes a Step further, and delivers his Sentiment of the Source of Life and Origin of Animals with great Simplicity. ' It ' is my Opinion, ſays he, that what we call Heat ' is both immortal, and views, and thinks, and ' hears, and knows all things, both things ' that now are, and that are to be hereafter. ' In the Beginning when all was in Confu- ' ſion, the greater Part of this Heat, iſſuing ' forth, mounted to the higheſt Region of the ' Heavens; and this the Ancients ſeem to me ' to have named the *Ether.* The next Portion ' from below, called *Earth*, is cold and dry, ' and variouſly agitated, in ſome parts of which ' there was likewiſe much *Heat.* The third ' Portion, the *Air*, occupied the middle Space, ' being ſomething warm and fluid : and the ' fourth, *Water*, the neareſt to the Earth, be- ' ing the moſt humid and thickeſt of them ' all. While theſe therefore were all whirling ' round in confuſion, much *Heat* was left in ' the Earth, in ſome Places more, in ſome leſs, ' and in others a very little ; but in number- ' leſs Particles. Now it happened in proceſs ' of time, that the Earth being dried by ' the *Heat*, the included Portions of it pro- ' duced Putrefactions, with Membranes as it ' were, or Wrappers about themſelves. Theſe ' being long cheriſhed by the genial Warmth,

ſuch

' fuch Parts of the included Mafs as confifted Lett. 10.
' of the drieft unctuous Subftance, with the leaft
' Moifture, were quickly condenfed and turned
' into *Bones*: But fuch Parts as were more
' humid and vifcous, cou'd neither be con-
' folidated by the Heat, nor remain in a State
' of Fluidity; and therefore affuming a Form
' different from the reft, they became ftrong
' Mufcles and Nerves. The Veins on the con-
' trary containing a cold watery Subftance, it's
' more glutinous Surface concocted by the Heat
' turned into a Coat or Membrane, and the
' remaining congealed Moifture, overcome by
' the Warmth, was diffolved, and remained
' a Fluid. In the fame manner the Throat,
' the Stomach, the Belly and all the Entrails
' of the Animal Body were compleated [b].
Thefe the Phyfician enumerates, and defcribes
their Formation too minutely to be followed
without lofing fight of our Purpofe.

You will obferve, that the Ancients afcribe
this generative Power to the new-formed Earth,
lately feparated from the other Elements, and
retaining many Particles of vivifying etherial
Fire. But the fanciful *Arabs*, having received
this Doctrine when they applied themfelves to
the Tranflation of the *Grecian* Authors, carried
it a degree ftill higher; and feem to imagine it

G 3 not

---

[b] HIPPOCRATES, SECT. III. In the little Treatife which fome
will have infcribed Περὶ Σαρχῶν, and others Περὶ Ἀρχῶν.

Lett.10. not impoffible, that in a benign Climate fome
Parts of the Earth, even in it's prefent condition, may be fo tempered, as in a long Courfe
of Years (God fo ordering it, and affording the
fame Concurrence he does in ordinary Generation) to produce a perfect Animal. So fays
the famous *Ebn Sina*, whom we call *Avicenna*,
one of the four learned *Arabs* fufpected of being
no found *Iflamites* [c], for which he was ftrenuouf-
ly refuted by his more orthodox Countryman
Ebn Rofhd [d]. But another contemplative Genius
of the fame Nation *Ebn Tophail*, in his elegant
Letter publifhed by our excellent Dr. *Pocock*,
has adopted the fame Opinion, and built upon it
the Story of his felf-taught Philofopher; a Man
fprung from the Earth, who without ever feeing a human Creature, by Dint of Reafon,
comes to the Knowledge of an Eternal neceffarily exiftent BEING, Creator and Ruler of all.

‘ WE HAVE been told by our pious An-
‘ ceftors, fays the *Imam* [e], that among the Iflands
‘ of *India*, there is one, lying directly under
‘ the Line, where *Men* are produced without
‘ Father or Mother ; and in it there grows a
‘ Tree, which inftead of Fruit bears *Women* ;
‘ the fame whom *Almafudi* calls the Damfels
‘ of *Wakwak*. For of all the Regions of the
‘ Earth

[c] Believers in *Mahomet*'s Religion, called *Iflamifm*.
[d] AVERROES.
[e] A Title given to eminent Men in *any* Profeffion by the *Arabs* ;
not confined to the Priefthood.

' Earth that Ifland enjoys the happieft Tem-Lett.10.
' perature of Air and Climate, by virtue of
' the pure fupreme Light rifing above it, and
' fhedding it's Influences upon it. —— Here, a
' certain depreffed Spot, having contracted Moi-
' fture, the Clay lying under it began to fer-
' ment, and fermented fo long until it acquired
' the requifite Qualities of *Hot* and *Cold*, *Wet*
' and *Dry*, in equal and due Proportion. In
' this great Mafs of fermenting Matter,
' fome Parts of happier Temper than others
' were apter to mix and coalefce for Gene-
' ration : But the moft perfect Temperature
' prevailed in the *Middle*, equal and benign
' like the Heat of the human Conftitution.
' Here the Matter was in higheft Agitation ;
' but while every Part fermented, there wou'd
' arife, as we fee in vifcid Matter boiling in
' a Pot, great Bubbles of different Figures. Now
' it happened that in the very middle of the
' fermenting Mafs, there was a fmall glutinous
' Subftance blown up into a Bubble, divided
' in two by a flender Film, and full of an aerial
' Spirit of the moft perfect and befitting Tem-
' perature. To this, by the Direction of the
' moft high God, a Soul joined itfelf, and ftuck
' fo clofely to it that it cannot be disjoined
' neither by Senfation, nor even in Thought ;
' there being a perpetual uninterrupted Irradia-
' tion of this Soul from God, in the fame
' manner as there is a perpetual Influx of Light

G 4   ' from

Lett. 10.' from the Sun, to enlighten the World. But
' as among the great Variety of Bodies of dif-
' ferent Texture, there are some that reflect not
' a single Ray of the solar Light, such as per-
' fectly pure *Air* ; others that do reflect a little
' tho' dimly, such as *opaque Bodies of broken*
' *Surface*, which as they vary in reflecting the
' Rays, for the same Reason differ in their
' *Colours*; and others in fine, that perfectly re-
' flect the influent Light, such as all polished
' Bodies, *Mirrors*, *Gems*, and the like ; and to
' such a degree, that these Mirrors, if made
' concave in a certain Proportion, generate Fire
' from the collected Beams: In the self-same
' manner, this Spirit issuing from God upon
' all his Creatures, leaves not the smallest Ve-
' stige of it's Virtue upon some of them, be-
' cause of the Defect of the requisite Disposi-
' tion ; such are all *inanimate* Things, unsus-
' ceptible of Life, like unillumined Air in the
' former Comparison. Others again, where it
' leaves some obscure Traces of it's Power, as
' in the different kinds of *Plants*, which ac-
' cording to their different Textures correspond
' to opaque Bodies in the same Comparison :
' And lastly, those on whom the Impression of
' this Influx is most conspicuous, the various
' Orders of *Animals*, whom We compared to
' polished resplendent Surfaces. But among
' these polished Bodies themselves, as some re-
' ceive more copiously the infused Light be-
' cause

' caufe they are of the fame Figure with the
' Sun whom they refemble, fo there are like-
' wife certain Animals who receive more kindly
' the Emanation of Spirit, becaufe they re-
' femble that Spirit, and are formed after it's
' Image. Such in particular is MAN, of whom
' is meant that faying, *God made Man ac-*
' *cording to the Image of himfelf* [a]. If this
' Refemblance be fo ftrong and predominant,
' that it deftroy and as it were abforb their
' Likenefs to every other Thing, fo that the
' Blaze of its Splendor kindles and confumes
' whatever it reaches, it then refembles thofe
' ardent concave Orbs, which reunite the Rays
' and fet all Things on fire. This happens
' to infpired Prophets only; as we fhall fee more
' particularly in it's proper place [b].' Then,
after a Soul had joined itfelf to the new-formed
Heart, the ingenious and eloquent *Arab* goes
on to defcribe the Formation and Structure of
the other noble Parts with fuch Skill in Anato-
my and vivid ftriking Metaphors, as wou'd go
near to perfuade you, That it was not impoffible but fuch a wondrous Frame as the human
Body, might be formed in a Mafs of fermented
Clay.

IT will perhaps affift your Belief, if after
hearing the knowing Stoïc, the great Phyfician,
and

---

[a] From the CORAN.
[b] Epiftola (*i. e.* Commentariolum de) HAI EBN IOKDHAN.

Lett.10. and *Tophail's* contemplative Son, you will again listen to our eminent philosophical Divine.

'The Opinion, says he, of Animals rising out
'of the Earth at first, was not peculiar to *E-*
'*picurus*, on whose account it hath lain under
'some Odium : the *Stoïcs* were of the same
'mind, and the *Pythagoreans*, and the *Egyp-*
'*tians*, and I think all that supposed the Earth
'to rise from a *Chaos*. Neither do I know any
'harm in that Opinion, if duely limited and
'stated ; for what Inconvenience is it, or what
'Diminution of Providence, that there shou'd
'be the Principles of *Life*, as well as the
'Principles of *Vegetation* in the new Earth?
'—— As to the spontaneous Origin of Living
'Creatures, *Moses* plainly implies, that there was
'a particular Action or Ministry of Providence
'in the formation of the Body of *Man*; but
'as to other Animals he seems to suppose that
'the Earth brought them forth as it did Herbs
'and Plants ᶜ.

'THE truth is, there is no such great Dif-
'ference betwixt *vegetable* and *animal* Eggs,
'or betwixt the Seeds out of which *Plants*
'rise, but that we may conceive *all Animals*
'rise, and the Eggs out of which the one as
'well as the other rose, to have been *in the*
'*first Earth*: and as some Warmth and In-
'fluence

ᶜ GEN. Ch. 1. V. 24, compared with V. 11.

' fluence from the Sun is required for the Ve-
' getation of Seeds, fo that Influence or Im-
' pregnation, which is neceffary to make ani-
' mal-Eggs fruitful, was imputed by the An-
' cients to the ETHER, or to an active and
' pure Element, which had the fame effect up-
' on our great Mother the *Earth*, as the Irra-
' diation of the Male hath upon the Female's
' Eggs: ———

Ether, *all-mighty Father, Source of Life,*
Into the Bofom of his joyful Wife
In genial Showers came down. ——

' 'Tis true, *Animal-Eggs* do not feem to be
' fruitful of themfelves without the Influence
' of the Male; and this is not neceffary in
' *Plant-Eggs* or vegetable Seeds: — But nei-
' ther does it feem neceffary in *all* animal-
' Eggs, if there be any Animals *fponte orta*, or
' bred without Copulation: and as we obferv-
' ed, according to the beft knowledge we have
' of this male-Influence, it is reafonable to be-
' lieve *that it may be fupplied by the Heavens*
' or ETHER. The Ancients, both the *Stoïcs*
' and *Ariftotle*, have fuppofed that there was
' fomething of an *etherial* Element in the Male-
' geniture, from whence the Virtue of it chiefly
' proceeded; and if fo, Why may not we fup-
' pofe at that time, fome *general Impreffion* or
' *Irradiation* of that purer Element to fructify
' the

Lett.10.' the new-made Earth ? *Moses* faith there was
' *an Incubation of the Spirit of God* upon the
' Mafs ; and without all doubt that was either
' to form or fructify it, by the Mediation of
' this active Principle : But the Ancients fpeak
' more plainly, with exprefs mention of this
' *Ether*, and of the Impregnation of the *Earth*
' by it as betwixt *Male* and Female [d] : a Notion
' which St. *Augustin* faith *Virgil* did not take
' from the Fictions of the Poets, but from the
' Books of the Philofophers [e].'

So much then for the firft Part of the Poet's
Tale, of the Rife of all things from CHAOS,
the Formation of the *Earth* through the Mediation of LOVE, the Expanfion of the *Heaven*, and the Production of every Species of
Plants and Animals through their conjunct O-
peration. Will you now follow the fame fagacious Guide while he explains the Sequel of
the Story, and paints the fecond Scene of the
Creation ? I mean the fubfequent State of Things
to the firft Settlement of the Univerfe. This,
according to the ancient Tradition, was the
happy *golden Age* in the Infancy of the World.
' For as foon, fays *Hefiod* [f], as the Gods
                                    were

---

[d] Tum Pater omnipotens fœcundis imbribus ÆTHER
     Conjugis in gremium lætæ defcendit, et omnes
     Magnos alit magno commixtus corpore fœtus.
                                    VIRGIL.

[e] De CIVITAT. DII. Lib. IV. Cap. 10.

[f] 'Ὡς ὁμόθεν γεγάασι θεοὶ θνητοί τ᾽ ἄνθρωποι,'
     Χρύσεον μὲν πρώτιςα γίν- μερόπων ἀνθρώπων——
                                    'Ως ι

‘ were born, and along with them mortal Men Lett.10.
‘ had fprung from the Earth, the firft Race of
‘ it's Inhabitants was of *Gold,* and lived happy
‘ like the Gods themfelves ; without Pain or
‘ Care, without Anxiety or Toil, fecure from
‘ the Blaft of old Age, or the Bane of Difeafe,
‘ they paffed their delightful Days in Youth's
‘ eternal Bloom. Their Life flowed with good
‘ Things ; the fertile Earth fpontaneons poured
‘ her Fruit ; the Heaven fmiled in perpetual
‘ Spring ; Rivers of Milk and Streams of Nec-
‘ tar ran through their Fields, and Honey dropt
‘ like Dew, from the verdant Oak. Thus they
‘ peaceful lived for Ages ; and at their Death,
‘ which refembled a balmy Sleep, they were
‘ transformed into beneficent *Genii,* girt in
‘ Robes of Air, Guardians of good Men ᵉ.

So the Poets fing ; and none of them fweeter
than your admired *Guarini*'s Mafter (for fo
I muft call *Torquato Taffo*) in his natural elegant AMINTA. Hear now their truly learned
Interpreter, explaining their Wonders, correct-
ing their Wanderings, and turning their Fables
into real Philofophy. ‘ The Ancients, fays he,
‘ make their *golden Age* begin immediately after
‘ the

῀Ωϛε Θεοὶ ϰ’ ἔζωον, ἀϰηδέα Θυμόν ἔχοντες,
Νόσφιν ἄτερτε πόνων ϰ̀ ὀιζύϑ·.
                                    ΗΣΙΟΔ. ΕΡ. ϰ̀ ΗΜ.

ᵉ Flumina tum lactis, tum flumina nectaris ibant,
  Flavaque de viridi ftillabant ilice mella.
                                    OVID. Metam. I.

Lett.10.' the Production and Inhabitation of the Earth
' (which they as well as *Moses* raise from *Chaos*)
' and to degenerate by degrees till the Deluge,
' when the World ended and began again.   But
' besides a *golden Age* in general, which was
' common to all the Earth, they noted some
' parts of it that were more golden, if I may so
' say, than the rest; the *Elysian* Fields, fortu-
' nate *Islands*, Gardens of *Alcinous, Hesperi-*
' *des*, &c.   These particularly answer to PA-
' RADISE.

' THEIR Characters or Marks of the gold-
' en Age were first, *Ver erat æternum*, as
' *Ovid* terms it, *an eternal Spring*.   They sup-
' posed that in the Reign of *Saturn*, who was
' an ante-diluvian God, TIME flowed with
' a more even Motion, and there was no di-
' versity of *Seasons* in the Year : But

Jupiter *antiqui contraxit tempora Veris,*

' as they express it, in their way, who seldom
' give any severe and philosophical Account of
' the Changes of NATURE.   Yet what was
' accounted fabulous or hyperbolical in this Re-
' presentation, we see to have been really and
' philosophically true.   The second Character
' of the golden Age is the *Longevity* of Men
' and other Animals —— to which *Josephus* the
' *Jewish* Historian says the Authors of all the
' learned Nations, *Greeks* or *Barbarians*, bear wit-
'   ' ness.

'nefs. The third, the *Fertility* of the Soil, and Lett.10.
' Production of Animals out of the new-made
' Earth: It's Fruits at firft were fpontaneous,
' and the Ground without being torn and tor-
' mented, fatisfied the Wants or Defires of *Man*:
' When Nature was frefh and full, all things
' flowed from her more eafily and more pure
' (fays the good Doctor, not very philofophi-
' cally, but in an honeft Effufion of Heart,
' and fincere Admiration of his favorite new-
' born Earth) like the firft-running of the
' Grape or the Honey-Comb: But *now* fhe muft
' be fqueezed and preffed, and her Productions
' tafte more of the Earth and of Bitternefs.
' —— *Then*, nothing violent, nothing frightful,
' nothing troublefome or incommodious to
' Mankind came from above, but the Counte-
' nance of the Heaven was always fmooth and
' ferene. —— I have often thought it a very
' defirable Piece of Power, if a Man could but
' command a *fair Day* when he had occafion
' for it: 'Tis more than the greateft Prince
' upon Earth can do; yet they never wanted
' one in that primitive World, nor ever faw
' a *foul* one: But they had conftant Breezes
' from the Motion of the Earth and the Courfe
' of the Vapours, which cooled the open Plains,
' and made the Weather *temperate* as well as
' fair. For their Spring was perpetual; their
' Fields always green; their Flowers always
' frefh, and the Trees always covered with
' Leaves

Lett. 10. ' Leaves and Fruit : Metals and Minerals they
' had none, and the happier they; no Gold nor
' Silver, nor coarfer Ore.

' As to *Men* and *Animals*, we have already
' fpoke of their Longevity : They were not only
' longer lived, but larger and ftronger than they
' are at prefent. The State of every thing that
' has Life is divided into the Time of its *Growth*,
' *Confiftency*, and it's *Decay*; and when the
' whole Duration is longer, every one of thefe
' Parts, though not always in like Proportion,
' will be longer. The Growth therefore, both
' in Men and other Animals, lafted longer in
' that World than it does now, and confe-
' quently carried their Bodies to a greater Height
' and Bulk : And I am very ready to believe
' that their *Stamina* were ftronger, and their
' Bodies greater than ours; and any Race of
' ftrong Men living long in Health, wou'd
' have Children of a proportionable Stature. In
' like manner their *Trees* would be both taller,
' and every way bigger than ours ; in no dan-
' ger of being ftruck with Thunder, or blown
' down by Winds and Storms, though they had
' been as high as the Pyramids of *Egypt* ; the
' Fowls of Heaven making their Nefts in their
' Boughs; and under their Shadow the Beafts
' of the Field bringing forth their Young.

' LET us next take a Profpect of the *moral*
' *World* at that time, or of the *civil* and *artifi-*
' *cial* World ; what the Order and Oeconomy of
' thefe

' thefe was, what the Manner of living, and Lett. 10.
' how the Scenes of human Life were dif-
' ferent from *ours* at prefent.

   ' The Ancients, efpecially the Poets, in their
' Defcriptions of the *golden Age*, exhibit to us
' an *Order of Things*, and a Form of Life very
' different from any thing we fee in our Days;
' but they are not to be trufted in all Parti-
' culars : They many times exaggerate mat-
' ters on purpofe, that they may feem more
' ftrange or more great, and by that means
' move and pleafe us more. A *moral* or *phi-*
' *lofophic* Hiftory of the World well writ, wou'd
' be a very ufeful Work ; to obferve and re-
' late how the Scenes of human Life, have
' in feveral Ages changed the Modes and Forms
' of living; in what Simplicity Men began at
' firft, and by what degrees they came out of
' that Way by Luxury, Ambition, Improve-
' ment or Changes in Nature : then, what new
' *Forms* and *Modifications* were fuperadded by
' the Invention of *Arts*, what by *Religion*,
' what by *Superftition*. This wou'd be a View
' of Things more inftructive, and more fatis-
' factory, than to know what King reigned in
' fuch an Age, and what Battles were fought,
' which common Hiftory teacheth, and teach-
' eth little more. Such Affairs are but the
' little Under-Plots in the *Tragicomedy* of the
' World ; the main Defign is of another nature,
' and of far greater Extent and Confequence.

H

' As

Lett.10.   ' As the animate World depends upon the
          ' inanimate, fo the *Civil* World depends upon
          ' them both, and takes it's meafures from them.
          ' NATURE is ftill the Foundation, and the
          ' Affairs of Mankind are a Superftructure that
          ' will be always proportioned to it.' —— No-
thing more certain than thefe general Maxims
laid down by this great Man, with equal Per-
fpicuity and Elegance; and fo far he may be
followed without the leaft hefitation: But now
he takes a Step further, and affumes the Hypothefis of his ingenious Theory, the fmooth
Shell of the new-formed Earth, enclofing the
great Deep or Abyfs of Water, whofe Difruption he believes occafioned an univerfal Deluge, and produced the Inequalities of the prefent terraqueous Globe.

          ' THE perpetual Equinox, fays he, of the
          ' primeval Earth, the Smoothnefs of it's Sur-
          ' face, the Calmnefs of the Air, Serenity of
          ' the Heavens, without Cold, violent Winds,
          ' Rains, Storms, or Extremity of Weather of
          ' any kind, wou'd require little Protection from
          ' the Injuries of the Air in that ftate: where-
          ' as now one great Part of the Affairs of Life
          ' is to preferve ourfelves from thofe Inconve-
          ' niencies by *Building* and *Cloathing*; two
          ' things which were then, in a manner, *need-*
          ' *lefs*, or in fuch plainnefs and fimplicity that
          ' every one might be his own Workman. *Tents*
          ' and *Bow'rs*, things of eafy and fudden Struc-

I   ' ture,

‘ ture, wou’d keep them from all Incommo-
‘ dities of the Air and Weather, better than
‘ stone Walls and strong Roofs defend us now ;
‘ and Men are apt to take to the *easiest* ways
‘ of living, till *Necessity* or *Vice* put them up-
‘ on others that are more laborious and arti-
‘ ficial. They fed not upon *Flesh* in those pri-
‘ mitive Ages; but only upon Fruits and Herbs,
‘ as seems to be plainly confirmed by the *Li-*
‘ *cence* God Almighty gave *Noah* and his Post-
‘ erity to feed upon Animals : *Every moving*
‘ *thing that liveth shall be Meat for you:*
‘ whereas before, in the new-made Earth, he
‘ had only prescribed them for their Diet, *every*
‘ *Herb bearing Seed, which is upon the Face*
‘ *of the Earth, and every Tree in the which is*
‘ *the Fruit of a Tree yielding Seed*; and of this
‘ *natural* Diet they wou’d be provided to their
‘ hands, without further Preparation, as the Birds
‘ and Beasts are.

‘ Here is a World indeed without Pro-
‘ metheus, or the use of Fire and the sub-
‘ sequent *Arts* ; and with a very different Face
‘ and Aspect from what it now wears. For
‘ of these Heads, *Food* and *Cloathing, Building*
‘ and *Traffic*, with that Train of Arts, Trades
‘ and Manufactures that attend them, *the*
‘ *civil Order of Things* is in a great measure
‘ constituted and compounded : These make the
‘ *Business* of Life, the several Occupations of
‘ Men, the Noise and Hurry of the World;

H 2   ‘ these

Lett.10.' thefe fill our Cities and our Fairs, our Ha-
' vens and Ports; yet all thefe fine things are
' but the Effects of Indigency and Neceffitouf-
' nefs, for the moft part needlefs, and unknown
' in the firft happy State of Nature.

' THE ANCIENTS have told us the fame
' things *in effect*; but telling them without
' their Grounds, which they themfelves did
' not know, they looked like *poetical Stories*
' and *pleafant Fictions*, and with moft Men
' paffed for no better. WE have fhewn them
' in another Light; with their Reafons and
' Caufes, deduced from the State of the *na-*
' *tural* World, which is the Bafis upon which
' they ftand : And this doth not only give them
' *a full and juft Credibility*, but alfo lays a
' Foundation for After-Thoughts and further
' Deductions when they meet with Minds dif-
' pofed to purfue Speculations of this nature[i].'

Now, my ingenious Friend! whom the
Gayety of Life does not hinder from reading,
nor even from thinking, (for they go not
always together;) there is a lucky Circumftance
in thefe Accounts of the Creation as they come
to us from the *Egyptian* or *Grecian* Mythologifts. It is the fame that *Socrates* mentions
in two *apocryphal* Lines of *Homer* concerning
the human and divine Appellations of *Cupid*.
He calls them fuch, becaufe they are not to
be

---

[i] Dr. T. Burnet's SACRED THEORY of the EARTH.

be found in the *authentic Canon* of the Poet's Lett.10.
Works, but were only handed down in a Tradition current among thofe who called themfelves his Pofterity. To thefe apocryphal Verfes,
fays the fmiling Sage, *We are at liberty to give
or withhold our Affent as we have a mind* *.

As for your curious Requeft, that I fhou'd
always fubjoin my own Sentiments of the feveral *Schemes* of the Ancients and Moderns, you
will give me leave only fo far to comply with
it, as to declare, that I find it impoffible for
me to keep pace with this great Genius, while
he profeffes *his full and firm Belief* of the
Theory of the Creation as he has defcribed it.
His Memory I highly honour, and admire the
Strength of his Fancy, and Compafs of his
manly well-digefted Learning ; but cannot accompany him throughout his amufing Plan, for
Reafons that imply too many Premiffes, and
wou'd require too fevere a Difcuffion to be read
with pleafure by a Perfon of your Vivacity :
befides that it muft be a Point of important
Neceffity, that either involves me in *Controverfy*
in Writing, or in *Difputes* in Converfation.
But if thefe beautiful Sketches awake your
Curiofity to ftudy the Sacred Theory of the
Earth, and you fhou'd then wifh to know it's
weak Sides, you will find Objections againft it's
Orthodoxy in a *Dutch* Divine, *Leidecker*'s Commentary on the *Mofaic* Account of the Creation,

H 3 and

* Τούτοις δὴ ἔξεςι μὲν πείθεσθαι, ἔξεςι δὲ μή.

Lett. 10. and the Inconſiſtency of ſo fine a Scheme plainly demonſtrated by no leſs Mathematician than the learned Mr. *Keil.* It is enough to my purpoſe, if the entertaining Light in which it's juſtly admired Author has endeavoured to ſet its Affinity, or rather Sameneſs with ancient Tradition, diſpel the Miſt that in your Opinion hung over *Mythology,* and ſhew you that the firſt Prieſts and Poets, the Fathers of Wiſdom, knew more and thought deeper than you were apt to imagine.

I always am

Yours, &c.

LETTER

LETTER ELEVENTH.

NO——My Friend! you need be under
no Apprehensions of having your Imagination bewildered or your Judgment misguided by these beautiful Allusions, and (as you
are pleased to call them) *fascinating* Representations of Nature: Besides the easy, *pleasing*
Cure I formerly hinted to you, two other
Considerations will prove effectual Antidotes
against the smallest Infection. The first, that
you know them to be *Fables* as they stand
literally, and therefore of no Meaning, but as
they point at some latent Truth. A Mind
aware of this admits nothing unexamined; but
while canvassing the wond'rous Tale is perpetually controuling it's own Fancies, and
improving in the wholesome Habit of sifting
the various Objects presented to it by the
mimic Faculty, whether they be Fantoms
or Realities. The other, that the most important and original of them, such as wou'd
be most likely to lead us astray, are upon strict
Examination by Men of the widest Learning
and exalted Genius, a BACON and a BURNET,
thought to be genuine and true. Such in part
is the Doctrine of the Creation, called the *Theogony* or Birth of the Gods; such the Division
of early Time into the *Golden, Silver, Bra-*

zen

zen and *Iron* Ages, and fuch in fine the Story of PROMETHEUS with which you feem to be fo delighted, and which is indeed equally inftructive and entertaining.

BUT there is ftill another Conveniency in this Method of Inftruction by *Fable* and *Allegory*, that muft effectually prevent any Fallacy, or hazard of being deceived: I mean it's *Condefcenfion* and *Pliablenefs* to all forts of Subjects, and Aptnefs to illuftrate indifferently various or even oppofite Opinions. For Mythology confines you to no Creed, nor pins you down to a Set of Principles, beyond which, you muft either not take a ftep, or lofe her Company. On the contrary, fhe permits, nay affifts you to contemplate at eafe, and like her eldeft Daughter the *early Academy* [a], follows complacent whitherfoever you lead. As you point, fhe exerts her creative Power, lays on her vivid though varying Colours, and diffufes interchanging Streams of Light on one and the fame Object. Witnefs the double View you have already had of the Rife of Things and Government of the World from *Orpheus* in the Defcription of PAN, and from *Hefiod* in his borrowed *Theogony*: and ftill plainer, in the double Moral of *Prometheus*, as fignifying either the *divine Providence* in the Formation of the World, and particularly of *Man*; or *human Forefight,*

[a] Nobis autem noftra ACADEMIA magnam licentiam dat, ut quodcunque maximè probabile occurrat, id noftro jure liceat defendere.   CICERO

Forefight, perpetually on the rack for the Ne-
ceffaries and Conveniencies of Life, fince the
Invention of *Arts* and the Ufe of *Fire*.

LET me however relieve you a little from
fuch gloomy Objects as ancient CHAOS and
dufky EREBUS, and give you a Specimen of
the Powers of this Enchantrefs, and of the various Shapes fhe affumes, on a Subject you
throughly underftand. But firft recollect the
Generation of *Cupid*, at the Birth of VENUS,
as the Son of PORUS and PENIA, (Plenty and
Want) and the Defcription of his variable Nature; and then liften to another poetic Tale.

' THE Goddefs of Beauty being pregnant,
' brought forth a delicate Infant they called
' *Cupid* or *Defire*, whom fhe gave to the *Graces*
' to be nurfed : But unhappily the Child neither
' throve in Perfon, nor put forth Feathers to
' garnifh his feeble unfurnifhed Wings. Un-
' der this Affliction his Mother and Nurfes
' had recourfe to the firft and moft ancient
' of the Oracles, the infallible *Themis*, who
' gave this Anfwer : That LOVE, it was true,
' came for the moft part, *fingle* into the World;
' but that he cou'd never truly grow nor at-
' tain his full Strength while he continued fo :
' that his Mother muft therefore bring forth
' another Son, and then the *one* wou'd thrive
' in virtue of the *other*; on condition tho',
' that if one of them fhou'd unfortunately die,
' the other cou'd not long furvive him. So
' faid

' said the footh-faying *Themis*; and *Venus* a-
'gain pregnant, brought forth another Son,
'*Anteros* by Name, or *mutual* LOVE. He no
'fooner came into Being, than his elder Bro-
'ther grew a-pace, inftantly his Wings fledged,
'and he took his flight to Heaven; there he
'affociated with the *Mufes*, was intimate with
'*Mercury*, kept fometimes company with *Hy-*
'*men*, and grew in favour with every God
'except the implacable *Momus*.'

So far, I dare fay, you think all goes well:
but a little patience, my Friend! See how the
Scene changes in the hands of another Mythologift. ' This growing Favour, the blind ca-
'pricious *Cupid* did not know how to im-
'prove. He grew infolent and vain, and be-
'haved with Arrogance to the fuperior Pow-
'ers. It was his pleafure to fow Difcord a-
'mong the Inhabitants of Heaven, and make
'Enmity reign where Peace and Concord
'fhou'd for ever dwell. Implacable Feuds raged
'among the Gods and Goddeffes on his ac-
'count, fo that the well-ordered celeftial State
'began to totter, and threatned irretrievable
'Ruin. In this Extremity, the Rulers of Hea-
'ven called the Gods to a folemn Affembly,
'in order to provide a proper Remedy for the
'growing Evil. LOVE was accufed and con-
'victed of being a public Incendiary, and a
'Difturber of the State. The Queftion of
'Pains and Penalties was put, and it was carried
　　　　　　　　　　　　　　　　' by

'by the Suffrage of the twelve great Gods,
'that *Cupid* fhou'd for ever be banifhed from
'the bleft Abodes; fhou'd be a Retainer to
'*Ceres* and *Bacchus* on Earth, and have his
'Wings ftript of their Feathers by *Saturn*,
'that he might be no more able to rife from
'the Ground, or again infeft the Confines of
'Heaven.'

Shou'd you chance to ftop a little at this Story,
and weigh it's Circumftances, it wou'd be no
fmall Entertainment, I imagine, to over-hear
the Soliloquy that wou'd break from a Man
fo nicely qualified, to judge of it's Propriety:
Unlefs the *Favours* you have received from the
Fair fhou'd put a Biafs on your Underftanding,
and difpofe you to patronize the hood-winkt
God againft the impartial Poet. 'Tis very
'hard, methinks,' I hear faid in a Sigh,
'Haplefs *Cupid!* always loaded with Ca-
'lumnies, and fuffering for Crimes not thy
'own! 'Tis very hard! LOVE! the Cordial
'of Life, the Refiner of Manners, the Band
'of Society; the Wifh of the Wife, and Re-
'ward of the Brave! Banifhed from Heaven,
'doomed to grovel on Earth, to depend on
'our loweft Appetites, and to have his Pinions
'plumed by every paffing Year! Is there then
'nothing noble or exalting in a generous Paf-
'fion? Nothing permanent, nor proof againft
'the Stroke of Age? Does every Charm fly
'with youthful Bloom? And will the Time
'indeed

' indeed come, when I fhall look unmoved on
' that Face I now idolize ; view indifferent that
' Perfon, now the Delight of my Eyes; or
' liften unenchanted to the Voice that now ra-
' vifhes my Heart ?'

TAKE Courage, my anxious Friend! Mythology is impartial, or to fay it better, indifferent; no farther oraculous than as fhe re-
prefents unchangeable Truth : The fame Faculty that degraded your favourite Deity, can
raife him to unfading Honours, and, with a
proper Management, make him the Source of
Happinefs and better Genius of the human Race.
' LOVE, fays the moft moral of all the Poets,
' is the greateft School of Wifdom and Vir-
' tue : and of all the Powers that prefide over
' human Affairs, *his* Influence and Sway is the
' fweeteft to Mortals. For pouring Joy un-
' mixed into either Heart, he fills them both
' with mutual Hope. Even his Toils are plea-
' fant, and his Wounds refrefhing : May ne-
' ver Friend of mine live exempt from the
' foothing Smart ; nor I be condemned to dwell
' among *lovelefs* Men! Attend ye Young, and
' liften ye Fair! Fly not from the proffered
' Blifs; but welcome the propitious Power, and
' wifely ufe his unenvious Bounty!
  ' AND THOU ! all-mighty LOVE ! Sovereign
' of Gods and Men, either teach not Mortals
' thy Way, but fhut their Eyes on Worth and
' Beauty, or mildly moderate a Lover's Pain,
                                        ' and

' and over-pay the Sufferings thou bringeſt with
' ſweet Returns of Love. So ſhalt thou be
' an highly-honoured God : but if thy Vota-
' ries ſigh and pine in vain, then that ſame
' Leſſon which thou giveſt ᴛᴏ Lᴏᴠᴇ, will rob
' thee of the Honours paid by Men ᵇ.'

Tʜᴇ happieſt Practice of that Leſſon is prettily painted by an ancient Tragedian, the Author of the Compariſon of the Power of Love
to the Effects of Wine. The Juice of the
Grape, ſays he, when mixed with Water, produces Health and Mirth ; when drunk pure
to exceſs, occaſions *Miſchief* and *Madneſs*. In
the ſame manner *Love*, when moderate and
gentle, is the Source of Pleaſure and ſoft Enjoyment ; but when intenſe and raging, turns
the moſt terrible impetuous Paſſion in the human Breaſt. Cᴜᴘɪᴅ therefore, continues the
elegant Poet, is armed with *two* Bows ; the
one he bends with the Aid of the *Graces*
ἐπ' εὐαίωνι τυχῇ, *for a happy ſmiling Lot* ; the
other with his *Bandage* on his Eyes ἐπὶ
ſυγχύσει βιοτᾶς, to the Confuſion and Miſery
of Life ᶜ.

Wou'd you wiſh to ſee him in one Shape
more ? Recollect the common trite Deſcription
of his Nature and Equipage : He is a winged
God, ever a Boy in Age and Stature, mounting
aloft at his pleaſure, ſhooting with a Bow, and
burning

ᵇ Eᴜʀɪᴘɪᴅᴇs apud Stobæum.
ᶜ Cʜᴀᴇʀᴇᴍᴏɴ apud Theophraſtum.

Lett.11. burning with a Torch: But according to *Ale-xis*, a celebrated comic Author, no one of all the Painters, Sculptors, Founders, or even Poets themselves, seem to have known any thing of the Nature of *Love*, nor in short any sort of Men who have undertaken to represent the Person and Qualities of this various God. For in himself he is neither *male* nor *female* ; neither truly God, nor yet meer Man; he is far from foolish, nor on the other hand, is he wise ; but being made up of different Ingredients brought and borrowed from different quarters, he changes his single Figure into a thousand shifting Forms. He is bold like the bravest Man, and timorous like the weakest Woman ; is thoughtless like an Ideot, and provident like a Politician ; he has the Fierceness of a wild Beast, the Hardness of the Adamant, and the Ambition of a deïfied Hero [d].

THUS you see how ductile and uncircumscribed the *allegorical* Art proves on a proper Subject : but how pliable soever this Mother of the Muses may be in her own Nature, and however condescending to her real Favourites, she is at first of very difficult access; bestows her Grace scantily, and very seldom upon a modern Poet. The Reasons of this Partiality wou'd be too long and some of them too invidious to be discussed by me : But you must

have

---

[d] ALEXIS apud Athenæum.

have obferved, that fhe has been fo profufe of Lett. 11. her Favours to the Ancients, that many of their Gods have double or triple Reprefentations. This wou'd occur to you in PAN the *Univerfe*, and PAN the Paftoral God of *Arcadia*; in VESTA the eternal Fire, and VESTA the Guardian of a Dwelling; and much more now, in LOVE a human Paffion; and LOVE the firft Principle that fettled the rolling Chaos and cemented the recent Creation.

DOES that Idea appear ftill ftrange and abftrufe to your Fancy? or have you rendered it familiar, by frequently reviewing the wondrous Tale of the Rife of all Things from the blind unactive Mafs, where, I know not how long, they had lain blended together? Let me give it a little bright'ning, by a new Proof of the Power and Wealth of Mythology on that interefting Subject.

'Tis obfervable, fays one great Interpreter of myftic Tradition, that the Ancients, in treating of the *Chaos*, and in raifing the World out of it, ranged it into feveral Regions or Maffes, and in that order, fucceffively rifing one from another, as if it was a *Pedigree* or *Genealogy*; and thofe Parts or Regions of Nature, into which the Chaos was by degrees divided, they fignified commonly by dark and obfcure Names, as *Night*, *Tartarus*, *Oceanus*, and fuch like: And whereas the Chaos when it was firft fet on work, ran all into Divifions and Separa-

tions

Lett. 11. tions of one Element from another, which afterwards were all in fome meafure united and
affociated in the primigenial Earth, the Ancients
accordingly made CONTENTION the Principle
that reigned in the Chaos at firft, then LOVE ;
the one to exprefs the *Divifions*, the other the
Union of all Parties in this middle and common
Bond *.

THIS Notion of the Formation of the World
was explained before ; but view the fame Object now in another Light, and as it is drawn
by the fame mafterly Pen.   There is one remarkable Doctrine amongft the Ancients, partly
fymbolical ; the Propriety and Application of
whofe *Symbol* hath been little underftood.   'Tis
their Doctrine of the *Mundane Egg*, or their
comparing the World, and efpecially the original Compofition of it to an EGG.   This feems
to be a mean Comparifon : what Proportion,
or what Refemblance is there between the
World and an Egg ? And yet I do not know
any fymbolical Doctrine or Conclufion that hath
been fo univerfally entertained by the *Myftæ*
or *Wife* and *Learned* of all Nations.   By the
World in this Similitude they do not mean
the great Univerfe ; but this fublunary World
which we inhabit.   And now do but reflect
upon the Theory of the Earth, the Manner
of it's Compofition at firft, and the Figure of
it

* DR. BURNET's Theory, Book I. Ch. v.

it when compleated, and you will need no other Interpreter to underſtand this Myſtery.

WE have ſhewed that the Figure of it was *oval*, and the inward Form of it was a Frame of *four Regions* encompaſſing one another, where that of *Fire* lay in the middle like the *Yolk*, and a Shell of Earth encloſed them all. This gives a Solution ſo eaſy and natural, and ſhews ſuch an Aptneſs and Elegancy in the Repreſentation, that upon a View and Compare of Circumſtances, one cannot doubt but that we have truly found out the Riddle of the *Mundane Egg*. But, to be more particular, the Earth reſembles an Egg, not ſo much for its external Figure, tho' that be true too, as for the inward Compoſition of it, conſiſting of ſeveral Orbs, one including another; and in that order as to anſwer the ſeveral *elementary* Regions, of which the new-made Earth was conſtituted. For if we admit for the Yolk a *central Fire*, and ſuppoſe the Figure of the Earth *oval*, and a little extended towards the Poles (as probably it was, ſeeing the *Cortex* that contains it is ſo) thoſe two Bodies do very naturally repreſent one another, as if a Scheme were made to repreſent the interior Faces of both a *divided Egg*, or the *Earth*; where, as the two *inmoſt* Orbs wou'd repreſent the Yolk, and the Membrane that lies next above it, ſo the exterior Region of the Earth is as the *Shell* of the Egg, and the Abyſs under it as the

I

White

Lett.11.*White* that lies under the Shell. And confidering that this Notion of the *Mundane Egg,* or that the World was *oviform,* hath been the Senfe and Language of all Antiquity, *Greeks, Latins, Egyptians, Perfians* and others, I thought it not unworthy our notice in this place, feeing it receives fuch a clear and eafy Explication from that *Origin* and *Fabric* we have given to the firft Earth ; and alfo reflects Light upon the Theory itfelf, and confirms it to be no Fiction ; this *Notion,* which is a kind of Epitome or Image of it, having been conferved in the moft ancient Learning. —— Had the Works of *Orpheus* been preferved, I fhou'd hope for as much Inftruction from them alone, as to the *Origin* of the World, as from all that is now extant of the other *Greek* Philofophers. He underftood in a good meafure, *how the Earth rofe from* Chaos ; what was its external Figure, and what the Form of its inward Structure. For the Opinion of the *oval* Figure of the Earth is afcribed to *him* and his Difciples ; and the Doctrine of the *mundane Egg* is fo peculiarly *his,* that it is called by *Proclus* the Orphic-Egg: not that he was the firft Author of that Doctrine, but the firft that brought it into *Greece* from *Egypt,* or the *Eaft.*

And now, I hope, you are fully convinced, that Mythology leaves us at liberty to think and reafon as we lift ; and therefore can lead

us

us no further aſtray than we ourſelves have a Lett.II.
mind to follow. You have ſeen how variouſly
it repreſents the Riſe of Things, according to
the different Opinions of the Sages concerning
them ; like a Mirrour that reflects whatever Object is held before it, and in the Colours it
then wears, whether genuine or not. You will
ſee its Complaiſance ſtill plainer in the mythical Account, not now of the Riſe, but of the
Government of the World, by the Father of
the Gods and Men, all-mighty *Jove*, and by
ſome few of the inferior Deities, the *Fates* and
Fortune, *Hecate* and *Pandora*, whom I intend
to ſelect, and explain their Natures for your
Entertainment.

I am

Yours, &c.

I 2   *LETTER*

LETTER TWELFTH.

OUR ingenious Countryman, Sir *Thomas Brown,* fays he had two Books from which he drew his Theology. ' One of them ' in Writing dictated by GOD himſelf; the ' other by NATURE his Hand-maid ; that ' univerſal and patent Manuſcript whoſe won- ' drous Leaves are expoſed to the Eyes of all ' Men. Thoſe who never ſaw the Author of ' Nature in the former have often viewed ' him in the latter, which was the early Scrip- ' ture and Theology of the Heathens. The ' ſupernatural Stop in the Sun's Courſe created ' not ſuch Admiration in the Minds of the ' *Iſraelites,* as his diurnal Motion did in the ' Underſtanding of the Philoſophers ; nor were ' the former ſo ſtruck with Miracles, as the ' latter with the moſt common Productions of ' Nature. Theſe ancient Sages far ſurpaſſed ' the Chriſtians in Reach and Capacity in this ' myſterious Learning. They knew how to ' join and ſpell out theſe hidden Characters ' much more ſkilfully than we, who take ' only a tranſient ſuperficial View of theſe ' vulgar Hieroglyphics, and fooliſhly underva- ' lue a Theology extracted from the faireſt ' Flowers of the Univerſe.'

THAT

THAT in reading this we may not injure
the knowing and ingenuous Phyſician, let us
remember that he wrote upwards of an hundred Years ago; when neither a *Boyle* nor a
Newton had yet aroſe, and trod the Path pointed
out by that mighty Genius, the immortal
BACON; to abandon Subtlety and Syllogiſm in
Philoſophy, and betake ourſelves to Obſervation
and Experiment for the Inveſtigation of Nature's Operations, and to Geometry applied to
them for her general Laws. Natural Science in
his Days wore but an aukward Face; and the
beſt of *his* ſeems to have been drawn from the
Ancients. Had he ſeen *Nieuentijt's Religious
Philoſopher*, or that plain primitive Man Mr.
Derham's Phyſico-Theology, (a Book with whoſe
pious Simplicity I am infinitely delighted) he
muſt have altered his Opinion; and much more,
if after a Demonſtration of the Structure of the
World, and of the eternal Laws by which the
heavenly Bodies revolve inceſſant in their Orbs,
he had read the deep Deſcription of its Author,
as the concluſive Stroke of the mathematical
Principles of natural Philoſophy by *Sir Iſaac
Newton*. But at the Time in which he wrote,
his Obſervation was not altogether groundleſs;
tho' I have nothing to do with the Compariſon he makes between the Ancients and Moderns, farther than to fulfil my Promiſe, and
give you a View of the Doctrine of the former
concerning that Power they believed to be

Pater

Lett.12. *Pater Hominumque Deûmque,* Father of the Gods and Men.

AND firſt, by inſpecting their Records, and comparing their Relations it comes to be abſolutely uncertain *where Jupiter* was born. The Stories of his Birth in a Cave of the Iſland *Crete,* or at *Thebes* in *Bæotia,* or on a Mountain in *Arcadia,* are but ſo many Traditions of the ſeveral Places where his Worſhip firſt grew famous in *Greece* and was celebrated with the greateſt Pomp. The Reaſons of its being ſo in *Crete* and *Thebes* are very evident becauſe of *Minos* and *Cadmus,* two *Aſiatic* Princes Founders of thoſe States, having brought their national Rites into *Greece:* But the *Arcadians* being addicted to War and Paſturage, in a rough mountainous Country, became afterwards a rude fierce People in compariſon of their politer Neighbours and yet retained more Traditions concerning the Birth, Education and Adventures of the Gods among them than the more knowing Tribes of the *Peloponneſus.* This I take to have been owing to their early Inſtruction, firſt by the Deſcendants of *Inachus,* and then by the *Danaïds,* in the Religion and Rites they brought from their ſeveral Countries; of which *Jupiter's* Worſhip in particular made a prime Part, as appears from the great Antiquity of his Oracle at *Dodona;* and theſe Traditions were preſerved among the hardy *Arcadians* rather than among the Nations inhabiting

inhabiting the fertile Shores, for the same Reason that the ancient *British* Language is preserved among the Mountains of *Wales* rather than among the Gardens of *Kent*, or the Fields of *Devon*.

IT rarely happens that a Religion professed in different Nations continues strictly the same as to Doctrine and Worship in them all: Variations usually ensue; and entail Disputes among the distant Votaries. If we survey the Religions now prevailing over the World, we will hardly find two Nations exactly agreeing in their Profession and Practice; while the zealous of each, hold their own particular Belief to be the only true Doctrine of Heaven. 'Tis thus I wou'd understand what *Cicero* relates of the Tradition of the ancient Divines concerning *three Jupiters*; the first and second of whom shou'd have been born in *Arcadia* of the ETHER and CELUS, and the third of SATURN in *Crete* [a]. The Creed-makers of the several Temples, and Directors of the solemn Rites have probably adopted the Doctrines and sanctified the Ceremonies peculiar to each Place; if they did not purposely contrive some Article of Dissent, or separate Usage, as a Badge of Distinction from the Rival-Worship. All Ages and Nations have afforded Examples of this envious unsocial Spirit; and none more flagrant

I 4 than

[a] Principio tres Joves numerant ij qui *Theologi* nominantur; ex quibus primum et secundum natos in Arcadia, alterum patre *Æthere* ——— alterum patre *Cælo*, ——— tertium Cretensem, Filium *Saturni.* De Natura DEOR. Lib. III.

Lett.12. than the Devotees of the Rival-Temples on the two Mountains (their common Situation in the Eaſt) *Moriah* and *Gerizzin* [b].

BUT the more authentic Tradition fixes neither the Time nor Place of *Jupiter's* Birth, but only agrees unvariably in his Parents, that he was the Child of *Saturn* and *Rhea*: that is, Men in all Nations who had any Religion have worſhipped a Supreme Being from Time immemorial, whom they believed not to have created the World out of nothing, but to have firſt ranged its diſordered Parts, and ever after to rule it at his pleaſure. Two remarkable Circumſtances are recorded of *Rhea's* Delivery of JOVE, which tho' apparently different, or even contradictory, are exactly of the ſame Significancy: The firſt and beſt known bears, that his gloomy Parent, relentleſs TIME, had ſwallowed up all his former Progeny and covered them in Obſcurity and Oblivion; and the ſecond, that the terrible TITANS (jarring Principles of the Chaos) had themſelves ſat by *Rhea* in Childbirth, and received and tore in pieces all the Male-Children as ſoon as they were born [c]:

that

[b] The *Jews* called the *Samaritan* Temple, in a Word of *Greek* Derivation, פלטאנוס Πελεθῦ ναὸς, the *Dunghill-Temple*, and שקר *Sichar* (inſtead of *Schechem*) a Lye: And the *Samaritans* in return called the Temple of *Jeruſalem* בית קלקלתא the *Houſe of Dung*, and ſince its Deſtruction בית מכתש Ædes Plagæ, the *Houſe of Calamity*.

[c] Ὁπποΐε κεν δέ 'PE'H τίκlεν, παρὰ τὴν δ' ἑκάϑηντο
ΤΙΤΗ͂ΝΕΣ, κỳ τέκνα διέσπων ἄῤῥενα πάνlα.
See Page 49, Note x.   ΕΠΗ ΣΙΒΥΛ:

that is, deſtroyed all the various Combinations Lett. 12.
into which the Chaos had run, until a ſuperior vivifying Power was produced, of all-
mighty Influence to unite and preſerve them.
‘ It was when firſt he reared his etherial Head,
‘ that all Things ſpontaneous appeared in their
‘ proper Forms, the great Goddeſs *Mother-*
‘ *Earth*, the lofty Tops of the re-echoing
‘ Mountains, the wide-ſpread *Ocean*, and
‘ whatever the immenſe Heaven contains within
‘ it ᵈ.’ Before that, they had lain o’erwhelmed
in the unfathomable Abyſs, the Seminary of
Being and Exiſtence, where this ſupreme
Power tells his Conſort ſhe could produce nothing without him ; not tho’ ſhe betook herſelf
to the utmoſt Boundaries of the Earth and
Sea, where *Iapetus* and *Saturn* (DESIRE and
TIME) are ſitting joyleſs without a Ray of the
enlivening Sun, or genial Breath of a refreſhing
Gale ; but deep *Tartarus* circumfuſed around
them ᵉ.

Some ſuch Idea as this of *Deſire* and *Time’s*
being ſhut up in perpetual Darkneſs until they

were

ᵈ Ὦ βασιλεῦ διὰ σὴν κεφαλὴν ἐφάνη τάδε ῥεῖα,
Γαῖα θεὰ μῆτηρ, Ὀρέων θ᾽ ὑψηχέες ἔχθαι,
Καὶ Πόντϱ, κὴ πάνθ᾽ ὑπόσ᾽ ὑρανὸς ἐντϱ ἔλαξε.

OΡΦ. ΥΜΝ.

See Page 86, and Page 91, Notes ᶜ and ᵈ.

ᵉ ———————— Οὐδ᾽ ἔικε τὰ νείατα πείραθ᾽ ἵκηαι
Γαίης κὴ πόντοιο· ἵν᾽ ΙΑΠΕΤΟΣ τε ΚΡΟΝΟΣ τε
Ἥμενοι, οὐδ᾽ αὐγῆς ὑπερίονϱ ηελίοιο
Τέρπονται, οὔτ᾽ ἀνέμοισι, βαθὺς δέ τε ΤΑΡΤΑΡΟΣ ἀμφίς.

See Page 87 and 88, Note ᵃ. ΟΜΗΡ. ΙΛΙΑΔ. Θ.

Lett. 12· were delivered by a superior Principle of *Light*
and *Being*, seems to have been wandering thro'
the Mind of the celebrated *German* Mystic [e],
when in his enigmatical way, he says, " *No-*
" *thing* hungreth after *Something*, and the
" Hunger is *Desire*. So that Nothing is filled,
" and yet remains Nothing; it is only a Pro-
" perty, to wit, *Darkness*. This is the Eye of
" the Abyss —— the eternal Chaos, wherein
" all, whatsoever Time and Eternity have, is
" contained —— its peculiar and proper Name
" is *Jeova*, (Existence)." Had this muddy
Metaphysician been inspired by any gayer Muse,
each of these abstract Notions had assumed a
Person and Character, and like *Saturn, Iapetus*
and the *Titans*, acted their Parts in the *Drama*
of the Creation.

But you will readily observe in all poetical
Accounts of the Generation of the World,
that Jupiter is *Saturn's youngest* Child;
that is to say, the last and latest Production of
Time; and cou'd therefore have no hand in
its original Creation. Among the Philosophers
it was quite otherwise : few of them had any
Notion of the Rise of the Universe from *Nothing*; but they supposed *Jupiter* to be the
eternal Principle of Life (so his Name plainly
imports) that first modelled the mighty pre-
existing Mass, and now governs and keeps it in
order. The most authentic Fragment of the
old mythological Philosophy, preserved by

[e] Jacob Behm.   *Diogenes*

Diogenes Laertius, is a Summary of PHERE- Lett.12.
CYDES SYRIUS's Doctrine concerning the Rise
of Things and Beginning of the World.
' *Jupiter,* says he, and *Saturn,* and *Ceres*
' were eternal ; and *Ceres* obtained the Name
' of ΓΑΙΑ' (*generating Earth*) after that *Ju-*
' *piter* had preferred her to Honour ʳ.' These
few Words wou'd bear a large Commentary,
were there now any need to explain them
to *You.* They contain the oldest philosophical Creed in the concisest Terms ; as if
he had said, ' MIND and TIME and MAT-
' TER were eternal, and MATTER be-
' came a fruitful Mother after the all-mighty
' MIND had put honour upon it by endow-
' ing it with a Capacity of Generation.' Take
a little leisure to view these three Ideas,
and to compare their Operations with whatever Accounts you have elsewhere heard of
the Beginning of Things ᵍ, you will find it well
employed ; and the Subject requires it.

THE Poets, on the other hand, understood
Jupiter to be a *material* Principle, of the
purest

ᶠ ΖΕΥΣ μὲν κ̀ ΚΡΟΝΟΣ ἦσ ἀεὶ κ̀ ΧΘΩΝ ἦν. ΧΘΟΝΙ
δὲ ὄνομα ἐγένετο ΓΗ, ἐπειδὴ αὐτῇ ΖΕΥΣ γέρας διδοῖ.

ᵍ Ὡς οὐρανός τε Γαῖα τε ἦν μορφὴ μία——
Ἐπεὶ δ' ἐχωρίσθησαν ἀλλήλων δίχα,
Τίκτυσι πάντα, κ' ἀνέδωκαν ἐς Φάος
Δένδρα, πτηνὰ, θῆρας, οὓς θ' ἅλμη τρέφει,
Γένος τε θνητῶν.—— ΕΥΡΙΠΙΔ. παρὰ τῷ ΕΥΣΕΒ.
Προπαρασκ. βιβ. αα

Lett.12. pureſt Nature indeed, the vital vivifying ETHER, which they took to be the firſt original Source of Life, and celebrated him accordingly. It was he who quelled the Rebel-*Titan*-Gods, and eſtabliſhed Harmony and good Order in the Creation; and it is *be* who by his immediate invigorating Power produces and orders all things in Heaven and in Earth, being now the ſupreme Parent and Ruler both of Gods and Men.

Jupiter omnipotens, rerum, regumque, deûmque, Progenitor, genitrixque. ——

WHEN the elegant and unfortunate *Ovid* ſat down to write his *Faſti*, and was beginning to conſider the Name and Nature of JANUS, from whom the Month of *January* and Entry of the Year is denominated, a ſudden Light ſhone around him as he ſat; the wondrous Form of the two-faced God preſented itſelf to his View, and encouraged the terrified Poet to aſk what he pleaſed concerning his Origin and Power. Addreſſing himſelf therefore with Reverence to the heavenly Viſion, he firſt enquired *which of the Gods be was? Since even* Greece *bad no ſuch* Deity; and received this Anſwer:

' I am old CHAOS, the ancienteſt of Things:
' This ambient Air, and the three remaining
' Elements Fire, Water and Earth, were once
' one undiſtinguiſhed Maſs.———Whatſoever
                                        ' thou

' thou fee'ft around thee, the azure Heaven, Lett. 12.
' the fleecy Clouds, the pathlefs Sea, and ⌣⌣⌣
' boundlefs Earth open and fhut by my pow-
' erful Hand. Sole Guardian I fit of the
' immenfe World, whofe eternal Hinges are
' only turned by me. —— I prefide over the
' Gates of Heaven attended by the *Seafons*;
' and guide even JOVE in the Circumvolution
' of the Sky: Hence I am called JANUS [h]:'
And hence we may fee both what the Ancients underftood by *Jupiter*, and how many
ways they had of expreffing his Dependance
upon the other Parts of the Univerfe, and the
Neceffity he lay under of governing it according
to their feveral Natures.

BUT the Birth of *Janus* did not finally
fettle the new-made World: Other Deities
were afterwards produced, who put the laft
hand to this mighty Frame. ' For after *Chaos*
' and Confufion difappeared, fays the Mufe of
' Memory to the fame Poet [i], and Nature had
' feparated

[h] ME CHAOS antiqui (nam res fum prifca) vocabant;
  Afpice quam longi temporis acta canam :
Lucidus hic Aer, et quæ tria corpora reftant,
  Ignis, Aquæ, Tellus, unus acervus erant. ——
Quicquid ubique vides, Cœlum, Mare, Nubila, Tellus,
  Omnia funt noftrâ claufa, patentque manu.
Me penes eft unum vafti cuftodia Mundi,
  Et jus vertendi cardinis omne meum eft. ——
Præfideo Foribus Cœli cum mitibus Horis
  It, redit, officio Jupiter ipfe meo.
Inde vocor IANUS.   FASTORUM Lib. 1. §. 4.
[i] POLYMNIA one of the three ancient Mufes, denominated
from πολλὴ μνεία great Memory. See *Lucian's* Treatife of
                                   Dancing.

Lett.12.' separated into its several Portions, tho' the
' Earth had sunk down with its Weight, and
' drawn after it the Sea, and the Heaven had
' mounted aloft with the etherial Fires, yet
' neither Heaven nor Earth remained unmoved
' in their proper Place, nor would the lesser
' Luminaries give way to the Sun : Some vulgar
' God would often usurp *Saturn*'s Throne, and
' any stroling upstart Deity wou'd put himself
' on the level with old *Ocean*, and take place
' of ancient *Tethys*. Things continued in this
' uncertain State until *Honour* and *Reverence* be-
' got MAJESTY, who filled Heaven and Earth,
' the Day she was born. *Awe* and *Dread*
' sat down by her, and all the three, being
' defended by *Jove*'s Thunders from the At-
' tacks of the *Titans*, have never since stirred
' from the Side of [k] this God, *who now rules*
' *Supreme, having rightly ranged all the Im-*
' *mortals, and allotted to each their particular*
' *Dignity* [l].' In short, to have a just Conception of ancient *Jove* let us first recollect *Zeno*'s
Definition of NATURE, *Ignem esse artificiosum*
ad g ignendum progredientem via [m], that it was

a

Dancing, and *Plutarch*'s *Table-Conversations*. *Polyhymnia* was
a later Name. *Hesiod* and the old *Grecian* Writers make but
four Syllables of it.

[k] A; sidet illa Jovi : Jovis est fidissima Custos ;
     Et præstat sine vi Sceptra tremenda Jovi. OVID. Fastor. V.
— ——————— Ἒυ δὲ ἱκαϛα

ʾΑϑὶ τωάτοις διέταξεν ὁμῶς κὴ ἐπέφραδε τιμὰς.
                         ΗΣΙΟΔ, Θεογον,

[m] Cic. de Nat. Deor. Lib. II.

a plaſtic Fire, ever generating by Rule; and Lett.12.
then obey the moſt philoſophical of all the
Poets, while he bids us

> *Look up and view th'immenſe Expanſe of*
> *Heaven,*
> *The endleſs* ETHER, *in his genial Arms,*
> *Claſping the Earth : Him call thou God and*
> *Jove* ª.

AND now, my Friend! judge of the Propriety of his Deſignations and Claim to Dominion, when you have read what the other
eminent Author (no *minute* Philoſopher) takes
to be one of the higheſt Steps in the Scale of
Creation. ‘ ETHER, ſays he, or pure invi-
‘ ſible *Fire*, the moſt ſubtile and elaſtic of all
‘ Bodies, ſeems to pervade and expand itſelf
‘ throughout the whole Univerſe. If *Air* be
‘ the immediate Agent or Inſtrument in natural
‘ Things, it is the pure inviſible *Fire* that is
‘ the *firſt natural Mover or Spring* from whence
‘ the Air derives its Power. This mighty
‘ AGENT is every where at hand; ready to
‘ break forth into Action, always reſtleſs and in
‘ motion, actuating and enlivening the whole
‘ viſible Maſs, equally fitted to produce and
                                ‘ to

ª Ὁρᾷς τὸν ὑψȣ̃, τόνδ' ἄπειρον ΑΙΘΕΡΑ
Καὶ γήν πέριξ ἔχονθ' ὑγραῖς ἐν ἀγκάλαις·
Τȣ̃τον νόμιζε, τόνδ' ήγȣ̃ ΘΕΟΝ. ΕΥΡΙΠΙΔΗΣ.
      Whence old Ennius has taken his,
Adſpice hoc Sublime candens, quem invocant omnes
Iovs ᵈ.

Lett.12.' to deftroy, diftinguifhing the various *Stages*
' of Nature, keeping up the perpetual Round
' of Generation and Corruption, pregnant with
' ' Forms which it conftantly fends forth and
' reforbs; fo quick in its Motions, fo fub-
' tile and penetrating in its Nature, fo exten-
' five in its Effects, it feems no other than the
' *vegetative* SOUL, or *vital* SPIRIT of the
' World ª.'

HERE is the true *Jupiter*, the Source of Generation and Principle of Life, that *cæleftis,
altiffima æthereaque Natura, id eft, ignea, quæ
per fe omnia gignat,* as *Cicero* defcribes it; *that
heavenly, moft high, etherial, that is, igneous
Nature, which fpontaneous begets all Things,*
the fuppofed Parent of Gods and Men. Let
us next confider his *Juno.*

' THE AIR º, fays the fame fagacious Au-
' thor, is the Receptacle as well as Source of
' all fublunary Forms —— the great Mafs or
' *Chaos* which imparts and receives them.
' The Atmofphere that furrounds our Earth
' contains a Mixture of all the active volatile
' Parts of all Vegetables, Minerals, Foffils and
' Animals. Whatever perfpires, corrupts or
' exhales, impregnates the Air, which being
' acted upon by the folar Fire (here is literally
' *Conjugis in gremium lætæ defcendit)* pro-
' duceth within itfelf all fort of chemical
' Operations;

ª See alfo the Introduction to BOERHAVE's *Chemiftry.*
º HPA, the *Greek* Name of *Juno,* is but a Tranfpofition
of the Letters of ʾAn̲p̲ the *Air.*

'Operations; difpenfing again thofe Salts and Lett.12.
'Spirits in new Generations which it had re-
'ceived from Putrefactions.——The A I R there-
'fore is an active Mafs of numberlefs different
'Principles, the general Source of Corruption
'and Generation, in which the Seeds of Things
'feem to lie latent, ready to appear and produce
'their Kind whenever they light on a proper
'*Matrix.* The whole Atmofphere feems *alive.*
'There is every where *Acid* to corrode and
'Seed to engender in this common Seminary
'and Receptacle of all vivifying Principles ᴾ.'

SMALL is the Sketch I have here made out
of thefe combined Powers; if you incline to fee
their Operations acutely inveftigated, and nobly
defcribed in a manly philofophic Language, you
may confult the Original from which I have
taken it. There you will find the true Foundation of the Marriage made by the Poets between
thefe Kindred-Gods; and a little Reflection upon
their feveral Natures will now fecurely lead you
thro' the Sequel of the Fable. No wonder if
the 'mighty AGENT, pregnant with Forms,
that keeps up the Round of Generation,' fhould
affume a thoufand different Shapes to accomplifh
his Ends, and transform himfelf into the Figures
of all the Animals that people the Earth and
Sea: and as little, if the active Mafs that furrounds our Globe, the AIR, whofe wondrous
elaftic

ᴾ Berkeley's SIRIS, §. 137, &c.

K

Lett.12. *elaſtic Spring* produces ſuch Convulſions at the
Approach of *Fire*, ſhould be frequently em-
broiled with her imperious Mate. The repeated
Adulteries of this generative Power, and the
perpetual Jarrings between him and his Spouſe
will now give no great Scandal ; nor when we
conſider at what Seaſon of the Year the *Air* is
moſt impregnated with *etherial* Seed, when it
is, that all Nature teems, and every Tribe is
prone to Generation, will we wonder at the
Cuckow's being the Bird of *Juno*, carved on the
top of her Scepter in *Argos* ; or at *Jupiter's*
transforming himſelf into this Meſſenger of the
genial Spring, when he firſt enjoyed his reluctant
Queen :

> *It Ver, et Venus, et Veneris prænuntius ante*
> *Pinnatus graditur Zephyrus veſtigia propter* [b].

As Truth once lighted up ſhines on every thing
around it, the ſame Thread of Reflection will
guide us thro' the Labyrinth of a greater Myſtery.
For this Matron-Goddeſs, and Patroneſs of Marriage, became once a year a pure unſpotted Virgin, upon bathing herſelf in a ſacred Fountain
in the *Argive* Territory : This grand Secret
tranſpired ſome way from the ſolemn Initiations
into her Myſteries ; and the Name of the Spring,
Canatho, which produced the miraculous Alteration [*]. It has probably been a hot Mineral
that acquired new Strength upon the Turn of
the

[b] T. Lucret. Lib. V.　　[*] Pausan. Corinthiac.

the Year, and perhaps by Ebullition ^q, or Exhalations emitted on a Change of the Temperature of the *Air*, might be a Mark of the returning Spring, and thereby a Source of Gain to the artful Prieſt, and a Trap for the credulous People. When the Fountain diſcoloured with the Ablutions, no doubt, of the Goddeſs, or ſeemed to boil in virtue of her bathing, the *Air* was again in a proper Temper for Generation; *Juno* was again become a Virgin, and it was time to perform the annual Solemnity. Thus you ſee how Circumſtances that ſeem quite trivial in themſelves, and little ſilly-like Tales come to repreſent ſome of the greateſt Changes in Nature. They appear mean only when they are not *underſtood*; and have therefore a Right either to be ſtudied e're they are contemned, or to uſe Mr. *B* * * * *'s Reply to a Lord-Mayor, who full of his bulky Dignity was anſwering diſdainfully, ' he did not underſtand him:' *Sir, I cannot mend your Underſtanding.* Even the *Contradictions* that ſhock us in a curſory Survey of ſeveral Parts of Mythology evaniſh upon a ſtricter Search, and appear not only conſiſtent with Truth, but eſſential to the Subject. *Jupiter* is honoured with the Epithet of *beneficent*ʳ, and loaded with that of *pernicious*ˢ——He is *Jove*

K 2 the

ᵠ ڪي Canaa ſignifies to grow red, muddy; to mix Water with any thing that diſcolours it: and in Hebrew קִנְאָה Kenah, in pl. קִנְאוֹת Kenaoth (Canatho) burning Jealouſy, boiling Wrath.

ʳ ΖΕΥΣ σωτήριⓈ. ˢ 'Ολοὸς.

Lett.12. the *Deliverer*, and *Jove* the *Deſtroyer*. *Apollo* his Son is the Source of Health and Author of the Plague : he is *Apollo* the *Soother* [t] and *Apollo* the *Tormentor* [u], and as of his Father, ſo the beſt and the worſt things are ſaid of *Apollo*. How ſhall we reconcile theſe Extremes? By remembering what theſe Powers repreſent : By recollecting what the learned laſt-quoted Author ſays of ETHER or the pure inviſible *Fire* that pervades and expands itſelf throughout the whole Univerſe ; " that it is equally fitted to *produce* and to de- " *ſtroy*; keeping up the perpetual Round of *Ge-* " *neration* and *Corruption*, pregnant with Forms " which it conſtantly *ſends forth* and *reſorbs*."

As for *Phœbus*,—the Influence of the *Sun*, and his various Effects both upon human Bodies, and upon all the animal and vegetable Race, nicely account for his jarring Attributes. I will not enter into the detail: Your great Phyſician has explained the firſt Part of this Influence in a Treatiſe worthy of its Author [v], which to you who know him, and my Eſteem of him, is the higheſt Commendation in my power to give it: But that this God's *muſical Capacity*, which fell not within the Deſign of that admirable Work, ſhould produce various, and even claſhing Effects; that the ſame Faculty (the Power of Muſic) ſhould be the Source of great Pleaſure and

[t] ΑΠΟΛΛΩΝ μειλίχιⒼ⸱.
[u] Eſſe quidem *Apollinem*, ſed *Tortorem*. Sueton. in Auguſto.
[v] De Imperio SOLIS ac LUNAE in corpora humana. R. MEAD, M. D.

and great Pain, is a Speculation too curious to be flightly paffed over. You may conceive of it thus.

A STRAIN of Poetry ftretched beyond its due Bounds turns to a Strain of Madnefs; and that fame foft Vein of native Mufic, which when the Mind is in its natural State, breathes nothing but Harmony and Love, if raifed to an extravagant unnatural Pitch, racks the lab'ring overburthened Breaft, and breaks loofe in Rage and foaming Ecftacy. Wild Looks, amazing Poftures, Soul-roufing Sounds, commonly ufh- ered the furious dithyrambic Song; and when heightened by Wine and proceffional Worfhip were as fo many Steps that led to the tortured bacchanal State of toffing and roaring; and, like ravening Wolves or enraged Bears, rending in pieces whatever came in the way: driven to the Defarts and wandering in the Woods, Danger was their Delight, and Mifchief their Paftime^w.

K 3 In

^w ——— Quæ in nemora, aut quos agor in fpecus
Velox mente novâ ?—Ut mihi devio
 Rupes et vacuum nemus
Mirari libet! O Naïadum potens
 Baccharumque valentium
Proceras manibus vertere Fraxinos
Nil mortale loquar: dulce periculum eft
 —Sequi *DEUM!* HORAT. Lib. III. Ode 25.

——— Μαινάδες
Χωρῦσι δ' ὡς' ὄρνιθες ἀρθεῖσαι δρόμῳ
Πεδίων ὑπὸ τάσεις——ὥςε πολέμιοι
Ἐπεισπεσῦσαι, πάντ' ἄνω τε κỳ κάτω
Διέφερον. ΕΥΡΙΠΙΔ. ΒΑΚΧΑΙ.

This Bacchic Paffion is prettily imitated by the Cavalier Marino, in his *Sampogna*, Idillio III. Arianna.

Chi

Lett.12. In this woeful State, the beautiful Order, the divine Harmony of the human Breaft is defaced, the delicate Economy of the Paffions reverfed; Diffonance and Torture rack the diftorted Soul, and wretched *Marfyas*, the Rival of Mufic, (the diforderly Din of the Paffions, the wild Shout of Joy, or piercing Yell of Grief[x]) is inevitably feized; firft whipt by *Minerva*[y], the Goddefs of Wifdom, and next hung up on a Pine[z], and truly flea'd alive.

Of the Blood that dropped from the rude Mufician, fprung the *Panifci* and *Satyrs*; half Men, half Goats; great Dancers and Pipers, but with a Strain of their Original, lewd, petulant and mifchievous. It was not long however before *Apollo* repented of his Cruelty: the Paffions foon fubfide; the Mind returns by degrees to its natural harmonious State; and the Strings of his Lyre, which he had thrown away in the bitternefs of Remorfe, were gathered up
by

Chi mi fpigne, chi mi tira?
Qual Vertigine m' aggira?
O che fogno! o che vaneggio!
Danzar gli arbori quì veggio:
E' pur notte ò mezzodì?
No, ò Sì? —

[x] So his Name plainly fignifies, מָרְוַח Marfecha, Marfyha, Marfyas, *Vociferatio præ dolo. e aut gaudio*; *Exultatio, Luctus*: *a Syrian Term, as* Marfyas *is a Syrian Story*.

[y] PAUSAN. Atticis.

[z] It is an Allufion to his Name, which by the fimilar Sound would be ftriking in the original Tale; מָרִישָׁה Merifha, Trabs: Syriac for a Beam.

by the MUSES, the mild Powers [a] of Invention
and Meafure, who that they might no more be
obnoxious to the like Difafter, added the **ΜΕΣΗΝ**
or *Middle-String* : a ftrange Remedy one would
think ; but an effectual. It is the *Chord* that
makes Mufic uniform and fedate; that prevents
the ecftatic Leaps, the irregular Bounds, the
Diffonance and Difproportion that fet the Paffions in an Uproar, and pour Madnefs and Mifery
into the human Soul. The Abufe of modern
Mufic, I mean the confining it to awake or
footh the moft effeminate Feelings, deprives us
almoft of any Conception of the ancient Extent
and Power of this heart-melting Art. But to a
delicate Ear, *that Sound can fcarce be formed*
which bears not a relation to fome Paffion and
carries not a Refemblance of fome inward Sentiment. The tender Structure therefore of the
Mind can be fooneft reached by its correfponding
Sounds, and delighted or diftracted according to
their Combinations.

This is one of thofe elegant Strokes in the
ancient Mythology, little underftood, it is true,
but fo very appofite, and expreffive, that under
fome Apprehenfion left you fhould imagine it
contrived or ftrained, I beg leave to conclude
with affuring you, that it is related from the
Original without Alteration.

I am, &c.

[a] Vos lene confilium datis, et dato
    Gaudetis almæ !   HORAT. Lib. III. Od. 4.

K 4   *LETTER*

LETTER THIRTEENTH.

I AM juſt returned from a ſhort Tour I had long promiſed to make in *D* * * * * *, and find myſelf doubly in your debt for a couple of Letters.——The kind one by Mr. *R* * * * * brought me welcome Accounts of your growing Health, and very certain Proofs of your Good-humour. It was put in my hand juſt as I was going to take horſe; and the Hurry of Company that flocks about one in the Country left me not an Hour's Leiſure to anſwer it. My Journey would have been every way agreable but for ſome Remains of the Ill-humour raiſed in that County by the late Election: Families in oppoſite Intereſts carry it ſo high that, like Rival-Courts, or if you pleaſe, Rival-Toaſts, a Viſiter in one is but coldly received in another.

I WILL frankly confeſs to you the Vanity (if it be ſo) of my Wiſh, that my Friends ſhould like me the better, the longer they know me ; and particularly that they ſhould ever find me incapable of ſo *mean* a Vice as Flattery, which at once proſtitutes Truth and Manhood. In confidence of this Indulgence, I will venture to tell you, that your laſt Epiſtle gave me exqui-ſite Pleaſure. The juſt Sentiments of Men and Manners, and that true Taſte of Life which with high Delight I perceive to be growing upon

you,

you, will be a conſtant Fund of Entertainment Lett. 13.
to us both. How elegant is every Period of
it! and how true! What an honeſt Indignation
it expreſſes againſt your *vulgar Gentlemen,*—
‘ unfeeling Souls! incapable of Friendſhip, or of
‘ any higher Taſte, than *Bagatelle* et *Bruta-*
‘ *lité !*—While at the ſame time, how amiable
the Contraſt! The eaſy, well-bred, generous
Man, enjoying the true Reliſh of Life himſelf,
and imparting like the Sun a Flow of Joy and
Contentment to all about him. Well, Mr. * * * *
I begin to believe it becomes no body ſo well as
a real Gentleman *to be wiſe:* his genteel Manners and polite Language give a Grace to Wiſdom itſelf. They ſmooth the rugged Paths of
Philoſophy, unbend the Brow of auſtere Virtue,
lend a new Luſtre to Learning, and poliſh every
Talent in Life. Your unaffected Reflections
upon the moſt important Subjects, and under
very various Aſpects of Things, gave riſe to theſe
Sentiments, and confirmed me in the Opinion,
that it is not in the retired Hermitage or lonely
Cell, we are to look for the moſt exalting Principles or the nobleſt Practice.——Worth, Truth,
Conſtancy, Contempt of Death, Improvement
of Life, with all the ſhining Train of genuine
Virtues. No——I find a Gentleman who lives
much in the World; who has ſeen, and like
Solomon, ſhared in its Joys, can really believe
that the Meaſure of a happy *Lot* is not the
Number of Days or accumulated Years; but

a

Lett.13. a Difcharge of the Duty of our Station, be it long or tranfient, with Dignity and Honour. To fuch a one we may fay with great Propriety,

> *Fælix, qui potuit rerum cognofcere Caufas,*
> *Atque metus omnes et inexorabile Fatum*
> *Subjecit Pedibus, ftrepitumque* ACHERONTIS
> *avari !*

AND now, my Friend, that the worft is paft, I feel a pleafing Serenity fucceed the Gloom that for fome Weeks hung over my Mind. I can now think of *T* * * * * without a Sigh; or rather perceive a filent Smile fteal upon me at the mention of the agreeable Name; and have a ftrong Inclination to imitate the Doctor of *Derry*, who told his Patient, he muft not relapfe for three Days, until he fhould return to attend him. You muft not have fuch another Fit until I can perfuade myfelf to be lefs anxious about you: for I would not undergo the painful Apprehenfions, nor live in the reftlefs Agitation that toffed and tortured me during your laft Sicknefs, for any Confideration. It is, I know, infeparable from a real Affection: *Quis enim fecurus amavit ?* But then a Gentleman of your thorow Good-nature, will certainly out of regard to one who loves you, take every Precaution in your power, not to give him Pain. I am fure this will have weight with you: add to it the Warning you have had from your Conftitution, not to trefpafs againft it, nor truft it too far to

its

its fuppofed Strength. Henceforth let no Perfuafion, no Company, no Temptation induce
you to rifque that without which Life and all
its Enjoyments are taftelefs and burthenfome;
and in this refpect,——*Fix your firm Refolve,*

Wifdom to wed and pay her long Arrear.

GREAT Reafon has a noble Author to fay,
that it is *Cowardice, meer Cowardice,* that de-
ters Men from Virtue and plunges them in Vice,
when one round hearty Refolve would rid them
of a Train of Miferies. 'Tis of a piece with
an uncommon Phrafe employed by a juft and
happy Writer, if there be one in Antiquity,
Sapere aude; DARE to be wife. No Habit or
Courfe of Life to which we have been accuftomed but requires *Courage* to throw it off:
And yet there is not a Friend or Companion
you have, at leaft none worth keeping, who
will like you the worfe for being truly temperate. Let him even be a little loofe himfelf, in
his inmoft Soul he muft approve of you, and
efteem you the more for being unlike him: For
well knows my Friend, there is no neceffity to
lay afide Pleafantry and Good-humour, in order
to affume Temperance and Integrity. We may
be as ferene, nay as gay as we pleafe; and have
much better Reafon to be fo, when once we
have come to contemn *Vice,* and all the flavifh
Crew of Fears, Remorfes, endlefs Purfuits
and infatiate Cravings that attend her. It is
true,

Lett.13.true, the utterly Abandoned, the refolutely Wicked will look upon you as a Man of *another* Party, and turn your Conduct into Ridicule if they can. But would you wifh for *their* Approbation?—for *their* Applaufe—whofe Friendfhips are Leagues in Wickednefs, only cemented by fimilar Lewdnefs? To pity the Perfons of the Vicious, and affift them even in the Ills which their Follies have brought upon them is one of the firft Leffons of Virtue and Dictates of Humanity. Are we therefore to love, efteem, or keep them company? Are we to behave to them as we would to Men exempt from their Faults and adorned with the oppofite Virtues? Such a one is a fad worthlefs Fellow, without Morals or Conduct: you can truft him with nothing.——' But, faid a noble Perfon of your
' Acquaintance, he is a fhrewd witty Dog, and
' very entertaining; I'll fend and have him here
' while I ftay in the Country. Mr. *B* * * * *
' my Neighbour is a knowing accomplifhed
' Gentleman; but he is devilifhly fober, and
' looks fo ftay'd and fpeaks fo accurate that
' I cannot bear him. Here *John!* Take a
' Horfe, and ride quickly over to *F*......*m*,
' and tell *Will Waggifh* that I expect him here
' to fpend the Week with me; and defire
' the Servants, if Mr. *B* * * * fhould call
' To-day or To-morrow, to tell him that I
' a'nt at home.——I'm gone a vifiting, d'ye
' hear? and don't know when I return.'......

INATTEN-

INATTENTIVE People, efpecially the mif-called Men of Pleafure (the meereft Drudges of the human Race) by living fome time in this way, come at laft to think every Thing decent and lawful that fuits their Inclinations : While they are in a Career of Diverfions, they really look upon Honour, Integrity, and Virtue as empty infignificant Sounds.

Virtutem Verba putant, ut Lucum Ligna—

So indeed they are to thofe who have no *Feeling* of the Things; fuch Perfons receive much the fame Benefit from all that can be faid in Commendation of Worth and Wifdom, as the late ferene Dauphin of *France* did from all the elaborate Editions of the Claffics publifhed for his Ufe. To them I would only recommend to go more *thorowly* to work, and if the Joys they purfue be genuine, to devote themfelves wholly to them. They are but puny ftarveling Rakes in comparifon of fome of their Predeceffors. I remember to have read of a celebrated Debauchee among the Ancients, the Bufinefs of whofe Day it was, *to get drunk at Night*. This wife and ingenious Perfon (for fo to be fure he thought himfelf) prepared for the Evening Campaign with great Addrefs and Affiduity. He flept long, eat delicately, rubbed, bathed, aired and walked, juft as much as would beft fit him for the dear Fatigue of *being drunk*. When that grand Point was attained, like a

Man

Lett.13. Man of Spirit, who had acted his Part with Dignity, and fully reached the Purpose of Life, he ordered his Servants every Evening to lay him on a magnificent Couch, and carry him in pro-cession with decent Funeral-Pomp from his Salon thro' a Suite of Rooms to his Bedchamber, calling out triumphantly all the way, ΒΕΒΙΩΚΕ ---ΒΕΒΙΩΚΕ, *He hath lived, he hath lived*; the Form of Funeral Service for the *Dead*.

SERIOUSLY, my Friend, Intemperance, or Vice of any Species is but a sickly inconsistent Thing; and we are obliged to make great Allowances to be able to bear with it. You hate the whole, and you both hate and contemn the half-Knave: a Man who falsifies his Word, who eludes his Promises, shuffles in his Answers, or swerves in his Dealings, draws your Aversion; and most justly. But why hate by halves?——why censure one Vice severely and connive at another? Be consistent in your Judgement and Liking: Love not the private easy Companion in the public mercenary Traitor; nor approve the pretended Patriot, be he ever so flaming, in the private immoral Profligate *. I do not say that what is good in a vicious Character is not to be approved; nor deny but that the same Character may in different respects be

virtuous

---

* It was an Ordinance in the admirable Constitution of *Sparta*, when any Person notoriously vicious made a wholesome Proposal to the Public, that some Man of known Probity should mount the Rostrum, and repeat the same Proposal, that it might pass into a Decree and be enacted in his Name.

virtuous and vicious; much lefs do I embrace Lett. 13.
the Stoical Paradox, that all Vices are equally
pernicious and criminal: But I lay it down as
a facred Maxim, That every Man is wretched
in proportion to his Vices; and affirm the nobleft
Ornament of a young generous Mind, and the
fureft Source of Pleafure, Profit and Reputation,
in Life, to be an unreferved Acceptance of
VIRTUE. Take the lovely Gueft but once
into your Bofom, refolve ftrictly and fteadily to
follow her Dictates, fhe will diffufe a Joy and Serenity thro' your Soul, a Confidence and Courage thro' your Speech and Conduct, fuch as no
corrupt Heart ever felt, or guilty Hand put in
execution. This refpects the important Parts of
Life; as to the *pleafant*, they follow their
Betters. The fweeteft Ingredient in Mirth is
Innocence; it heightens and refines the Humour, and doubles the Relifh of every Enjoyment. I have feen many bad Men brutally
merry; but never one of them quite open, eafy,
and unchecked in his Mirth. That abfolute
Serenity, that fupreme Eafe is the fole Gift of
VIRTUE. To her Chofen alone, fhe gives to
tafte Gayety and Pleafure *unmixed*; to drink
of the pure Stream that flows fpontaneous
from confcious Worth, and Beneficence to
Men: To all others it is dafhed and imbittered
in proportion to the Crookednefs of their Minds,
Inhumanity of their Tempers, and Intemperance of their Lives.

3

SHALL

Lett.13. SHALL I wrong you in suppofing you apprehenfive of fuch a ftrict Refolution, as if it
would lead you into thorny Paths, or confine you to a narrow Track, full of Scruples
and Peevifhnefs ? Truft me, it will not.
On the contrary, *Wifdom's Ways are Ways
of Pleafantnefs, and all her Paths are Peace.*
The peculiar Felicity of fuch a Temper of
Mind, owing beyond controverfy to our divine original Frame, is the *Simplicity* of its
Directory. You need no intricate Syftems,
nor abftrufe ambiguous Rules to lead you the
Road of Happinefs: *One* plain Principle will
prove an unerring Guide in this flow'ry Path,
for ever ftrew'd with frefh Contentment and
unrepented Pleafure. Would you be exempt
from Uneafinefs ; *Do no one thing you know,
or but fufpect to be wrong.* Would you enjoy
the pureft Pleafure ; *Do every thing in your
power you are convinced is right*[b]. A little
Attention to the *inward Monitor* we lamely
call Confcience, will difcover him to be your
beft Friend, faithful and true ; fond and forward to do good, while he muft be dragged
reluctant even to doubtful Evil : for to approve of it open and undifguifed, neither the
Songs of the Sirens could ever allure, nor the
Tortures of Tyrants ever compel him. No
fooner does the Species of any Conduct, or Idea
of

[b] ——πάντων δὲ μάλιϛ' αἰχύνεο σαυτόν.

Χρυσ. ΕΠΗ.

of any one Action strike upon the Understand-Lett.13.
ing, than it is immediately remitted to this in-
corrupt Judge, who transmits it to the *Will*
brightened with his Approbation or blackened
with his Dislike; and if the inward Oeconomy
be found, it is put in execution as good, or rejected as base, according to the Mark of his Sovereign Controul. Deceived he may be in particular Instances, when Falsehood is presented
to him in the Garb of Truth; but bribed or
biassed he never can, from the general Rectitude of his Intention, singly to promote the
Welfare of Men, by assuring them, nay by
making them *feel* that their Happiness depends
upon their acquitting themselves fully and fairly
of the Duties of Humanity. How often have
you heard it said of a private Gentleman, *He
wou'd not do an ill thing for the World?* Glorious Character! and I hope more frequent than
is commonly believed *——a Character to be
courted, or to say it better *deserved* by every
Man who wishes to live happily; and to taste
genuine Pleasure.

Cou'd my Friend now take one other Step
with me? I know he *can* and fain wou'd I
assure

* Lasciando i Precetti di tanti savi Filosofi, diremo in poche
Parole, bastar ch' uno sia, come si dice, *Huomo da bene*; che in
questo si comprende la Prudenza, Bontà, Fortezza e Temperanza
d'animo, e tutte le altre condizioni che ad honorato Nome con-
vengono: ed Io stimo quel solo esser vero Filosofo morale, *che
vuol esser buono*; ed à ciò gli bisognano pochi altri Precetti che tal
Volontà. Cortegiano del C. B. Castiglione.

* L

Lett.13. aſſure myſelf *He will.* If the Happineſs of our Lives depend upon our Obedience to this *Home-Cenſor* lodged in every Man's Breaſt, it muſt needs increaſe in proportion to our Attention to his Dictates, and diminiſh according to our Negligence. What a Thought is there ? what a Fund of uncloying Pleaſure pointed out to a noble Youth in the Bloom of Life, as yet untainted with Vice and fond of real Fame ? To live without Remorſe, in bliſsful Ignorance of *inward Pangs,* we muſt do no one thing we but ſuſpect to be wrong ; to be truly happy, we muſt do whatever we believe to be right : But wou'd you exalt and refine this Happineſs, you muſt be *at pains* to examine what is right, and *at pains* to put it in Execution d. Startle not at the word ; for in exact proportion to your Pains will be your Pleaſure. In the ordinary Occurrences of Life, ſuch a Conduct will procure you Peace and Plenty at home, and Reſpect and Confidence abroad; but in public Stations it leads to the higheſt pitch of human Felicity, and puts the Man who honeſtly aims at it in the direct Road to Heroiſm and Immortality.

Look around you, my Friend, and obſerve, whether the happieſt (I do not ſay the richeſt) be not at the ſame time the beſt and wiſeſt of your Acquaintance ? while you can ſcarce meet

a

---

d Τᾶτο ἐςὶ τὸ ἅιτιον τοῖς ἀνθρώποις πάντων τῶν κακῶν, τὸ τὰς προλήψεις τὰς κοινὰς μὴ δύναϑαι ἐφαρμόζειν ταῖς ἐπὶ μέρυς. Ἀῤῥιαν. εἰς ΕΠΙΚΤ. Βιβ. γ. §. κϑ.

a Wretch who has not been made fo by Vice or
Folly; it is finely faid by our old Englifh Satirift,

𝕸𝖚𝖈𝖍 𝖜𝖔 𝖜𝖔𝖗𝖙𝖍 𝖙𝖍𝖊 𝕸𝖆𝖓 𝖙𝖍𝖆𝖙 𝖒𝖎𝖘𝖗𝖚𝖑𝖊𝖙𝖍 𝖍𝖎𝖘 𝕴𝖓𝖜𝖎𝖙𝖙𝖊 [e],

A *Mifrule*, that affects the Offender himfelf
in the firft Place, and but confequentially thofe
who are connected with him. Such a Perfon,
we fay, is loft to all *Senfe* of Honour or Shame.
Think a little what may be the Meaning of
that Expreffion. Is it not, that by a Courfe of
Immorality he has vitiated his natural Perceptions of Right and Wrong, and dulled his Tafte
of Beauty and Virtue? This we commonly call,
in a ftrong Metaphor, *a feared* Confcience, becaufe it is callous and unfeeling; and then, the
inward Monitor lofes a great Part of his Power;
his Voice becomes faint, and his Dictates feeble;
tho' it rarely happens that he is fo intirely perverted but that he roufes at Intervals, and fpeaks
in a Tone that makes his Tyrant tremble. But
he is much oftner *cheated,* than *born down*; as
when our moral Rectitude is mifguided, a falfe
Species of *Good* paffed upon us inftead of the
true, and the deluded Fancy taught to fubfti-
tute fome perverfe partial End in which to place
its Happinefs, inftead of the free Exercife of its
native Faculties *in doing good.* This is done by
the Excefs fometimes of one Paffion, and fome-

L 2 times

---

[e] VISION of *Pierce Plowman.*

Lett.13. times of another: Love, Ambition, Envy and Avarice take their turns in the fucceeding Stages of Life, and prefent us with their Favourites in impofing Lights; which——no fooner vanifh, than the Objects appear in their genuine Colours, and this upright Cenfor revokes his Approbation.

But the grand Sorcerefs, *fly Superftition*, approaches with an Air of Sanctity, and hoodwinks unhappy Men, not for any one Period as the other Paffions, but alas! for Life. *Enfnared and hampered by the Soul*, as our comic Poet fays, they look at things only thro' the magic Glafs which the Enchantrefs holds up to them, and ftart amazed when prefented to them undifguifed. Thro' it they fee *Nature reverfed*, the World turned upfide down, and curfe the Creation to oblige its Author.

You, my Friend, are in little hazard of this gloomy Goblin: You know that Virtue, when genuine and fincere, gives a Dignity to human Nature; and can believe the nobleft Genius of Antiquity when he fcruples not to affirm That the Breaft of a Man, adorned with Juftice, Humanity, and Regard to the Laws, is the moft auguft Temple that can be reared to God. It is from *Syrens* of fofter Afpect and fweeter Voice, you have more to fear, tho' you have lately had a fufficient Difcovery of their hidden Deformities. You have had a View of their nether Parts, and feen that the fair Face and alluring Song only

serve

ſerve to conceal the devouring Monſter. Wou'd
you effectually avoid them ?——Betake yourſelf to
Knowledge, Virtue, and the Duties of a MAN :
' For when the all-wiſe Creator had formed
' the two Contraries, *Pleaſure* and *Pain*, he
' found it impoſſible to reconcile the implacable
' Enmity ſubſiſting between their oppoſite Na-
' tures :——but as there was likewiſe a Necef-
' ſity that they ſhould at times occupy one and
' the ſame Subject, he blended their Extremities,
' and joined them ſo inſeparably, that the one is
' never found in any great degree without the
' other.   One ſole Species of Joy eſcaped the
' fatal Tye, to wit the *Pleaſures of the Under-*
' *ſtanding* or contemplative Delight.   She alone
' ſtretched herſelf beyond the Extremity of
' Pain, and leaving all her Siſter Pleaſures to
' wander with their grievous Aſſociate on the
' Sides of Mount *Olympus,* (where the clear
' Sky is oft o'ercaſt) ſhe mounted to the Top,
' where ſhe baſks ſerene in ambient Light,
' ever-ſtreaming in perpetual Day.'

I am, &c.

L 3   *LETTER*

LETTER FOURTEENTH.

I SINCERELY congratulate your Return to Study and Retirement in fo eafy Circum-ftances and delicious a Situation: tho' I cou'd not chufe but fmile, at the Change of your Sen-timents along with your Practice. You not only read the old Stories of the Heathen Gods with pleafure, but are become a Judge of their Propriety; and I am taken to tafk for departing from the Standard of ancient Orthodoxy, the Writings of Homer, in making PAN to fpring immediately from *Chaos,* while, according to the infpired Poet, he was the Son of *Mercury* and Grand-fon of *Jove.*

THE Charge, I muft acknowledge, is juft: But with all due Submiffion to the Poet's Pre-tenfions to Infpiration I can not admit his Wri-tings to be the fole Standard, or even the pureft Source of primitive Mythology. The ancient Bards who firft went down to Egypt from Greece, have, in my opinion, a preferable Claim; and to the Fragments of their Compofitions, and efpecially to the *Orphic Hymns,* I wou'd at any time appeal from Homer in a Point of *myftical* Theology.

From HOMER! fayyou, the Prince of the Poets——the Father of Science——the Inter-preter of the Gods—and Inftructor of Men!——

Be

Be not furprized; I confefs my Opinion is uncommon, and muft appear highly heretical to a
young Convert, zealous for the authentic Canon,
the Bafis of his mythical Creed. But Tradition
and Truth, you'll allow, are not always of a
Side; elfe you and I, like our docile Anceftors,
had been paying Peter's Pence, procuring Maffes
to efcape Purgatory or making Pilgrimages to
St. Thomas a Becket: Nor would I have ventured on fo ticklifh an Affertion, had I not believed it capable of the cleareft Evidence. And
firft, the Practice of the ancient Devotion in the
heathen Church was not always favourable to
our admired Poet. An accurate Writer, well
verfed in the old Divinity; but moderate, like a
low-church Man, gives a formal decifive Teftimony upon this Point. It is Paufanias I mean,
in whom we fee a lively Inftance of a Man of
very good Senfe and great Learning being a true
Believer in the Religion of his Country. ' The
' Thracian Orpheus, fays he, was reprefented
' on Mount Helicon with ΤΕΛΕΤΗ, (*Initia-*
' *tion* or *Religion*) by his Side, and the wild
' Beafts of the Woods, fome in marble, fome
' in Bronze, ftanding around him. His *Hymns**

L 4

' are

---

* The Hymns which we now have under the Name of Orpheus are the very fame which were revered by the ancient
Greeks and ufed in their folemn Worfhip. Here is a convincing
Proof of that important Point. In the firft Speech of Demofthe-
nes againft Ariftogiton in a Caufe where Precedent was not favourable, ' Let us, fays the Orator, overlooking all Cuftom or Wont,
' judge righteous Judgment: let us reverence ΕΥΝΟΜΙΑ that
' loves Equity and preferves States; and fevere inexorable ΔΙΚΗ
' (RIGHT)

Lett.14.' are known by thofe who have ftudied the
'   ' Poets to be both fhort, and few in Number.
'   The *Lycomides*, an Athenian Family dedi-
'   cated to facred Mufic, have them all by heart,
'   and fing them at their folemn Myfteries.
'   They are but of the fecond Clafs for Elegance,
'   being far out-done by Homer's in that refpect.
'   But our R E L I G I O N has adopted the *Hymns of*
'   *Orpheus*, and has not done the fame Honour
'   to the Hymns of Homer *.'   For what reafon, pray, but that the former contained a
founder Doctrine and more orthodox Divinity
than could be compenfated by Flights of Fancy
or Smoothnefs of Verfe?   'Tis not therefore
without ground that I beg your Poet's pardon,
and prefer the Teftimony of a more ancient
                                             Bard,

'   (RIGHT) whom Orpheus, our Inftructor in the moft holy
'   Rites, places by the Throne of Jove, infpecting the Affairs of
'   Men (ᵃ).   Let each of us imagine her piercing Eye is now upon
'   us, and think and vote fo as not to difhonour *Her* from whom
'   every Judge has his Name.'
      Compare this with Orpheus' Hymn to ΔΙΚΗ or RIGHT.
      Fair Juftice' far-reflecting Eye I fing ;
      Who plac'd befide the Throne of Heaven's King,
         Infpects the Life of all the Tribes of Men (ᵇ).
And you cannot doubt but that the Hymn referred to by De-
mofthenes, is the fame you have in your Hand.

   (ᵃ) —τὴν ἀπαράιτελον κͻ σεμνὴν ΔΙΚΗΝ, ἣν ὁ τὰς ἀγι-
ωτάτας ἡμῖν τελετὰς καͺαδείξας ΟΡΦΕΥΣ παρὰ τὸν τῦ
Δι☉ Θρόνου φησὶ καθημείνην, πάντα τὰ τῶν ἀνθρώπων
ἐφορᾶν.   ΔΗΜΟΣΘ. κατ. Ἀριςογ. α.

   (ᵇ) Ὄμμα ΔΙΚΗΣ μέλπω, παλιδερκέος ἀγλαόμορφυ
    Ἥ κͻ Ζηιὸς ἄνακͺ☉ ἐπὶ θρόνου ἱερὸν ἵζει
    Οὐρανόθεν καθορῶσα βίον θνητῶν πυλυφύλων.
                          ΟΡΦΕΩΣ ῾ΥΜΝ. εἰς ΔΙΚΗΝ.
   ⁕ BŒOTIC.

Bard, PRONAPIDES, who paffed for his Mafter, Lett. 14. and who in his Poem infcribed the FIRST WORLD, or *primary State of the Univerfe*, plainly fays, That PAN, with his three Sifters the *Fates* were born at *one* Birth, not of *Mercury*, but of DEMOGORGON, the thinking active Genius that fet the mighty Mafs on work, and produced every thing out of primigenial *Chaos*.

THE other venerable Author of their religious Syftem, the old Man of *Afcra*, who fo pioufly fung the Births and Kindred of the Gods, is accufed by a knowing Divine in their way, of having corrupted the ancient Theology; and of having in particular perverted the Doctrine of *Saturn* the primeval God, by adding fabulous Circumftances of his own to the authentic Doctrine of his Anceftors. And in effect, the more we confider the Fragments of the very early Poets, the more we fhall be convinced of the Corruption of the original inftructive Mythology into a grofs Legend of imaginary Perfons, without *Morals* or *Meaning*. The ancient Hymns, fung in the Temples, were the moft genuine Pieces of Theology. I fay the *ancient*; for the modern were foon modelled according to the depraved Belief of the Country; as the unlucky Poet who drew a Sarcafm upon himfelf, by addreffing *Diana* with the Epithets of λυσσάδα! φοιβάδα! μαινάδα [a]! which by the by, if taken *cum grano falis* (as a *Scots* Divine
faid

M_{ad}! Lunatic! Raging-Mad!

Lett.14. ſaid in explaining a Myſtery) is no ill Deſcription of her Qualities or Effects [b]. The Ridicule
that lies againſt it flows only from that common
but deluſive Rule *of judging of divine things by
a human Standard:* whereas it is principally
here that Mr. *Bays*'s Maxim takes place, *When
you tye up Spirits and People in the Clouds to
ſpeak plain, you ſpoil all.* Some ſuch thing as
this, I take your Author to have meant, when
we are told, 'That the monſtrous Stories con-
'cerning the Birth and Actions of the Gods,
'were certainly underſtood by the *firſt Grecian
'Sages,* who brought them from Egypt ; but
'that afterwards, falling into the Hands of
'Men of warm Fancies, who thought they
'might invent as well as their Maſters, there
'were many traditional Stories tacked to the
'former, ſometimes untowardly enough, and
'ſometimes ſo as to make a tolerable Piece of
'the *literal* Relation, but confounding when
'applied to the *Allegory* [c].' And in another
place, diſtinguiſhing Mythology into *natural*
and *artificial,* he points at the ſame Source of
Corruption ; 'That while a Poet is intent upon
'his Compoſure, the *firſt* is apt to run away
'with the Story, and confound its own Off-
'ſpring,

[b] In the Battle of the Gods, ILIAD XXI, *Diana* is reproach'd
by *Juno* with being no Match for a Goddeſs, *Since* JOVE *had
only appointed her to be the Scourge of* WOMEN, *with Power to
kill them at her pleaſure.*

———— 'επεί σε λέοντα γυναιξὶν,
Ζεὺς θῆκε, ϰ᷄ ἔδωϰε ϰαταϰτάμεν ἤν ϰ᷄ ἐθέλησθα. Ἰλιαδ. Φ.

[c] ENQUIRY pag. 50. 2d. Edit.

' fpring, the *fyftematic* Mythology: whence Lett. 14.
' fpring *clafhing Circumftances, Inconfiftency in*
' *Facts*, and impenetrable Obfcurity in the
' Meaning of the Allegory [d].'

I confefs I cannot help thinking, that inftead of being improved, Mythology was fpoilt when intermixed with *Hiftory* and *human Perfons*: A Mixture that threw it off its Hinge; and from explaining Nature and inftructing Men, made it a Rhapfody of inexplicable Wonders. With graceful Propriety it may be *applied* to human Tranfactions, when the Subject of the Narration will bear the *Ambages et Deorum Minifteria* [*]; but it can never admit particular *Perfons*, as Parts of its original Compofition. Whenever *they* are introduced, the Story becomes a meer *unmeaning* Fable, and no Mythology. Nay the fewer of its own genuine Phantoms that are employ'd, the better; and the fimpler the Tale, the more elegant the Application. The learned Antiquary lately mentioned, *Paufanias*, in his Defcription of the Territory of E L I S lets us know there was an Altar erected there to an extraordinary Deity, Κ Α Ι Ρ Ο Σ ; (We wou'd call him *Opportunity*) and that there was an ancient Hymn fung at his Sacrifices, which celebrated the God *as the very youngeft of all Saturn's Children*: A plain Panegyric! and yet pregnant with

[d] Ibid. page 213.
[*] Poetical Machinery, and Interpofition of the Gods.

Lett.14. with inftructive Allegory. It contains all the Doctrine, which the later Greeks and Romans operofely painted in their *Occafio,* ftanding on a Globe, with Wings at her Feet, bald behind, and her Fore-top playing in the Wind ; and all the Moderns have moralized concerning the Shortnefs of Life, the Improvement of Time and happy Conjunctures.

In the fame manner, VENUS is beautifully faid both by the grave [e] and gay [f] among the Ancients to have in her Retinue, the ardent amorous Boy, the Sifter Graces in loofe Attire, *Aglaïa, Thalia* and *Euphrofyne* [g]; to be attended by Youth, a wayward Thing without her ; and her whole Train to be conducted by *Mercury* the God of Eloquence, and *Pitho* the Goddefs of Perfuafion ; and fo far is extremely intelligible: But when fhe is made to be in love with *Adonis,* (if a human Creature be meant, as I believe is not) or married to *Anchifes,* and made the Mother of a Mortal, fhe is quite out

[e] Ευχόμεν@ τῇ ΑΦΡΟΔΙΤΗ τὰς Μύσας παρεῖναι κ, συνεργεῖν· — κ, γὰρ οἱ παλαιοὶ τῇ Αφροδίτη τὸν ʽΕΡΜΗΝ συνκαθίδρυσαν, ὡς τῆς περὶ τὸν γάμον ἡδονῆς μάλιϛα λόγ𝛖 δεομένης· τὴν τε ΠΕΙΘΩ κ, τὰς ΧΑΡΙΤΑΣ, ἵνα πείθοντες διαπράτlωνται ἀλλήλων ἃ βούλονται, μὴ μαχόμενοι μηδὲ Φιλονεικοῦντlες. ΠΛΟΥΤΑΡΧ .Γαμ. Παραγ.

[f] Fervidus tecum Puer, et folutis
Gratiæ zonis, properentque Nymphæ ;
Et parum comis fine te, Juventus,
Mercuriufque.
Horat. Carm. Lib. I. Ode 30.

[g] To be *bright, blooming* and *gay.*

out of my Sight——: if it be not a pretty way
of saying the Hero was a Baſtard; and that
Anchiſes, while looking after his Cattle on
Mount *Ida* had met with a ſtraying Nymph,
by whom he had the pious Founder of the
Roman State.

' The moſt ancient Theology, ſays *Plutarch,*
' both of the Greeks and Barbarians, was
' natural Philoſophy involved in Fables, that
' figuratively and myſtically unveiled the
' Truth to the Learned,—as appears from the
' Poems of *Orpheus,* the Egyptian Rites, and
' Phrygian Traditions ᵍ.' A Maxim that if
kept in mind will at once enable you to diſtinguiſh
the pure primitive Doctrine from later Inventions,
and ſhew you the reaſon why I am ſo fond of
the Fragments of the Sages, as to prefer them
to the moſt laboured Productions of their Succeſſors: If you will keep my Secret, I will
own to you that I cou'd have liſtened to old
Pampho ſinging of mighty Jove, (or the vital
vegetative Power that fructifies the Earth) ' *as
wrapt in Dung, of Horſes and of Mules,*'
with as much pleaſure as to *Homer,* who is ſaid
by your Author or ſomebody he quotes, to
have refined upon this groſs Idea, and more
elegantly and unmeaningly to have made his
Jupiter ' *brandiſh the Thunders and compel the*
' *Clouds.*'

Of

ᵍ Περὶ τῶν ἐν Πλαταιαῖς ΔΑΙΔΑ´ΛΩΝ.

Παρὰ Ευσεβ.

Lett. 14. Of the twelve great Gods, the greateſt, according to the *Egyptians*, was PAN or the *Univerſe*, to whom the higheſt Honours were paid. Next to him ſtood *Latona* or Night : Vulcan was next in Dignity ; and then Iſis and Oſiris, with Orus, or *Light*, their Son. That is, in weſtern Language, That the Univerſe, comprehending Nature and all her Powers, lay o'erwhelmed in Darkneſs, until the igneous vivifying Spirit broke looſe, and diſpelled the Shade that for eternal Ages had been brooding over it: That then the Sun and the Moon ſhone forth, Parents of Light, preſiding over the Generation of Animals, the Vegetation of Plants, and the Government of the Whole. Inſtead of this, PAN with the later Poets is the Son of Mercury and Penelope,—*Vulcan* of Jupiter and Juno ; and *Latona* a fine-haired Lady who brought forth Apollo and Diana in *Delos* or the *Ortygian Iſle !* 'Twas not without reaſon that *Alexander* the Rhetorician accuſed *Heſiod* of having play'd the Plagiary and ' both ' plundered and ſpoilt *Orpheus*'s Theogony[h].'

BUT happy, my Friend ! is the Doctrine that depends upon *Allegory* ; and thrice happy if to that Allegory it join a ductile ſort of Myſtery that ſhields it from Abſurdities, and affords proper Solutions to its docile Profeſſors ! They need not be alarmed at ſeeming Contradictions: The

[h] τὴν Ὀρφέως ὑποκλέψας — κỳ παραφθείρας θεογονίαν. παρὰ Τζέτζω.

The Regions of Fable are wide and fertile: Lett. 14
They refemble *Rabelais*'s Iron-work Ifland, where
Swords grew from the Trees, and Scabbards
fprung like Mufhrooms from the Earth; but
fo exactly under them, that every ripe Sword
fell precifely into its own Scabbard without
miffing it an hair-breadth. PAN, if he cannot
in one Senfe, he may ftill in another be the
Son of *Mercury*, if as Cicero fays, the firft God
who bore that Name was not the Inventor of
Speech or Patron of Merchants; but the Off-
fpring of *Uranus* and *Phanes*, or which is the
felf-fame thing of *Celus* and *Dië*. The Reprefentations of old Hermes [i], liker the God of
Lampfacus than the chafte Power of Eloquence,
belong to this ancient Defcent; according to
which the Steps of Creation will be in this
Succeffion. From hoary *Chaos* fprang *Ether*
and *Light*, and from them arofe *Order* and the
Power of Generation. This *Power was put
in action by the fight of Proferpine*, and produced PAN or the Univerfe. Nor does *Mercury's*
common Pedigree differ widely from this
Genealogy, while he is called the Son of *Jupiter*
and *Maia* [k]; — which is as much as to fay,
' That the Order and Contrivance appearing in
' every part of this vaft Frame, and the Power
' of continuing it by Succeffive Generation is
' the

---

[i] ὀρθὰ ἔχων τὰ αἰδοῖα.   HΡOΔOT. Eυτερπ.
[k] From μάω cupio, perquiro: It came afterwards to
fignify a *Midwife*.

Lett.14.' the Child of *Ether* the Principle of Life and
' of *Maia*, Search or Defire.'

Thus you fee what kind of Perfons made up
the Syftem of the pure primitive Mythology,
and that as foon as *Hiftory* and *Hiftorical
Perfons* began to mix with it, fo foon it began
to be corrupted. Indeed, when any Adventure
happening to a human Perfon, or any fingular
Quality of that Perfon is *mythologically* narrated,
it is then properly *applied*, and not *corrupted:*
when, for example, the Fortunes of Ulyffes
are always governed by Minerva; or his Father-
in-Law's Genius for Stratagem, Thieving and
Equivocation is afcribed to Mercury, who had
adorned his Favourite *Autolycus* with his own
Talents; in all fuch cafes the Art is happily
enough employ'd, tho' ftill on inferior Subjects.
How foon it came to be debafed is hard to
afcertain. I believe as foon as it was mifunderftood; and that muft have been very early.
The grand and general Source of Confufion in
ancient Theology is the fame that perverts a
much purer at this Day, the *Stupidity* and
Superftition of the blind and credulous Vulgar,
always apt to take Reprefentations for Things,
as we fee daily happen in Popifh Countries. It
had arrived at fuch a pitch before the Age even
of *Heraclitus*, that fpeaking of their ordinary
Worfhip, he exclaims againft the grofs Abufes
introduced in it. ' The common People, fays
' he, pray to thefe fame Statues juft as if one
' was

' was to talk to the Walls of a Houfe, Lett. 14.
' knowing nothing about the *Gods* or *Heroes*,
' who or what they are, to whom they are
' praying [1].' And in whatever City or State
the common People had the fupreme Power, as
in many of the *Grecian* popular Governments,
it was fufpicious not to be of their Opinion, and
unfafe to endeavour to rectify it.

THE fecond Source of Corruption was more
particular, and flow'd from the Origin of their
Religion, and the Method in which it was
planted among them. The ignorant Tribes of
the rude *Greeks* received the firft Notices of
Gods, and crude Ideas of their Worfhip, from
politer People indeed, but whofe Language they
did not perfectly underftand, and confequently
could not conceive with great Exactnefs what
their civilized Mafters thought concerning their
feveral Deities and different Modes of Devotion. Thus the *Affyrians* and *Phenicians* were
taught by the *Egyptians*, the *Greeks* by the
Egyptians and *Phenicians* in the firft inftance,
and at fecond hand by *Thracians* and *Pelafgi*,
and taught the *Romans* in their turn. No
wonder then there fhould be Miftakes in Matters fo myfterious, and made more fo by the
abftrufe *fymbolical* manner of treating them.

M   Even

---

[1] Καὶ τοῖς Ἀγάλμασι τελέοισι εὔχονται, ὁποῖον ἄ τις
τοῖσι δομοίσι λεσχηνεύοιτο, ὅ τι γινώσκων θεὸς ἐδ᾽ ἥρωας
ὅτινες εἰσί.

ΗΡΑΚΛΕΙΤ. ϖαρ᾽ Ὀριγεν. κατὰ Κελσ.

Lett.14. Even in the after-intercourse of these Nations, when Commerce or Conquest had made them mutually acquainted, and their respective Religions were established in their several Countries, upon finding any Ensign or Attribute belonging to their domestic Deity ascribed to a foreign God, they immediately concluded it to be one and the same *Numen:* Or if they found a Rite of Worship, or solemn Sacrifice peculiar to their God at home, offered to another abroad, they never scrupled to identify the Divinity; as the ingenious *Plutarch* pleasantly imagined the *Jews* to have worshipped *Bacchus*, from their using the Figure of a *Vine*, and the Name of *Levi*, (Λεϋϊ) which he mistook for one of the *Bacchanal* Cries *.

THE first Poets were at the same time Philosophers: The latter was their proper Character, to which they made the other subservient, and used it as a Tool to convey their Instructions to Men. The second Race were mere Poets, who meant rather to amuse than instruct, and therefore selected the most striking Tales for the Entertainment of their Audience, and dwelt upon the most wondrous Circumstances of these Tales, with little regard to the Truth of the original Doctrine, or Justness of the Application. Corruption ensued in endless Deviations from the Intention of the first Sages, and by degrees, a total Oblivion of the Meaning of the Allegory. This the grand Critic seems to have had in view,

* TABLE-TALK, Book IV.

view, while he complains of the *Grecian* Poets,
as having only meant to gain Belief to themfelves, and imprefs on their Audience an Opinion of the Truth of their Doctrines ;— carelefs what became of Pofterity, and therefore at
no pains to give Reafons for their Affertions.
Upon the Queftion, 'If all Things be produced
' by the fame CAUSE, why fome are mortal
' and perifhing; and others, like the Heaven
' and heavenly Bodies, everlafting and perma-
' nent ? Thefe *Ancients,* fays he, having made
' the *Principles of Being* GODS, and all Things
' to have been produced by them, *Whatever,*
' faid they, *drank* Nectar *or tafted* Ambrofia
' *became immortal, and whatever tafted not this*
' *life-giving etherial Food became fubject to*
' *Death.* Now it is plain, that tho' they may
' have ufed Terms well known to themfelves
' in delivering the Doctrine of thefe *Caufes,* yet
' they are unintelligible to us : For if it was only
' to footh the Minds of their Hearers that they
' brought their *Nectar* and *Ambrofia* in play,
' then they are no real Caufes of Immortality
' and continued Exiftence: But if they give
' them as real Caufes as we underftand them
' How can any thing be immortal or eternal
' that ftands in need of Food to fupport it ? ▪
You have heard too much of the Rife of
Things, and Creation of the World, not to

M 2 conceive

▪ Μετὰ τὰ Φυσικ. Βιε. β. § δ.
See the Rife of the Fable in the Derivation of the Terms above.
Page 87. (b)

Lett.14. conceive what he means by the antient Poets
having *made* GODS *of the Principles of Being:*
But that thefe were their *only* Gods, is what
I will now prove to you from a more exalted
Strain of the fame Philofophy.   After a fublime
Defcription of *God* as the living, everlafting, beft
of Beings, and of the Motion of the Heavens,
and Difpofition of the Orbits of the Planets,
he infers the Heaven to be ONE, fince its eternal Mover is but *one:* ' But, continues he, there
' has been handed down to Pofterity from the
' firft Sages and Philofophers, a Doctrine left in
' the Form of a Fable, " That thefe Heavenly
" Bodies themfelves are Gods,——and that the
" Deity contains the whole Nature of things."
' As for the remaining Parts of our Theology,
' 'tis thought they were added for better per-
' fuading the Multitude, and for their Ufeful-
' nefs in promoting Obedience to the Laws, and
' the good of the People.   'Twas for this the
' Gods have been faid to be of human Shape,
' or to refemble fome certain Animals, with
' other Legends confequential thereupon, and
' conducive to the Purpofes above mentioned:
' From which ADDITIONS, if any one will
' feparate the original Principle, and take only
' this, *That the Ancients thought the primary*
' *Subftances of Things to be Gods,* he will both
' be induced to believe that they fpoke divinely
' upon the Subject; and according to the com-
' mon Fate (as every Science and Art is at firft
' in-

' invented and perfected as far as poffible, but
' afterwards corrupted and loft) that thefe O-
' pinions of the Ancients have in the fame
' manner, like fo many *broken Reliques*, reached
' our Times: And this is all we can fay concer-
' ning our religious national Doctrines, or thofe
' of their firft Inventers who publifhed them
' to Men ".'

Much more could he have faid, had he thought it proper to expatiate upon the Abufes introduced among the feveral Nations of *Greece :* But there is a peculiar Beauty in the Caution and Tendernefs with which he touches the public Religion of his Country. He fays enough to let Men of Senfe fee that he well underftood the Purity of its philofophical Origin, which he proceeds fo far as to call *divine,* and yet at one difcriminating Blow (foftned by a fort of Apology) he cuts off the whole Train of infignificant Deities and ridiculous Rites, which the Superftition of After-ages had entailed upon the primitive Theology.

His Mafter, the Honour of Antiquity, proceeds with yet greater Circumfpection : And becaufe the Regulation he has made of Religion in his Commonwealth, and the Opinion he delivers as the Reafon of it, are two ftrong Inftances how much the primitive Mythology was then corrupted, I will conclude this long Epiftle with a diftinct Account of both.

M 3

WITH

" Μετὰ τὰ Φυσικ. Βι. λ.

Lett.14.   WITH refpect to the firft, he enacts it as aLaw,
' That the current Traditions about the Gods
' fhou'd neither be talked of in private, nor
' ever mentioned in public : But fhou'd any
' one's Confcience be fo tender as to think he
' could not abftain from rehearfing them without
' Impiety, in that cafe it fhou'd be done; but
' only on certain folemn Days, and after offer-
' ing a great and expenfive Sacrifice.' The
Reafon he affigns for this Statute is, ' That the
' explaining and reconciling thefe Traditions is
' a Work of immenfe Labour and Difficulty,
' and unhappy is the Man who engages in it.'
From the Law it appears, that the Doctrines
originally taught concerning the Rife of the
Univerfe and Powers of its Parts were no longer
generally underftood; elfe they had never made
fuch impious Impreffions on Peoples Minds as to
oblige a humane Lawgiver to contrive a Method
by which (without abfolutely condemning or
abrogating the national received Faith) they
wou'd feldom or never come to their Ears:
That therefore the Vulgar believed the caftrating
of *Celus*, the dethroning of *Saturn*, the Re-
bellion againft *Jove*, his Wars, Adulteries and
Difafters *litterally*; took the Gods to be real
human-like Perfons, tho' of immortal Nature,
and were accordingly affected by their Example.
From the Reafon of the Law it is evident, that
the Traditions concerning the Gods were now
become inconfiftent, thro' the numberlefs Things
added

added to the fimple Doctrine juft mentioned by Lett. 14. *Ariſtotle* of the *primary Subſtances of Things being only Gods* ; infomuch that after infinite Labour it was no longer poffible to explain and adjuft them : Neither was it fafe for any Man to attempt it, if he did not fall in with the prevailing Opinions.   Mythology muft have been very corrupt, when it extorted from fo cautious a Writer, ' *That it ſcarcely deſerved a ſerious* ' *Conſideration* °.'   But hardly durft he have ventured fo far, had he been either an *Athenian* born, or had his great Pupil, and *Antipater* his Succeffor (with whom the Philoſopher was extremely gracious) lefs overaw'd that giddy State.

As for the *Roman* Mythology, their Poets carried it ftill a Step farther from the Original, and made it for the moſt part merely *legendary*; that is, compiled from the traditional Tales of the *Greeks*, without once confidering their Relation to the Subject.   Not but that they had a real Mythology of their own, rude indeed, and fimple like the Age in which it rofe, confifting moftly of rural Deities, Faunus and Silvanus, Pales and Pomona, Janus and Tellus, and fuch like : Their other Gods they had from *Aſia* and *Greece*, and their Rites principally from *Hetruria* : But their politer Poets write entirely in conformity with the modern *Grecian* Learning.

M 4   JUNO

° Ἀλλὰ περὶ μὲν τῶν μυθικῶς σοφιζομένων οὐκ ἄξιω μετὰ σπουδῆς σκοπεῖν.   Μετὰ τὰ. Φ. βιϛ. β.

Lett.14. JUNO in the Iliad of *Homer* is indeed a constant Friend to the *Greeks,* and a sworn
Enemy to the *Trojans;* but that cannot excuse
her belying her own Character, so far as to be
reconciled to a Mistress of her Spouse *Juturna,*
to save her Brother *Turnus's* Life. The good
Father *Bossu* does his best to account for this
Incongruity. With great Gravity, and Respect
for the Poet, he tells us that the Assembly of
Gods with which *Virgil* opens his tenth Book,
represents *the divine Nature divided into four
Persons,*— as it were into so many Attributes,
Jupiter, Juno, Venus and *Fate,* which he
says may be lawfully added to the other three.
That *Jupiter* is the Power of God, *Fate*
his Will, *Venus* his Mercy or Love to virtuous
Men, and *Juno* his Justice: That the Poet thus
condescends to accommodate himself to our rude
manner of conceiving celestial Matters, which
makes us imagine, thro' the Weakness of our Un-
derstandings, these Qualities to be incompatible
in the divine Nature. But it is pity the reverend Father should be obliged immediately to
metamorphose the Justice of God, and transform it into *Air,* as he does *Juno* in the very
next Page. There ' *Eolus* signifies the Exhala-
' tions and Vapours, and these Vapours rise into
' the *Air* represented by *Juno.*' Such Explications put me in mind of the *Argument,* as it
is commonly called, prefixed to the several
Cantos of the *Italian* epic Poets. *Dante* their
Leader

Leader muſt be allowed to have been originally an emblematical Writer, and his Work, tho' ſtrangely inſcribed a COMEDY, to be a true moral Fable : But his Succeſſors *Arioſto*, *Marino*, and even *Taſſo* himſelf, after indulging a luxuriant Fancy in all the Pomp of Deſcription, Wilds of Magic, and Mazes of Love, ſit gravely down and compoſe a Moral to each Book, which they call the ALLEGORY. Thoſe who can believe, and enter into it, receive double Pleaſure ; being at once delighted with the flow'ry Deſcriptions, and inſtructed by their ſuppoſed Meanings : For after all, in this Obſervation upon the learned *Boſſü*, I am very conſcious of having unwiſely for myſelf tranſgreſſed a Rule, *Never to ſcan mythological Matters too nicely.* Could I have believed him, and been fully perſuaded of the Truth of the Myſteries he ſaw in the Poet, it muſt have doubled my Admiration, and conſequently my Enjoyment.

Pol me occidiſtis Amici !

You know the reſt,——and that I truly am,

Yours, &c.

LETTER

LETTER FIFTEENTH.

I WILL make you no Compliments upon
the Ingenuity of your Objections, but tell
you bluntly, they were welcome to me upon
many accounts : They let me fee you were now
fully entered into the Subject, and I hope into
a Habit of Study and Way of Thinking you will
never repent: At the fame time, they made
me review fome things in different Lights, and
with different Connexions from what I had ever
done before.

You afk firft, whether the Meanings we
afcribe to ancient Fables, be not for the moft
part *Conjectures* of the Moderns, who admire
every thing that is ancient, merely becaufe it is
fo, and torture their Brains to find out Meanings and Myfteries which the Authors or their
Cotemporaries never thought of? Let me anfwer
you by another Queftion, *Can you now believe
it ?* Can you read a Fable of *Efop*, and imagine it means nothing? No more can you now
read one of the old Fictions, without looking
for the moral or natural Leffon latent in the
wondrous Tale. Take our great Lord *Bacon*'s
little Book *De Sapientia Veterum*, read it coolly,
and difbelieve if you can. But to anfwer more
directly ; I fay they are not mere modern Inventions, but what a very learned Writer [a]
wou'd

[a] Pere SIMON. Hift. Crit. du V. T.

wou'd fain perfuade us of Tradition, ' That by Lett. 15.
' its means *a Body of Religion* is preferved in
' the holy Catholic Church independent of
' written Records,' holds true in the learned
World ; a Body of mythological Doctrine having
been preferved from the earlieft Ages until now,
and handed down from Generation to Generation, varied indeed like its Betters, according
to the Run of the Times, but ftill retaining
enough of its original Purity to free it from the
Sufpicion of a Counterfeit.

 ' The greater Part of thofe who firft began
' to enquire into Nature, and fearch into the
' Rife and Caufe of the Univerfe, thought the
' *Principle* of all Things lay in that fingle
' Species we call MATTER. For *that* of
' which every Thing confifts, of which every
' Thing is formed at firft, and into which it is
' refolved at laft, the Subftance or Subject-mat-
' ter remaining ftill the fame under a thoufand
' Variations, *That*, they faid, was the *Principle*
' and *Materia prima* of every Thing that
' exifts. As for example, We do not fay
' barely *that a Man is*, when he is either a
' good Man, or a good Mufician ; nor do we
' fay *that he is no more*, tho' he fhou'd lofe his
' Probity and Skill in Mufic, becaufe the Sub-
' ject-matter, the *Man*, ftill remains, tho'
' ftript of thefe Qualities. It is the fame in
' other Things ; there muft be fome certain
' Nature or Being, either one, or more than
        ' one,

Lett.15.' one, which remains ftill indiffolvable and uni-
'form, while all other Things are made of it.

' But with refpect to this *primary Subftance,*
' whether it be one or more, and of what
' Species, they did not agree in their Opinions.
' Thales, who introduced that Philofophy,
' faid it was *Water*, and affirmed that the Globe
' of this Earth confifted of *Moifture condenfed.*
' He was probably led to this Tenet, by obfer-
' ving the Nourifhment of every thing to be
' humid, by feeing Heat itfelf generated from
' Humidity, and Animal-Life extinguifhed where
' it fails. But *that* of which any thing is pro-
' duced or generated, and without which it can-
' not fubfift, is its *Principle* and *Origin.* For
' thefe Reafons therefore, he feems to have
' efpoufed this Opinion, and likewife becaufe
' he faw the *Seeds* of all Things to be of a *moift*
' Nature, whofe Principle of Being is *Water.*
' Some there are, who believe that long before
' this prefent Generation, the very ancienteft
' of the Philofophers, who firft of all treated
' of the *Nature of the Deity*, entertained the
' fame Opinion concerning the *Creation.* For
' they made *Ocean* and *Tethys* to be the Parents
' of Generation, and the Oath of the Gods,
' called *Styx* by the Poets, the moft ancient and
' auguft of Beings: For the moft ancient is
' the moft honourable, and the moft honourable
' is that by which we fwear [b].' As this Tefti-

mony

[b] Μετὰ τὰ Φυσικ. βιϐ. α.

mony has dropt from the fevereft Pen that ever Lett.15. wrote upon the Subject, it plainly evinces that the firft Philofophy was thought to be couched in Mythology ; or in other Words, *That the early Fables were framed to convey a Doctrine which is not a mere Conjecture of the Moderns.*

You afk next, Whether there be not many of the ancient Fictions we do not now underftand at all ? Some I believe there are into whofe Meaning we have not yet penetrated— ; not very many ; owing in the firft place to the *Corruption* of the pure genuine Mythology, which ftript it of all Meaning, and of which you are now fufficiently apprifed; and next, to the SECRET RITES at *Initiations,* fo carefully kept from unhallowed Eyes, but which yet daily clear up. There remain but few Parts of Antiquity upon which the Sagacity and Labours of the Learned have not poured new Light : Rites and Doctrines before unintelligible are by degrees explained ; and lately, a very learned and lively Writer, in attempting to demonftrate the divine Legation of *Mofes* from an uncommon Topic, has taught us, *en paffant,* how the Ancients veiled their folemn Leffons of Immortality and a future State. It is certain that Mythology, as it now ftands, is not to be underftood without a wide and accurate Knowledge of the *religious Rites* of the feveral Nations from whom the *Greeks* received their Gods ; becaufe upon fome fignificant Ceremony concerning the Nature,

or

Lett.15.or traditional Tale concerning the Exploits of
the Divinity depends the Key to the Legend,
and fometimes the very *Name* of the God himfelf. As the early *Egyptian* Rites were all
eftablifhed by Law, were all recorded, were all
typical and fymbolical, the Type or Symbol
came by an eafy Tranfition, not only to fignify
obfcurely, but directly to exprefs the Thing
typified : a grand Source of Error and Incertainty in the Foundation of the Allegory ! But
befides the original Type, any remarkable part
of the divine Service, any myftical Mixture as
in the Rites of *Ceres*, any ftriking Pofture as
in the Feafts of *Pan*, any uncouth Garb of the
Hierophant or Prieft, or any uncouth Quality
afcribed to the *Numen*, was enough to fix an
Epithet, and that Epithet to wear gradually into
a Name [c].

YOUR Conclufion therefore, tho' very natural and very common, ' That what you do not
' readily underftand has really no Meaning,' is a
little too hafty, as you fhall fee in the very Example you propofe of an unmeaning Fable.
' What cou'd *Homer* intend, fay you, by mak-
' ing *Juno*, for inftance, promife the youngeft
' of the Graces in Marriage to the God of
' Sleep, if he wou'd feal the Eyes of all-mighty
Jove

---

[c] *Jupiter* from Ζεῦ πάῖερ. *Ceres* from *a Sheaf* in Syriac. So
ΦΟΙΒΟΣ, ΑΠΟΛΛΩΝ, ΉΡΑΙΣΤΟΣ, ΑΦΡΟΔΙΤΗ,
ΔΙΩΝΗ, from their refpective Qualities.

' Jove for a little Space ? ᵈ Was it only to Lett. 15.
' adorn his Story with more Machinery, and
' throw more Life and living Perfons into his
' Dialogue ? ' Tho' it had been fo, he would
have been little to blame. But one fingle Reflection will convince you, that fuch a Marriage
was propofed with the higheft Propriety : Think
how frefh and how fair one rifes from foft balmy
Sleep,—how ghaftly and haggard even a fine
Face looks after undue Watching, and you muft
inftantly believe, that the *youngeft* of the *Graces* ᵉ
is indeed *married* to the foothing Power of Sleep.
What is it that fpoils fo many fine Complexions,
that deadens the brighteft Eye, and blafts the
Bloom of the gayer Females? Is it not keeping
bad Hours, and divorcing the youngeft of the
Graces from the God of Sleep: 'Tis this unnatural part of high Living that chiefly pales
the rofy Lip, difarms the fparkling Look,
and robs a Beauty of her native Grace ; a Confideration, you will allow, fo weighty, that if it
do not prevail, we may defpair of ever feeing a
happy Reformation. The other Sifters are difpofed of with equal Significancy ; the eldeft a
Miftrefs to Vulcan, there being little *Grace*
without a genial Warmth, and the higheft when
it is lighted up to a Glow; while the remaining
Sifter is a conftant Attendant upon the Queen of
Love. Were Mythology in all its Branches
equally

ᵈ ΙΛΙΑΔ. Ξ.
ᵉ Πασιϑεὰ, *Pafithea,* All-divine.

Lett.15 equally intelligible with the Functions of the Graces, there would be little reason to complain of its Corruption. But tho' it had not been directly spoilt by injudicious Episodes tacked to the simple original Fable, some Parts of it may have become inexplicable thro' the Loss of the *Traditions.*

THE COURSE of *Time* since the World began, may according to VARRO be divided into three Periods; the unknown, the fabulous and the historical. The *unknown* comprehends all that Space which the Ancients supposed to have passed from the beginning of Things, and of which we have not the least Knowledge. All that was then transacted, in their Opinion escaped the keenest Sight, and lay concealed— *beyond the utmost Stretch —— of mortal Ken.* The *fabulous* began with the earliest Notices of Things, that is, in ancient Style, with the Birth and Marriages of the Gods, and continued thro' the heroic Ages until Records and History introduced Certainty, and unfabled Truth: Then commenced the *historical* Period, which has happily kept the same Evidence till now.

INSTEAD of this accurate Partition, the early Poets sung, ' That SATURN sprung of ' *Celus* and *Ops*, lurked long out of sight of ' Heaven, and likewise devoured his own Pro- ' geny assoon as they were born [f]: This is plainly

---

[f] Itaque nec TEMPORIS Partus nec Abortus extant in Faftis. BACON.

plainly the *unknown* Period, the Χρόν℧. ἄδηλ℧. Lett.15.
of the Philofophers. ' He rendered his Father
' *Celus,* continued the Bards, incapable of Ge-
' neration; and was himfelf treated in the
' fame manner by *Jupiter* his eldeft Son, who
' together with *Juno, Ceres, Pluto* and *Nep-*
' *tune* (the Air, the Earth, the Abyfs, and the
' Ocean) were produced without his Know-
' ledge and preferved againft his Will. They
' confpired againft their relentlefs Parent, feiz-
' ed and bound him with a Cord of Wool,
' never to be loofed while almighty *Jove* holds
' the Reins of Government.' Here is the *fa-*
bulous Period, Χρόν℧. μυϑικό;, in the Sequel
of the Story, comprehending the Birth and Adventures of the Gods, and the hiftorical Period
Χρόν℧. ἱϛορικό's in the Conclufion. TIME,
tho' it glide filent and almoft imperceptible,
is faft bound in the Revolutions of the heavenly Bodies, the fofteft and fureft Bond in Nature : Their unerring Courfe fubjects it to Hiftory, and chronological Rules, and will continue to keep it indiffolubly chained, while
the beauteous Frame and harmonious Order of
the Univerfe remains the fame.

HITHERTO the Fable of *Saturn* is pretty
confiftent and intelligible : But why did he
fall in love with *Philyra?* Why transform
himfelf into a Horfe and fhake Mount *Pelion*
with his Neighing, to become the Father of
N *Chiron,*

Lett.15.*Chiron,* and Grandfather of *Ocyroe?* [t] The *Tradition* is loft that fhou'd explain it : at leaft I have met with nothing on the Subject that gives me Satisfaction. It wou'd not be difficult to frame Conjectures from their feveral Names, which allude to the Verdure of the returning Seafons, (*Saturn's* annual Children) and Swiftnefs of their paffing [u]; but the Ground-work is wanting on which they muft be woven to appear genuine and fatisfactory. Another Inftance will make this ftill plainer.

Suppose that amidft the Calamities that frequently befel the *Jewifh* Nation the Book of their Law, whofe Prefervation is almoft a Miracle, had perifhed ; and with it, as of other Incidents, the Memory of the brazen Serpent erected by their great Law-giver had been irretrievably loft, what cou'd we have now made of the Serpents erected at this day as *Talifmans* [v] all over the Eaft in imitation of that divine Pattern? We might have groped in the dark, attributed them perhaps to the Power of *Mercury's Caduceus,* the magic Rod with twining Snakes; or to *Efculapius'* Badge of Life and Health, a fingle Serpent wreathed round

---

[t] —— Ipfe Jubam cervice effudit equina
Conjugis adventu pernix Saturnus, et altum
Pelion hinnitu fugiens implevit acuto.
Virgil. Georg, III.

[u] Φιλυρα χλωρα, Φιλυριν☉ χλωρος.   Σουιδ
'Ωκυροη from ωκυς and ρέω. She was a Prophetefs.

[v] See Glycas' Annals, Part III.

round his Staff; or to the myftical Veneration of the *Egyptians*, who have moft of thefe *Ta-lifmans*, for that Reptile, to which they ftill facrifice * amidft all the Strictnefs of the Mahometan Doctrine concerning the Unity of God, and the Precifenefs of the Chriftian Cophtis : But we cou'd never have been throughly fatisfied of the real Rife of that Rite without the *original Tradition*. There are many Cuftoms both in facred and civil matters, now prevailing over the World that are upon the fame uncertain Footing. Mankind in this refpect are exceffively docile, fhall I fay, or ftupid. A Rite once received is carefully kept up, and even fpreads, when the Reafons of its Inftitution have been long forgot, or are quite unknown. A learned Father of the *Latin* Church has recorded a Complaint of *Seneca*, ' that after the example of the wicked *Jews*, ' (fo he calls them) the greater part of the ' World had begun to lofe the feventh Part ' of their Life in Idlenefs and Neglect of ne- ' ceffary Bufinefs, in which Cuftom the Van- ' quifhed had given Law to the Victors.—— ' Yet they, the *Jews*, fays he, know the Caufe ' of their own Rite, while moft of our People

N 2　　　　　' are

---

* The *Egyptian* Arabs believe the Soul of *Ogli Haffan* the Son of *Sheik*, to be transformed into a Serpent that lurks in the Cleft of a Rock near his Tomb, and works abundance of miraculous Cures.

　　　Dr. *Pocock's* Obfervations on EGYPT.

Lett.15. ' are doing what they can give no Reason *why*
' *they do it.*' [x]

Now the original *Egyptian* RECORDS are
wholly loft; as few of the *Affyrian* or *Phenician* remain: What Notices we have of them
have tranfpired in their communication with
neighbouring Nations, and reached us at *fecond* or *third* Hand from the Fountain. In
what thick Darknefs muft this have involved
fome of their religious Practices? Hear the La-
mentation of a true Difciple of theirs, whofe
Character is uncommon, and his Writings worth
your Confideration.

JAMBLICHUS and his Mafter PORPHYRY
were two of the moft extraordinary Men in
the later Ages of Learning: Both *Platonifts*,
of an exalted Genius, and unblemifh'd Morals;
but bigottedly biaffed to their national Rites
which were then beginning, not to be called
in queftion (that the Philofophers had often
done at their peril) but to fall in difcredit with
the Populace; and therefore, one would think,
in favour with the Sages. *Porphyry* after the
Death of *Plotinus* was efteemed the greateft
Philofopher of his Age: Yet his vaft Learning and piercing Thought cou'd not prevent his
attempting to make an unhappy Affociation between

---

[x] Cum interim ufque eò fce!eratiffimæ genti confuetudo con-
valuit, ut per omnes jam terras recepta fit, victi victoribus
leges dederunt.—Illi tamen caufas ritûs fui noverunt, et major
pars populi facit, quod cur facit ignorat.
SENECA de Superftitione, apud Auguftin. de C. D. Lib. VI.

tween *his* Philofophy and Religion ; nor the Lett. 15.
unhappy Effect of fo prepofterous an Attempt
as the reducing *divine* Myfteries to the Standard of *human* Underftanding.*—He trefpaffed
againft the invariable Maxim of the wife *Strabo,* ' That a mixed Multitude of Men and Wo-
' men can never be governed by abftract Rea-
' fon, nor led by Rules of Philofophy. They
' muft be ftruck with fenfible Objects, allured
' with *Elyfian Fields,* and terrified with *Tri-*
' *dents, Gorgons* and the forky *Bolts* of thun-
' dering Jove.' He accordingly became one
Inftance, among many, of the Truth of the
Obfervation made by the moft learned of the
Apoftles in his Converfe with the politer Nations, *That his Doctrine was to the* Greeks
Foolifhnefs. Nor does the Philofopher feem to
have been much better fatisfied with the *Grecian* or even *Egyptian* Theology. He made
a fruitlefs Reformation upon the one in a famous Treatife often quoted by the Fathers, *Of
Oracular Knowledge,* and is full of Doubts and
Difficulties about the other. Thefe he has propofed in a celebrated Letter to *Anebo* or *Nec-
tanebo* an *Egyptian* Prieft, fuppofed to be ini-

N 3 tiated

* In *mathematicis* ac *phyficis* per quædam antecedentia, five
Axiomata feu tu Principia voces, quæ refellere nequeas, mox
certæ combinationis artificio concluditur id quo ipfe ftare compel-
laris. At contrà *in divinis* Silentium defideratur, Contentio re-
fpuitur, Syllogifmus irridetur. Igitur quodcunque concludendum
fuerit, eidem itatim acquiefcendum eft.
I. Reuchlin. De Verbo mirifico. Lib. I. Cap. 15.

Lett.15. tiated in their Myfteries, and therefore capable of giving the defired Solution.

St. Austin is of Opinion, that in this Letter *Porphyry* rather expofes the Abfurdity of believing in thefe dubious Deities, than feeks Satisfaction concerning their Sanctity and Godhead [z]; and *Eufebius* retails Scraps of it, fometimes to fhew that the Gods of *Egypt* were no fpiritual immaterial Beings, but Parts of the material World [a]; and fometimes as unfufpected Evidence of the Inconftancy of the *Grecian* conjectural Theology [b].

But Jamblichus more firmly perfuaded of the Reality of his Religion, and of confequence, more zealous than his Mafter, carries the matter fo far, as to make the accurate Knowledge of the ancient Rites, and pious Practice of the folemn Invocations, the ultimate End and fupreme Attainment of his Philofophy. By *their* means and theirs alone he believed *Mankind* cou'd be raifed above their frail mortal Nature, cou'd be intimately united to the Gods, and in fome meafure made Partakers of their divine Power. This learned Man, a Lover of Myfteries, and a great *Afcetic*, affuming the Perfon of Anebo the *Egyptian* Prieft, has minutely anfwered his Mafter's Letter: So minutely, that while he difcuffes every Scruple and
expatiates

[z] Porphyrius, confulenti fimilia et quaerenti, et prodit artes et facrilegas evertit.
De C. D. Lib. X. §. 11.

([a]) ΠΡΟΠΑΡ. Βιϐ. ς.   [b] Βιϐ. ιδ. κεφ. 1.

expatiates upon the Powers and Properties of
the feveral Orders of the *Gods, Demons* and
Genii, his Anſwer has ſwelled to a pretty large
Treatiſe, *Of the Myſteries of the* Egyptians.

AMONG other ſhrewd Queries, *Porphyry* had
aſk'd, ' *What the barbarous unintelligible Names*
' *of the Gods wou'd be at ? and of the intelli-*
' *gible, Why in our ſolemn Invocations are the*
' *foreign Appellations preferred to thoſe in a*
' *known Tongue ?* ' To this the perſonated
Anebo anſwers :

' THERE is a *myſtical* Reaſon to be given
' for ſuch Uſage. Confider —— why have the
' GODS fanctified the whole Language of the
' *holy* Nations, the *Egyptian* and *Aſſyrian ?*
' For that ſame Reaſon we chuſe to make
' our Addreſſes in the Dialect *neareſt a-kin* to
' the Divinity ^c. This manner of Speech was
' likewiſe the *firſt* and *moſt ancient* of Tongues ;
' and they who firſt learned the Appellations
' of the Gods, having handed them down to
' us cloathed in their own Language, as be-
' ing peculiarly capable of expreſſing the Eſ-
' fence and Attributes of the divine Nature,
' we to this day unchangeably retain the ſa-
' cred Sanction of ſuch Tradition : for if any
' thing be proper to the Gods, it muſt be Per-
' manency and Exemption from Change.——
' Befides, the *eaſtern* Languages, which we
' call *barbarous,* have great *Emphaſis,* great

N 4

' Con-

εὐγενεῖ διαλέκτῳ.

Lett.15.‘ Concifenefs, are lefs liable thro’ a multiplicity
‘ of Words to Ambiguity and Variations [d],
‘ and are therefore better fitted for the higheft
‘ purpofe, *Prayer to the Immortals.* Away
‘ with Sufpicions then, that fall far wide of
‘ the Truth, as if thefe ancient Names were
‘ ufed becaufe the God invoked had been an
‘ *Egyptian*, or had formerly fpoke the *egyptian*
‘ Tongue: let us rather think, that the *Egyp-*
‘ *tians* having firft of all the Nations on Earth
‘ enjoy’d the Prefence and Converfation of the
‘ Gods, thefe fame Gods take moft pleafure
‘ in being invoked according to the *egyptian*
‘ Forms: Forms not devifed by Impoftors,
‘ nor contrived by cunning Men; but what
‘ above all things are moft immediately iden-
‘ tified with the divine Nature, unite us moft
‘ intimately to it, and have almoft the Vir-
‘ tue and Efficacy of the Gods themfelves [e].
‘ Can *thefe* be fantaftic Fictions, without which
‘ no holy Rite can be pioufly performed? And
‘ much lefs can they be, as you feem to in-
　　　　　　　　　　　　　　　　‘ finuate,

[d] Whence I conclude the Philofopher’s Proficiency in them to
have been but flender, or his Prejudice ftrong.

[e] Here is the Source of the Power afcribed to Words and
Invocations of invifible *Numens*, which they called ΘΕΟΥΡΓΙΑ.
It came from the CHALDEANS, and along with it the Superftition about writing certain Names. *Nomen quod folis quatuor
Punctis rite ordinatis* CHALDAEI *depingere folent, quo n. con-
fuetudinem modo pariter affumfere* HEBRAEI[*]. Hence the Rab-
binic Miracles wrought by the *Tetragrammaton* and *Shem-ham-
phorafh*; in virtue of which the travelling *Jew Benjamin* tells,
that *David Elni*, a Magician, performed a Journey of ten days
in one.

[*] REUCHLIN de Verbo mirifico, Lib. II.

' finuate, *Coverings* or *artful Concealments* of Lett.15.
' human Paffions and human Frailties impi-
' oufly afcribed to the Deity: No — thefe fa-
' cred Appellations, adapted to, and expreffive
' of the Natures of the Gods, are not drawn
' from *this State of Mortality*; but on the con-
' trary, from the peculiar Attributes of the Gods
' themfelves: Nor while we are ufing thefe
' awful Names have we Notions of the Na-
' ture of the *Gods* contrary to the reality of
' the divine Effence; but according to *that*
' *very Nature*, and according to *Truth*, as it
' has been delivered down to us from the *Firft*
' who inftituted thefe facred Rites of Wor-
' fhip, we invariably perfift in them: for, as
' I faid, if any thing befit divine Inftitutions,
' it is *Immutability*. I conclude therefore, that
' we ought to preferve the ancient Terms and
' Forms of Prayer inviolate, like Sanctuaries, in
' the fame order and condition we found them,
' without addition or diminution of a Syllable.
' A contrary Conduct has been the Caufe that
' both the authentic Forms of Worfhip are
' now almoft obliterated, and the very Names
' of the Gods effaced; fo many Changes hav-
' ing been introduced thro' the *Grecian* Itch
' for Novelties and Contempt of Laws, that
' nothing has kept fteady and permanent. For
' the *Greeks* are naturally *Innovators*, driven
' hither and thither by their own Levity.
' They have no fixed Principle to ferve as Bal-
' laft,

Lett.15.' laſt, in themſelves ; nor do they preſerve what
        ' of that kind they receive in *Tradition* from
        ' others: but quickly forſaking it, they tranſ-
        ' form and confound every thing thro' an end-
        ' leſs Search of new Things and new Terms.
        ' Whereas the Nations by them called *barba-*
        ' *rous*, being conſtant in their Cuſtoms and
        ' uniform in their Manners, keep invariably
        ' to the ſame Forms of Speech and Worſhip ;
        ' and on that account are both agreeable to
        ' the GODS, and pay their Devotions in accep-
        ' table Stile, which it is unlawful for any Man,
        ' at any time to change.'

IT MUST have been in virtue of ſome of
theſe *wonder-working Forms* that this pious
Philoſopher called forth EROS and ANTEROS,
two *Genii* reſembling beautiful Boys, out of the
Fountains bearing their Names ; and was frequently ſeen at his Devotions by his peeping
Servants, caught up into the Air, and the Colour of his Garments changed to a bright Pur-
ple. Had his Doctrine been obſerved, we
ſhould have better underſtood the real Senſe
of the ancient Lawgivers, and been leſs at a
loſs in tracing that Religion to it's Source, which
from EGYPT and the EAST overſpread the
weſtern World. It's Authors, no doubt, did
their beſt to procure that Satisfaction to Poſterity by repeated Sanctions, that none of their
Inſtitutions ſhould be altered: For what Founder, civil or religious, but wou'd wiſh his Re-
                                    gulations

gulations to be facred, and punctually practifed Lett. 15.
while there are Men to obferve them?

BUT the perpetual Flux of fublunary Affairs; the Cataftrophies of Nations and Vicif-
fitudes of Dominion fo inevitably abforb the
Manners, Language and Religion of a Country, that no *buman* Forefight, nor Reach of
Thought has yet founded an unvaried Church,
or eftablifhed an everlafting State. In vain did
the *Medes* and *Perfians* ordain their immutable
Statutes; in vain did the great ZOROASTER,
tho' feconded by *Dodonean* JOVE [a], forbid the
barbarous myfterious Terms to be changed; in
vain did the *Egyptians* or *Affyrians* inftitute
fignificant folemn Rites, or the *Greeks* and *Romans* appoint annual Feafts, and enter into Societies to perpetuate their Celebration. All is
obliterated and covered in Oblivion. *Adonis* is
no more loft and found in *Egypt*; *Mylitta's*
Temple ftands no longer open for the Ladies at
Babylon; the glorious *Olympics* are forgot in *Elis*,
and *Auguftus'* Birth-day flips unheeded over in
fpight of his Temples and *Flamens*, or the
Socii Auguftales facred to his Memory.

WHEN therefore nothing but the *Rite* remains, whether preferved by ftupid Practice,
or barely recorded in Hiftory, and the TRA-
DITION is loft, that fhou'd explain it, no
wonder

[a] Ἐχρηϛηριάζοντο ἐν τῇ ΔΩΔΩΝΗ οἱ Πελασγοὶ εἰ
ἀνέλωνται τὰ οὐνόματα τὰ ἀπὸ τῶν βαρβάρων ἥκοντα· κϳ
ἀνεῖλε τὸ μανϑήϊον χρᾶϑαι.   ΗΡΟΔΟΤ. Εὐϊέρπη.

Lett.15.wonder the Allegory fhou'd be dark, and continue a proper Subject for critical Conjectures. But this, as I faid, is not often the Cafe: Symbols carry natural Marks that ftrike a fagacious Mind, and lead it by degrees to their real Meaning. A Hint in one Author brightens the Obfcurities of many others; as one fingle Obfervation of *Macrobius* proved the Clew to Abbé *Pluche*, how juftly I fay not, to unravel the whole Myftery of the *Egyptian*, *Affyrian* and *Grecian* Gods: Nay, the very Ruin of the ancient Rites has contributed not a little to their Illuftration. How little foever it may feem plaufible at firft view, it is very certain that the *Roman Conftitution*, for inftance, cou'd never have been fo accurately learned from *Roman* Authors, (who took no care to explain what every body knew as well as themfelves) as from the knowing polite *Foreigners**, who lived at *Rome*, and wrote, not for *Romans*, but for the Inftruction of their own ingenious Country-men that knew little about *Rome*, but it's Conquefts and Power. Much in the fame way, it is not from the Votaries of the feveral Religions into which the ancient Devotion had fplit, that we are to learn the Detail and Intention of their Ceremonies: it is rather from Foreigners, or even from *Enemies*, who pry'd into their Myfteries in order to expofe them. Accordingly, there are many Gods and Goddeffes among the *Greeks* and *Romans*, whofe

Powers

* POLYBIUS, DIONYSIUS of *Halicarnaffus*, APPIAN. *&c.*

Powers and Attributes we fhou'd fcarcely have underftood without the affiftance of the *Chri-ftian* Fathers. All the early pious Pen-men have contributed their Mite, and the moft zealous for Profelytes, *Clemens the Alexandrian*, and the learned *Arnobius* have furpaffed the reft in explaining and confuting the Modes of Idolatry. Lett.15.

HAD all the Nations of the World been of the *Eaftern* Caft; had they been as ftubborn as the *Jews*, as thoughtful and fullen as the *Egyptians*, as folemn and filent as the *Affy-rians*, we had been lefs indebted either to Friends or Enemies for the Knowledge of their religious Opinions or Practices ; the Rites had then reached us unvaried, and the Traditions been handed down inviolate like the MISHNA. But they fell unluckily into the Hands of the GRECIANS, an ingenious fanciful People, who, as no Friend of their Religion fays[b], ' excelled ' all Mankind in Genius and Invention: They ' adopted the greater part of the firft Tradi-' tions, which they amplified and made more ' marvelous with beautiful Epifodes of their ' own. They diverfified them afterwards with ' a thoufand Colours, as having no other ' Intention than to footh the Mind with the ' Pleafures of Fable. Hence *Hefiod* and the ' celebrated CIRCLE † of ancient Songfters ' introduced

---

[b] ΦΙΛΩΝ ὁ Βύβλιۍ.

† A Collection of *Cofmogonies*, or Suite of Hiftories of the Creation, that made the ancient BODY of DIVINITY. See below, Note ۍ.

Lett.15.' introduced their Generations of the Gods,
' their *Giant-Wars*, and *Titan-Fights*, and
' Caſtrations of Deities of their own Con-
' trivance.   Their alluring Fictions hurry us
' ſo along, that they have even got the bet-
' ter of Truth *.   For our Ears being accu-
' ſtomed to theſe Tales from our Childhood,
' and pre-poſſeſſed with the Tradition now
' of many Ages, preſerve their fabulous Doc-
' trine like a ſacred Truſt.   This co-operat-
' ing with Time, has rendered the once re-
' ceived Belief ſo indelible, that to tell real
' *Fact* ſeems mere Trifling, while the ſpurious
' Parts of the Narration paſs for the genuine
' Truth.'

THESE are the chief Reaſons of the great
Variety of Opinions concerning ancient Rites ;
and of the many Diſputes among the Learned
about the Origins, Names, Powers and Enſigns
of the Gods, and therefore of the many long
Letters you have received on this Subject, from

Yours, &c.

* Ἔνθεν ΗΣΙΟΔΟΣ οἵτε ΚΥΚΛΙΚΟΙ περιηχημένοι,
Θεογονίας κ̀ Γιγαντομαχίας κ̀ τιτανομαχίας ἔπλασαν
ἰδίας κ̀ ἐκτομάς. οἷς περιφερόμενοι ἐξενίκησαν τὴν ἀλήθειαν.
Παρ᾽ ΕΤΣΕΒ. Ευ. Προπαρ. βιβ. α.

LETTER

LETTER SIXTEENTH.

I N the fluctuating State of the Religion of *Greece*, when every body believ'd in what God, and worshipped him in what manner he pleafed, a fhrewd Man and great Traveller took it into his head to reform their Creed, and new-model their Syftem of Divinity. For this purpofe he ftretched his travelling Privilege, talked of Lands where he had never been, and of Things which he had never feen, and which indeed exifted no where; but were meer Creatures of his licentious Imagination. He told in what Country, and of what Parents each of the Gods was born, how they were educated, where they lived, and pointed out the Place of their Death and Burial.——He gave a Detail of their Tombs and Temples, whofe Dimenfions and Materials he defcribed, and brought home their Infcriptions like a modern Antiquary. This was the famous EUHEME-RUS the *Meffenian*, a fort of Adventurer and Sea-Captain employ'd by *Caffander*, Author of the new Doctrine, *That all the Gods adored by the* Greeks *were deïfied* MORTALS.

THE Reception this Doctrine met with in *Greece* was different, according to the different Characters of the People. The Devout were fcandalized, the Vulgar ftartled, the Phi-

2　　　　　　　lofophers

Lett.16.lofophers fmiled, and the Half-thinkers, like
thofe of our own Days, greedily fwallow'd a new
Topic from which to ridicule the received Religion. But in general *Euhemerus* was look'd
upon as little better than an Atheift; his *Pan-
chaian* Ifle in the Eaftern Ocean, his Temple
and Tomb of *Triphylian* Jove, with his golden
Columns and Infcriptions, were treated as impious Romances, and his Opinions only regarded by a Species of *Efprits forts* † in *Greece*
and *Rome*, among whom was old Father *Ennius*,
who tranflated his *Sacred Hiftory* into Latin.

BUT this, which was formerly a grand religious Controverfy, is now turned a Point of
pure Speculation. What in the Days of *Po-
lytheïfm* raifed the Indignation of the Priefts,
and inflamed the rival-Zeal of the Fathers of
the Church, now raifes a little Squabble among
Antiquaries, as a Queftion of meer Curiofity:
Whether, to wit, *all the Gods of Antiquity
were not once mortal Men?*

THAT the primitive Philofophy, upon which
the feveral Religions of the Ancients were originally grafted, was foon corrupted, appears already pretty evident: that it was fo by the
Introduction of *human Perfons* into it as Gods,
appears in part from the fame Reafoning: But
as many of the Fathers[c], and feveral learned
Men

---

[c] EUHEMERUS, omnes tales Deos, non fabulofâ Garrulitate,
fed hiftoricâ diligentiâ homines fuiffe, mortalefque confcripfit.
AUGUSTIN. De C. D. Lib. VI. Cap. 6.
† Daring Wits.

Men of late, for whofe Memory and Character I have a real regard, have revived the
Opinion of *Eubemerus*, it becomes worth
while to review that Hypothefis, and confider,
whether it be well founded ?

It is paft doubt that many of the Gods,
and efpecially of the Heroes worfhipp'd in
Greece, had been mortal Men : as mortal as
Pater Quirinus, or *Divus Julius*, or any of
their infamous Succeffors, who had Priefts, and
Shrines, and Sacrifices decreed to them after
Death. The Queftion regards neither the later
Grecian nor *Roman* Deities, but the primary
great Gods of *Affyria* and *Egypt* *, the im-
mediate Offspring of Chaos, and Progeny of
Oceanus and *Tethys* ; whether *thefe* were meer
Men deified by Superftition and Ignorance, or
contrived Types and Reprefentations of the Rife,
Progrefs and Powers of the Univerfe?

The Patrons of the former Opinion, faid
with great Plaufibility, that it was very true
the Gods had been allegoriz'd, Meanings invented, and much Ingenuity employed in adap-
ting them to the ancient Fables : But that
the Allegory *came too late*, after the *Platonic*
Philofophy had difpelled the grofs Notions of
Idolatry, and dark Superftition had fled before
the Light of divine Truth: ' That then

O   ' the

---

* Νομίζυσι δ' ὦν 'Αιγύπλιοι, ὸδ' ΗΡΩΣΙ ὀυδέν.
ΗΡΟΔΟΤ. 'Ευ7έρπτ.
This Teftimony is decifive as to Egypt.

Lett.16. ' the fabulous fublime Theology pompoufly
' delivered by the Ancients, was undertaken by
' certain modern Profeffors of Philofophy, and
' explained according to a Sett of Principles
' confonant to found Reafon, fuch as, *a* MIND
' *the Creator of all Things*; *incorporeal pre-*
' *exiftent Ideas*; *intellectual rational Powers*;
' after which, the Fables thus dreffed out with
' their new Explications, were produced with
' greater Pomp than before.——While in the
' mean time, the Gods worfhip'd in all the
' Towns and Villages where Idolatry prevailed,
' *were wholly, without exception, Spectres of*
' *dead Men, or Images of Mortals long fince*
' *departed*ᵃ.'

THIS is fo far true, that the later *Platonifts* did certainly attempt to reform the Heathen Rites ; to purge the old Religion, and
new-model it upon the Purity of their Philofophy : And it is as true, that their Attempt
fo to do, proved a full Accomplifhment of their
Mafters Prophecy, of its being ' a heavy labo-
' rious Tafk, and the Work of no very happy
' Man.' But *their* ill Succefs, in reducing the
ancient Fictions to modern Refinements, concludes nothing againft the Doctrine of the primary Gods having been originally intended and
contrived to exprefs the Parts and Powers of
NATURE,

ᵈ Πάντες πανδημεὶ νεκρῶν εἴδωλα, κ̀ ἀνδρῶν πάλαι
καʼ οἰχομένων εἰκόνες.   ΕΤΣΕΒ, Πρεπ. Βι6. β.

NATURE, which is all that is requiſite for Lett.16.
our Entertainment. Nor is even *that*, perhaps abſolutely neceſſary, ſince we often allow ourſelves to be deceived for Amuſement,
nay, and lend a helping hand to carry on the
Cheat. Yet our Pleaſures are purer when
founded on Realities, and inſtead of being meer
Chimera's of our own Fancies, come recommended by Antiquity, conſecrated by Nations,
and cheriſhed by the greateſt *Genii* among Men.

EUHEMERUS therefore and his Followers, e'er we join in mortalizing the firſt
Divinities, muſt ſatisfy us, Why the poetical
Sages, Inſtructors of Mankind, termed their
grand Work, the Baſis of their Doctrine, not
only a THEOGONY, or an Account of the
Birth and Pedigree of the *Gods*, but a Cos-
MOGONY [e] or an Account of the Birth and
Creation of the *World?* or plainer ſtill a Cos-
MOPOEIA [f] *a making or framing of the Uni-
verſe?* The *Platonic* Philoſophy had no hand
in the *Coſmogonies* or Hiſtories of the Cre-
ation written by *Taaut* or *Thoth*, by *Linus*,
by *Orpheus*, by *Muſæus*, by *Epimenides*, by
Melampus, by *Pherecydes*, by *Antipho*, by
Thamyras, by *Dromocritus*, by *Parmenides*,

O 2   by

[e] ΔΙΟΓΕΝ. ΛΑΕΡΤ. Προοιμ.
[f] Σουϊδ. ΠΑΛΑΙΦΑΤΟΣ.

Lett.16.by *Acuſilaus, &c* *. or in any Part of the famous *Epic Cycle* ᵍ, that from CHAOS the Riſe
of Things, deduced the mythical Hiſtory down
to the *Trojan*-Times: Nor can any unbiaſſed
Mind peruſe *Heſiod*'s Theogony, and not perceive that he intends and plainly *profeſſes* to
deſcribe the Origin, and repreſent the Government of the World ʰ: And that the Plan
of his Work, tho' interwove with many a
disjointed Tale, is ſubſtantially the ſame with
Orpheus's ΙΕΡΟΣ ΛΟΓΟΣ or HOLY WORD, in
which we are told the great Theologue of
the *Greeks,* and Pattern of pious Poets explained Points of no leſs Importance than *the Births
of the Gods, the Creation of the World and Formation of Man* ⁱ. 'Tis plain therefore, the
Allegory *did not come too late:* It was not framed after the Fable, like modern Predictions,
after

* ΗΣΙΟΔΟΣ πρῶτον μεν Χάος γενέϑαι φησί.—κ̀ϳ
μετὰ τᾶτο, δύω τᾶτω γενέϑαι, Γῆν τε κ̀ϳ ῎Ερωῖα. Παρ-
μενίδης δὲ τὴν γένεσιν λέγει, Πρώτιϛον μὲν ῎Ερωῖα ϑεῶν
μητίσαῖο πάντων· Ἡσιώδῳ δὲ κ̀ϳ Ἀκυσίλεως ὁμολογεῖ.
　　　　　　　　ΠΛΑΤΩΝ. ΣΥΜΠΟΣ.

ᵍ ῎Αρχεται μὲν ἐκ τῆς ὀυρανᾶ κ̀ϳ γῆς μυϑολογυμένης
ῥίξεως.　　　　　　Φωτιῶ. βι ᴇ̄. ἐλϑ.

ʰ ῎Ειπατε δ' ὡς τὰ πρῶτα ϑεοὶ κ̀ϳ Γαῖα γένοντο,
Καὶ πωῖαμοὶ, κ̀ϳ πόντῶ ἀπέιριτῶ ὀίδματι ϑύων,
῎Αϛρα τε λαμπετόωνῖα, κ̀ϳ ὀυρανὸς ἐυρὺς ὕπερϑεν,
῾Οι τ' ἐκ τῶν ἐγένοντο ϑεοὶ.——　　ΘΕΟΓΟΝ.

ⁱ Θεογονιάς, κ̀ϳ κόσμυ κτίσιν, κ̀ϳ ἀνϑρώπων πλαϛργίαν.
　　　　　　　ΤΙΜΟΘ. παρὰ Κεδρψν.

after the Event : It was underſtood and receiv'd Lett.16. from the Beginning.

How fitly theſe Fables were contriv'd, how juſtly they repreſented Nature, and what Purpoſes they ſerved among Men, are quite different Conſiderations; and wou'd require a different Diſcuſſion, were it neceſſary to point out Beauties or Blemiſhes that are better felt than deſcribed ; that ſtrike and pleaſe in proportion to every one's Genius and Capacity : For it is no vulgar Happineſs to be entertained with this alluſive ſhadowy way of writing, nor vulgar Penetration to comprehend its Force and Extent : A peculiar Caſt of Mind is neceſſary to diſcover the Art of an ingenious Fiction, and truly judge of its Propriety and Elegance.

‘ The human Genius, ſays an Oracle in
‘ Learning[k], is of two ſorts ; Men of dry diſ-
‘ tinct Heads, cool Imaginations, and keen
‘ Application : They eaſily apprehend the *Dif-*
‘ *ferences* of Things, are Maſters in Contro-
‘ verſy and excel in Confutation ; and theſe
‘ are the moſt common. The ſecond ſort
‘ are Men of warm Fancies, elevated Thought
‘ and wide Knowledge : they inſtantly perceive
‘ the *Reſemblances* of Things, and are Poets,
‘ or *Makers* in Science, invent Arts, and ſtrike
‘ out new Light wherever they carry their
‘ Views.’

O 3

[k] Bacon. Org. nov.

Lett.16. ' Views.' Thefe are more rarely produced, eafily
〰️fmothered, and therefore appear at great Intervals.   This acute Obfervation holds true,
not only of particular Men, but of whole Nations : The *Eaftern*, contemplative, fabulous,
and metaphorical : the *Weftern*, blunt and plain,
fticking to Fact, and content with naked
Truth.   When M. *Voltaire*, whofe Sallies furprized and diverted us here fome Years ago,
fhew'd his HENRIADE to M. *de Malezieux*,
he was told by that able Judge, after a due
Commendation of his beautiful Poem, that it
wou'd not be much relifhed by his Country-
men the *French* ; for, faid he, *ils n'ont pas
la Tête Epique*.   With equal, or greater reafon he might have faid *ils n'ont pas la Tête
Mythologique*.   They have indeed neither Dignity of Manners to fupport the one, nor Strength
of Genius and Extent of Fancy to tafte the
other.   In Life they are wholly occupied with
their *Savoir vivre*, and in Poetry with pretty
little ingenious Pieces compofed by the *Abbés*
to read in the Ruëlles to the Ladies[1] : No
wonder their late Authors fhou'd lean to the prevailing profaïc Tafte [m] ; and that even fuch Men
as the Abbé *Banier* and M. *Fourmont*, whom I
mention

---

[1] Tout le Secret de la Poefie françoife confifte à faire de
petits Vers aifez, ou l'on fe contente de renfermer quelque
forte de Delicateffe de Sentimens doux et paffionnez dont on
fait l'Effentiel de la Poefie.

P. Rapin. REFLECTION xxxi.

[m] De toutes les Nations de l'Europe la nôtre eft la moins
poetique.   VOLTAIRE Difcours fur le P. E.

mention with the Honour due to their Learning, Lett.16. fhould favour a Syftem rejected by the greateft Men of every Age, and deftructive of all true Poetry.

IF *Heaven* and *Earth*, *Ocean* and *Slime*, *Ether* and *Air*, *Fire* and *Water* be *human* Perfons deified, of what Type, or Symbol of any one Thing in the Univerfe may we not fay the fame *? The Rife and Relation of thefe Parts of the Creation to one another, their various Oppofitions, Conjunctions and Effects were myfterioufly fung by the firft Sages under the Wrappers of Births, Marriages, Wars, Imprifonments, and other Figures taken from the Affairs of Men: They have been fo read and underftood for more than three thoufand Years, except when Ambition, Humour, or Intereft have made it proper to find out that they were Mortals. ' Mankind, fays the elegant ' *Fontenelle*, have an invincible Courage for ' what they are once fond of: Every one be- ' lieves the Difcovery refufed to others has been ' referved for himfelf. Ten thoufand Years ' hence there may be a Sett of *Litterati*, who ' will boaft of confuting Errors that have been ' received for fixteen thoufand before; and they ' will find People difpofed to believe that in

O 4　　　　　　' reality,

* Principes Dei COELUM et TERRA. Hi Dei iidem qui Æ-gypti SERAPIS et ISIS, et S. *Harpocrates* digito fignificat, ut idem princeps in Latio, SATURNUS et OPS. TERRA enim et COELUM, ut *Samethracum* Initia docent, funt DEI MAGNI, et hi quos dixi, multis Nominibus.

M. TER. VARRO. De Lingua Latina Lib. IV.

Lett.16. ' reality, the World is then juſt beginning to
⌣⌣⌣ ' open its Eyes.

THE Abbé BANIER's learned Work will
open a wide Scene to your View: He endeavours to explain, the Riſe, Progreſs and Extent of what we call *Paganiſm :* He traces
the Principles from which the various Modes
of Superſtition firſt ſprang, and points out their
Effects upon Life and Manners. This Part of
it is full of Inſtruction. There we ſee the Paſſions and Affections moſt neceſſary for private
Happineſs and the Preſervation of Society groſsly
perverted, and find a large Detail of

Quantum Relligio potuit ſuadere malorum.

But while you read the cool Reflexions of this
unpoetical Writer, it will not be amiſs to car-
ry a Conſideration or two along with you.
Firſt, that he writes upon an *Hypotheſis,* or
Suppoſition, that the Fables of the Ancients are
hiſtorical [n]; that is, that there are real human
Perſons couched under the Names of *Saturn*
or TIME, *Jupiter* or HEAVEN, *Juno* or
AIR, *Neptune* or SEA, *Ceres* or EARTH,
and is every where endeavouring to trace that
Hiſtory to its ſuppoſed Original. This is the
Plan on which he writes, and which it muſt be
acknowledged to his Honour he has the good
Senſe not always to follow. For he makes

a

[a] La Mythologie et les Fables expliquées par l'*Hiſtoire.*

a neceſſary Diſtinction between the *firſt Gods*, Lett.16.
whom (after *R. Moſes Ben Maimon*, as I judge)
he takes to be the heavenly Bodies, and, af-
ter-deified *Heroes*°. But neither does this Diſtinction remount high enough to the Principles of Creation, nor extend wide enough to
all the Powers of Nature ; nor does the learned Author, keep cloſe to it in the Proſecution of his Work ; but biaſſed and clogged
by his Hypotheſis, inſtead of the primary
Powers that produced, and permanent Parts that
compoſe Heaven and Earth, he is conſtantly in
queſt of tranſient Mortals.

His chief Proof which he brings from *Herodotus* is ſcarce concluſive. That Author does
not ſay that the *Greeks* thought all the Gods
were born of Men ; but only that tho' eternal they had a human (not a mortal) Nature ;
or, which is the real Senſe, were of the Shape
and Figure of a Man ; whereas the *Perſians*
thought that Notion fooliſh and abſurd, as indeed it is. The Word ἀνϑρωποφυὴς, *made like
a Man* †, has miſſed the learned Abbé ; and
Inattention

° Je pretens prouver que les Dieux non ſeulement des Grecs,
mais encore des Nations d'ou ils les avoient reçus, ayent été
des Hommes, ſi vous en exceptez les Aſtres, &c

Mythol. Liv. V. Chap. 3.

† That this is the true Meaning of the Word appears from what
Hecatæus ſays of *Moſes* the *Jewiſh* Lawgiver, almoſt in the ſame
Terms with what *Herodotus* ſays of the *Perſians* ; that Ἄξαλμα
μὲν ϑεῶν τὸ σύνολον ὀυ κατεσκεύασε, διὰ τὸ μὴ νομίζειν ᾽ΑΝ-
ΘΡΩΠΟΜΟΡΦΟΝ.

Lett.16. Inattention to what he certainly knew, that even the *Epicureans*, who defined the Deity to be TO AIΩNION KAI TO MAKAPION; the ETERNAL and the BLESSED, yet affirmed he had the moſt beautiful of all Figures, that of *a Man*; for which they are deſervedly ridiculed, not by the Vulgar, who thought ſo too, but by the other Philoſophers, who had founder Sentiments of the divine Nature[p].

YOU ARE not therefore to expect poetical Entertainment from an Author, who writes upon this Plan, nor to have the fair ſide of Mythology ſet in an advantageous Light : Not a word of the Wiſdom of the Ancients, the Depth of their Conceptions, Strength of their Fancies, or Services in civilizing the Savage Tribes of Men. On the contrary, whether from a proper Deference to his Profeſſion, or from ſome other View, he is conſtantly endeavouring to render the ancient Mythology *odious*, and with ſuperfluous Pains confuting ſtrenuouſly what no body now believes. In ſo doing he may by ſome be thought to have acted

ΘΡΩΠΟΜΟΡΦΟΝ ἔιναι τὸν ϑεὸν· ἀλλὰ τὸν περιέχοντα τὴν ϟῆν 'ΟΥΡΑΝΟΝ μόνον ἔιναι ϑέον, χ̀ τῶν ὅλων κύριον. 'ΕΚΑΤΑΙΟΣ ϖαρὰ ΔΙΟΔΟΡ. τὸν Σι. ἐκ τῶν Φωτ.

[p] Habebit igitur Linguam DEUS, et non loquetur : denteis, fauces, palatum nullum ad uſum, quæque procreationis cauſâ natura corpori affinxit, ea fruſtra habebit DEUS ; nec externa magis quam interiora ; cor, pulmones, jecur, cæteraque, detractâ utilitate, quid habent venuſtatis? quandoquidem hæc eſſe in DEO propter pulchritudinem vultis (Épicurei.)

M. T. CICERO De Nat. Deor. Lib. I.

acted decently in his Station, or perhaps wise-ly for a Bishopric; and *thus* I wou'd chuse to understand his general Condemnation of the ancient Fables, and particular Arraignment of their Gods for permitting *Troy* to be sackt without good Reasons, rather than believe that he did not see the Danger of enquiring into the Nature and Attributes of the Deity upon Principles we do not fully comprehend. To judge of the Intentions of Providence by the Events that fall out in the World, Famines, Fires, Wars, Earthquakes, Pestilence or Storm, might lead the unwary into an inextricable Labyrinth. It is only with Assistance of superior Wisdom, that we can fully account for these dismal Shocks, that seem to make Mankind the alternate Sport of the Elements and their own Passions, and wind ourselves out of the Maze of clashing Principles.

But I am likewise apt to imagine that Imitation of a great Pattern whom he often quotes, has contributed to give this Turn to the Abbé's Pen; a Prelate of vast Parts, learned, eloquent, artful, and aspiring. By these Qualities he rose to the first Dignities of the *Gallican*-Church; while another of a finer Fancy and better Heart, humble, holy, and sincere, was censur'd at *Rome*, and disgraced at the *French* Court. Both were entrusted with the Education of *Princes*; and acquitted themselves of
their

Lett.16. their Duty in a very different manner. The one endeavoured to make his royal Pupil noble, virtuous and juft, a Father to his People and a Friend to Mankind, by the Maxims of the inimitable TELEMAQUE: the other, in his *Difcourfes upon univerfal Hiftory*, is perpetually turning his Prince's Eyes from Mankind to the CHURCH, as the facred Object of his Care, ' from whofe everlafting Stem who-
' ever feparates is loft, and for whofe Interefts,
' in the Extirpation of Herefy, and Aggrandize-
' ment of her Minifters, he is, like his Father
' *Lewis* XIV. to exert all the Power he has re-
' ceived from God ^q.' The one has employ'd the Charms of Mythology to make Virtue appear amiable to an afpiring Youth: the other employs his Eloquence in railing at it, and abufing thofe who ufe it. He can fcarce fpeak with Patience of the ancient Fables, or hear of an Allegory to explain them.

' The filthy Hiftories, fays he, of the Gods,
' their infamous Genealogies, their lafcivious
' Loves, their Feafts, their Myfteries, were all
' allegorized: It was the World or the Sun
' that was underftood to be the one fupreme
' God. It was the Stars, the Elements, Fire,
' Air,

---

^q Etudiez, MONSEIGNFUR, cette fuite de l' *Eglife:* ——
Employez toutes vos Forces a rappeller dans cette unité tout ce qui s'en eft dévoyé, et à faire écouter l' *Eglife :*——Recommandez à vos Défcendans l' *Eglife*, plus encore que ce grand Empire de vos Ancêtres.

Difc. fur l' Hift. Univer. Part. II. §. XII.

' Air, Water, Earth, and their various Com-Lett.16.
' binations that lurked under the Names of
' the different Gods, and Tales of their A-
' mours. Wretched and weak Refuge! For
' the Fables were ſcandalous, and all the Al-
' legories pitiful and forced.' No doubt ſome
of them were: But were they *all* ſo, M.
Boſſuet? You have need of clear Proof of your
Aſſertion: For ſo did not *Orpheus* think, nor
Pythagoras, nor *Plato*, nor *Zeno*, nor *Chryſip-
pus*, nor the Fathers of Learning who invented
Fables, nor the Reſtorers of it who explained
them, nor even *Origen* the Champion of our
Religion ʳ : Nay, nor you yourſelf when left to
your own quick Perceptions, and leſs intent upon
an unneceſſary Refutation of Idolatry. Nature is ſtubborn, and Truth is powerful : For
this ſame learned Prelate in the Sequel of this
very Diſcourſe, when his Zeal we may ſuppoſe was a little cooled, ſtruck with the Juſtneſs and Elegance of theſe individual Allegories of the Gods, has himſelf explained ſome
of them with great Beauty and Acuteneſs.

' O N E of the things, ſays he, that ſo
' much recommended *Homer*'s Poetry, was
' that

ʳ Τὰ ΛΙΝΟΥ, κ̀ ΜΟΥΣΑΙΟΥ κ̀ ΟΡΦΕΩΣ ποιή-
ματα, κ̀ ἡ ΦΕΡΕΚΥΔΟΥ γραφὴ· ―― τὸ μὲν τάγμα
τέ]ων τῶν σϳγϛαφέων ὀλίγον μὲν ἐφρόντισε τῶν αὐτόθεν
ἐντευξομένων· μόνοις δὲ ἄρα τοῖς τροπολογῆσαι κ̀ ἀλληϛορῆσαι
δυναμένοις ἔγϛαψε ἐκϛ-Θ τὴν ἰδίαν φιλοσοφίαν.
Κατὰ ΚΕΛΣΟΝ. βιϛ. α. See below Note v.

Lett.16.' that he fung the Superiority and Victories
' of *Greece* over *Afia*.' This Superiority lies
not in the Conqueſt of that Country by the
Greeks, and the actual Deſtruction of it's Capital: No; it conſiſts, according to the fagacious Biſhop, in the Arrangement and Diviſion of the GODS between the contending Nations. ' On the Side of ASIA was *Venus*, that
' is, Pleaſure, fooliſh Paſſion, and Effeminacy.
' On the Side of GREECE was *Juno*; that is,
' Matron-Gravity and Conjugal-Love; together
' with *Mercury*, Invention and Eloquence, and
' *Jupiter*, or political Wiſdom. On the Side
' of *Afia* was brutal and impetuous *Mars*;
' that is War made with blind Fury: On the
' Side of *Greece*, was *Pallas*; that is Military-
' Diſcipline and Bravery guarded by Judge-
' ment *.'

Naturam expellas Furcâ, tamen ufque recurret.

BUT perhaps theſe Allegories, thus explained, mean only to *pleaſe*; and are recommended
for meer Amuſement. *That*, in *my* opinion,
is enough; but not ſo in the eloquent *Prelate's*. ' The Poets, Parents of Allegory, that
' were in every body's Hands, according to
' *him*, *inſtructed* more than they *entertain'd*:
' The greateſt Conqueror look'd upon HOMER
' as his *Maſter* in the Art of Government.
' *That*

* Diſc. ſur l'Hiſt. Univ. Part III. §. V.

' That mighty Poet taught Men as much to
' Obey, as to Command : For both he, and
' so many other Bards, whose Works are equal-
' ly grave and agreeable, aim at nothing so
' much as to celebrate the *useful Arts of Life :*
' They breathe nothing but the public Good,
' Love of their Country, Social Virtue, and
' that wonderful Civility of Manners we ad-
' mire among the *Grecians :*' Nay, upon these
very Allegories lay the chief Stress of the public
Instruction. ' By *their* means every *Greek*
' came to believe that Understanding and true
' Courage was his natural Character ; and of
' consequence cou'd not bear the Thought of
' being vanquish'd by a *Barbarian* ; which, in
' his Opinion, wou'd have been a Sacrifice of
' Virtue to Effeminacy, of the Mind to the
' Body, and of real Valour to brutal Strength
' depending upon Numbers'.' Strange Effect of
these pitiful, forced Allegories! One wou'd almost
be tempted to think that the injured GENIUS
of ancient Mythology had first stript M. *de
Meaux* of his priestly Prejudice, and then forced
his Pen to make *Amende honorable* for abusing
its Offspring. For this is not all: the same
great Prelate has grievously forgot himself when
he extols the Wisdom of *Egypt,* the Mother-
land of Mythology, and represents the *Egyptians,* it's Foster-Fathers, as kept in the steady

3 Practice

' Ibid.

Lett.16. Practice of Virtue, by a daily Meditation on the Meaning of their fignificant Rites. ' One
' of their fineft Contrivances, he fays, to pre-
' ferve their facred Maxims, was to clothe them
' with certain Ceremonies that imprinted them
' upon People's Minds : Thefe Ceremonies were
' gone about with deep Reflexion ; and the fe-
' rious thoughtful Temper of the Nation pre-
' vented their degenerating into unmeaning
' Forms.'

But were not the Stories of their *Gods* particularly fcandalous ? No : they were particularly
ufeful to nourifh the nobleft Paffion of the human Breaft. ' One of the things, continues
' this ftaunch Churchman, inftilled with the
' greateft Care into the Minds of the *Egyp-*
' *tians,* was a Veneration and Love of their
' Country. EGYPT, they faid, was the Dwel-
' ling of the *Gods,* where they had reigned
·' for Millions of Years; the Mother of Men
' and Animals, which her Plains, impregnated
' by the River, had produced, while the reft
' of Nature was curfed with Barrennefs. The
' Priefts who compofed their Chronicles, com-
' prehending innumerable Ages, *filled them*
' *with Fables and Genealogies of their Gods,*
' *only to imprint the Antiquity and Pre-emi-*
' *nence of their Country upon the Minds of*
' *the People* ".'

BE

* Ibid. §. III.

B E it fo, M. *de Meaux!* They anfwered a Lett. 16. noble End in fo doing: But it was not folely for that Purpofe thefe Fables and Genealogies were either invented in *Egypt*, or propagated over the *Eaft.* They were full of higher In-ftruction, conveyed plainly to the Wife, tho' veiled from the Vulgar. Of which I will pro-duce one unexceptionable Witnefs, as free from Sufpicion of Prejudice in their favour, as you were of practifing the *Maxims of the Saints* *, when you were perfecuting their Author. ' In ' *Egypt*, fays the moft learned of the Fathers, ' the Priefts have a fecret Philofophy concern-' ing the Religion by Law eftablifhed, con-' tained in their national Scriptures ; while the ' common People only hear certain Fables ' whofe Meaning they do not underftand. ' Were any one to hear thefe Fables from a ' *private Man*, and imagine he underftood ' them without converfing with any *Prieft*, ' or learning from one of *that* Order the *Egyp-* ' *tian fecret Doctrine*, he wou'd be extremely ' ridiculous. What I have faid of the Learned ' and Illiterate among the *Egyptians*, may be ' likewife faid of the *Perfians*, who have fo-' lemn Rites performed by the Wife-Men (*Ma-* ' *gi*) with Knowlege of their Reafons and In-' ftitution ; while the fuperficial Multitude con-' tent themfelves with the meer outward Rite

P ' or

---

* A Treatife writ by M. *de Fenelon*, and made the Pretence of profecuting him.

Lett.16.' or infignificant Symbol: And the fame holds
' true of the *Syrians* and *Indians*, and of all the
' Nations, that have Fables and Scriptures ˅.'

THE Teſtimony is clear and deciſive: With
it I leave M. *Boſſuet*; who might have
diſplay'd his great Learning and magiſterial
Eloquence without Animadverſion, had he
more regarded Truth, and the injured Merit of
the greateſt Modern that has done Honour
to Mythology. It is not eaſy to aſcertain what
ſhou'd make ſome warm Eccleſiaſtics (for the
wiſer are far above ſuch Weakneſs) ſo angry at the
Allegories of the ancient Poets, *now* when all
danger from their Deities is over. Of old indeed, when Temples and Revenues belonged
to them; when the Wealth and Dignities of
the Church were annexed to the allegorical
Devotion, and veſted in its Teachers, no wonder the good Fathers ſhould fulminate againſt
the wild and impious Worſhip: But *now*, when
the Struggle is long ſince over, when the Father of Gods and Men has not had ſo much
as a Lamb offered, nor his Daughter a ſingle
Grain of Incenſe burnt upon any Altar for near
a thouſand Years, it is hard to tell what ſhou'd
awake their prepoſterous Zeal, or make them
ſo eager to mortalize the Emblems of Antiquity. Is there not, as I was hinting, ſome
Infection

˅ Τὸ δ' αὐτὸ κ̀ περὶ Σύρων, κ̀ Ἰνδῶν, κ̀ πάντων, ὅσοι
κ̀ ΜΥΘΟΥΣ κ̀ ΓΡΑΜΜΑΤΑ ἔχυσι, λεκτέον.

Κατὰ ΚΕΛΣ. βιϐ. α.

Infection in the Cafe? Some fecret Operation like *Plato*'s Loadftone ʷ, that communicates it's Virtue from the primary Paffion through many inferior Links, (Iron-Rings all hanging by this original Magnet :) Thefe Rings fucceffively ope- rating in the Votaries of *Apollo*, were Poets, Players, Rhapfodifts, and all the Retinue of the Mufes down to the loweft Link, the affect- ed Spectator, where Enthufiafm ftopt. In the fame manner, has not the reading the flaming Invectives ˣ of the primitive Fathers who were actually in the Struggle, a little infected their Followers with the fame fiery Spirit and inde- cent Language ʸ? *Eufebius* cannot endure to hear that the old Theology fhou'd be appli- cable to the Powers of Nature, or capable of Allegory and a latent Meaning; but will needs

P 2

have

ʷ ΙΩΝ, ἢ περὶ Ἰλιάδ⊙.

ˣ Τὸν σὸν Μισοπώγωνα, εἴτ᾽ οὖν Ἀντιοχικὸν—τότε μὲν ἡ πορφυρὶς μέλαν ἐποίει, κỳ οἱ πάνΊα τὰ σὰ θαυμάζονΊες κόλακες· νῦν δὲ πώγων ἐςὶ περιφθειρόμεν⊙, κỳ περι- συρόμεν⊙, κỳ τοῖς συμπεπΊωνηκόσιν ὁμῦ γελώμεν⊙.

ΓΡΗΓ. Ναζ. κατὰ Ιουλ. 6ασ. ϛηλιτευτ. β.

ʸ Thefe polite, thefe civilized, thefe philofophical Nations deified the worft of Things, and the worft of Men ; and re- plenifh'd Heaven with fuch a Rout of Deities, as made it look more like a Jail full of Rogues and Villains than an Habita- tion of the Gods.——For when all is done, they were nei- ther better nor worfe than mortal Men. *Saturn* and *Jupiter* were known Tyrants in *Crete*, *Apollo* a common Fidler, the *Mufes* Servant-Maids, *Efculapius* a Tooth-drawer in *Arcadia*, *Venus* a known Strumpet to *Cinyras* King of *Cyprus* not long be- fore the *Trojan* War. Thefe, and like thefe, were the Gods they worfhipped. Dr. PARKER's Demonft. Part II. §. 39.

ᶻ ΣΤηλιτ. α.

Lett.16. have its Authors to have meant it grofsly and literally of Gods, as underftood and believed by the Vulgar. He is fo full of this, that he finifhes the firft and begins the fecond Book of his *Gofpel-Preparative* with affuring us, ' That thefe Theologies of the *Phenicians* and *Egyptians* were no *Fables*, nor poetical Fictions concealing a different Senfe : But the Record or Teftimony, as *they* wou'd fay, of profound and pious Divines, containing a Doctrine older than all the Poets and Hiftorians, to the Truth of which the Names and Notions of the Gods yet received over all the Towns and Villages of *Phenicia*, bear witnefs, and the Myfteries yearly performed in each : That this is plain both from other Writers, and particularly from the Confeffion of the moft approved Theologues ; ' that the firft and oldeft Sages, Authors of ' the Doctrine concerning the Gods, had no ' Eye to *Nature* in their Compofitions, nor ' allegorized the Tales concerning them ; but ' reftricted their Meaning to the Letter of ' the Narration.'— So that, he concludes, we need not go in queft of ftrained Applications to Nature, of which the Facts themfelves afford a plain Confutation.

ANOTHER Father of a clearer Head, tho' warmer Heart, goes not quite fo far ; he feems to allow a little unwillingly, the firft Fables to have had Allegories ; but fays, moft juftly as

' to

to the later *Grecians*, that the Doctrine they Lett.16.
contain'd was unfixed and variable. ' Let an-
' cient *Orpheus*, says he ironically, present him-
' self before a solemn Assembly with his en-
' chanting Song and harmonious Lyre, that
' drew Woods and Wild Beasts after it: Let
' him invoke his *Jupiter* in the wondrous
' Words and transcendant Conceptions of his
' Theology :

Most great, most glorious Jove! *tho' wrapt in
Dung,
Of Horses, Sheep and Mules* —— *

' Then let him consider their marvelous and
' allegorical Meanings ; and let his Doctrine,
' quitting these Portents, bewilder itself among
' the Depths and Precipices of a vague Theo-
' ry ² :' which last Stroke, by the by, I believe was meant as a Hit at *Porphyry* and
Jamblichus, the then Patrons and Props of the
new-modelled Mythology ª.

WITH better Sense St. AUSTIN, after ex-
posing the Absurdity of their Worship, starts
the Objection ; that these same Rites have natural Allegories ; that is to say, they are Explications of the Laws of Nature, by which

P 3   the

---

* See above p. 173.
² ΣΤΗΛΙΤ. α.
ª ῎Ουτ῀ ὁ λόγ῀ σὸι τῶν Πορφυρίε ψευσμάτων κὶ ληρη-
μάτων (ἀντιτάτ]εϑω) οἷς ὑμεῖς ὡς ϑείαις Φωναῖς ἀϳάλλεϑε.
᾿Αυτοϑ. β.

Lett.16.the World was created at firſt, and by which
it ſtills ſubſiſts: ' As if, ſays he, natural Al-
' legories were the Matter in queſtion, and not
' divine Truth; or that we were diſputing what
' were the Rules of Nature, and not what was
' the Rule of God!' This is touching the Point:
For how properly he diſtinguiſhes between the
Laws of Nature and the Will of its Author, otherwiſe than between Cauſe and Effect, is not to our
preſent purpoſe; but the Diſtinction between
them as *Objects of Worſhip* is highly perti-
nent; and at the ſame time that it decides the
Queſtion between him and his then Adver-
ſaries, it leaves the ancient Sages in full Poſſeſ-
ſion of their Allegory.

But why then does both he and the greater
part of the Fathers favour the morralizing Scheme
introduced by *Eubemerus*; that all the Gods of
the Ancients were once Men? For two Reaſons: Firſt it was a cheap and ready Method
of Confutation, that rid them of all the Gods
at once, like *L****'s ſhorteſt Way with the
Diſſenters:* Next it was the moſt *odious* Light
in which they cou'd repreſent them. All the
Ancients believed that dead Bodies were *impure,* and that whatever touched them was
polluted and unholy until it underwent a
proper Purification. This gave them a kind of
Horror at whatever had a relation to a Corps,
and made them ſhrink with Averſion from
Sepulchres and Places of Burial, which they
called

called *Sacred*[b] in the firſt and worſt meaning of the Word. The moſt hideous Form
therefore in which the ancient Temples cou'd
be dreſs'd up, was to repreſent them as Tombs;
and make the Worſhip performed in them paſs
for *funereal Rites* to the Carcaſſes of departed
Mortals. To prove this, *Clemens* of *Alexandria* has made a large Compilation in his Miſ-
cellanies[c] tranſcribed entire by *Euſebius*, and
often referred to by the other Fathers: And
as the Aſſertion was true *in part*, and that moſt
People had neither Learning nor Leiſure enough
to make the grand Diſtinction †, it came
to be generally admitted as true *in whole*. The
ſucceeding Fathers took it upon the word of
their Predeceſſors, and tranſmitted it to the
Monks, who faithfully handed it down to later
Times[d]. Under this Prepoſſeſſion many learned
Moderns have gone upon various Scents in queſt
of the human Origin of the ancient Gods.
Their ſeveral Attempts reſemble the different
Syſtems of Philoſophy contrived to account for

P 4   the

[b] —— Inteſtabilis et *ſacer* eſto.   Horat.
[c] Περὶ τȣ̃ νεκρᾶν ἔιναι τάφȣς τὰ καλȣμένα ἀυτῶν ἱερὰ
τῶν Θεῶν.

ΚΛΗΜ. ΣΤΡΩΜ.

† See Aristotle, above p. 180.
[d] Por feitos immortais e ſoberanos
No Mundo, a os Varões esforço e arte
Divinos os fizeram, ſendo humanos:
Que *Jupiter, Mercurio, Febo,* e *Marte,*
Eneas, e *Quirino,* e os dous *Thebanos,*
Ceres, Palas, e *Juno* com *Diana,*
Todos foram de fraca carne humana.

Lusiad. Cant. IX.

Lett. 16. the Phænomena of Nature. The Authors of these Syftems are commonly fo full and fond of one Principle of their own Invention, or at leaft of their own Applying, that by *it's* fole means they muft needs explain the Structure, and unravel the Myfteries of the Creation. This *Gilbert* attempted by *Magnetifm*, Dr. *More* by his *hylarchic* or Matter-ruling Genius, and M. *des Cartes* by *Matter* and *Motion.*

In the very fame manner, the excellent Abbé *Pluche*, whofe Works I read with real delight, reduces the whole Gods of Antiquity to certain Statues or emblematical Figures fet up in public Places in *Egypt* by way of Almanach, to warn the People of Seed-time and Harveft, or like Heralds to proclaim Peace and War : Our learned and unwearied Traveller Dr. *P****, circumfcribes them to a few of the firft *egyptian* Kings : The Abbé *Banier* to real hiftorical Perfons, or dead Men deified ; and the greater part, *Voffius, Bochart, Huet*, and of late M. *Fourmont*, will have the Gods to be *Scripture Worthies*, and their Legends to be *hebrew Tales* mifunderftood.

But Mythology is a vaft and various Compound ; a Labyrinth thro' whofe Windings no *one* Thread can conduct us ; ' fince all ' the Powers of Heaven and Earth, whatever is, ' whatever acts, whatever changes, whatever re- ' mains the fame, is by fome congruent Image

' to

' to its peculiar Nature, varioufly painted in this Lett.16.
' mimic Mirror of the Univerfe.' The primary
great Gods reprefent its principal Parts and
Powers, the numerous *inferior* Train exhibit
either the under-parts of the World and their
Influences, or they belong to human Paffions
and human Tranfactions as connected with them:
The reft are *Men* adopted into the number
of Gods, and frequently *blended* with the
original Deities.—To imagine all *thefe* can be
reduced to *one* Clafs, and their infinite Relations, Explications, Applications and Mifappli-
cations, through fucceeding Ages of different
Tafte, and diftant Nations of different Manners, can be traced and laid open by any *one*
however ingenious Syftem, is believing an Im-
poffibility. It is like feeking a full View of
the World with the Light of a Taper; and an
Attempt to fubject the Vagaries of heated Fancy
on fuch Subjects as Religion and Philofophy to
a fimple Uniformity. It may fhew great A-
cutenefs, and greater Learning, as indeed it has
done; but turns out at beft a pretty ingenious
Hypothefis, like *Des Cartes' Vortices* or *Epicurus' Atoms*; a Fiction in the main with fome
mixture of Truth.

' THE finding all the Gods of the Ancients,
' fays a learned Antiquary, to be *Jewifh Pa-*
' *triarchs*, feems unfupported by every thing,
' but a pious Intention of doing honour to the
' Bible.

Lett.16. ' Bible. For by what we can collect from
﹏﹏﹏﹏ ' *Pagan,* or even *Jewish* Antiquity, the Hiſtory
' of *that* People was leſs celebrated or known
' than of any People whatſoever : But known
' or unknown, continues the ſame Author, it
' is ſomewhat hard, methinks, that they will
' not allow *Greece* the honour of producing
' one ſingle *Hero* ; but that they muſt all be
' fetched from *Paleſtine.* One wou'd have
' thought the Number of the *Pagan*-Worthies,
' and the *Paucity* of the *Jewiſh,* might have
' induced our Critics to afford *thoſe* ſome home-
' ſpun Heroes of a ſecond rate at leaſt : But
' this, it ſeems, would look ſo like a ſacrile-
' gious Compromiſe, that an *Expedient* is con-
' trived to leſſen this Diſparity of Numbers ;
' and MOSES alone is found to be *Apollo, Pan,*
' *Priapus, Cecrops, Minos, Orpheus, Amphion,*
' *Tireſias, Janus, Evander,* and *Romulus,* and
' about ſome twenty more of the *Pagan* Gods
' and Heroes. So ſays the learned and *judici-*
' *ous* Mr. HUET, who not content to ſeize
' all he meets with as lawful prize within
' the Waſte of *fabulous* Times, makes cruel
' Inroads into the cultivated Ages of *Hiſtory,*
' and will ſcarce allow *Rome* to have its own
' Founder. Nay ſo jealous are they of this
' fairy Honour paid to the Scripture, that I
' have met with thoſe who thought it much
' incroached on, if we ſhou'd believe there

3   ' was

' was any other Origin of *Human-Sacrifice,* Lett. 16.
' than the Command to *Abraham* to offer up
' his Son. This contending for fo extraordi-
' nary an Invention puts one in mind of thofe
' Grammarians who from a due Regard to the
' Glory of ancient Times, will not admit either
' the Great or Small Pox to be modern Difcove-
' ries, but vindicate thofe ineftimable Bleffings to
' all-knowing Antiquity *.'

A PREJUDICE therefore derived from the *Fathers,* and a pious Defire to put honour upon the *Jews* have led many Men aftray. Mif-guided by thefe, they have taken a flippery Road where *Refemblances* are miftaken for *Proofs,* of the God and Mortal's being one and the fame Perfon. A Road full of Mazes, and frequented by Phantoms that promife to direct, and then deceive you. Many great Men, whofe Names I truly honour, have wildly wan-dered in it, in fpite of the wideft Literature, and found, or *imagined* Refemblances, in vir-tue of which they concluded the moft different Perfons to be the fame Individual. An Ex-ample will better convince you of the Fallacy of this way of reafoning; and in that very In-ftance where they think themfelves leaft obnoxi-ous to Delufion, I mean the Identity of the *Jewifh Lawgiver* with the *God of Wine.* The chief

---

* DIVINE LEGAT. Book II.

Lett.16. chief Points of Refemblance, collected with infinite Pains and Pomp of Learning, are thefe.

I. BACCHUS was born in *Egypt*, put into
a Rufh-Bafket, and committed to the River:
So was MOSES. II. *Bacchus* had two Mothers, and was very comely: So had *Mofes.*
III. *Bacchus* was bred in *Arabia*, from whence
he iffued and led wondering Nations after him
by miraculous Feats: So did *Mofes.* IV. *Bacchus* was a Legiflator, and had a two-fold Law
engraved upon two Plates * : So had *Mofes.*
V. *Bacchus* is painted with Horns, and always
accompanied with a Dog: So is *Mofes* ᶠ. VI.
In fine *Bacchus* and the *Bacchants* handled
Snakes unhurt, brought Streams with a Stroke
of their *Thyrfe* from the Rock, made Fountains flow with Wine and Milk, and Honey
diftill under their Steps: So did *Mofes* in every
point.

Now to fhew how ticklifh it is to truft
to thefe Co-incidencies, let us fuppofe that
we had known the Hiftory of *Romulus* the
Founder of *Rome* with no more Certainty (as
it is not with much) than we do the Conqueror
of the *Eaft*'s; that we had only a fcattered
Tradition about him equally vague with the
myftic Hints about the *Nyfean* God. In that
Cafe, what fhould hinder fome fagacious Sage
to

* ΔΙΠΛΑΚΑ ΘΕΣΜΟΝ.
ᶠ *Kaleb* in *Hebrew* and *Kalb* or *Kelb* in *Arabic* fignify a
Dog, the Name of *Mofes*'s chief Favorite.

to affirm, that *Romulus* and *Moses* are one and
the fame Perſon.   For I. ROMULUS at his Birth
was expoſed in the River for fear of a great
King: So was MOSES.   II. *Romulus* was ſpa-
red by the Water, and moſt fortunately preſerved : So was *Moſes*.   III. *Romulus* was educated as a Shepherd, and kept his ſuppoſed Father's Flocks : So did *Moſes*.   IV. *Romulus* de-
feated and killed the King who had cauſed
him to be expoſed : So did *Moſes*.   V. *Romulus* led forth Tribes to new Seats, was a Lawgiver and Founder of a State : So was *Moſes*.
VI. *Romulus* introduced a Senate or Court of
Elders into his new Polity: So did *Moſes*.
VII. *Romulus* was both King and Prieſt; and
had a Brother more prieſtly than himſelf:
So was *Moſes*, and had a Brother the ſame.
VIII. *Romulus* conquered Kings, and with
Hands lifted up to Heaven, averted a Defeat,
and obtained a Victory : So did *Moſes*.   IX.
In fine, *Romulus* diſappeared from among Men,
prone to worſhip him as a God, the manner
of his Death, and Place of his Burial being
equally unknown : So did *Moſes* in every point.
If therefore the ſimilar Circumſtances of their
Fortune and Atchievements prove *Moſes* and
Bacchus to be the ſame Perſon, much more
muſt the ſame ſort of Evidence prove *Moſes*
to be *Romulus*; and then, by the grand Rule
of Reaſoning, *Bacchus*, *Moſes* and *Romulus*
muſt

Lett.16. muſt neceſſarily identify, and the *Italian* and *Arab* (if *Bacchus* be a Mortal) muſt be loſt in the *Jew*.

THE Limits of Truth and Falſhood are not always eaſily fixed : But eſpecially in *mythical* Matters, their Barrier at this Diſtance of Time, is often like *Mahomet's* Bridge [s] ; finer than a Hair, ſharper than the Edge of a Sword, and ſo beſet with Briars and barbed Thorns on each ſide, that to paſs it without ſupernatural Aſſiſtance is next to impoſſible. What clearer Evidence of this than the Variety and Contra-riety of the claſhing Syſtems ? While ſome will have all the Gods of Antiquity to have been *Egyptian* SIGN-POSTS [h] ; others *Egyptian* KINGS [i] ; others *Theſſalian* PRINCES [k] ; others *Jewiſh* PATRIARCHS [l] ; others KINGS of the ſeveral Countries where they were worſhip'd, or the COUNTRIES themſelves [m]. But if you deſcend from the general Syſtem to Particu-lars, even thoſe who agree in the main dif-fer widely in the detail. Of thoſe, for in-ſtance, who transform the Heathen Gods into *Jews*, ſays one, *Saturn* is *Adam*, *Rhea* and *Atê* is *Eve*, *Jupiter* is *Cain*, *Prometheus A-bel*, *Lamech Apollo*, *Jabal* is *Mercury*, *Noë-ma Venus*, *Bacchus Noah*, *Janus Noah*, and *Phaëton*

----

[s] *Al Sirât*, in *Arabic*, the Paſſage over Hell to Paradiſe.
[h] M. l' Abbé *Pluche*.   [i] Dr. P * * *   [k] M. *le Clerc*.
[l] *Voſſius*, &c.   [m] M. *Bianchini*.

Phaëton Elias in his fiery Char[n]. No, says
another, *Saturn* is *Noah*, *Sem* is *Pluto*, *Cham*
Jupiter, *Japhet Neptune*, *Nimrod Bacchus*,
and *Phut Apollo*[o]. No, says a Scholar of the
former, *Saturn*, *Jupiter*, *Pluto*, *Neptune*, *Bac-*
chus, *Mercury* and the whole Train of the
Gods center in *Moses* alone, and all the Goddesses in *Zipporah* his Wife, or *Miriam* his
Sister[p]. No, no, you are all wrong, says another, happy in a Discovery hid from the Critics, for three thousand Years, CELUS or the
Heaven is *Terah*, *Saturn* is *Abraham*, *Rhea*
Sarah, *Keturah Ceres*, *Hagar Pallas*, *Isaac*
Jupiter, *Rebecca Juno*, *Ishmael Pluto*, the
good *Jacob* the Giant *Typhon*, *Leah* is *Dione*,
Rachel Venus; their Maid *Zilpah* is a younger
Rhea, and *Bilha* one of the *Fates : Diana*
was their *Family-midwife*; and their *Nurses*,
Bed-makers, *Chamber-maids*, *Dressers*, &c.
made the *Artemides* or Nymphs of *Diana*'s
Train[q].—— Such is the Evidence that results
from imaginary Resemblances between real
and fictitious Persons; and upon such Evidence,
supported by equivocal Allusions and tortured
Etymologies, have the plainest Allegories been
rejected, and emblematical Gods metamor-
phosed into the Chiefs of a vagrant Tribe,
and the Implements of their Seraglio.

BUT

[n] *Kircher, Vossius,* &c.   [o] *M. Bochart.*
[p] *M. Huet.*   [q] *M. Fourmont.*

Lett.16.   But if contrariwise you pretend to argue, not from a *Resemblance* between *Persons*, real or fictitious; but to fix a Person from the *Circumstances of a Fable*, your Footing is still more slippery.   Mythology is not only a perfect *Proteus* herself, but communicates a transforming Virtue to all she touches; for that Person human or divine is not so real, whom with two or three Epithets muttered like Charms, and a small Variation of his Pedigree, she can not change into a Shadow.   What Person more real than *Samson*, or whose Feats of Strength are to be more literally understood ? Yet he and they are allegorized away by a very learned Man into the Subtleties of the Sceptical Philosophy.   As *Atlas* and *Hercules* of old, because of their celestial Science were said to support the Heaven on their Shoulders, in the same manner, says he, the bodily Strength attributed to *Samson*, is to be understood *figuratively* of the Powers of his Mind, whose superior Penetration convinced him of the Incertainty of all things, and made him a *Sceptical Hero*.   His first Exploit was to kill the Lion, in whose Mouth he found delicious Nourishment.   The presumptuous *Dogmatist* is the Lion, out of whose Mouth he draws Arguments to confound him, and nourish himself in his own *Scepticism*.   *Samson's* Foxes set on fire the Corns of the *Philistins*.   The

Causes

Caufes of Doubt collected by the Sceptic, and tied together in one Chain of Argument, burn up and lay wafte the Sciences, the Growth and Produce of the dogmatic Philofophers. *Samfon* carries off the *Gates* of their Town and fets them upon a Hill. The *Senfes*, the Inlets or Gates of Knowledge are fhewn by the Sceptic to be fo evidently fallacious, that it turns to a Demonftration expofed to public View. The dogmatical *Philiftins* feize this flippery *Samfon* at laft, fhear off his Speculations the Produce of his Head, where his great Strength lay; and tye him with their mighty infurmountable Argument, ' That if there be nothing certain, then the Foundation of Scepticifm is incertain likewife: So that he muft either chufe to perifh himfelf, or allow that Propofition to be certain, *that there is nothing certain*.' He chufes the former, includes his own fundamental Maxim in the general Doubt, and to be avenged for his two Eyes, involves himfelf and his Enemies in the fame inevitable Ruin. But the prime Hieroglyphic in all his Story and the moft pat for our Purpofe is the *Jaw-bone of an Afs* with which he gave his Enemies fuch a notable Overthrow: With this natural Emblem of *Ignorance* and *Inconcern* he laid the bold Afferters of Infallibility by hundreds at his feet. He confounded the Pride of the felf-fufficient Sophifts; fhew'd them they were but Affes; and weary with

Q   difputing,

Lett. 16. difputing, he drank fweetly of the Stream of Contentment that flows from a due Senfe of our own Incapacity, and delivers us from the vain Purfuits and endlefs Difappointments that attend prefumptuous Searches, and mock our Attempts to know beyond our mortal Nature and finite Capacity [i].

LET me now fet before you another Allegory; the Explication of a Fable contrived by the Devil, fays a Man of immenfe Learning, in order to expofe a Prophecy before its Accomplifhment. It is the Story of SILE-NUS, the Tutor and Companion of *Bacchus*; whofe Name he derives from *Shil*, or *Silan*, in the fame manner as from *Shir* a Song the *Phenicians* derived their *Shiran*, and the *Greeks* their *Syrens*. ' It is faid of *Shilo*, that to him ' *fhall the People be gathered for Inftruction*, ' and therefore *Silenus* is extremely learned, ' the Preceptor of the young *Bacchus*, and ' in *Virgil* fings of the Rife of Things, from ' *Chaos*, and the Formation of the World, ' which is a real *Cofmogony. Shilo* is repre- ' fented as *tying his Foal to the Vine, and* ' *to the choice Vine the Colt of an Afs. Si-* ' *lenus* is always lolling upon his broad backed ' Afs, (*patulo ut femper Afello*) and an infe- ' parable Companion of the God of the Vine. ' *Shilo* is to *wafh his Robes in Wine, and his* ' *Garment in the Blood of the Grape*, like
those

[i] LA MOTHE LE VAYER. Opufcule Sceptique.

'thofe *who tread in the Wine-Prefs.* To tread Lett. 16.
'the Grapes is the particular Function of *Si-*
'*lenus.* But nothing is fo impious, as that they
'feign him to be always drunk, and his Veins
'diftended with laft Night's Liquor, becaufe
'it is juft fubjoined of *Shilo, his Eyes fhall*
'*be red with Wine.* The Conclufion of the
'Prophecy is, *and his Teeth fhall be white*
'*with Milk* ; and therefore *Silenus*'s Food is
'Cheefe curdled with Fig-Juice, and the Milk
'of a Cow †. The Devil, concludes this great
'Scholar, could not contrive a more ugly Tale,
'to profane the moft holy Myfteries of our
'Religion, and expofe them to the Ridicule
'of wicked Men [k].

BUT now fee how the Tables turn! The
Devil, according to another eminent Author,
had not the leaft hand in the matter; but as
he will needs have *Abraham* to be *Saturn,*
Ifaac Jupiter, and *Efau* to be *Bacchus,* and
Ofiris from his dwelling in Mount *Seir* ; fo
he pretends, that *Silenus* can be none other than
Efau's Father-in-Law *Ana,* called likewife the
Seirian (tho' he was a *Hivite*) and that his
Name is a Compound of *Seiri-ana, Sir-enab,*
Silenus.

' BOCHART's *Silenus,* derived from *Schilo,*
' is, he fays, a moft extraordinary thing: It
' is

† Καὶ τυρὸς ὀπίας ἐςὶ, ἡ βόος γάλα.
ΕΥΡΙΠΙΔ. Κύκλωψ.

[k] S. Bocharti CANAAN. Lib. I. Cap. 18.

Lett.16.' is true, the other Circumſtances of that
' Prophecy agree pretty well with the Pre-
' ceptor of *Bacchus*; but what is that but
' explaining one Myſtery by another? The
' whole Detail of *Jacob's* Prediction [1] has
' hitherto been a perfect Riddle, and is ren-
' dered ſtill more ſo by the Zeal of the Com-
' mentators.   What I dare affirm is, that from
' *Schiloh*, whoſe Meaning we know not, M.
' *Bochart* ought not to have deduced the
' Term *Silenus*. *That* God is called *an old*
' *Satyr*; and his Name was anciently pro-
' nounced *Seirênos*.   Now if we recollect that
' the Satyrs of *Bacchus's* Retinue were none
' other than *Eſau's* Troop of *Sēirim, Seirians*,
' then the old *Seirian, Ana*, is the true *Si-*
' *lenus* [m]. This *Ana*, we are told, found *hot*
' *ſprings* in the Deſart while he was feeding
' his Father's Aſſes; or as others read, found
' *Mules* ; and probably made uſe of them in
' his Expeditions with *Eſau* preferably to any
' other Animal, as having been the Inventer
' of their Propagation.   Hence *Silenus* is al-
' ways mounted on his *Aſs*, always accom-
' panies *Bacchus*, and ſchools the God amidſt
' his Conqueſts [n].'   What pity that the fair
Abolibama,

---

[1] Genes. XLIX. ℣. 10.

[m] It is no ſtrained Etymology of Σειλη̄νος from σείω *quatio,*
and λη̄ν℘ *Torcular :* But I believe it really comes from لسان
Silan or *Sailan* Fluxus, Fluxibilitas, and יין *Iaa* Vinum. The
n in *Silan* is only accidental.

[n] M Fourmont, Reflex. Crit. ſur les Hiſt. &c. Liv. II.
Sect. 3. Ch. 14.

Abolibama, *Ana*'s Daughter, and *Esau*'s be-
loved Lady fhou'd not be found to be the
forlorn *Ariadne?* That his Mother *Rebecca*
fhould not be SEMELE inftead of *Juno?* or
his eldeft Son Duke *Eliphaz*, fhou'd not be
Bacchus' firft-born *Staphylus* ᴾ, tho' plainly
meaning a *Grape*; Nature's firft Step in the
Production of Wine.

WHOEVER goes in queft of Similitudes to a
fav'rite Object, will be fure to find, or to imagine
he finds them: neither Learning, nor Ingenuity
can fecure him from Illufion : nay the warmer
his Fancy, the more flippery is his Footing;
and the wider his Views are, without a cool
and mafterly Judgment, they but furnifh more
Phantoms to lead him aftray. The *three States*
which a great Man * had conceived the World
was fucceffively to pafs thro', had fo poffeffed
his Imagination, that he believed them to be
typified by the *Jewifh* Temples. The firft
(*Solomon*'s) reprefented the Earth before the
Flood; the fecond, inferior to the firft, reprefented the prefent fhattered State of the Globe
fince the Difruption of its fine Shell by
the Deluge ; and *Ezechiel*'s Temple, the moft
beautiful of all, is to figure with the new Form,
which this fecond Temple of the World will
affume after the Conflagration. The *Cab-
balifts* have a Notion that the Tabernacle made

Q 3   by

ᴾ Σταφυλὸς.
* Dr. T. BURNET.

Lett.16. by *Moses* was a Model of the Univerſe in mi-
niature; but when they come to explain every
Part, they are as much at a loſs how to adjuſt
them, as the truly learned Doctor muſt have
been to tell, What State of the Earth was repreſented by the *Jewiſh* Temple built under
the later Kings, and deſtroy'd by *Titus Veſpa-
ſian?* Thus you ſee what comes of Attempts
to take Things off their natural Hinge, and
hang them upon our own ingenious Suppoſi-
tions: It proves an untoward Machine, which
neither Learning nor Genius can keep a going.

BUT after wandering thro' ſo many different
Schemes, wou'd you be content to have all
the various Gods of the Ancients ranged, and
ſet before you in one comprehenſive View?
They fall naturally into *three* Claſſes, and
had Worſhippers ſuited to them of *three* different Characters. I. The PARTS and natural
POWERS of the Univerſe, called out of *Chaos*,
ſaid the Poets; formed in *Chaos*, ſaid the Philoſophers †, by an all-wiſe MIND that firſt
regulated and ſtill keeps them in order. II.
GENII, or ſpiritual abſtract Subſtances, ſuppoſed to exiſt in, or preſide over theſe Powers;
and III. HUMAN Creatures deïfied. The
Worſhippers of the *firſt* were the wiſe and knowing

† Δόξειε δ' ἂν κ̀ Ησίοδ῾ ὀρθῶς λέγειν, ϖοιήσας
ϖρῶ]ον τὸ ΧΑΟΣ.——ὡς δέον, ϖρῶτον ὑπάρξαι χώραν τοῖς
οὖσι, διὰ τὸ νομίζειν, ὥσπερ οἱ πολλοὶ, πάν]α ἔιναί τι,
κ̀ ἐν ΤΟΠΩ.   ΑΡΙΣΤΟΤ. Φυσικ. Αχροασ. βιε. Δ.

ing *Few*, who believed in one fupreme God, governing all the fubordinate Powers of the World.
The Worfhippers of the *fecond* were the middle
fort of People, of good Senfe in the Affairs of
Life; but who had no Leifure nor Inclination to
queftion the received Religion. The Worfhippers of the *laft*, and of every thing that had
the Name of a God, were the unthinking Multitude, ftanding in awe of their Statues, and
fwallowing the literal Legend.

PYTHAGORAS taught that GOD, the firft
Caufe, was imperceptible, invifible, incorruptible, and only to be apprehended by the pure
intellectual Faculty of the Soul. The pious
peaceful NUMA forbid the making any Statue
or Image of *God*, after the Likenefs of mortal
Man or other living Creature; it being neither
holy in itfelf to liken the Supreme exalted
Nature to any bafer Being, nor poffible to attain
the Knowlege of God otherwife than by the *Underftanding*. While fome natural Philofophers,
Materialifts, were bungling like *Spinofa*, or
bewildered like *Des Cartes*, in their incoherent
Schemes, ANAXAGORAS brought forth his
divine Principle, *That when all things lay
mingled in one mighty Mafs, a* MIND, *all-
wife and all-powerful, mildly interpofed, feparated the jarring Parts, and reduced them
into order*; and in fo teaching, fays a fevere
Judge, ' *be feem'd like one who fees among the*

' *Blind.*

Lett. 16. ' *Blind* [a].' ANTISTHENES the Parent of the
Cynics affirmed, that *God* cannot be viewed
with our mortal Eye, becaufe he refembles no
vifible Thing; fo that we need not imagine it
poffible to frame any Idea of him from Statues,
Pictures, or any material Reprefentation [b]. XE-
NOPHANES, with his wonted Tartnefs, faid, that
if the Ox or Elephant cou'd carve or paint, they
wou'd certainly reprefent God under the Form
of their own Species, and juft with as good
reafon as *Phidias* and *Polyclete* had imagined
he refembled a Man. Even the pious *Xenophon*,
devout almoft to Superftition, the great Patron
of Sacrifice and Divination, if we may truft a
learned [c] Father, cou'd fay, that tho' we might
well difcover the Immenfity and all-mighty
Power of *God*, as he moved and governed all
Things, being himfelf immovable, yet it is
impoffible to conceive the Form of his Countenance, or know his real Afpect. Nay much
later, and in more bigotted, becaufe more flavifh
Times, the inquifitive ADRIAN ftill prying
into Futurity, and canvaffing all the hidden
Things in Heaven and Earth, built many a
beautiful Temple, with ne'er a Statue or Image
of the Divinity within it, nor e'er a Beaft or
Burnt-Offering allow'd in the Worfhip. A
Song in honour of the God, or Hymn to the
Hero,

[a] ΑΡΙΣΤΟΤ. Μετὰ τ. φ.
[b] Apud *Theodoret. Cyrenenf.*
[c] *Arnob.* adv. *Gentes.*

Hero, folemnly performed on appointed Days, Lett. 16. was all the Oblation he thought cou'd be acceptable to the divine immaterial Nature.

I Should make a long Letter, or rather a Book by itfelf, were I to tell you all that the ancient Sages, or Plato fingly, has faid upon this Subject. I referve the divine Philofopher for fome Opportunity when I can do him more Juftice: Let me conclude this part of the Proof of my Diftribution of the Gods and their Votaries with the Words of his great, and for the honour of Learning, I wifh I cou'd not add, ungrateful Scholar; a Man of the *keeneft* Parts that ever wrote: ' God, fays he, is always
' the Object of Admiration; and the more
' he is viewed, the more marvelous he appears.
' For God is *Life*; as the Action of Mind
' is Life. He is the Source of *Action* and
' *Motion* : and felf-exiftent Action is *his* Life,
' tranfcendent, and eternal. We affirm there-
' fore, that God is the living, everlafting, best
' of Beings; and that Life eternal, and unin-
' terrupted Duration is the peculiar Attribute
' of God, and conftitutes his Godhead [d]. From
thefe Teftimonies I infer, that the wife and knowing *Few* among the Ancients acknowleged *one* all-wife Mind that firft regulated the Parts and Powers of the Univerfe, and ftill keeps them in Order.

But

[d] ΑΡΙΣΤΟΤ. Μ. Τ. ΦΥΣ. β.6. λ.

Lett. 16.　Bu t what will you fay, when for *Examples*,
of the *Middle* fort of People, I produce Men
of no lefs Note than the learned *Varro*, and
contemplative *Plutarch?* I am forry for it;
the Acutenefs of the firft, and Piety of the
laft, might have done honour to greater *Reach:*
but hear the Creed of the former. ‘ As for
‘ my part, fays he, I believe that God is the
‘ Soul of what the *Greeks* call ΚΟΣΜΟΣ, the
‘ Universe; and that the *World* itfelf is God*:
‘ But as a wife Man is fo denominated from
‘ his *Mind,* tho’ he confift of Mind and Body,
‘ in the fame manner the World is called
‘ God from the *Mind* that predomines.　It
‘ is divided into two Parts, *Heaven* and *Earth*;
‘ and Heaven into other two, *Ether* and *Air*;
‘ and the Earth into *Water* and *Land.*　The
‘ higheft of thefe is the Ether, next Air, then
‘ Water, and laftly Earth.　All which four
‘ Parts are full of living Souls; the Ether and
‘ Air of Immortal, the Land and Water of
‘ Mortal.　From the utmoft Circumference of
‘ Heaven to the Orbit of the Moon, inhabit
‘ etherial Minds, *the Hoft of Heaven,* who are
‘ not only underftood, but *feen* to be the cele-
‘ ftial Gods.　Between the Moon’s Orbit and
‘ the Height to which the Winds and Rains
‘ afcend are aerial Beings not to be perceived
‘ by the Eye, but only by the Mind; and
‘ they

* It is the Orphic Doctrine : See ΠΟΙΗΣ. ΦΙΛΟΣΟΦ
publifhed by H. Stephens.

' they are called *Heroes, Lares,* and *Genii* ᶜ.' Lett. 16. This is the Sum of his Creed ; and of a piece ︷ with it is his Syſtem of Divinity.

THERE are, he ſays, three kinds of Theo-logy, or three Methods of treating of the Nature of the Gods: one *mythical,* another *natural,* and a third *political.* They call that mythical which is moſt employ'd by the *Poets*; the natural belongs to the *Philoſophers* ; and the political to the *State.* In the firſt I named, many things are feigned contrary to the Nature and Dignity of the Immortals; ſuch as that one God ſprang from a Head, another from a Thigh, another from Drops of Blood ; here we are told that the Gods ſtole, that they committed Adultery, that they ſerved as Slaves to a mortal Man; and in ſhort, here we find every thing aſcribed to the Gods, which not only a Man, but the vileſt of Mankind cou'd be guilty of. The ſecond I mentioned is the Subject of the Books of the Philoſophers, where you find many Queſtions put about the Gods; as, Who they are ? Where they are ? Of what, and what kind of Race ? Of what Duration? If they be from Eternity? if they ſpring from Fire as *Heraclitus* thought ? if from Numbers as *Pythagoras?* if from Atoms as *Epicurus?* With many other ſuch Diſquiſitions, which our Ears can better bear in private within the Walls of a College, than in public Meetings abroad.
The

ᶜ Apud *Auguſtin.* de Civ. Dei. Lib. VII. Cap. 6.

Lett. 16. The third fort of Theology properly belongs
to the Members of a State, and fhou'd be
known and exercifed efpecially by the Clergy.
It prefcribes what Gods ought to be publickly
worfhip'd, what Sacrifices it is proper for every
one to offer, and what holy Rites to perform.
The firft Theology is chiefly adapted to the
Stage; the fecond to the World; and the third
to the State[f]. That is to fay, that *M. Varro*
thought the chief Ufe of Mythology was *Di-
verfion*; that the Books of the Priefts were
calculated for *Policy*, and the real Nature of
the Gods was given, as *Solomon* fays of the
World, for Men to *reafon on*. How far he
carried his own Enquiries you have already
feen; and fhall now fee that the good *Plutarch*
did not carry his much farther.

In his Treatife *of reading the Poets*, he is
very careful to make a Youth diftinguifh when
the *Name* of a God means directly the *divine
Spiritual Subftance*, or is only applied to certain Powers of which the Gods are Authors
or Directors. ' Thus when *Homer* invokes
' *Jove, moft glorious, moft great, fitting on
' high, and governing all things*, it is, he fays,
' the GOD himfelf: But when the Poet fuper-
' adds *Jupiter* as the Caufe of all the Mifchief
' that followed upon the fatal Strife between
' *Agamemnon* and *Achilles*——*Done was the
Will*

[f] Ibid. Lib. VI. Cap. 5.

' *Will of Jove* * —— it is no more the God, Lett. 16.
' but FATE. For the Poet does not think
' that *Jupiter*, the moſt beneficent of the
' Gods, contrives Miſchief to Men ; but very
' truly and properly points out the natural
' *neceſſary* Connexion of Things : to wit, that
' Proſperity and Victory is deſtinated to the
' State, to the Camp, to the Commander, who
' is moſt ſober and vigilant : but if abandoned
' to Paſſion, they come, like the diſſolute *Grecian*
' Chiefs, to ſplit and mutiny, Diſorder enſues,
' and a diſmal Exit ˢ.'

BOTH theſe learned Men believed in diſtinct
ſpiritual Subſtances, bearing the Names of *Jupiter* or *Apollo*, or of any particular Deity :
and if a *Varro* and a *Plutarch* did ſo, what
may we conclude of the greater Part of the
Senators of *Rome*, or Stateſmen of *Greece*, who
perhaps never called one of their Gods
in queſtion ; or if they did, had but little
Leiſure for ſuch Speculations. As for the *Vulgar*,
their Credulity in later, as well as ancient
Times, is ſo glaring, that it wou'd be loſing
Labour to exemplify it : But you ſometimes
find among them a ſolemn conceited Dunce,
who at the ſame time that he believes the
literal Legend, how groſs ſoever and palpable

it

* *Plutarch* is favourable to the Poet: *Jove's Will* plainly
relates to the Petition cf *Thetis*, and *Jupiter's* Purpoſe in conſequence of it, to put honour upon *Achilles* by reducing the
Greeks to ſuch diſtreſs as ſhould oblige them to implore his
Aſſiſtance

ˢ Πῶς δεῖ τὸν νέον ποιημάτων ἀκούειν.

Lett.16.it be, thinks himſelf inſpired and a Favourite of Heaven. As a Character of this kind is entertaining in Theory, tho' odious in the Original, I will give it you as drawn by the greateſt moral Painter that ever handled a Pen.

THE *Athenian* EUTHYPHRO was not only a religious, but a prophetical Perſon; and particularly remarkable for a moſt ſcrupulous Conſcience that trampled upon all human Conſiderations of Duty, Conſanguinity and Gratitude, when they ſtood in the ſmalleſt competition with his ſuppoſed Piety. He happened to meet with *Socrates* while the Philoſopher was attending the Court for capital Crimes, ſome time before his Trial; and having heard what he was accuſed of, he condeſcended to encourage him, and made no doubt but he *(Socrates)* wou'd manage his Cauſe with Spirit and Succeſs, as he himſelf hoped to do his own— ' What, ſaid the Sage, have *you* a Trial likewiſe to come on! Pray what may it be —do you proſecute or defend? *Euth.* I am the Proſecutor, *Socrates!* *Soc.* And of whom pray? *Euth.* Of one whoſe Proſecution ſeems as mad to the World, as my Prophecies ſeem wild to the People of *Athens.* *Soc.* Who may that be, *Euthyphro?* *Euth.* My own Father. *Soc.* Your *Father!* good Sir? *Euth.* Yes, my very Father. *Soc.* Well— but what is the Crime? of what do you accuſe him? *Euth.* Of nothing leſs than

Murther

Murther. *Soc.* Heavens! *Euthyphro!* Sure the
greater Part know not how to do things as
they ought to be done; that is not every
body's Talent; but only their's, who like *you*
have been bleſſed with great Attainments in
Piety and Wiſdom.——— *Euth.* Ay, *Socrates*,
with great Attainments indeed! *Soc.* But pray,
give me leave, was it any near Relation that
was killed by your Father?— to be ſure it
was; for you wou'd never proſecute your
Parent for the Death of a meer Stranger.———
Euth. Ridiculous! Why do you imagine, *Socrates*, there is a bit of difference, in a matter
of Bloodſhed, Whether the murthered Perſon
be your Kinſman or not? or that this is not
the ſingle point to be conſidered, Whether the
Man were *juſtly* killed? And if juſtly, to ſay
no more of it; if not, to proſecute the guilty
Perſon, tho' he ſlept with you in the ſame
Bed, and eat at the ſame Table: For the Pol-
lution and Infection of Guilt is the ſame to
you, if you wittingly aſſociate with the Criminal,
without ſanctifying yourſelf and him by a legal
Proſecution of the Crime. The Perſon murthered was a Doer of mine; and Overſeer of
the Ditchers and Labourers at our Farm in
Naxos: he one day got himſelf drunk, and
in his Liquor fell upon one of the Workmen
he had a pique at, and diſpatched him: Where-
upon my Father had him ſeized, and thrown
into ſome Hole or Ditch, bound hand and
foot,

Lett.16. foot, fending a Meffenger hither to *Athens* to take Advice of the Judge of *Criminals*, what was to be done with him. But in the mean time he never minded the Man he had bound; but neglected him as a Murtherer in the Ditch; as if it were no matter whether he perifhed or not; as in fact he did; for Cold, Hunger and Bonds killed him before the Return of the Meffenger. And it is for *this*, *Socrates*, that my Father himfelf and all my Friends are enraged at me, becaufe for the fake of a Murtherer I profecute my Parent who neither killed him, as they are pleafed to fay, nor if he had killed him a thoufand times, as he was guilty of a Murther, fhould any body mind what was done to fuch a Wretch; befides that, it is a horrid thing for a Child to profecute his Father for Murther. Thus they talk; — but little— very little, are they acquainted with God : or in what refpects *he* reckons things *holy* or *impious* in the Actions of Men. *Soc.* And do you then, *Euthyphro*, really imagine that you have fuch infallible Knowlege of the Things of *God*, and can fo affuredly difcern between what is *impious* and what is *holy*, that, the Cafe being as you fay, you have no Perplexity, left you fhould be perhaps doing a wicked thing in a capital Profecution of your own Father — ? *Euth.* No—not the fmalleft : For then my Knowlege wou'd be of little avail — and your Friend *Euthyphro* wou'd

differ

differ nothing from any common Man, unlefs he underftood all thefe things with the utmoft Certainty and Exactnefs. *Soc.* Well then, my dear Friend! Since it muft be fo as you fay, I wifh above all things to become your Scholar, that I may be able to cope with this fame *Melitus* who has accufed me of debauching my young Companions, and inftilling wicked Notions into them about the Gods. For Heaven's fake, therefore, do — tell me what you fay you fo accurately know, and inform me, what it is you call real *Piety*, and what *Impiety?* and inftruct me about Cafes of Murther and fuch other weighty Matters..... But to do this the better, tell me firft, whether Holinefs be one fingle Thing, always confiftent with itfelf, and always the fame in every Action: and *Unholinefs*, if I may ufe the Term, be not always its oppofite, confifting of one individual Quality that renders any Action or Thing *unholy*, that is fo. *Euth.* Why to be fure, *Socrates*, it muft be fo. *Soc.* Well — now tell me precifely what it is you call *holy*, and what *impious?* *Euth.* I call that holy, for example, what I am now doing; the profecuting any Tranfgreffor either for Murther or Sacrilege; or *any* Perfon committing fuch a Crime; be it your Father, be it your Mother, or who it will: and the not profecuting them I fay is unholy and impious. For confider, *Socrates*, and I will give you a ftrong Proof that

R

fuch

Lett.16.fuch muft be the Law of God, as I have already faid to others; and that it muft needs be a juft and righteous Thing to proceed againft the impious, and not to fpare, *whofoever* it be. Do not all Men believe *Jupiter* to be fupremely good, and fupremely juft? And yet all agree that he laid his Father *Saturn* in Fetters, becaufe he devoured his own Children; and that *Saturn* himfelf had even caftrated his old Father *Celus* upon fome fuch account: This every body believes; and yet People blame me for profecuting a guilty Parent, and contradict themfelves in fo doing — while they praife in one what they blame in another, and fay clafhing Things of the *Gods* and *Me*. *Soc.* Why *Euthyphro!* that is the very Reafon, why I wou'd chufe, if poffible, to avoid *Melitus*'s Accufation; becaufe when I hear any body telling or talking fuch ftrange Stories of the Gods, I ufe to give them but a forry Hearing; for which caufe they pretend that I tranfgrefs, and am criminal. . . . But if *You*, my Friend, who to be fure know all thefe Matters fo perfectly, affirm them to be true, we muft e'en yield the Point, and believe along with you. For what cou'd *I* pretend to fay to the contrary, who have fo often confeffed that I know little about them? And therefore in the Name of *friendly Jove*, tell me truly, Do you in your Confcience believe that the Things told of *Jupiter* and *Saturn* and the other Gods really happened, and

were

were in Fact tranſacted as they are litterally Lett. 16.
told? *Euth.* That I do moſt firmly, *Socrates,*
and know and believe ſtill *ſtranger* — more
miraculous Things than theſe, of which the
reſt of Mankind know little or nothing. *Soc.*
And you are perſuaded that there was actually
War in Heaven; —— Enmities, Strifes, and
dreadful Battles among the bleſſed Gods? and
believe thoſe Relations of the Poets and other
pious Writers, in rememb'rance of which our
Worſhip is ſo diverſified with ſignificant Ceremonies; as particularly at our grand Feſtival *,
when *Pallas'* ſacred Robe ᵇ crouded with ſuch
curious Repreſentations is carried in ſolemn
Proceſſion from the Town to her Temple in the
Cittadel: Shall we believe all that to be really
true, *Euthyphro*—? *Euth.* True—Sir! Ay,
and not only all that, but a great deal more;
things that when you hear them, I am ſure
will *aſtoniſh* you, *Socrates*; and which, if you
pleaſe, I will inſtantly rehearſe to you concerning the Tranſactions of the Immortals.
Soc. Why that may be, Sir: But as we are at

R 2   preſent

---

* The PANATHENAIA.

ᵇ It has probably been in imitation of the Robe made by
Jupiter, the Emblem of the Univerſe, deſcribed by the grand
Mythoʹogiſt. ΖΑΣ ϖοιει φαρϟ μεγα τε κ̀ καλον· κ̀
ἐν αὐτῶ ϖοικιλλει Γῆν κ̀ Ὠγενον, κ̀ τὰ τῆ Ὠγένε δώμα-
τα. ΦΕΡΕΚΤΔΗΣ. MINERVA, or *Science*, (ſo her Name
ſignifies) ſprung from the Head of JOVE, contrived the Texture of the Univerſe; and to HER in Sacred Proceſſion is
carried the *Robe* it's *Emblem.* See her Picture drawn more divinely than ever *Grecian* drew it. PROV. VIII. §. 22.

Lett.16.prefent engaged upon another Subject, we will,
if you pleafe, wave the relation of thofe Wonders
until a more proper Opportunity [i].

THIS knowing confcientious Perfon appears
in the Sequel of the Dialogue to know little
of the Duties of Life, and lefs of real Religion:
Things, we muft allow, that are too often feparated; but not by thofe who have any juft
Notion of *Nature*, or of the Wifdom and
Goodnefs of it's *AUTHOR*.

Yours, &c.

ΕΥΘΥΦΡΩΝ, ΠΛΑΤΩΝΟΣ.

LETTER

LETTER SEVENTEENTH.

' 'TIS enough, *my Friend!* I afk no more:
' You are quite fatisfied that the primary
' Gods of the Ancients were intended to re-
' prefent the Origin and Economy of the
' Univerfe: and that the Aim of the early
' Sages might have been to introduce an awful
' fort of Science fit to inftruct the Wife and
' reftrain the Multitude. That this Science
' was artfully convey'd in fuch Images as
' were apteft to ftrike the raweft Fancy, while
' they gave infinite Scope to the moft elevated
' Capacity. That it was no wonder fuch a
' *perfuafive Power*, fhou'd tame Savages,
' polifh Barbarians, and extort a little Attention
' from the wifeft of every Age fince it firft
' exerted it's Influence upon Men.' But, fay
you, has not this enchanting Faculty been made
fubfervient to bad purpofes? Has fhe not patronized the Interefts of Vice, and painted it's
Enormities in lovely tho' lying Colours? She
has, when mifapplied or mifunderftood: but
no more than the other Powers of Poetry,
the Influences of Eloquence, and even of
Religion itfelf. Their Charms have all been
proftituted to ferve the worft of Caufes; to
ridicule Virtue, to undermine Liberty, to banifh
Morality, and vilify their Patrons and Profeffors.

Witnefs

Lett.17.Witneſs the wild Wit of an *Ariſtophanes* [k], the Eloquence of a *Curio* [l] or a *Cleon* [m], the ſeeming Sanctity of moſt Sectaries [n], the Fury of the *League* [o], or ſly Hypocriſy of Father *Girard* [p]. For what good thing is it that has not been ſome way abuſed ? *Mythology* is but an Inſtrument, and may, like a Sword, ſerve the beſt of Ends in defending your Country,

or

[k] The Comedy inſcribed the CLOUDS is an execrable Attempt to expoſe one of the wiſeſt and beſt of Men to the Fury and Contempt of a lewd Multitude, in which it had but too much ſucceſs.

[l] He firſt patronized, and then for an immenſe Bribe, betray'd the Cauſe of Liberty, and proved the chief Incendiary of the Civil War.

[m] A profeſſed Rogue ; eloquent, humorous, and prone to promote bad and depreſs good Men.

[n] I ſhall mention two : *Mazdac,* a *Perſian* Prophet, under *Coſru Cobad,* preached a Community of *all* Things, as the ſole Way to Peace among Men. He had many thouſands of Followers, and among the reſt *Cobad* himſelf ; from whom he obtained a Night of the Queen ; and had certainly taken it, but for *Anuſhirwan* her Son's humble Entreaties ; who, as ſoon as he came to the Throne, cut off *Mazdac* the Impoſtor's Head.
ABUL-FEDA.

About the Year 1125, *Tanchelin* a Fanatique, drew a great Part of *Flanders* after him. He appeared pompouſly dreſſed, in Cloath of Gold, with his Hair in Ringlets, curiouſly intertwiſted with Loopings of the ſame. He gave ſumptuous Entertainments, and aſſumed mighty State. His chief Doctrine was that Chriſt's Obedience had freed us from the Obligation of the Law ; that the Euchariſt was of no avail for Salvation, and that the pretended Miniſtry of Biſhops and Prieſts was an Abuſe in Chriſtianity. His Diſciples were ſo beſotted with him, that they drank his Urine, and took it as a ſingular Favour, that he would abuſe their Wives and Daughters in their Preſence.
MEZERAY.

[o] Under Pretence of preſerving Religion it occaſioned inexpreſſible Miſery : The Aſſaſſination of two Kings, the horrid Maſſacre at *Paris,* and the Deſolation of *France,* were the chief Fruits of the holy League.

[p] A Jeſuit, that firſt ſtupified and then abuſed his Female Penitents : a recent Story.

or Friend in danger; and the worſt by enabling you to murder both. You ſeem to comprehend ſo truly how the Ancients applied it, that I wou'd not mention the Virtues they aſcribed to this myſterious man-taming Science, had not their *Education*, and of conſequence their Way of thinking been ſo different from ours, that their Conceptions give us new Hints, and are delivered in a more genuine manly Language than is compatible with our Manners. But before I mention the various Purpoſes it ſerved, it will not be amiſs to review the general *Source* of the Gods, and conſider the Intent of their moſt ſolemn Ceremonies, as they are deſcribed by the greateſt *Greek* and *Roman* (the Pattern and Copy) whoſe Writings have reached our Times. Lett. 17.

Astronomy and Idolatry, naturally conjoined of old, came hand in hand from the Eaſt. The firſt of Mankind who inhabited *Greece*, ſeem to me, ſays Plato, to have had no other Gods than thoſe worſhipped by many of the Barbarous Nations at this day; the *Sun* and the *Moon*; the *Earth* and the *Stars* of Heaven[q]; inſomuch, that they had not at firſt Names, not even for the Seven Planets. The Reaſon of this is, that the firſt who obſerved their Courſe, was not a *Greek* but a *Barbarian*. For it was in Countries bleſt with fair Weather and fine Summers,

[q] ΚΡΑΤΥΛΟΣ.

Lett.17. fuch as *Egypt* and *Syria*, that are remarkably
fo, where we find the firft Obfervers of the
Heavens. Their Inhabitants, feeing the whole
Chorus of the Firmament at once, and
always bright, as living in Parts of the World
far remov'd from Rain and Clouds, have tranf-
mitted to us, and difperfed over all, Obfervations of the Heavenly Bodies, verified by
the Experience of ten thoufand Years or upwards[r]. Where by the Inhabitants of *Syria*
the Philofopher points at the *Chaldeans*, the
greateft Obfervators of the World.

But the *Jewifh* Doctors proceed fo far as
to name the Man, and condefcend upon the
precife Time when firft Mankind began to
commit Idolatry; and as they have generally
fome fort of Foundation wrefted from the Letter
of the Scripture for their Figments, they build
their Opinion, that *Enos* firft introduced Star-
worfhip, upon an extreme obfcure Sentence in
the Original, which they tranflate, *Then was
Profanation committed in calling upon the Name
of the Lord*[s]. Upon this Foundation the moft
learned of the Rabbins, *Mofes* the Son of *Maimon*, introduces *Enos* difcourfing thus: ' Since,
' faid he, God has created thefe heavenly
' Bodies,

[r] Παλαιός γὰρ δὴ τόπ⊙ ἔϑρεψε τὰς πρώτας ταῦτα ἐν-
νοήσαντας, διὰ τὸ κάλλ⊙ τῆς ϑερινῆς ὥρας, ἣν ΑΙΓΥΠ-
ΤΟΣ τε ᾗ ΣΤΡΙΑ ἱκανῶς κέκτηται.

ΕΠΙΝΟΜΙΣ.

[s] GENES. IV. §. 26.

'Bodies, and placed them on high in their
'exalted Spheres; since he has put honour
'upon them, and uses them as his *Ministers*,
'it is but reasonable that *We* shou'd praise
'and extol, and put honour upon them like-
'wise: For this is the Intention of the blessed
'God, that we shou'd magnify and reverence
'whomsoever he hath magnified; just as a
'King desires that *his* Ministers shou'd be
'honoured, which is doing honour to the
'Prince himself.'

No SOONER, continues the Rabbi, had this Doctrine, sunk into their Minds, than they immediately began to rear Temples to the Stars, to do sacrifice, to praise and exalt them in Words, and bow down before them; thro' a perverse Opinion of thereby obtaining the Favour of *God* who made them. This was the Foundation of Idolatry; and thus such of it's Votaries spoke and thought as understood it's real Origin ; never imagining that there was no God beside these visible Stars: And for this reason the same Doctor, a Man of great Authority among the *Jews*, expressly prohibits his Disciples, to look up and contemplate the Beauty and Order of the Heavens, lest they shou'd be tempted to worship them ; or to fix their Eye upon an Image to admire it's Symmetry, lest in so doing it shou'd seduce their Heart; or lastly to read any Books concerning the Reasons or Rites of any other Religion than their own:

Nay,

Lett.17. Nay, fays he, we will not fo much as turn
our Thoughts upon the *Origin* of a different
Worfhip, or confider how fuch an Opinion
cou'd fpring up in the Mind of a Man (in
direct contradiction to his own Practice, in this
very Treatife *of the Worfhip of the Stars)* left
we be betray'd by our own Meditations: for
human Reafon is too feeble and confined for
Men, by it's means, to attain the genuine Truth;
fo that fhou'd every one indulge his own narrow
way of thinking, every thing in the world wou'd
quickly go to ruin.

SUPPOSE, for example, a Man fit down to
fearch into the Origin of Idolatry; fometimes
he doubts of the *Unity* of the Deity, whether
there may not poffibly be two or more active
life-giving Principles governing the World ;
fometimes he confiders whether the World
were really *created* (produced of nothing) or
exifted from all Eternity: then he falls a
fearching, what is by Nature *fupreme,* and
what *fubordinate?* what neceffarily pre-exifts,
and what neceffarily is the effect of it ? At
other times he is perplexed about *Prophecy,*
and doubts in his own Mind whether it be *real,*
or perhaps a *Delufion?*——whether the LAW*
came indeed from Heaven, or was the Device
of a cunning Man ? In this wavering ftate, he
knows not the Rules by which he ought to
proceed, in order to arrive at the Truth ; and

fo

* The five Books of MOSES, called the *Pentateuch.*

ſo by degrees ſlips into the Opinion of the Epicureans, who deny the Providence of God, or any kind of Intercourſe between him and Men. Againſt this we are expreſsly warned in our Law, where we are commanded *not any more to walk after our own Heart, and after our own Eyes to commit Whoredom* ' : As if it were written, ' Let none of you follow his own Underſtanding, which is weak; nor flatter himſelf that by his own Reaſon and Meditation he can acquire Knowledge of the Truth.' For as our Sages have ſaid, *from following our own Heart comes Hereſy; and from indulging our Eyes comes Whoredom* * ; meaning ſpiritual Whoredom.——Now a *Jew* who turns *Epicurean*, is no longer a *Jew* in any thing he does; nor are ſuch to be again received tho' ever ſo penitent; becauſe it is ſaid ' All that go in to her ſhall not return, nor tread any more in the Path of Life".' But they are all *Epicureans* who conſult the Thoughts of their own Hearts——with whom it is not lawful to converſe or to anſwer them a Queſtion; ſince it is written, *Come not thou near the Door of her Houſe*, and that all their Reaſonings lead to Idolatry.

Would not you imagine from hence that the reverend Rabbins had a good mind to erect

among

Numbers XIII. §. 39.

* כך אמרו חכמים אחרי לבבכם זו מינית
ואחרי עיניכם זו זנות

" Proverbs II. §. 18.

Lett. 17. among themſelves a ſort of Inquiſition? As in
fact the Diſcipline is extremely ſevere which
they exerciſe over thoſe they call *Minnim*[v],
Men of a Kind (Heretics): They treat them
as if they were Creatures of a different *Species*
from the holy genuine *Jews*; and frequently
include *Chriſtians* in the Appellation, whom
they look on as Sectaries and Schiſmatics, that
have ſeparated from the everlaſting Stem of their
divine Catholic Religion. Were it in the Power
of Prieſts in many Countries, as much as it is
in their Will, to make their *Anathemas* effectual,
a great Part of the World would be in a ſorry
Plight: But, Thanks to Liberty and Learning,
the bitter Curſes of the Rabbins are equally
harmleſs to us *Britons* as the *Vatican* Thunders:
—happy, that we need only take ſo much of their
Doctrine, as illuſtrates the Philoſophers Aſſertion,
that the firſt Gods were the *Sun*, *Moon* and
Stars, whoſe Worſhip came into *Greece* from
the *Eaſt*.

But let us, if you pleaſe, take one Step
further back; and to facilitate our penetrating
into ſo remote Antiquity, let us keep Nature
ſteadily in view, and not be ſtartled at a
Paradox that ſeems to preſent itſelf, to wit,
That things of ſuch oppoſite Natures as *Philoſophy* and *Idolatry* had yet one and the ſame
Origin. Men, ſays the grand Critic, were firſt
prompted

[v] מין *Species.* מינא *Specialis.* מינים *(Minnim)* Spe-
ciales, Hæretici, Chriſtiani.

prompted to apply themfelves to Philofophy Lett. 17.
by *Admiration* and *Wonder*: their early Wonder
turned upon the moft obvious Matters of Doubt
and Speculation : afterwards, advancing by little
and little, they began to enquire concerning
things of more difficult Comprehenfion; fuch
as the Reafons of the Changes of the Moon,
of the Returns of the Sun, and Motions of
the Stars: and at laft they came to enquire
into the Generation and Origin of the Univerfe
itfelf. But the Man who *wonders*, who is
at a ftand how to account for what he fees,
is ftill ignorant, and ftill in fearch of the
Truth. Wherefore every real Philofopher is
in fome refpect a *Mythologift*, a Lover of Fable
and Allegory: For a *Fable* commonly confifts
of Wonders; and in order to comprehend thefe
Wonders, and difpel the Ignorance that occafions them, Men applied to Meditation and
Philofophy ".

THAT the fame Paffion was the Source of
Idolatry needs now no Proof: The Story told
by the *Arabian* Divines ˣ of *Abraham*'s being
brought up in a dark Cave, and at his firft
coming forth, being fo ftruck with the Appearance of the Stars, that he worfhipped fucceffively *Hefperus*, the *Moon*, the *Sun*, as his
Creators, while they rofe one after another ;
the

ʷ ΑΡΙΣΤΟΤ. μ. τ. φ.
ˣ Ab. Ecchellens. Arab. Hift. VI.

Lett.17. the Story, I fay, tho' good painting, is too long
for my Patience.   I prefer a more authentic
Picture of the moft early Idolatry, from that
admirable Draught of eaftern Manners, *the
dramatic Hiftory of* Job.   ' If, fays the truly
' pious *Arab*, I gazed upon *Orus* (the Sun)
' when he was fhining, or upon *Iärêcha* (the
' Moon) when rifing in her Glory ; and my
' Heart went fecretly after them, and my
' Hand kiffed my Mouth, then may fuch and
' fuch Miferies attend me ʸ.'   In mild Climates
and ferene Skies the Worfhip of the Sun
muft be very enfnaring.   It is the moft obvious
and general Species of Idolatry,—varied into a
thoufand Shapes,—widely fpread, and of the
longeft Continuance : nor is it any wonder,
that Men ignorant of a higher Caufe fhou'd
adore fo bright an Object, at whofe Recefs the
World mourns, the Heavens lowr, the Stars
abfcond, and the Earth is ftript of her Fruits
and Verdure : whereas, all Nature fmiles at his
Return ; the Seas are calm, the Rivers clear,
the Sky ferene, the Air benign, and Birds and
Beafts, and Plants and Men revive at the touch
of his enlivening Ray.   No wonder the lofs
of this Adonis *, or mighty Lord, fhou'd be
loudly lamented in *Affyria*, in *Egypt*, in *Phenicia*, and in all the Countries tinctur'd with
their

ʸ Job XXXI. §. 26.

* אדון Adon, Dominus.   אדני Adoni, Dominus meus.

their Traditions *: or that his Return to impregnate the World with genial Vigour fhou'd
be welcomed with the higheft Demonftrations
of Joy. With whom fhou'd the fufceptive
Power of Generation, the mild VENUS, be in
love † ? whofe Abfence fhou'd fhe mourn when
he goes a hunting thro' the Monfters of the
Zodiac, and approaches too near the frozen
Bear ‡, but this mighty Source of Life and
Love? Moft naturally wou'd the *Chaldeans*
call him *Baal* ˣ, Lord of the World; the
Phenicians Beelfamen ª, Lord of Heaven; the
old *Egyptians Orus* ᵇ, or Light and Fire ; the
Arabians

---

* See a long and accurate Account of their Mourning for
ADONIS in *Herodote's Euterpe*, and in *Plutarch de Ifide et Ofiride*,
to which join *Ezechiel's* Women bewailing *Thammuz*.

 † *Alma* VENUS *Cæli fubter labentia Signa*
  Quæ Mare navigerum, quæ Terras frugiferenteis
  Concelebras ; per TE *quoniam Genus omne Animantum*
  Concipitur, vifitque exortum Lumina SOLIS:
  Nam fimul ac SPECIES *patefacta eft verna* DIEI,
  Et referata viget genitalis *Aura Favoni*
  Aïreæ primum Volucres, te DIVA, *tuumque*
  Significant Initum, *percuffæ Corda tuâ vi* —
  Omnibus incutiens blandum per Pectore amorem
  Efficis ut cupide generatim Sæcla propagent.
            LUCRET.

‡ Ἄρκ1ǫ (the North.) See BION's elegant Ode on the
Death of ADONIS.

ˣ The moft inquifitive curious Traveller that ever view'd a
Country, the natural and wife *Herod tus*, who was an Eye-
Witnefs of the Magnificence of his Temple, and Rites of his
Worfhip, calls him ZEYΣ BHΛOΣ *Jupiter* the *Lord*. *Ju-
piter* is of his own addition to explain the Nature of the God
to the *Grecians* for whom he wrote. *Bel* or *Belus* fhews the
Chaldee pronunciation then prevailed inftead of *Baal.*

ª בעל שמים *Baal-Shamaim :* Chald. בעל שמין *Beel-
Semén* Lord of Heaven.

ᵇ אור *Ur* —*Orus.* See JOB XXXI. §. 26. and *Jamblichus* of the *Egyptian* Myfteries.

Lett.17. *Arabians Ourotaalt*[c], the fupreme Light ; the *Perfians Orofmades*[d], the gracious Light ; and the later *Perfians Mithras*[e], the moft Excellent ; while the other Parts of the vifible World, the Moon, the Earth, the Sea, the Air, and the brighteft Stars, received a proportionable but inferior Reverence.

THE Gods in whofe Worfhip all the EGYPTIANS agreed, were no more than *Ifis* and *Ofiris*, the Sun, Moon and Earth : for *Ifis* is fometimes *Diana*, tho' for the moft part *Ceres*[f].

THE ancient PERSIANS neither built Temples nor raifed Altars ; but facrificed on the Tops of the higheft Mountains to the whole

---

[c] It would appear that in the Age of *Herodotus* the *Arabic* was a little nearer the other *Aramean* Dialects than it is now אור *Ur*, *Fire*, the *Arabs* now call نور *Nouro*, *Light*, and نار *Naëro*, *Fire* : and עליון *Ee'ion*, the *Exalted*, is pretty nearly غلو *Elin* and its Synonime ― طلب, whence *Ourotaalab*, according to the Genius of the Language, *the moft high, or Supreme Light*, and thence *Herodotus* formed his OU-ROTALT. It was well he was fo nigh it. See below Note †.

[d] See above p. 60.

[e] From the *Chald.* יתיר *excellens, præftans, major* ; with the fervile (מ) מיתרא MITHRA. It fignifies likewife *Plenty, Abundance* ; and alludes to *Jupiter pluvius*, for مطر *mater*, fignifies to give *Rain*, to pafs in a rapid Courfe, and make to fwim in Plenty ; all Effects afcribed to the Sun, as is well known to thofe who underftand the Symbols of the MITHRIAC SA-CRIFICE.

[f] Θεὸς γὰρ δὴ ου τὰς αὐτὰς ἅπαντες ὁμοίως Ἀιγύπτιοι σέβουται, πλὴν ΙΣΙΟ'Σ τε, κỳ 'ΟΣΙΡΙΟΣ, τὸν δὴ Διό-νυσον ἔιναι λέγουσι.

HPOΔOT. ETTEPΠH.

whole *Circumference* of Heaven, whom they
called *Jove*; and to the *Sun*, the *Moon*, the
Earth; to *Fire*, *Water*, and the *Winds*, and
to *thefe alone* they facrificed from the Beginning[g]. *Strabo* fubjoins *Venus*, meaning, I
fuppofe, *Aftarte* the Queen of Heaven, whofe
Rites they had learnt of the *Affyrians* and
Arabs *.

THE firft ARABS themfelves had abfolutely
no Gods but the *Sun* and the *Moon*, as we
are told by *Herodotus* †, and the later were
Zabians all the Time of their Ignorance ‡
and adored the Hoft of Heaven, until they
were converted to the Worfhip of the one
true God by *Mahomet*.

S   THE

[g] Τύ͵οισι μὲν δὴ μουνόισι θύεσι (οἱ Πέρσαι) ἀρχῆϑεν·
ἐπιμεμαϑηκασι δὲ ϗ τῇ ΟΥΡΑΝΙΗ θύειν, παρά τέ
Ἀσσυρίων μαθό͵τες ϗ Ἀραϐίων· καλέεσι δέ Ἀσσύριοι τὴν
Ἀφροδίτην ΜΥΛΙΤΤΑ, Ἀραϐιοι δὲ ΑΛΙΤΤΑ, Πέρσαι
δὲ ΜΙΤΡΑΝ.   ὁ αὐ͵. ΚΛΕΙΩ.

* ΣΤΡΑΒ. Γεωγρ. βιϐ. ιε. in fine.

† ΔΙΟΝΥΣΟΝ δὲ θεὸν μοῦνον, ϗ τὴν ΟΥΡΑΝΙΗΝ
ἡγέονται εἶναι·——ὀνομάζεσι δέ τὸν μὲν Διόνυσον ΟΥ-
ΡΟΤΑΆΤ· τὴν δὲ Ὀρανίαν ΑΛΙΛΑΤ. I take this
Alilat to be a different Goddefs from *Alitta* mentioned above,
Note (g) : The former to be *Venus* (the Star called *Allat*,
the Goddefs, worfhip'd by the Tribe of *Thakif*, whofe Temple
was deftroy'd by *Mahomet*'s Command the ninth of the *Hejira*,
that is the Year before his Death) the latter to be the לילית
of the *Chaldeans*, and the هلال or هلة *Illato*, the New Moon
of the *Arabs*.

‡ So they call the Condition in which they lived before
Mahomet.

Lett.17. THE Inhabitants of ancient *Meroë*, the Metropolis of ETHIOPIA, did facrifice to none of all the Gods, but to *Jupiter* and *Bacchus* ; that is, in Terms of *eaſtern* Divinity, to the *Heavens* and the *Sun*, whom they moſt devoutly worſhipped, and made Peace or declared War, as directed by their Oracle *

THE oldeſt Gods of the GRECIANS appear in their moſt ſolemn and ancient Oath, to have been Father *Jupiter*, the all-ſeeing *Sun*, the all-bearing *Earth*, the *Rivers* and *infernal Powers* [h].

THE ſame appear to have been the Gods of the ancient GOTHS, whoſe ſolemn Form of Swearing was, ' So help me *Freia* (*Ceres*
' or Earth) *Thor* (*Jupiter*) and *Attin*, or
' *Odin* (*Neptune*) the Almighty, as I ſay the
' Truth [i].'

THE Gods worſhipped by their Fore-fathers the ancient SCYTHIANS, were principally *Veſta*, the Bond of the Univerſe, *Jupiter* whom (with high Approbation of *Herodotus*) they called ΠΑΠΑΙΟΣ or *fatherly*, and his *Wife* the Earth :

next

* HERODOTE's THALIA. ΜΕΡΟΉ, λέγεται ἶναι Μητρόπολις τῶν ἄλλων ᾿Αιθιόπων· οἱ δ᾿ ἐν ταύτῃ ΔΙΑ θεῶν ἠ ΔΙΟΝΥΣΟΝ μούνους σέβονται· τέτες τε μεγάλως τιμῶσι. ὁ ἀυτ. ΕΥΤΕΡΠΗ.

[h] ΖΕῪ πάτερ! ἴδηθεν μηδέων, κύδιςε, μέγιςε!
ΗΕΛΙΟΣ θ᾿ὃς ἀπ᾿ ἐφορᾶς, ἠ πάντ᾿ ἐπακούεις ?
Καὶ ΠΟΤΑΜΟΙ, ἠ ΓΑΙΑ! ἠ οἱ ὑπένερθε καμόντες
Ανθρώπες τίνυσθον ——— ΟΜΗΡ. ΙΛΙΑΔ.
EDDA Sæmundi apud Hickes.

next to thefe they worfhipped the *Sun*, *Venus* Lett. 17.
Urania, (the Moon) and *Hercules* and *Mars*,
Powers of War[k]. Their Neighbours the
Maffagetes acknowledged no God, but the
Sun alone[*].

THESE were originally the Gods of the
greateft Nations: They were afterwards mul-
tiplied firft by the Knowledge of the Philofophers, then by the Fictions of the Poets,
and moft of all by the Ambition, and Avarice,
of the Priefts, and Superftition of the credulous
Vulgar. The Philofophers quickly ceafed from
making Additions to their Number. Some of
them attempted afterward to reduce it: while
the wifer accepted of the current Tradition,
and contented themfelves with taking the beft
Precautions in their power againft it's bad Influence upon Morality. *Plato* in his *Timæus*
pays a decent Compliment to the Religion of
his Country, that though it's facred Doctrines
were delivered by the Defcendants of the
Gods without requifite Proof or proper Evidence, yet they were to be received and believed, both in Obedience to the Laws, and
as coming from thofe who were *fprung* from
the feveral Deities, and fhou'd beft know the
Matters of their own Kindred. In conformity
therefore, fays the complacent Philofopher, to
their Traditions, let this Account of the Ge-

S 2   neration

[k] ΗΡΟΔΟΤ. ΜΕΛΠΟΜΕΝΗ.
[*] ὁ αὐτ. ΚΛΕΙΩ.

Lett.17. neration of the Gods be received by us and delivered to others: ' That of HEAVEN and
' EARTH were born *Ocean* and *Tethys*; and
' *Saturn,* and *Rhea* and their Children.   That
' of *Saturn* and *Rhea* sprang *Jupiter* and *Juno,*
' and the Brother-Deities whom we all know;
' that when all these who either openly circum-
' volve in Heaven in our sight, or only appear as
' the Gods think proper, were compleated, the
' great GOD, Parent of the Universe, called
' them together and spoke thus.'   His Speech
to the new-created Deities is of higher
Import than to decide a Question of meer
Mythology; as you may perhaps hear at a
fitter Opportunity: this Introduction to it
plainly shews what regard a wife and knowing Man thought was due to the *established
Religion*; and that the *primary* Gods of the
Ancients were not understood to be deified
Mortals, but Parts of the mighty self-moving
Frame created by the first Cause [i] : that *such* was
the Sense of the *Authors* of this Doctrine, as
such it had the Sanction of the Lawgivers, and
was received by the States of *Greece.*

HERE then is the Origin of a Distinction and
the Reason of a Phrase frequently misunderstood; the *Dii majorum et minorum Gentium,*
Gods of the greater and lesser Nations: the
former were the Gods worshipped by the
                                                    Egyptians

[i] HERMES ille ægyptius, quem *trismegistum* vocant, alios
Deos dicit a summo DEO factos, alios ab Hominibus.
                        AUGUSTIN. De C. D. Lib. VIII. §. 15.

Egyptians, *Affyrians*, *Grecians*, and other great Lett. 17.
and wife Nations, all agreed in deifying thefe
primigenial Parts of the Creation: the latter
were afcititious; or Gods adopted from obfcure
People among whom their Worfhip had taken
it's Rife. Thefe, the Philofophers and wifer
of the Priefts would not allow to be Gods,
fuch as the *Theban Hercules*, *Efculapius*, *Caftor*,
and *Pollux*, becaufe they had once been Men[k].
The others were the *Cabeirim* or Mighty Gods
of the *Eafterns*, and the *Confentes*, the unani-
mous or co-operating Gods of the *Romans*,
worfhipped over all the World; but whofe
Rites and Myfteries were particularly famous
in the Iflands *Samothrace* and *Lemnos*, and at
Eleufis in the Neighbourhood of *Athens*. They
were originally but *two*, *Heaven* and the *Sun*, the
only Gods of the *Ethiopians*, from whom *Egypt*
itfelf is faid to have drawn both it's Religion and
Learning: *Thefe* were worfhipped in *Samothrace*, and the *Egyptians* made them firft *fix*,
then *eight*, and long afterward *twelve*, at which

S 3   number

---

[k] Relatum eft in Literis, doctiffimum Pontificem Scævolam
difputaffe tria genera tradita Deorum: unum à Poetis, alterum
a Philofophis, tertium a Principibus Civitis. Primum genus nu-
gatorium dicit effe, quod multa de Diis fingantur indigna Secundum, non congruere Civitatibus, quod habeat aliqua fuper-
vacua, etiam *quæ obfit Populis noffe*: qualia funt, non effe Leos
Herculem, Æfculapium, Caftorem, Pollucem; proditur enim a
doctis quod *Homines* fuerint.

Ibid. Lib. IV. §. 27.

Lett. 17. number the *Dii Cabiri dicti* Gods called *Cabirs* or *Mighty* rested in most Nations[1].

WHO these Gods were, and what was the Import of their Mysteries you may learn in one Sentence from the eloquent *Roman* already mentioned. In his first Book of *the Divine Nature*, he pretends to decline treating particularly of the holy august *Eleusis*, whither Nations came to be initiated from the utmost Ends of the Earth ; nor will he search *Samothrace*, nor enquire too curiously . what are the Objects of Worship hid in *Lemnos* amid the Thickets of a gloomy Wood, to which there was no access but in the Silence of Night : But he adds, ' When they are explained, and ' their real Import examined, the NATURE ' of THINGS (the *Universe*) is rather laid ' open than the Nature of the Gods[m].' The Powers and Parts of the Universe were therefore the ancient *Cabir* or *mighty* Gods, and their mutual Connexions, Operations and Productions were typically represented in their Mysteries.

[1] There is no doubt of this in the polite States ; and here is a Proof that the same number prevailed among the fierce People, that under the Name of *Getes, Goths, Almans, Normans*, &c. overran the *West*.

Cold era aeſei qoð ꞇuinigir ———.

Twelve are the Aeſers *to be worshipped.* ODIN's Surname is ASA, the *Asiatic* ; and from him the twelve Gods are called *Asas* and *Acsars*. The *Goths* were originally *Asiatic Tartars*.

EDDA ISLAND. Mythol. XIX.

[m] Praetereo *Samothrac am*, eaque quae *Lemni*, nocturno aditu occulta coluntur, silvestribus sepibus densa ; quibus explicatis ad rationemque revocatis, RERUM magis NATURA cognoscitur quam DEORUM.

CICERO.

Myfteries. ' As for thofe, fays the fame great
' Author, who will have the Gods whom
' the World adores to be mortal Men taken
' up to Heaven for their Bravery, Power, or
' Fame, are they not void of all Religion
' themfelves. Yet this is the whole Plan of
' *Euhemerus,* who prefumes to narrate how
' the Gods died, and to point out their Places
' of Burial. But by fo doing, whether does
' he feem to have promoted Religion, or to
' have ruined it from the Foundation ?

By great Chance, the Names of four Gods
of the *Lemnian* Myfteries have been preferved
to us in a Citation from the Hiftorian *Mnafeas,*
AXIEROS, AXIOKERSOS, AXIOKERSA and
KADMILUS. They found very barbarous, and
have fufficiently exercifed the Sagacity of the
Etymologifts; their ingenious Conjectures might
have had better fuccefs had they more attentively confidered *who the Gods were* whofe
Names they were attempting to explain. The
Knowlege of Things is the beft Interpreter of
Words; and *Mnafeas* has left us a general Hint
that the firft is *Ceres,* the fecond *Pluto,* the
third *Proferpine,* and the fourth *Mercury:* but
by not attending fufficiently to the Nature
afcribed to thefe Deities, Men of great Genius
have loft fight of the Subject, and ftruck quickly
off to other Views.

THE

Lett.17. THE ΘΕΟΙ ΚΑΒΕΙΡΟΙ, *Cabir-Gods*, were originally *Egyptian*. When *Cambyses* the Son of *Cyrus*, was playing the Mad-man at *Memphis* after his Return from the unhappy *Ethiopian* Expedition, he not only murdered his Brother and best Servants in the Palace, but going abroad he broke up the Tombs of the Dead (hallowed Things in *Egypt*) and profaned the Temples of the greatest Gods. Among the rest he burst into the ancient Temple of *Vulcan*, and made himself extremely merry with the little pigmy Statue of the God : But after that he would needs enter the Sacred Shrine of the *Cabir* or *Mighty Gods*, into which it is impious for any Man to set his Foot but the Priest : Here he not only scoffed and blasphemed, but likewise burnt the Statues of the Gods. These, says *Herodotus*, resemble that of *Vulcan*, ' *whose Children they pretend to* ' *be* ª.' The *Cabir-Gods* therefore are the Powers and Produce of FIRE impregnating Mother-Earth in the mysterious Work of Vegetation ; and in this view their hard Names become of easy Derivation *. The first is the prolific

---

ª ΚΑΒΕΊΡΩΝ τ᾽ ἀγάλματα ὅμοια ἐςὶ τοῖσι τῦ ΗΦΑΙΣΤΟΥ. Τύτυ δὲ σφέας παῖδας λέγυσι εἶναι. ΗΡΟΔΟΤ. ΘΑΛΕΙΑ. HERACLITUS said that the GODS (*i. e* the World and it's Parts) were originally from FIRE.

* ΦΕΡΕΚΤΔΗΣ λέγει ἐκ Καβείρας τῆς Πρωτέως κỳ Ηφαίς-υ, Καβείρυς τρεῖς κỳ νύμφας τρεῖς Καβειρίδας γενέδαι· τὰ δ᾽ ὀνόματα αὐτῶν ἐςὶ μυς-ικά.

ΣΤΡΑΒ. βιβ. ι. Θεολογυμ.

prolific *Strength* or *Warmth* of the *Earth* itfelf°; Lett. 17.
the fecond the latent *Strength* of *Grain*ᵖ or
Power to expand itfelf by Heat and Moifture;
the third that genial *Warmth exerted*ᵖ and
in Action, or the vegetative Life of a growing
Plant, and the fourth is the *Servant*, or *Creature*
of thefe *Gods*ʳ, laborious, inventive, and prone
to Propagation ˢ.

EXPERIENCE fhews that the greateft Wonders ceafe to be fo when they are frequently
feen. Some of them pafs daily before our
Eyes

° From יַעַן, in HIPH. הוֹעִין, in *Arabic* جد Roboravit,
Virtute et Potentiâ imbuit, by tranflation, Concepit, gravida
fuit, אֶרֶץ Erets Terra: But as the CABIRS came of *Vulcan*,
I prefer the *Chaldee* אָזִי Aazi, fuccendit, accendit, calefecit,
as the truer Compofition. The Word runs through the *Eaftern*
Languages. ﺟﺯ Azza Bullivit, ferbuit, accendit, commovit,
expreffing particularly *Fermentation*.

ᵖ From the fame and גֶרֶם Gheres Frumentum. The few
Fragments remaining of the *Hebrew* afford but narrow Notions:
The *Syriac* and *Arabic*, copious Dialects, extend our Views of
their primitive Analogy. In the latter غرس Gharas, fignifies
to *plant*, غرس Ghirfo Mucus, or generative *Slime*, (pag. 173.)
كرس, Kirfa, Dung, and Urine of Cattle, غريس Gharifo,
the firft *Shoot*, or *Germ*, from whence Aazi-gherfa, Proferpine;
the Derivation of whofe *Greek* Name ΠΕΡΣΕΦΟΝΗ, fee in
the Note on *Sanchoniathon* below.

ᵠ The Feminine of the former.

ʳ From قديم Kadimon or Kadim, Minifter, Famulus, and
الله Ilahon Deus. Kadm-iloë. ΚΑΔΜΙΛΟΣ and ΚΑΣΜΙ-
ΛΟΣ, Mercury.

ˢ Supra. page 175. and join to it from *Herodotus* Ὅς-ις
δὲ τὰ Καβείρων ὄργια μεμύηται, τὰ Σαμοθρήϊκες ἐπι-
λεῦσι, οὗὗ ὢ νὴρ οἶδε (διὰ τίτὰ τῦ ἘΡΜΕΩ ἀγάλματα ὀρθὰ ἔχυσι τὰ αἰδοῖα.)

ΕΥΤΕΡΠΗ.

Lett.17.Eyes without Notice or Reflexion.   The Sun
rifes, the Moon changes, the Stars revolve, in
the View of thoufands blind to fo auguft a
Scene.   The Vapours mount, the Rains de-
fcend, the Rivers flow, the Tides return unheeded by the Bulk of Mankind: and much
more unheeded fpring th' unnumbered Tribes
of the vegetable Race, except in fo far as they
contribute to the Suftenance or Conveniency
of our Lives.   We feed upon the Fruits of
Mother-Earth, without confidering what fecret
vivifying Power renews her Bofom with annual
Pregnancy: what latent Virtue enables a Seed
apparently dead to transform itfelf into a thriving
Plant, or tow'ring Cedar; and what *Nymph*
or *Hamadryade* animates and feeds the endlefs
earth-born Family?

It had perhaps been well, cou'd I have
introduced the Explication of the Nature of
thefe hidden Deities, and the Import of their
enigmatical Names, with fome ftriking Ceremony.   Cou'd I under Cloud of Night have
led you trembling through the thick Mazes
of a wild Wood into a Grotto's Gloom; and
there hear a folemn Voice pronounce thefe
fearful Names,   *Aaxi-Erez! Aaxi-ghêrez!
Aaxi-ghêrza!* and at every Sound made the
facred Image of the God to pafs tremendous
before you: Then have invoked the KADM-
ELOE to fhew their Operations typified in
amazing Symbols, you might poffibly have
ftared

ſtared like a young Convert, turned Votary of Lett. 17. the *Cabir*-Gods, and never forgot their Rites while you lived.

AND now, my Friend, I ſuppoſe with your Aſſent I may venture to aſſert it to be a common Miſtake, ' that Mythology belongs only to POETS; or to Poets preciſely as *ſuch*, I mean Makers or Compoſers of Verſe. They have long, it is true, monopolized the Muſes, as if they favoured none of the Sons of Science but themſelves; and along with that Encroachment they have appropriated their Method of inſtructing by Fable and Allegory: But anciently it was not ſo: the inſpiring Muſe confined not her Influence: the Poet was not her ſole Favorite: no, nor ever ſo much as when he was a real Philoſopher. FABLE was the firſt Garb in which *Wiſdom* appeared; and was ſo far from being peculiar to the Singſong Tribe, that the Fathers of Science both Civil and Sacred adopted it as the beſt of Means both to teach and perſuade. What Branch of Knowledge but has borrowed aſſiſtance from this mimic Power? What Piece of abſtract Speculation has ſhe not coloured with Imagery, or what practical Precept has ſhe not enforced with Examples? Even in Converſation and Buſineſs, to what do we more commonly allude than to ESOP's *Cock*, or his *Fox*, or his *Dog* deceived with his own Shadow? When a corrupt Reſident lately meant

to

Lett.17. to delude his Country, and fell her to the common Enemy, he reprefented the fole Means of her Safety, her Union with *Great-Britain*, as hunting with the *Lion* who wou'd afterwards devour her[t]. Often, indeed, have *Politics* borrowed the Drefs and Language of Fable ; a Language in which you can fay without Offence a thoufand ticklifh Things not elfe to be mentioned: Things that would wound a tender Ear, and fhock a darling Paffion if nakedly told, glide gently down, like a bitter Pill in a mild Vehicle, when wrapt in a foothing Tale. Witnefs in Sacred Writ, the Story of *Nathan*, of the Widow of *Tecoa*, and to keep near the fame Country, witnefs the inexhaufted PILPAY; whofe fertile Fancy has painted the Courts of the *Eaft*, and exemplified the Fate of Favourites in a thoufand Tales, fitted to every Maxim of State.

WOULD you have a fmall Tafte of this political Mythology? Here it is ; a Sketch from a fuperior Genius, equally capable of excelling in other Parts of Science, as he does in his own Profeffion. ' WHEN *Jupiter* firft ' heard of the Death of his Son *Sarpedon*, in ' the Rage of Grief he called *Mercury*, the ' Meffenger of the Gods, and gave him Orders ' to go inftantly to the *Fates*, and bring from ' them the ftrong Box in which the eternal Decrees were laid up. *Mercury* obeyed ' went

[t] Lettres de M. VAN HOEY.

' went to the fatal Sifters, and omitted nothing
' a wife and well inftructed Minifter cou'd
' fay to make them obtemperate the Will of
' *Jove.* The *Sifters* fmiled, and told him,
' that the other End of the golden Chain,
' which fecured the Box with the unalterable
' Decrees, was fo fixed to the Throne of *Jove,*
' that were it to be unfaftened, his Mafter's
' Seat itfelf might tremble.' This elegant
Apologue is capable of a fublime Application:
but in meer human Affairs, were a Prince
about to fap the Foundations of his own
Grandeur, or a Minifter about to difconcert
the Meafures, or deftroy the Men that kept
him in play, cou'd there be any thing more
appofite than to tell the Anfwer of the Fates
to almighty JOVE?

BUT though there be no Science unadorned
by Allegory, it is in THEOLOGY that it tri-
umphs and fits upon it's Throne: that Method,
I mean, of teaching by Types, Allufions and
Parables, fo common in the *Eaft,* and with
which all their Compofitions, facred and civil,
fo much abound. Yet it is a ftrong Phrafe
ufed by a learned Prelate, ' That the Fables
' which were profane in other oriental Nations
' were *fanctified* in SYRIA, and confirmed
' by the Authority of *God* himfelf:' Not
meaning, to be fure, the myfterious Tales or
religious Doctrines of the neighbouring Nations,
Egyptians, Phenicians, or *Arabs* to have been
adopted

Lett.17. adopted and fanctified in *Paleftine*; but that the *Method of inftructing by Fable* was em-ployed by the Heaven-infpired Pen-men in the Land of Promife, as well as by the Priefts in *Egypt* and the Magi of the *Eaft* ᵘ : and in effect, fome of the greateft Divines in all Ages have been the moft eminent Type-makers. A Prophet can fcarce open his Mouth but in Figure and Allufion; and the greateft Wifdom is frequently couched in the darkeft Sayings. *Origen, Philo,* and *Tertullian,* Men of warm Fancies, if they be not the greateft Type-makers, are the greateft *Type-finders* in Anti-quity; and accordingly it was, and ftill is, a principal Part of facred Inftruction, fays a very knowing and modeft *Jew,* to fearch into the ' *myftical* Expofition of the Law, and *parabo-* ' *lical* Hiftories, not to be underftood according ' to the Letter, but in a *figurative* Senfe, with ' defign to inftruct us in fome ufeful Precept ' of Morality, according to the known Practice ' of the *Orientals* ᵛ.' Another learned Man of the fame Nation, but converted to *Chri-ftianity,* declares the *allegorical* Meaning to be highly neceffary for preferving the Pu-rity of our Religion; which moft certainly wou'd be infected with *Judaifm,* if we kept ftrictly to the *Letter.* ' We fhou'd be ob- ' liged,

---

ᵘ Quas Parabolas in Nationibus de quibus differui profanas modo vidifti, eæ Sanctiones factæ funt in *Syria,* et Dei ipfius authoritate roboratæ.

P. D. HUET. De Orig. Fab. Romanens.

ᵛ Is. ABENDANA, Polity of the JEWS.

' liged, he fays, to re-eftablifh Circumcifion, Lett.17.
' renew the Sacrifices and Burnt-Offerings,
' and reftore the whole Train of the legal
' Ceremonies. Nor cou'd we without the
' myftical Meaning, well anfwer the Enemies
' of the Law and the Prophets, when they
' afk in derifion, Why ever God laid fuch
' abfurd Commands upon Men as to cut their
' Fore-fkins, kill a Lamb, or confecrate a red
' Heifer ?' But does not the knowing Convert
go too far in favour of *Allegory*, when he
concludes ' that the Laws of *Sparta* or *Athens*
' would appear more reafonable than the *Jewifh*
' taken without their myftical Meaning, and
' it's Explication ▼ ?'

WE are indeed told, that Truth, *naked*
Truth, in facred Matters, is like the Sun in his
Brightnefs, which mortal Eye cannot ftedfaftly
view, without being dazz'led : but Allegory, the
Picture or Semblance of Truth, is compared
to the *Iris*, the reflected *Image* of the Sun,
which we behold with Wonder, and gaze on
with Eafe. She is faid to be the Daughter
of *Thaumantias*, or Child of *Admiration* ; a
Paffion when mixed with Delight the moft
attractive and commanding in the human Breaft.
The Mind therefore, fays a pious Philofopher,
attaches itfelf with higher Satisfaction to the
Rain-Bow of FABLE, than to the refplendent
Sun of *fimple* TRUTH.

CERTAIN

▼ SIXTI SENENS. Biblioth. Sac. Lib. I.

Lett.17. CERTAIN it is, that our Sight turns too familiar with Objects it can command, and with which it is daily converfant. They lofe their Dignity by degrees, and ftrip themfelves of the ftriking awful Appearance they formerly wore. ' The facred Horror of a ' holy Cavern, fays an admired *Italian*, a reli- ' gious Darknefs, a devout myfterious Dim- ' nefs, or dubious Confine of Night and Day, ' produce incredible Reverence in the Wor- ' fhipper, and inhance the cloudy Majefty of ' the half-feen Object.' But how fhall we underftand what that eloquent Author immediately fubjoins, when he firft defires us to reverence *Truth*, and then afks, What other Religion in the World profeffes more openly to walk *in the dark* than our own? Does not GOD, continues he, make his Abode in the refplendent Abyfs of *inacceffible* Light?— and though he be faid, ' to have made Dark- ' nefs his hiding Place,' does he not for all that dwell in the pureft Splendor ; which being too dazz'ling an Object for the human Eye, is therefore held forth to us under the Name of *Darknefs?* Is not *Faith*, which flows from him, an obfcure myftical Revelation —— it's Inftruments, meer *Symbols*, it's Oracles the *Prophet*'s full of a thoufand Adventures that have all the Appearance of Type and Allegory[a]? It is far out of my way to anfwer thefe
Queftions :

---

[a] AGOST. MASCARDI Difcorfi morali Parte I.

Queſtions: but whatever Difficulties they might
raiſe in *Italy*, I am inclined to believe, that
a *Proteſtant* who throughly underſtands his own
Principle, is the fitteſt to remove them.

So far however, we may ſafely aſſent to this
learned Writer, that the End of ſacred Allegory
was the Inſtruction of Mankind, which it
obtained by two natural Effects of it's Influence
on their Minds: Firſt it impreſs'd them with
an Awe of Religion, by the Majeſty and Obſcurity of the allegorical Meanings: and next
enforced the Precepts of Virtue, and under
cover of *pious Rites* recommended the Practice
of them to the People. How juſtly the
Opinion may be founded I pretend not to
determine; but it has been long believed ' That
' the Divinity loved to be *veiled*; and that
' it's myſterious Subſtance diſdained to be
' convey'd in plain Words into polluted Ears.'
Numenius, the celebrated *Pythagorean*, having
through I don't know what Caprice, undertaken
to publiſh an Explication of the *Eleuſinian* Myſteries, had proceeded but a little way in his
Work, when ſome Goddeſſes appearing to him
in a Dream, ſhew'd themſelves ſtanding naked,
in an indecent Poſture and infamous Place.
From thence they chid him bitterly for his
Attempt to divulge their Myſteries, as if thereby he had proſtituted their Honour. For
the ſame Reaſon *Diagoras* was baniſhed from

T *Athens,*

Lett.17. *Athens*, and a Price set upon his Head; and
M. Attilius the Duumvir was condemned as
a Parricide by the *Roman* Senate for having
only employ'd a common Clerk to copy over the
Sibylline Verses. In such a Temper, and under
such Impressions, Men wou'd naturally fall to
allegorize; that is, to hide their Conceptions of
divine Things under Coverings and Symbols,
and accordingly the Countries where Allegory
was most cultivated have been the most celebrated for their Religion.

E G Y P T above all the rest, the Mother-
Land of Mysteries is said to have hatched the
better Part of the Rites that prevail over the
World. ' It is a frightful Thing, says an emi-
' nent Divine, to consider their immense Di-
' versity. Yet they all agree in many Points;
' they have almost all the same Principles
' and Foundation; they agree in *Thesis*, pro-
' ceed by the same Steps, and keep even Pace
' with one another: nor is it any wonder,
' *since they all took Birth in the same Coun-*
' *try and Clime* ; all of them invent and fur-
' nish Miracles, Prodigies, Oracles, solemn My-
' steries, holy Prophets, sacred Festivals, certain
' Articles of Faith and Creeds necessary for
' Salvation '.' It is for this Reason that the
first Poets, Masters in Allegory, *Linus*, *Or-*
pheus and *Musæus*, all instructed in *Egypt*,
were

---

y P. Charron de la Sagesse. Liv. II. Ch. V. Page 351.

were called *Theologues*[z]; and that such high Merit is afcribed to them in taming and civilizing rude Mankind[a]. Their Method of doing it by *Parables* and enigmatical Fictions they learned, if we may believe a Father of the Church, from the *Jewifh Prophets*; nay and many of their mythological Tales tend to typify the Attributes and Actions of the *true God* according to the fame Author[*]. Whatever be in that Affertion, great was the Veneration anciently paid to thefe Sages, and little lefs to their Succeffors. It was faid of HOMER, for inftance, ' that as a Poet, he had in a ' manner *formed* and *difciplined* barbarous ' *Greece*; that for Inftruction in the Manage- ' ment of all human Affairs he deferved to ' be taken up and got by Heart ; and in a ' word, that it wou'd be the Heighth of Wif- ' dom to model one's whole Life and Conver- ' fation upon this divine Poet[b]:' And taking all thefe venerable Bards together, they

T 2   were

---

[z] Extiterunt Poetæ qui etiam THEOLOGI dicerentur, quoniam de Diis carmina faciebant ; ex quorum numero fuiffe perhibentur *Orpheus, Mufæus, Linus.*

             AUGUSTIN. de C. D.

[a] Vivendi rationem quam moralem civilemque Sapientiam licet appellare, primi omnium mortalium prifci POETÆ indagaverunt.

       PATRICIUS de Regno. Lib I. Tit. 2.

[*] CLEMENS of Alexandria.

[b] Ὡς τὴν ΕΛΛΑΔΑ πεπαίδευχεν οὗτ☉ ὁ ποιητὴς· ᾗ πρὸς διοίκησίν τε ᾗ παιδείαν τῶν ἀνθρωπίνων πραγμάτων, ἄξι☉ ἀναλαβόντι μανθάνειν· ᾗ κατὰ τῦτον τὸν ποιητὴν πάντα τόν ἁυτῦ βίον κατασκευασάμενον ζῆν.

          ΠΛΑΤΩΝ. Πολιτει. 1.

Lett.17. were generally allowed to be the *Fathers* as it were of Wisdom, and *Leaders* in the Way of Knowlege. Their *allegorical Art* was adopted into every Part of Life, and every Science was treated in *Metaphor* and *Allusion.* The first *Historians,* as well as the first *Philosophers,* were Mythographers or Writers of Fables[c]. After what you have heard, I suppose the last may be pretty intelligible; but how is it possible to transmit real *History* in a Fiction? It is, I must acknowlege, a little strange; but read *Homer's* Account of the Wall raised by the *Greeks* round their Ships and Camp, and particularly the Destruction of it by *Neptune* and *Apollo,* (the *Sea* and the *Sun*) after their Departure, and you will see an elegant Conjunction of Fact and Fable. But there are two curious Instances of this Method of Narration in the most natural Author that ever wrote, and in the plainest of his Writings[d]; that wond'rous *Journal* of *Cyrus's* Expedition against his Brother, kept by XE-NOPHON; the most delightful instructive Record that ever preserved Virtue from Oblivion.

AFTER the first Repulse which that hand-ful of hardy *Greeks* had given the perfidious *Persian,* they marched to the Banks of the *Tigris.* ' Here, says their General and Histo-
' rian,

c Ὁι πρῶτοι ΙΣΤΟΡΙΚΟΙ και ΦΥΣΙΚΟΙ μυθογράφοι. ΣΤΡΑΒΩΝ. Βιβ. α.

d ΞΕΝΟΦΩΝΤ. Ἀναβάσεως, βιβ. γ.

' rian, we came to a great City, deferted and
' wafte, called *Lariffa*, formerly inhabited by
' the *Medes*. It's Wall was twenty-five Foot
' thick, an hundred high, and two Parafangs
' in Circumference, built of Brick with a
' Stone-Foundation of twenty Foot. This City
' was befieged by the King of *Perfia*, when
' he drove out the *Medes*; but it was not in
' his power to take it, until the SuN *covered*
' *himfelf with a Cloud, and kept under Dark-*
' *nefs, until the Inhabitants failed, and then*
' *it was taken.*

From thence the Army made one March
of fix Parafangs to a vaft Wall furrounding a
wafte City, by name *Meffpila*, formerly inhabited by the *Medes :* The Foundation of hewn
Stone finely ftreaked, fifty Foot thick and fifty
Foot high, upon which ftood a brick Wall of
the fame thicknefs, and a hundred Foot high,
fix Parafangs in Circumference. ' Hither the
' *Median Queen* is faid to have fled when the
' *Medes* were deprived of the Empire by
' the *Perfians*; whofe King laid Siege to it;
' but could neither take it by Storm, nor
' through Length of Time, until JUPITER
' *thunder-ftruck the Inhabitants, and then it*
' *was taken.*

THESE two improbable Tales look quite
foreign and diffimilar as they ftand interwove in
the plain perfuafive Narration of that memorable
Retreat ; and evidently bear the *Afiatic* alle-

gorical

Lett.17. gorical Stamp both in their Turn and Expreſſion. The *Eaſterns* to this day tell all
grand Tranſactions *mythologically*; and are ſo
accuſtomed to the *figurative* Stile, that it enters
even into common Life. XENOPHON in his
Paſſage through *Aſia*, has picked up theſe
Traditions from the People of the Country,
and inſerted them into his Journal juſt as he
received them: I ſuppoſe that *one* of theſe
Towns has been taken either while the Inhabitants were under Conſternation during an
Eclipſe of the *Sun*, or from ſome thick *Vapour*
raiſed by the Stagnation of the Canals drawn
from the River; and the *other* during their
Amazement at the Thunder's burſting juſt over
their City.

POETRY, PHILOSOPHY and LEGISLATION,
originally conjoined in one and the ſame Perſon,
came in a few Generations to be ſeparated into
three different Characters *. The *Philoſopher*
and *Legiſlator* ſtuck long together, and were
never throughly disjoined; but *Poetry* which at
firſt had been only a *Servant* to the other
two, came quickly to forget her Station; to ſet up
for herſelf, and take looſe Flights, which ſhocked
the Philoſopher's Reaſon and the Lawgiver's Morality. Hence the early Grudge between the Pro-
feſſions ᵉ; Wit and Wiſdom at variance; and, in
ſome States, Laws made to reſtrict *Muſic* and regulate

ᵉ Παλάια μὲν τις διαφορὰ Φιλοσοφία τε κ̀ ποιητικῇ.
* See Page 178.   ΠΛΑΤΩΝ. Πολιτ. ι.

gulate *Poetry*. But except in a very few, the *Bard* for the moſt part got the better: His amazing Tales, his harmonious Numbers, his ſeeming Sanctity and Pretences to Inſpiration, gave him a great Aſcendant over his Competitors. He ſpoke to the Paſſions, and touch'd the weak Sides of Mankind, and could not fail to become *popular*. The *Prieſts* quickly ſaw it, ſtruck wiſely in, joined Intereſts with the *Poet*, grafted their Rites upon his Verſe, and ſecured his Reputation with their own Eſtabliſhment. *He* celebrated their Temples; *they* recommended his Tales. *He* aſſured the Multitude that every conſecrated Place was a School of Piety; *they* explained every Allegory into a Leſſon of ſome Virtue, or Cure of ſome Malady of the human Mind. No Man, they ſaid, cou'd ever hear the dreadful Puniſhments deſcribed, that await thoſe who tranſgreſs the Laws of Religion and Humanity, without feeling ſome Impreſſions of the *Awe* they are calculated to raiſe: That *Lycaon*, for inſtance, was transformed into a Wolf, and others changed into Trees, Birds, Stones, or condemned to diſmal Tortures below, or puniſhed in their own Perſons, or in their wretched Poſterity. But whoever ſoundly believes them (as the Bulk of Mankind once did) will be throughly ſhaken; and ſo terrified while the Impreſſion laſts, as either to abſtain from ſuch like Crimes, or at leaſt have recourſe to thoſe who are imagined to have Power from the

T 4 Gods

Lett 17. Gods to abfolve them. In fhort, continued the Priefts, Nothing fo efficacious to footh a difturbed Confcience, to rowze a dejected or curb a haughty Spirit, as a pleafing Rite or religious Allegory. Our fecret Luftrations, our folemn Proceffions and facred My-fteries are fo many fovereign Charms to allay the Storm of the human Breaft: They give a loofe to fome of them which muft be evaporated either this or a worfe way, and calm others through a kindly Perfuafion of the Good-will of the Gods being procured by their Performance. Our public Feafts where *Dancing* and *Exercife* is ufed are of the firft Sort; fuch as the Progrefs of *Cybele*, the Siftrums of *Ifis*, and above them all, the Ladies Delight, the Proceffions of *Bacchus* [f]: Returned from *thefe*, the

---

[f] An ingenious Phyfician, in his Treatife of the *Tarantula* fays, though there be many really bit by that venomous Spider, yet the *Women*, (by far the greater number of the Patients) frequently counterfeit the Diftemper by feigning it's ufual Symptoms. For when they fall into any Languifhment, either through Misfortunes, unfuccefsful Love, or Ailments peculiar to the Sex, the lafting Grief brought on them by fuch Accidents degenerates into Melancholly and Defpair. This is fed partly by their Solitude, living like *Nuns*, and forbid the Converfation of Men be it ever fo innocent; and chiefly by the fultry Climate, (*Calabria*) hot nourifhing Food, their own aduft Conftitution, Idlenefs, and fuch like. In this gloomy State, nothing delights and refrefhes them fo much as *Mufic* and *Dancing*: And to have their Fill of it, which is alone allowed to thofe ftung by the *Tarantula*, *they fay they are bit*; and their Palenefs, Dejection, Difficulty of Breathing, Palpitations, and perverted Imagination, like a Delirium, give a Colour to the Cheat. This is fo common in the South of our Country (*Italy*) that thefe violent Dancings, fo highly delightful to the Women, are turned into a Proverb, and called *il Carneualetto delle Donne*, the Ladies little *Carneval*.

G. BAGLIVI. Diff. VI. de Tarant.

the weary Worſhipper, being at a proper Pitch for ordinary Life, can afford to ſit quietly down at home, and mind his private Affairs. But if upon any Diſaſter, the Mind be ſeized with brown-eyed Melancholly; if evil Omens, or long Solitude bring Dejeƈtion and Gloom, then a *ſecret Sacrifice*, an *Expiation*, or other holy Ceremony is the Cure: after it's pious Perfor-mance the Cloud is diſpelled, the Gloom gives way, and the happy Devotée, now ſatisfied with himſelf, and in good Terms with the Gods, ſees every thing look gay; the World ſmiles; his Heart is full of the ſweeteſt Hopes, and all about him partake of his Good-nature and Affability: So powerful is the Virtue of our ſacred Inſtitutions! But if upon a Repe-tition of theſe Rites at proper Intervals, that Serenity of Mind be procured which makes the Happineſs of Life, muſt it not be acknow-leged that their Authors were wiſe, and Friends to Mankind?

Such was the Language of the ſacred Order among the Ancients. The *Poets*, frequently moved by internal Impulſe, gave their cor-dial Aſſent; and even the *Philoſophers* partly approved the ſame Doƈtrine. The old thought-ful Heraclitus called all holy Rites Akea, Cures: And a later Sage, and zealous Diſciple of the Prieſts, gives us this Detail of their Reaſons. 'Some of the Rites, ſays he, that 'are daily performed in the Temples have a ſecret

Lett. 17. ' fecret and ineffable ' Caufe of their Inftitu-
' tion : Others have been confecrated to the
' Gods as their peculiar *Symbols* from the Be-
' ginning of Time : Others reprefent them in
' different Afpects (as genial NATURE has
' expreffed invifible Proportions in vifible Forms.)
' Others are meant as Marks of Honour, and
' aim at fome certain Refemblance or Attri-
' bute of the Superior Nature. The fecond
' Clafs have been framed for *our* Good, in
' order to deliver *us* from diforderly Paffions,
' or to rid us of other Diftempers to which
' we poor Mortals are obnoxious.' In confequence of thefe Principles he explains the ftrange,
and moft fhocking Inftance of their Rites, the
Confecration of the Phallus, into an ' *Emblem*
' of the POWER of Generation, whofe pro-
' lific Virtue is thereby invoked to impregnate
' the Univerfe ; for which reafon that Cere-
' mony is for the moft Part performed in
' the *Spring*, when the whole World receives
' a kind of Regeneration from the Gods.' As
for the *obfcene Forms of Speech* thought to be
indifpenfable Parts of the Service, they are
Remedies, or rather *Antidotes* againft impure
Paffions ——. ' All our Affections, he fays,
' like

' SATURNALIORUM originem illam mihi in medium pro-
ferre fas eft, non quæ ad arcanam Divinitatis naturam refertur,
fed quæ aut fabulofis admixta differitur, aut a phyficis in vul-
gus aperitur: nam occultas et manantes ex MERI VERI fonte
rationes ne in ipfis quidem *Sacris* ennarrare permittitur ; fed fi
quis illas affequitur continere intra confcientiam tectas jubetur.
MACROB. Saturnal. Lib. I. §. 7.

' like a stemmed Torrent, grow more violent, Lett. 17,
' the more they are reftrained : But when they
' are gently indulged, and permitted mode-
' rately to exert their native Powers, they
' are quickly fatisfied ; after that, being foothed
' by a fort of Charm, they yield to Perfuafion
' that wou'd have ftormed at Violence. Thus
' as we come to reftrain our own Paffion, by
' feeing the Rage of other Men, and it's dif-
' mal Effects reprefented upon the Stage, in the
' fame manner by feeing obfcene Sights in the
' Temples, and hearing obfcene Words, we
' are delivered from the Mifery infeparable
' from the Actions '.'

WHETHER this might not fometimes be
true, I fhall not at prefent enquire. That it
was frequently otherwife I am very certain;
and therefore perfectly agree in Opinion with
one of the wifeft and moft learned Writers of
Antiquity ᵍ, when after a high Commendation
of the *reformed* Roman Rites, he defires that
no body wou'd fuppofe him to be ignorant of
the Ufe of the *Grecian* Fables. Some of them,
he knows, explain the Works of Nature in
gloomy myfterious Initiations ; others are compofed to comfort unhappy Men under Affliction ;
others to relieve us under Trouble of Mind,
to rid us of Terrors and purge off black Opinions ; and others for various laudable Purpofes.
But

ᶠ ΙΑΜΒΛΙΧ. ΒΙΒ. Γ. §. 15.

ᵍ ΔΙΟΝΥΣ. ΑΛΙΚΑΡ. Ἀρχαιολογ. βιϛ. β.

Lett.17. But, says he, tho' I be as much apprifed of this as any Man, yet I would incline to ufe them cautioufly, and rather approve the *Roman* Theology: For I confider that the Advantages to be reaped from the *Grecian* Legends are but fmall, and confined to the few who have been at Pains to enquire into their Origin: Now there are not very many who are well inftructed in this fort of Philofophy; while the rude unthinking Multitude commonly underftand thefe mythical Narrations in the *worft* Senfe; and fall into one of two Evils: Either an utter Contempt of Gods immerfed in fuch Mifery; or into an opinion that they need abftain from nothing bafe or unlawful, fince they have the Gods themfelves for their Patterns.

You fee he allows the *Grecian Allegories* to contain a real Philofophy; and that thofe who are capable of enquiring into their Origin may be highly profited both in Speculation and Practice. In the former they unfold the Myfteries of Nature; in the latter they afford infinite Materials to moralize? A well-difpofed Perfon may there find fomething fitted to every Condition in Life. Wou'd we live contented with our Lot, and not aim at higher things than are confiftent with Mortality? Let us recollect the Fate of the *Giants* that attempted to fcale the Heaven, and the Fall of ambitious *Bellerophon* from his winged Horfe.

WOU'D

Wou'd we guard againſt Pride and an un-**Lett.17.** bridled Tongue? There is wretched *Marſyas* hung up before our Eyes, and *Niobe* weeping for her Children till ſhe was turned to a Stone. Wou'd we ſooth our Minds under the Viciſſitudes of Fortune, and Calamities of Life? Let us liſten to the Complaints of *Apollo,* uttered in doleful Strain upon the Banks of *Amphyrſſus* while he was doomed to feed *Admetus'* Sheep. *Lycaon* howling through the Woods, is a loud Warning to the Wicked and the Cruel; *Ixion* for ever rowling on the reſtleſs Wheel, to the Lewd and Lawleſs; and *Tantalus* tortured amid Streams with Thirſt, to the Covetous and Inſatiable. On the other hand, there is *Hercules* and the Train of *Heroes* who by Virtue and glorious Deeds have obtained Heaven and Immortality: or if you aſpire not ſo high, the *Elyſian* Fields and Groves, the Abodes of the Bleſſed, ſtand open to the *Pious,* and to thoſe

Qui ſui memores alios fecêre merendo.

These are ſome of the trite and obvious Leſſons to be learned from Mythology: What an Inſtructreſs then muſt this creative Faculty prove, when employed by a maſterly Hand to paint the Charms of Virtue, and Deformity of Vice? To trace their ſeveral Sources, pull off their Diſguiſes, and point out their Tendencies

through

Lett. 17. through all the Windings of the human Heart? Form to yourfelf the Idea of a monftrous many-headed Beaft : Nay, fhrink not from the Savage ; he is nearer a-kin to us than we are aware. Imagine fome of thefe Heads to be of tame, and others of wild Animals, which fhoot forth all around the Creature by turns, and germinate at it's pleafure. With this Beaft imagine the Nature and Genius of other *two* Animals to be compounded, that of a Lion, and that of a Man, fo as to make only *one* Creature of all the three, but in whofe Conftitution the multifarious *Monfter* fhall predomine, then the *Lion*, and leaft of all the *Man.* Conceive it to be fo vefted with the human Figure, that to thofe who cannot fee within it, but only view the Out-fide, it fhall appear to be *one* fingle Animal, and that *a real* MAN. Then imagine it allowed to act according to the feveral inward Springs of it's heterogeneous Frame ; and after that, think coolly with yourfelf, *what Management would be moft conducive to it's real Happinefs* ——? Whether to feed and cherifh the *various Beaft,* to nourifh the *Lion*, and ftarve the *Man*, fo as he fhou'd be dragged whither fo ever the other pleafed ; while they are fighting, biting, and devouring one another, or to keep the Monfter at under ; to *tame* the Lion, and *cherifh* the human Creature ? In plainer Terms, Whether it be better to indulge the Inftincts

of

Lett.17.

of an Ape, a Hog, a Fox, or Goat, and *Lion-like* to tear whatever opposes them; or to curb these sprouting Motions, and act *like a Man?*—to temper the native Fierceness of our Make with the mild Principle of Humanity; and chasten our *apish animal* Inclinations with the Majesty and Decency of a *superior Nature*[a]?

PROTEUS is said by those who wou'd deduce all Fable from *History*, to represent the various *Ensigns* used by the Kings of *Egypt*. *Plato* laughing, makes him an Emblem of the quackish Sophists, *Lucian* of the Players, *Eustathius* of Flatterers, *Cassiodorus* of Traitors, and St. *Austin*, which is the nearest, of *Truth*; for the real Allegory of *Proteus* is of deep philosophical Import: But the immense Diversity of the *human Heart*, the Vicissitudes in it of Virtue and Vice, the Successions of wavering Thought, the Storms of Passion, Contrasts of Desire, and Change of Pursuits, make it, if not a true, at least a happy Application, to call it a *perfect Proteus*; now Fire, now Water, then a lifeless Lump; by and by a Lion; then a Bull, a Snake, or any Animal whose Instinct and Affections it pleases to assume[1].

'T is thus that Fable takes the Harshness from dry Philosophy, and by mixing its Precepts with Imagery makes them not only easy to apprehend,

[a] ΠΛΑΤΩΝ. Πολιτ.
[1] AGOST. MASCARDI. Part. I. Disc. 2.

apprehend, but their Impreffions both agreeable
and lafting.   For no Meafure of Verfe, no
Strength of Figures, no Pomp of Language,
nor Art of Compofition has fuch an infinua-
ting Influence upon a young Mind as a *well-
told wond'rous Tale.*

AFTER all, what fhou'd hinder one of a
poetical Turn, laid down perhaps on the Bank
of a Brook, or feated on the Brow of a Clif,
commanding the Ocean, and viewing the
auguft Spectacle around him ; the Beauty
and Order of the Heaven, the Oeconomy
and Concord of the Earth and Sea — ; then
confidering the Chain of Caufes that keep the
mighty Frame fteady and invariable, what
fhou'd hinder him, I fay to liften attentively
to a Sage, who fhou'd approach and tell him ;
' Sir ! I'll give you the Clew by which to trace
' thefe latent Powers and fatisfy your Curiofity.
' The great Foundation of Knowlege is the
' Principle of *Contradiction* or *Identity* ; that
' is to fay, that a Propofition cannot be true,
' and falfe at the fame time ; fo that A is A,
' and cannot be *not* A, which fingle Principle
' is fufficient to demonftrate all Geometry :
' but if you intend to apply it to *Nature*,
' you muft affume *another* Principle, that of
' a *fufficient Reafon*, or that nothing happens
' without a REASON why it happens fo rather
' than otherwife ᵏ.'   He retires, and another
advances—

ᵏ M. LEIBNITZ.

advances—— ' Sir! it is impoſſible that a Moun- Lett. 17.
' tain can be without a Valley; that the Whole
' ſhould be leſs than a Part; that two and two
' ſhould not make four, and that a Thing ſhould
' be and not be at the ſame time. To ſuppoſe it
' otherwiſe would be turning Theology and Re-
' ligion into Ridicule, an Abſurdity of worſe Con-
' ſequence than any thing I have mentioned [1].'

SUPPOSE after theſe two great Men, and
great they really were, an old myſterious Mythologiſt ſhou'd preſume to ſucceed, and ſing
or ſay this ancient Tale, ' That the Goddeſs
' THEMIS [m] prior to the Formation of the
' Univerſe had three eternal Daughters, *La-*
' *cheſis, Atropos* and *Clotho,* upon whom the
' ſupreme conſulting MIND, her Huſband, be-
' ſtow'd the higheſt Honour. They were
' called the FATES, (*Lots* or *Shares* parcelling
' out the World) and had Power irremiſſibly
' to diſtribute Good or Evil to Mortals. I have
' likewiſe heard, might the Bard ſubjoin, what

U   I

[1] M. BERNIER Eccⅼairciſſ.

[m] *Poſſibility* or *Aptitude,* the Wife of JOVE, to whom ſhe
bore the *Fates. Orpheus* ſays to her,

Πρώτη γὰρ τελείας ἁγίας θηλοῖς ἀνέφηνας
'Εκ σέο γὰρ τιμαὶ μακάρων μυςήρια θ'ἁγνά.

THOU *firſt to Mortals* ſacred Rites *revealed'ſt:*
From THEE *the Worſhip paid to every God,*
From THEE *their hallowed Myſteries proceed.*

That is to ſay, that the eternal Relations of Things conſidered
as influencing the Structure and Government of the World,
were the Source of Religion, or of the Worſhip of theſe ſuperior *Powers,* whoſe Connexions and Operations the Prieſts
endeavoured to *imitate* in their Rites, and *repreſent* in their
Mythology. See Page 51 and the Notes, and Page 88, Note [b].

Lett. 17. ' I do not fo well comprehend, that they were
'the Children of NIGHT, or of that Dark-
'nefs that preceded the Birth of PAN; that
'they were elder than TIME, and, what I
'better believe, that they preceded even an-
'cient CHAOS [n], but came to Maturity and
'Power when PAN firft fprang from its eternal
'Womb. But wou'd you, Sir! have a more
'intelligible Genealogy, tho' the fame in Sub-
'ftance with the firft and laft; the *Fates* were
'the Daughters of NECESSITY [o]: their Ha-
'bitation is the Recefs of a gloomy Cavern,
'where they live wrapt up in impenetrable
'Darknefs, but whence they daily fly out in-
'vifible, and govern Heaven and Earth, Gods
'and Men, according to their immutable Pre-
'fcription.' To which of the three Inftructors
wou'd a Man of Tafte liften with moft Pleafure?——To the laft, fay you, without doubt;
but it wou'd ftill increafe, if he condefcended
to fpeak a little plainer. That, my Friend,
he can never do while he keeps to his Character
as a Mythologift : But we fhall, if you pleafe,
call an Interpreter or two, an Ancient and a
Modern; and after hearing them, you may
better judge of his abftrufe Genealogies.

THERE are, fays the one, certain eternal
immutable *Relations* of Things, according to
which the World was framed, and by which it

is

---

[n] *Lycius Delius*, older than HOMER, (perhaps OLEN the
Lycian, Apollo's Poet in *Delos.*) See PAUSAN. Arcadic.
[o] From PLATO's *Timæus.*

is still governed. The Properties of a Triangle
can never agree to a Sphere, nor those of a
Sphere to a Cone. Every Piece of Matter requires a commensurate Space, and all Existence
necessarily implies Duration : The same Body
cannot have the Firmness of Iron and Fragility
of Wood, the Consistency of Earth and Fluidity
of Water. It cannot be crooked, and at the
same time streight ; heavy and yet light ; a
Circle and yet a Square. Each of these Properties is an eternal Law, by which Nature does
and must proceed. For the Powers necessarily
resulting from these immutable Relations were
so ordered by their great Creator, as by the most
admirable Mechanism to govern the Universe,
and preserve the divine Harmony and Order in
which it moves : while the apparent natural Ill
in the World is the slight Concomitant of a
much greater and more general Good.

It is my Opinion, says another, that the
Divine Nature is but one, tho' called by numberless Names, according to the several Operations and Productions which are ascribed to
God. We call him *living*, as the Author of
Life ; *eternal*, as he is from everlasting to everlasting ; *thundering* and *etherial*, from these his
Operations above ; *fruitful, generative* and *pa-
ternal*, from his Productions below ; *Saviour*
and *Deliverer* with the highest Propriety ; and
to include all, he is denominated *heavenly* and
earthly, after the various Effects of his Power

and

Lett. 17. and Providence, being himſelf the CAUSE of all things.—As to what is called NECESSITY, I take it to be nothing but his eternal and immovable Eſſence; to which the Fable of her Daughters the *Parcæ* and their fatal Spindle plainly points. They are three in number, according to the triple Diviſion of Duration into *paſt*, *preſent* and *to come*. Their ever-running Thread is partly ſpun and wound up, partly juſt drawn out and twiſting, and partly as yet on the Diſtaf. *Atropos* (Irreverſion) the eldeſt, ſevers the *Paſt*: *Lacheſis* (Allotment) the ſecond, lays out the *Future*: And *Clotho* (the young Spinſter [p]) is always furniſhing what is *Preſent*: So that the grand Tranſaction of Time is not ill repreſented in the Drama of the Fable. 'But, as *Plato* hath nobly ſaid, all this is nothing but GOD himſelf, who, according to 'ancient Tradition, having the Beginning, 'Middle and End of all Beings in his Power, 'keeps one ſtreight ſteady Courſe according to 'NATURE, with his inſeparable Adherent '*Juſtice*, always ready to avenge the leaſt Deviation from its *divine Law* [q].'

AFTER reading this beautiful Solution, methinks I hear you muttering to yourſelf, 'THEMIS 'the Wife of JOVE,—Mother of the FATES!

'*Poſſibility*—

[p] There are different Arrangements of the FATES; this ſame Author makes *Lacheſis* over-rule *Futurity*; and *Plato* makes her Province the *Preſent*, and *Atropos*'s *Futurity*: I have followed the Order that beſt ſuited the Subject, and the Import of their Names.

[q] ANONYM. περὶ Κοσμȣ̃.

' *Poſſibility*——*Aptitude*——*Structure of the*
' *World*—*Source of Worſhip*—*Three Siſters*—
' *Triple Duration, all governed by one all-wiſe,*
' *all-juſt and almighty* NATURE!' Glorious
comprehenſive View, if that be indeed the
Meaning of the Tale, and we be ſecure from
Illuſion in the Application! I well know you
are not eaſily ſatisfied; and in the preſent Caſe
there is but *one* Way to obtain Satisfaction; that
is to know the real Sentiments of the great
Maſters of Life and Philoſophy; *who thought
for themſelves,* at the ſame time that they were
comparing the Opinions of all their Neighbours,
and particularly ſearching into the Treaſures of
the *Eaſt*; to know, I ſay, their real Sentiments
of the Riſe and Government of the World, and
compare them with the alluſive Tale. But how
is that Knowledge to be attained? I heſitate
a little to anſwer the Queſtion: yet muſt
ingenuouſly tell you, that if you indeed wiſh
to enter into the Spirit of the early Sages, and
view their genuine manly Conceptions of *Nature*
and *Truth*; if you wiſh to feel their elevated
Genius, and be truly acquainted both with their
Head and their Heart, you *muſt of neceſſity be
Maſter of their* LANGUAGE. No Interpreter,
no Commentator, no Copier can ſave you from
this Condition: Were *Mercury* himſelf to deſcend at your Prayer, and reſume his ancient
Office, you wou'd receive at beſt but faint, often
falſe, often disfigured Ideas from his Interpre-

tation.

Lett 17. tation. What the judicious *Cervantes* says of
Poetry, holds equally true of elegant Prose, and
indeed more or less of all kind of Writing; ' That
' all Attempts to translate Verse into a different
' Language have always come short of the
' Beauty of the Original, let ever so much La-
' bour be employ'd, or Abilities shewn in the
' Translation '.' But all Fable is *Poetry*, and
the truest Species of it is *Fable*. In this, you
have often heard, the earliest Authors wrote;
and even the unfabled Accounts, if I may so
speak, of the grand Transactions of ancient
Chaos, and the Rise of Things, are, in the Opinion of a knowing Divine, *poetically* and enig-
matically told. ' The Reflections, says he, that
' are made in several Parts of the divine Wri-
' tings upon the Origin of the World and the
' Formation of the Earth, seem to me to be
' writ in a Stile something approaching to the
' Nature of a *prophetical* Stile, and to have
' more of a divine Enthusiasm in them than the
' ordinary Text of Scripture; the Expressions
' are lofty, and sometimes abrupt, and often
' figurative and disguised; as may be particu-
' larly observed in that beautiful Speech of Wis-
' dom recorded by *Solomon*; which is yet so ob-
' scure, that no two Versions I have met with
agree in the Translation of that Verse :—and it
' commonly

ʳ Todos aquellos que los Libros de Verso quisieron bo/ver en
otra Lengua——quitaron mucho de su natural Valor : que por
Cuydado que pongan; y Habilidad que muestran jamas llegarán
al punto que ellos tienen en su primer nacimiento.

D. Qu i x. Lib. I. § 6.

' commonly happens ſo in an *enthuſiaſtic* or pro- Lett. 17
' phetic Stile, that by reaſon of the *Eagerneſs*
' and *Trembling* of the Fancy, it does not al-
' ways regularly follow the ſame even Thread of
' Diſcourſe; but ſtrikes many times upon ſome
' other Thing that hath *Relation* to it, or lies
' *under* or *near* the ſame View '.' Is it poſſible,
do you think, to underſtand the bare Meaning,
not to mention the Beauty and Spirit of ſuch a
Way of Writing by *Tranſlations?* No—nor is it
in many Caſes poſſible to make any Tranſlation at
all, without loſing not only the Elegance, but
half the Senſe; of which there is ſo pregnant
an Inſtance in the Author lately quoted, where
he explains the various *Greek* Names of *Fate,*
that I dare challenge the greateſt Linguiſt in *Europe* to make it perfectly intelligible to a Perſon
unſkilled in the Original '. *Plato* ſays prettily,
that a Poet is ΤΡΙΤΑΤΟΣ ΑΠΟ ΤΗΣ ΑΛΗΘΕΙΑΣ,
three Removes from Truth, whoſe primary genuine Eſſence, according to him, is the divine
IDEA, the *Model* of the Creation. The viſible

U 4

Forms

' Dr. T. BURNET's Sacred Theory.

' Ο'μαι δὲ τὴν ΑΝΑΓΚΗΝ ἐκ ἄλλο τὶ λέγεσθαι πλὴν
τῦτον (τὸν ΘΕΟΝ)· ΕΙΜΑΡΜΕΝΗΝ δὲ διὰ τὸ εἴρειν τε. κỳ
χωρεῖν ἀκολύτως· ΠΕΠΡΟΜΕΝΗΝ δὲ διὰ τὸ πεπερα-
τῶσθαι πάντα, κỳ μηδὲν ἐν τοῖς ὅτι ἄπειρον εἶναι· κỳ ΜΟΙΡΑΝ.
μὲν ἀπὸ τῦ μεμερίσθαι· ΝΕΜΕΣΙΝ δὲ ἀπὸ τῆς ἑκάςῳ
διανεμήσεως· ΑΔΡΑΣΤΕΙΑΝ δὲ ἀνικφύδρασον αἰτίαν ἕσαν
κατὰ φύσιν· ΑΙΣΑΝ δὲ ἀεὶ ὅυσαν. Περὶ ΚΟΣΜΟΥ.

In the firſt and two laſt Names of FATE, I apprehend the
Author to have miſtaken the Etymology.

Lett.7. Forms of Things make the firſt Step from it ;
our Conceptions or Ideas of them the ſecond ; and
the Poet's Allegories, or *Figures* of theſe Conceptions, the third. A Tranſlation therefore
muſt be a Remove further off ; and if he vary'd
the Figure, which he cannot avoid in Languages of different Genius, he muſt be the *fifth*
from Truth. Slight and ſlippery is the Hold
of her at that Diſtance ; and abſurd the Plan
of ſearching for her in a Tranſlation ! For do
but conſider ; the greateſt Men of Antiquity,
tho' endow'd with the ſublimeſt Underſtandings,
ſpent their Lives in Study, with an Application
and Docility amazing to a Modern. When
Pythagoras impoſed a ſeven Year's Silence on
his Diſciples, he told them that he required
but one half the Time which he had himſelf
ſpent among the Prieſts in *Egypt*, (where he
ſubmitted to *Circumciſion* into the bargain) in
order to gain Admittance into their Order, and
participate of their myſtical Science. *Democritus*
ſpent a long Life, in an unwearied Reſearch of
Truth, under the Direction of the *Chaldean* Magi,
the *Egyptian* Prieſts, the *Indian* Gymnoſophiſts,
and of *Leucippus* the *Grecian* Author of the *Ato-
mic* Philoſophy. *Theophraſtus* is characterized by
Plutarch ΦΙΛΗΚΟΟΣ ΕΙΤΙΣ ΑΛΛΟΣ, *inquiſitive
if ever Man was,* and continued ſuch beyond
his ninetieth Year. His Maſter *Ariſtotle*, tho'
of ſuch Penetration as to be called by *Plato* the
Genius of *Nature,* ſtudied for twenty Years
under

under the Direction of that great Man, who, Lett. 17. e'er he obtained himself the Title of the *divine Philosopher*, had been successively the Scholar of *Socrates*, of *Archytas*, of *Eudoxus* and *Eurytus* near double that time, besides a Voyage we are told he made to the grand School of Religion and Learning, the Kingdom of *Egypt*. Are *these* Men's or their more metaphorical Master's Sentiments to be truly and justly learned in Translations? Numberless are the Mistakes which I cou'd point out in the most elaborate, authentic, and often revised Versions; but I shou'd be unwilling to depreciate well-meant Endeavours, whose Miscarriage detracts nothing from their primitive Merit. I chuse rather to give you a pleasant Instance of this kind, to which I was Witness myself.

It is not very long since a Gentleman, who did Honour to his Country while he resided at *Constantinople* in a public Character, and who is now still more conspicuous by his Merit and Services, happened in Conversation to mention the Subtlety of the *Mahometan* Doctors, the Piety and Devotion of their Disciples, and prodigious Extent of their Religion. As he is a Man of superior Knowledge and Probity, his way of speaking surprized an ingenious Youth who happened to be in the Company, and awaked a Curiosity natural to a young Mind, to see the *Basis* upon which so vast an Edifice leaned. He accordingly got a *French* Translation

of

Lett.17 of the CORAN by their Conful *du Ryer,* and fat eagerly down to read it. But he was amazed beyond meafure when he cou'd fcarce make out half a Page of common Senfe together. ' *This* ' the Foundation, faid· he, of a mighty Reli- ' gion! this the Decider of fubtile Difputes! ' and Rule of refined Morals! Impoffible. ' Sir *E* * * * * *F* * * * * to be fure ' knows the *Eaft* better than any Man in *Bri-* ' *tain*; but what can be the Influence of fuch ' Stuff as this?'

As ill Luck wou'd have it, an old *Latin* CORAN fell into his Hands much about the fame time, which is utterly unintelligible; and inftead of a Foundation of Faith feems to be the Produ&ion of Madnefs and Immorality. This compleated his Aftonifhment; particularly *Sura* XII. in relating the Hiftory of *Jo-feph's* being fold by his Brothers into *Egypt,* and of his Miftrefs's Paffion for him, (who, as her beft Excufe, invited a Sett of Ladies *to fee him,*) there is in that Tranflation an Expreffion about the Women, at his Entrance into the Room, too indecent to be repeated; but at which the Tranflator in a marginal Note exclaims, *O fœdum et obfcœnum Prophetam!* O the obfcene and filthy Prophet! My young Gentleman cou'd ftand it no longer: he came flying to me with his Tranflation and Amazement, which appeared fo painted in his Looks, and fuch Eagernefs to tell it, that I
cou'd

cou'd scarce hear him with tolerable Gravity; Lett.17. nor can I yet think of it without Laughter. In end however I took out the Book, view'd the Verse, and assured him there was neither Trace nor Vestige of such an Expression in the CORAN; but on the contrary a very modest Term that signifies to *prize highly*, or *greatly commend.* Then looking here and there thro' the pretended Translation, I found it did not deserve the Name; and recommended to him a *new* one done by a modest learned Man * of equal Capacity and Candour, and who, for the Honour of our Country, I wish had met with the Encouragement due to his Merit. This satisfied my young Friend *in part*; to do it *wholly*, and to let him see that that Book, which we justly think replenished with Folly, may yet be the Object of Admiration, and almost Adoration † of greater *Numbers* of Mankind than any Book extant, as indeed it is, I read to him, from an *Eastern* Author, the Story of a deep Remorse and high Profession of Repentance it once produced in a Royal Breast.

THE powerful King of *Carisme*, possessed of the finest Countries of the *East*, (the ancient *Persia*, *Media* and *Parthia*, and the mighty Tract lying to the East and South of the *Caspian Sea*

* Mr. G, SALE.

† The orthodox *Moslems* believe the CORAN to be eternal and uncreated; having been writ from everlasting on the same Table by God's Throne that contains the divine irreversible Decrees, whence the Angel *Gabriel* copied it, and at proper Seasons brought it to *Mahomet*.

Lett. 17. Sea all the way to *India*) had connived at a barbarous Murder committed againſt the Law of Nations in the Perſon of an Ambaſſador from the great *Genghis-can*, and a Caravan of *Mogol* Merchants put cruelly to death in his Capital. That Northern Conqueror, bred in Hardſhips, the School of Heroes, iſſuing from the Mountains of *Tartary*, with the Poſterity of theſe fierce Nations that formerly ravaged, and now poſſeſs *Aſia* and *Europe*, had extended his Fame and Power over a great Part of the *Eaſt* : But *Sultan* MEHMED King of *Cariſme*, elated with a Grandeur built upon the Ruin of the *Khalifs*, the *Seljuc* Sultans, and later *Grecian* Empire, deſpiſed *Gengis-can* and his rude *Mogols*. ' What tho', ſaid he to his Generals, ' they have vanquiſhed ſome barbarous Pagan ' Nations, unſkilled in military Arts; they ſhall ' find they have now to deal with different Peo- ' ple, the brave generous *Muſſulmen*, verſed in ' War, who have conquered *Fars* ", and all the ' reſt of *Iran* ˟; and whom no Nation, not ' the moſt warlike in *Aſia*, has yet been able ' to withſtand: Let us go and teach the raſh ' *Tartar* the Difference between Us and the ' *Pagan Barbarians* he has vanquiſhed.'

 ' The Generals obey'd: the Sultan's *Sangiac* ˟ ' was reared: the great Trumpet the *Kerrena* ' ſounded : the *Mangalay* ˟ marched : the Ar- ' mies met in the Plains of *Caracou*. A terrible   ' Battle

---

  ˟ PERSIA.   ˟ HIRCANIA.
  ˟ The Royal Standart. ˟ The Vanguard.

'Battle was fought; which lasted from Sun-
'rising till Darkness covered the Earth [y];' and
tho' the King of *Carisme*, and the noble Prince
Gelal-addin his Son, both did Wonders of Valour, yet on that fatal Day, of three hundred
thousand fighting Men they lost one hundred
and sixty thousand, and the Victory. It was
then that *Sultan* MEHMED, stript of his vast
Dominions, was forced to fly before the *Mogol*-
Conqueror : and pursued from City to City and
Fortress to Fortress, he wandered thro' Desarts,
until he arrived with a thin Retinue at a little
obscure Town upon the Banks of the *Caspian
Sea*. Here the once haughty and now humbled
Prince regularly assisted at the public Devotion,
which a poor *Imam* performed in a mean
Mosque at the five stated Hours of Prayer; and
one Day hearing the CORAN read, and Justice
and Mercy recommended, his Heart melted,
he burst into Tears, and made many ardent
Vows to Heaven; promising in a loud Voice, if
God would deliver him from the Dangers
hanging over his Head, and re-establish him in
the Throne of his Kingdom, that he wou'd re-
ligiously thenceforth keep the LAW, and govern
his People with Equity and Mildness.

I never saw deeper Attention than the curious
Youth gave to this Story, tho' brokenly read
from the *Eastern* Author : but as the Impression
was likewise very deep which the Absurdity of
the

[y] ABUL-CAIR, the Historian's own Words.

Lett.17. the Tranſlations and Difference of *Manners* had
made upon him, I found it farther neceſſary to
tell him, that tho' the CORAN, as being *principally* founded upon *Talmudical* Stories, and
next upon *our* Scriptures *miſunderſtood*, was
interſperſed with palpable Ridicule, yet the
general Deſign of it being to unite the three
predominant but confuſed Religions at that
time, *Zabians*, *Jews*, and heretical *Chriſtians*
in the Knowlege of *one* ſupreme God, and *one*
ſimple Worſhip *, it was no wonder, in the
Circumſtances of the Prophet and his People,
that it ſhould obtain Belief. To convince
him of this, I aſked leave to give him a faint
imperfect Idea of one Part of its Doctrine
upon the moſt ſublime of all Subjects, the
DEITY.

" GOD!——There is no other *God* beſides
" him. HE it is who *lives*, ſelf-exiſtent for
" ever and ever. HE it is whom Sleep can never
" ſeize, nor Slumbers approach. To him be-
" longs whatever the Earth contains ; whatever
" the Heaven ſurrounds : and *who*, againſt his
" Will, dares intercede for the Crime of another?
" HE, and HE alone knows all things; pre-
" ſent and to come ; while *Mortals* know no-
" thing but what his Pleaſure reveals. The
" Extent of his THRONE outmeaſures Heaven
" and Earth : the Preſervation of all they con-
" tain is no trouble to HIM. *He* is GOD, the
" *lofty*

* GOLIUS in Append. ad Gram. *T*. *Erpenii*.

" *lofty* one and the *great* † :"—and after reading Lett. 17.
it nearly in this manner, I affured the young
Gentleman, as I do you, that how noble and
exalted foever the Defcription may appear, it is
but a dim Shadow of the Energy, Majefty, and
Comprehenfion of the Original.

If the Ideas then and forcible Expreffions of
an illiterate *Arab* (for fuch was *Mahomet*) admit of no adequate Tranflation, what Chance
muft the deep Conclufions and refined chafte
Conceptions of an elegant *Grecian,* or allegorical
Theologue have to be genuinely reprefented in
a foreign Dialect ? Undeceive yourfelf, my
Friend ! Refolve to go to the Fountain-Head,
if you purpofe to drink of pure untainted Knowledge. *There* plunge into the Stream, and take
a Draught fufficient to quench a noble Thirft.
The *Socraticæ Chartæ* ª in particular, which
explain

—*Quid Patriæ debitum, et quid Amicis*;

What to our Country and our Friends is due;

and teach us *that* Sapere, *that Wifdom* and
Senfe which *Horace* fays is the Source of fine
Writing ª, are not to be learned in tranflated
Scraps. You muft, in the fame Author's Phrafe,
Socraticis madere Sermonibus— ' throughly im-
bibe the *Socratic* Doctrines,' e'er you be
admitted to view the Goddeffes Virtue and
Science in the fineft Drefs they have yet
appeared

† Coran, *Sura* II.
ª *Socratic* Writings; meaning Plato, Xenophon, Cebes
and Eschine's Works. ª De Arte Poetica.

Lett.17 appeared among Men. Mean time I'll give you a
Glance of them upon the same Subject, *the fatal
Sisters*, (which likewise includes the Doctrine
of Transmigration) to raise your Desire of
further Enjoyment. Cou'd I find *English* Terms
equivalent to the Eloquence of the Man whose
chosen Language was to be the Pattern of the
Speech of the Gods, I shou'd make no doubt
of its having the desired Effect; at present you
must be contented with my good Intentions,
and accept the Translation, if it be but barely
intelligible.

Assoon as the Soul, says an old *Grecian* Tradition, is separated from the Body by Death, it
takes its Flight towards its next Mansion; and
first arrives at a solemn sacred Region, where
the Earth opens in two great *Chasms*, and opposite to them, the Heaven in other two, con-
tiguous to one another. Betwixt these sit the
Judges of Men, who pass Sentence upon all
that arrive, and according to its Import, direct
the Souls of the *Just* to take their way by one
of the *heavenly* Passages, and those of the *Unjust*
to seek the nethermost of the *infernal* Roads;
leading to the Place of Punishment destined
for Tyrants, Traitors, Murderers and Oppressors;
but which is chiefly filled with Princes who
abused an absolute Power. The judged Souls
therefore immediately pass thro' *one* of the
earthly, or *one* of the heavenly Passages, and
depart for their respective Abodes: and thro'
the

the *other* two they as conſtantly arrive at the Let.17.
Place where the Judges ſit. Tnoſe who riſe
out of the *earthly* Gulph, come there in
wretched Plight, full of Filth and Mire; but
thoſe who deſcend the *celeſtial* Road, appear
bright and pure, like their Habitation: Both
ſeem to be newly arrived from a long Journey,
and with great Complacency go in a Body and
lodge in a *Mead*: There they ſalute as old
Acquaintance, and enquire at one another their
ſeveral Adventures; thoſe from under the Earth
aſking about the Things in Heaven, and the
heavenly Gueſts the Tranſactions below. The
former in relating their Fate, weep and wail
at the Remembrance of all the Miſery they
ſaw and ſuffered in their infernal Progreſs of a
thouſand Years; and the latter tell with Rapture their high Enjoyments, and Sights they
ſaw of ineffable Beauty.

AFTER having been ſeven Days in the Mead,
the Souls muſt remove on the eighth; and
making a Journey of four more, they arrive at
a Place, whence they diſcover a *ſtreight Body
of Light*, as it were a Column, reaching *thro'*
Heaven and Earth, nearly reſembling the *Iris*,
but more pure and reſplendent: At this they
arrive in one Day more, and behold the Extremities of the *Band* of Heaven, braced to the
Middle of the Column; for this LIGHT is the
Band of Heaven, embracing and keeping firm
its whole Circumference, like the under-gird-

X ing

Let. 17. ing of a Galley. Dependent from its Ends, hangs the *Spindle* of NECESSITY, which with its eternal Twirl makes all the celeftial Orbs to circumvolve; her *Diftaff*, with its *Hook*, are of Adamant, and her Whirl a Compound of this and other Materials; its Form the fame with thofe ufed on Earth, but fuch its internal Mechanifm, that within the great outer Whirl, which is hollow and perforated, lies juft fuch another, but lefs; and in the fame manner a third and fourth, and fo forth to the eighth, like Nefts of Boxes fitted to one another, being in all eight concave Spheres, lying in Circles one within another, whofe Edges appear above, but make the external Superficies of one fingle Sphere around the *Spindle*[b], which paffes clear through the Middle of the eighth and innermoft.—By the Twirl of the everlafting Spindle, the whole is carried round in the fame Circumvolution; but while it circumvolves, the feven inner Spheres move gently round in a contrary Direction: Of thefe the eighth revolves with the greateft Velocity; next to it, and equal with one another, the feventh, fixth, and fifth; the third appears to follow the fame Courfe with the fourth, the fourth with the third, and fifth with the fecond,

---

[b] Νῶτον συνεχὲς ἑνὸς σφονδύλου ἀπεργαζομένους σιρὶ τὴν ΗΛΑΚΑ-ΤΗΝ. I make no doubt but this muft either have been an Efcape in the great Philofopher, or, which is more probable, the blunder of a Copift; for the Senfe requires it fhould be σιρὶ τὸ ΑΤΡΑΚΤΟΝ, and I have tranflated it accordingly.

cond, and *the Spindle, with all its Orbs, turns*
upon the Knees of NECESSITY.

ALONG with every Sphere is carried aloft a
Syren, who utters one unvaried fimple Note,
but from whofe compofition with the reft, being eight in all, there refults a perfect Harmony. Befides thefe, there fit round the
Spindle, at equal Diftances, each upon her
Throne, the three FATES, Daughters of NE-
CESSITY, *Atropos, Lachefis,* and *Clotho,* ar-
rayed in white Apparel, with Garlands on their
Heads, and finging in Concert with the Melody of the *Syrens; Lachefis,* the *Paft; Clotho,*
the *Prefent;* and *Atropos,* things *to come.*
Clotho, at times laying her right-hand upon
the Whirl, drives round the outer Sphere, in-
termitting her Action: *Atropos,* with her left,
does the fame to the inner Spheres: And *La-*
chefis, with either Hand, pufhes round fometimes the one, and fometimes the other.

ARRIVED at this Place, the Souls go ftreight
to *Lachefis,* when a certain *Prophet* firft di-
vides them into Claffes; and then taking out
of *Lachefis'* Lap, *Lots* and *Patterns* of Life,
he fteps up to an exalted Throne, and proclaims, Thus fayeth *Lachefis* (Alottment) the
Child of NECESSITY, *Ye tranfient Souls! here*
is the beginning of a new Period, ending in
Death to the mortal Race: Deftiny fhall not
draw Lots for you, but you fhall choofe a Def-
tiny for yourfelves; whofe Lot is firft, let him

X 2 *firft*

firſt chooſe his Life, which once choſen, he muſt of neceſſity lead: But Virtue is free to all; which, as every one prizes or deſpiſes, more or leſs of it ſhall be his Share; the Blame be on the Choice, and GOD *be free!* And having thus ſpoke, he ſcatters abroad the Lots, and each takes up that which falls by him, not being permitted by the *Prophet* to touch any but his own well-known Number. Then the Patterns of all the various Kinds of Lives that are lived upon Earth, are ſet in order before them, many more than the Souls that are to chooſe: There you have the Lives of all ſorts of *Animals*, and all the ſorts of Lives led by *Men*. There you have Kingſhips and Sovereignties, ſome laſting for Life, others cut ſhort in the Middle, and ending in Beggary and Baniſhment. There are the Lives of *Men* celebrated for their Beauty and Comelineſs, for their Strength, Bravery, and glorious Toils, for their high Deſcent and illuſtrious Anceſtors; and of *Women* in the ſame manner: But there is no Diſtinction or Claſſing of Souls, becauſe of the Neceſſity there is that the Soul ſhould *change* according to the Life it chooſes, and theſe are infinite in Number, varied and mixed with the Extremes of Poverty and Riches, Sickneſs and Health, and with all their intermediate Degrees.

AND here indeed is the grand Danger, the Point that requires our prime Care, how to poſtpone

postpone every other Science, and, if possible, Let. 17. learn this supreme of Arts, *How to discern a wise worthy Life from an ignorant wicked one, and make our Choice accordingly.* For this Purpose we ought, while in *this* World, seriously consider what is the *real Value* of the Things most coveted in it; Beauty of Person, Strength, Wealth, Power, Honour, and high Birth, and what Effects they produce either singly, or intermixed and compounded with some of their Contraries; and when about to leave it, we ought to set out on our Journey to the Grave, with this Opinion bound to us as with an adamantine Chain, *That Virtue is Happiness, and Vice Misery, in all their Respects and Tendencies*; lest possibly our Mind should even there be struck with the Desire of Pomp, and such other dazzling Evils as supreme Power, Usurpation, and illegal Grandeur, for whose sakes Men make irreparable havoc of their fellow-creatures, and suffer yet worse Tortures themselves. On the contrary, we ought to stick to the *middle Life*, and fly the Extremes on either hand, both in this mortal State, and in that which succeeds; for this is the *Happiness* of MAN.

AND now, the various Models and Manners of Life being ranged in Order, so as every Soul may chuse in its Turn, the *Prophet* again proclaims, ‘ *The last by Lot, if he wisely choose,* ‘ *and worthy live, may assure himself of a*

X 3 ‘ *happy*

Let.17.' *happy Life; wherefore let neither the firſt in*
' *order be careleſs, nor the laſt deſpair.*' Then
the Soul advanced to whom the *firſt* Lot had
fallen, and choſe *the greateſt Kingdom*; but
through Senſuality and Folly did not ſuffici-
ently conſider the Circumſtances of the Choice,
nor perceive that it was inevitably accompanied
with Extirpation of his Family, eating his
Children, and other execrable Deeds; wherefore viewing it at more leiſure, the Soul was
confounded, and made a hideous Outcry, neither abiding by its Choice, nor the Conditions
fixed by the *Prophet*, nor taking Blame to itſelf, but loudly accuſing the Gods, and Fortune, and every thing rather than its own
Folly.   The Soul who made this wretched
Choice, was of the Number of thoſe who had
come laſt from Heaven, and who had lived its
former Life in a regular well-governed State [c],
where it had acquired the Habits of Virtue by
meer *Cuſtom*, without *Reaſon* or *Philoſophy*;
and of that ſort who come from Heaven, not a
few are catched in wrong Choices, as having
never taſted Miſery; whereas the far greater
part of thoſe who come from the Earth, have
both ſuffered themſelves, and ſeen the Sufferings of others, and are in no Hurry to make
their Choice; by which Means a Rotation of
Happineſs and Miſery prevails among the Souls,
to which the *Chance* of their various Lots likewiſe

[c] A Touch, as I conceive, againſt *Crete* and *Lacedemon*.

wife contributes. For fuppofe that one fhould always, when they come into the World, feek in earneft after Wifdom, if at the fame time their Lot do not happen to be the laft, that Perfon muft ftand a fair Chance not only to live happily on Earth, but in going and coming, never to travel the black infernal Road, but only the fmooth celeftial Way.

It is an entertaining Sight to fee how the feveral Souls pick out their different Lives, a Sight both piteous, and ridiculous, and ftrange; becaufe, for the moft part, they make their Choice from fome odd Circumftance of their former Life. There you may fee, for Example, the Soul that once animated the famous *Orpheus*, making choice of the Life of a Swan, through Hatred of the Sex that cruelly murdered him, and Difdain being again born of a Woman. *Thamyris*, the Poet and Mufician, chofe the Life of a Nightingale; and *Swans* and others of the *mufical* Tribe, exchanged their former for the State of Men. A remarkable Soul, that of *Ajax* the Son of *Telamon*, refufed to revive a Man, from a Memory of his Difgrace in the Judgment of the Arms, and chofe the Life of a *Lion*. After him, *Agamemnon's* Shade advanced to chufe; and that he might not be again murdered by a Spoufe, he preferred the Life of an *Eagle*. *Atalanta*, famed for her Speed, happening about the Middle of the Choice to fpy the Honours de-

ftined

Let. 17. ſtined to an *Olympic* Wreſtler, could not paſs
by it, but choſe the athletic Life of a Man.
On the contrary, the Son of *Panopeus*, *Epeus*
the Mechanic, preferred the Nature of an inventive artificial Woman, weaving curious
Webs, and contriving new Patterns of Needle-
work. *Therſites*, the Buffoon, took up with
the Life and Manners of a Monkey : And laſt
of all the Soul of the celebrated *Ulyſſes* advancing to chuſe, and recollecting all the Fa-
tigues and Dangers he had formerly under-
gone, and wiſhing now for Reſpite from the
Toils of Ambition, and Riſques of Battle,
went a great while about looking for the Lot
of a private, obſcure, unoccupied Man.   This
with Difficulty it at laſt found thrown ſome-
where aſide, and deſpiſed by all the reſt; and
taking it fondly up, ſolemnly affirmed, that
had its Lot been firſt in Order, and at full
Liberty to pick out among them all, this Life
it would have choſe, and none other.

OF the other Animals, in the ſame Manner,
many went into the human Nature, and many
into the different Species of their own, the
Cruel and Ravenous into the *Wild*, and the
Harmleſs and Gentle into the *Tame*, making
all the Mixtures and Combinations imaginable.
But when the Choice is over, and every Soul
has got the Life it is to live, they all proceed
in order to *Lacheſis*, who appoints a *Genius*
to each, the Guardian of the Life they choſe,
                                    and

and Accomplisher of its particular Lot. His
first Business is to lead them to *Clotho*, in order to ratify under her Hand, and from the
Run of the potent Twirl of her Spindle, the
Fate they elected for their own. After they
have been touched by it, he next leads them to
the Thread of *Atropos*, giving an irrevocable
Sanction to the Decrees of *Clotho*. From hence,
without once looking back, they all pass directly under *the Throne of* NECESSITY, and
through it they go. When all are passed, they
march together in sultry suffocating Heat to
the *Plain* of OBLIVION, a naked dreary Region, without Tree or any Thing produced by
Earth, and there they encamp by the Banks of
the River *Inconcern*, whose Water no Vessel
can hold. Of this every one must drink a certain Measure; and those who are not saved
from it by Understanding, drink more than
enough, while whosoever drinks forthwith,
forgets every thing, and falls asleep. But about
Midnight Thunders begin to break—Earthquakes ensue, and every Soul is of a sudden
hurried aloft, and some one way, some another, shoot like Stars into a new Birth.

TRY your Taste, my Friend, by these allegorical Images of the Rise and various Periods
of Mortality. If you can read this long Letter with Pleasure, I pronounce you no mean
Proficient in Mythology; and if the latter
Part of it give you particular Satisfaction, I
should

should think my Pains well-placed, and con-gratulate you on a higher Attainment. Ab-solve me, in the mean time, from my Promise of explaining *Hecate* and *Pandora*, or any other Allegory ; whoever understands the Doc-trine of the *Fates*, has a Key to the better part of the ancient Emblems. Let me therefore conclude with telling you two Things about this Relation of the invisible World. First, that the Philosopher does not tell it as origi-nally his own, but makes his Master (*Socrates*) repeat it as a Story told by one *Eros* a *Pamphy-lian*, who being wounded in a Battle, lay nine Days for dead on the Field, and the Carcasses beginning to putrify, was found sound on the tenth, and carried home to be buried. Two Days thereafter being laid on the funeral Pile, he came to Life after having been twelve Days dead, and related to his Friends all his Soul had seen in its Progress while dislodged from the Body. Next, that this Relation concludes his Body of *Politics*, as his *Timæus*, or History of the Creation, introduces his *Laws* ; being both employed as powerful Restraints from Vice, and Persuasives to the Practice of Piety and Virtue. Nor can I refuse myself the Plea-sure of observing, in favour of a more refined Theology, that the Doctrine. of the Ancients about their *Gods*, that is, of the *Creation*, and its constituent Parts, generally leads to the happy Idea of one *supreme eternal* Being,

from

from whom all Things firſt ſprang, and who Let. 17. firſt put, and now preſerves them in Order; or where it has no ſuch Tendency, it is a Child born by Superſtition to wild Fancy, full of crude Conceptions, which only amuſe without in-ſtructing. WISDOM never yet contrived a World without a GOD, all-mighty, all-boun-teous, all-wiſe at the Center. May You, *My Friend!* always ſo reaſon, and ſo live, as to think of him with Pleaſure!

I am, &c.

LETTER

LETTER XVIII.

IN good Earneſt, it would ſeem I have cut out more Work for myſelf than I was aware, and raiſed an inquiſitive Spirit, which I cannot wiſh entirely to *lay*, though I find it will coſt me ſome Pains to feed and keep it quiet.   It is indeed a natural and noble Curi-oſity, after hearing ſo much of the Allegory and Imagery in which the Ancients wrapt their Opinions concerning the Riſe of Things and Creation of the World, to enquire *what theſe Opinions really were when ſtript of their Cover-ings?* and an obvious Connexion, to take, as you have done, another Step, and aſk *whether they were falſe or true?*

To anſwer the *laſt*, would be to write upon the moſt abſtruſe Parts of *Metaphyſics* and *na-tural Philoſophy:* a Taſk I hope you will diſ-penſe with my undertaking, upon ſo eaſy Terms as telling you, that I believe they were neither abſolutely *true* nor *falſe*, but *mixed*, part *Truth*, and part *Falſhood* *; and as for the reſt, let me only remind you of the cau-tious Plan of the *Jewiſh* Education †: ſo far

I

---

* Vera ſunt quæ loquuntur POETAE, ſed obtentu aliquo, ſpecieque velata. LACTANT. Lib. I. Cap. II.

† ‘ In our Schools *natural Philoſophy* is to be learned from ‘ the firſt Chapter of *Geneſis*; upon which account it is called ‘ *the Study of the Work of Creation*; which being incumbered ‘ with

I can foundly direct you, on condition that you afk no farther: For fhould you next defire to know what *Rabbi*, what *Father*, what *Annotator* you muft take for your Teacher or *Hierophant*, I muft ftop fhort, and declare myfelf not a little at a lofs to whom I fhould preferably recommend you.

How the *private* Inftructors among the *Jews*, acquit themfelves of their arduous Tafk, is not perhaps worth enquiring; but the moft knowing of their *Writers* have taken different Roads, and explained many Things *oppofitely* to one another [a]. The fame Fate has attended the learned Moderns who have undertaken to adapt the fhort Hints we have of *natural* Things in holy Writ, to the Principles of Philofophy that prevailed in the feveral Ages in which they lived. Thefe Attempts were particularly frequent in the beginning of this, and end of the laft Century, when Knowledge of every kind ftreamed like Light through the weftern World; while others, who imagined

that

' with great Difficulties, is not wont to be publickly explained, ' but only in *private* to the Party that defires it. As for *Meta-* ' *phyfics*, neither is this Study to be otherwife attained to, it be- ' ing grounded upon the firft Chapter of *Ezekiel*, which is look'd ' upon as no lefs difficult, and therefore not to be explained but ' with the like Caution.' Is. ABENDANA. *Polity of the* JEWS.

[a] The *Jewifh* Commentaries are of three forts: 1. *Literal*; fuch as thofe writ by the *Carraim*, that by R. *Ben-Melec*, and a very few others. 2. *Allegorical* and *moral*; fuch as *Jarchi's*, *Ramban's*, and the far greater Part of their Writers. 3. *Kabbaliftical* and *myfterious*; fuch as the *Sepher Jetzirah*, or Book of Creation of R. *Akibah*, the *Zohar* of R. *Simeon Ben-Jochai*, and all the *Siphri* and their *Biutim*, i. e. *Illuftrations*, or Sub-commentaries.

Let. 18. that the current Opinions could not be so well reconciled with the sacred Doctrine, and who for that Reason believed them to be *false*, thought it advisable to frame a *new Philosophy*, that would better quadrate with the received System. With the same Views one very lately endeavoured to extract a Set of Principles by a sort of *Kabbala* founded upon Letters and a new Punctation, which should at once confirm our Belief, and highly improve our natural Knowledge. Yet all this Variety of different Methods, and different Interpretations, neither derogates from the Authority of the primitive Doctrine, nor is it any reason why some *one* of its Glossators should not have hit upon the Truth.

IT is true, such Attempts have been made directly contrary to the Advice of the pious Lord *Verulam:* ‘ The greatest Caution, he ‘ says, should be used against a Mixture of ‘ *Superstition* and *Theology:* It spreads wide ‘ Corruption through Philosophy, and does ‘ Mischief both to Systems and their Parts: ‘ For the worst of Things is *Error deified*, ‘ which ought to be regarded not as a *Defect*, ‘ but as a *Pest* of the Understanding when attended with groundless Veneration. Yet some ‘ of the Moderns have, with the utmost Levity, so far indulged themselves in this Illusion, as to endeavour to found a *natural* ‘ *Philosophy* upon the first Chapter of GENE-

SIS,

' SIS, the Book of JOB, and other Parts of the
' *holy Scriptures*; prepofterously fearching for
' the *Dead* among the *Living:* A Folly the
' rather to be reftrained, becaufe from the un-
' wholfome Mixture of Things *human* and *di-*
' *vine*, arifes not only a fantaftic Philofophy,
' but an heretical Religion. 'Tis therefore the
' moft falutary Method to apply *Faith* only
' in Matters *that to Faith belong* [b].'

WE accordingly fee fome of the wifeft Men,
thofe who beft underftand the real Interefts of
Religion, who have moft promoted it by their
Writings, and adorned it by their Lives, take
a quite different Courfe [c]. They fix the due
Limits between Faith and Philofophy: They
are at pains to fhew, that the great Ends propofed by the former, could be better compaf-
fed, and its great Objects more properly reprefented in a *popular* than a *philofophical* Strain;
and with comprehenfive Views, and enlarged
Hearts, have at once reverenced Truth, re-
moved Objections, and done Honour to their
Profeffion. Difference of Opinion there has
been, and will be while there are *Men*; and
the

[b] ORGANUM NOV. Parf. II. Aphor. 65.

[c] See Dr. SAMUEL CLARKE's *Demonftration*, &c. Part II.
Dr. BUTLER's *Analogy*, &c. Dr. A. A. SYKE's *Principles, Defence*, and *Treatife* of *Demoniacs*. Dr. T. BURNET's *Sacred
Theory*, Book II. Ch 8. and *Short Confideration* of the Excep-
tions againft it. Dr. FORSTER's *Ufefulnefs*, &c. in the INTRO-
DUCTION; and hear the great Chriftian Critic; ὅτι μὲν 'Οικο-
νομίαι εἰσί τινες μυϛικαὶ δηλούμεναι διὰ τῶν θείων γραφῶν, πάντες κ
οἱ ἀκεραιότατοι τῶν τῷ λόγῳ προϛιόντων σεπιϛεύκασι· τίνες δὲ αὖται,
οἱ ἐυγνώμονες κ ἄτυφοι ὁμολογοῦσι μὴ εἰδέναι. ΩΡΙΓΕΝ. Φιλοκαλ.
Κεφ. α.

Let.18. the more abstrufe the Subject, the wider the
Difference : But that does not hinder the *Good*
and the *Wife* of every Age, from perceiving
which Side has the greatest Tendency to promote Piety and Virtue, and befriending it to
the utmost of their Power.

Your *first* Question, What were the *real
Opinions* of the Ancients concerning the Creation of the World, though not quite fo knotty,
has yet its own Intricacy. They were very
various, and, like the Moderns, went widely
afunder, when they came to enter into any
Detail. The best View I can give you of
them, is first from a venerable *Phenician*
FRAGMENT that is faid to have stript the ancient *Cofmogonies* of Fable, in order to tell
plain historical Truth ; and next from the *Pythagoric* Doctrine concerning the Creation, explained and refined by the Master and Model
of *Athenian* Ingenuity.

THERE are few Remains of Antiquity more
famous, than the Comments and Controverfies
of Critics have rendered *a Fragment of a Phenician History tranflated into Greek.* It is
preferved by *Eufebius* in his Preparation for
the Proof the Gofpel, and contains, or pretends to contain, like the *Theogonies* of the old
Legiflators, the original Belief of the *Phenicians* concerning the Creation, or more properly
the *Formation* of the World, the Birth of the
Gods, and Invention of Arts, extracted by
SAN-

SANCHUNIATHON the Son of THABION, firſt Let. 18. from the hieroglyphical Books of *Taaut*, the primeval Archives of EGYPT, and then from the other *Phenician* Records. It is pity it ſhould have reached us in ſuch extreme Diſorder; mangled, interpolated, and in ſhort, *ſuch* as we might expect ſo abſtruſe a Piece coming to us at *fifth* hand. For I. TAAUT, the Inventer of *Letters,* and firſt *Recorder* among Men, wrote that Part of it relating to the Riſe of Things, in Signs or ſacred Sculptures [k]. II. Theſe Signs and Records were compiled by the *Prieſts,* and embodied with the other Books of the *Phenician* Theology. III. SANCHUNIATHON the Son of THABION extracted it from the *Phenician* Records and Books of *Taaut* ' *by conjecture from the ſacred Cha-* ' *racters, and Marks which his Sagacity found* ' *out, to enlighten us, intermixing it with his* ' *own Allegories* [l].' IV. PHILO, a Native of *Byblos,* tranſlated it from the *Phenician* of *Sanchuniathon* into Greek, with his own Interpolations and Comments; and V. EUSEBIUS gives it in Scraps from *Philo,* we know not in what Order, nor how much re-interpo-

Y   lated,

---

[k] Ταῦθ' εὑρέθη ἐν τῇ Κοσμογονίᾳ γεγραμμένα ΤΑΥΤΟΥ κ) τοῖς ἐκείνυ ὑπομνήμασι ἐκ τε ςοχασμῶν κ) τεκμηρίων ὧν ἑώρακεν ἢ ἀυτё διάνοια κ) εὗρε, κ) ἡμῖν ἐφώτισεν (ΣΑΓΧΟΥΝΙΑΘΩΝ) ΦΟΙΝΙΚΩΝ Θεολογία παρὰ ΕΥΣΕΒ.

[l] Ταῦτα πάντα ὁ ΘΑΒΙΩΝΟΣ παῖς, πρῶτος τῆς ἀπ' αἰῶνος γεγονότων Φοινίκων ἱεροφάντης, ἀλληγορήσας, τοῖς τε φυσικοῖς κ) παθεσιν ἀναμίξας, παρέδωκε τοῖς ὀργιῶσι κ) τελετῶν καταρχꙋσι ΠΡΟΦΗΤΑΙΣ. Ἀυτё.

Let. 18. lated, there being no lefs than *ten* Breaks, fome
of *Philo*, fome of *Eufebius*, in the Thread of
the Narration. I will give it you as free from
Mixture, and as genuinely *Phenician* as its
maimed Condition, and the little we can know
of a loft Language, permits.

SANCHUNIATHON's Hiftory of the CREATION.

‘ THE *BEGINNING* of all Things
‘ was a *dark breathing* AIR, or *Gale of*
‘ *darkfome* BREATH [m], and a *turbid* CHAOS
‘ obfcure as NIGHT: Thefe were infinite, and
‘ without End of Duration. But when this
‘ *Spirit* or *Breath* fell in LOVE [n] with its own
‘ Principles, and a *Mixture* enfued, that Mix-
‘ ture was called DESIRE [o]: This was the
‘ Source of all *Creation:* It did not know its
‘ own Creation; but of its Conjunction with
‘ that *Spirit* fprang MOOT [p], *Slime*; and of
‘ MOOT fprang the Seed of Creation, and the
‘ Generation of the Univerfe. It was framed
‘ in the Form of an EGG [q], and MATTER
iffued

[m] See Page 49—51, and efpecially 174.

[n] Page 49—85—94—97—125.

[o] Page 138.

[p] Τεῖο, fays PHILO, τινές φασιν 'ΙΑΥΝ· οἱ δὲ ὑδατώδης μίξεως σῆψιν. ORPHEUS and the *Greeks* call it the ἰλὺς πρωτογενής, *primigenial Slime*, before the Elements were feparated; allego-rizd. it turns to ΘΟΥΣ, *Tethys*, Wife of the Ocean, and Mother of the Gods.

[q] ΩΟΝ ἀιχὶ γνίσιως—.ΟΡΦΙΚ. See Page 128.

' iffued forth, and the Sun, and the Moon, Let.18.
' and the Stars both fmall and great.—Of
' the Air illumined by the fiery Gleam from
' *Earth* and *Sea*, Winds were generated and
' Clouds, whence enfued vaft Effufions of
' Water from above. Thefe, when fepa-
' rated and drawn from their Place by the
' *Sun*'s Heat, met in the Air in mutual Shock,
' and begot Lightening and Thunder.

' Now there were certain Creatures void of
' Sentiment of which other *intelligent Crea-*
' *tures* were made, called Zophasêmin[r],
' *Spectators of the Heaven.* Thefe at the Noife
' of the Thunders awoke; and, ftartled at the
' Crack, in Earth and Sea Male and Fe-
' male were moved.—Then of the Breath
' Colpias[s] (the *Voice of the Mouth of God*)
' and his Wife Bau[t] (*Darknefs* or *Night*)
' were produced Æon[u] *Exiftence*, and Pro-
' togonos *Firft-born*, Mortals[w]: Of them
' came Genos *Generation*, and Genea[x] *Race*
' or *Progeny* :—From *Generation* the Child of
' *Exiftence* and *Firft-born*, fprang three mortal
' Children, Light, Fire, and Flame[y].

Y 2 ' They

---

[r] צֹפֵי-שָׁמַיִן. Tzophe-Sêmaïn.

[s] קוֹל-פּוּ-יָה Kol-pi-iah.

[t] בֹּהוּ Bohou.

[u] From הָיָה *Fuit*; whence the *Greek* ΑΙΩΝ.

[w] Not everlafting, but tranfient. I take the Word ἀνδρας to be an Addition of the Tranflator.

[x] *Greek* Terms as plain as Ἀιων and Πρωτογόνος.

[y] See Page 35. The *Arcadians* went annually to a Vale called ΒΑΘΟΣ, *Depth*; where, near a miraculous Fountain, Eruptions of

Let. 18. ' They invented Fire by Attrition of Wood,
' and taught the Use of it : They likewise begot
' Children of transcendant Size and Strength,
' who gave their Names to the Mountains[z],
' *Cassius, Libanus, Antilibanus* and *Brathy.*
' Of these sprang MEMROUM[a], *Heaven's*
' *Height.*—MOTHERS then gave Names, as
' they prostituted themselves to the first MALE
' they met. — MEMROUM dwelt in *Tyre,*
' contrived Huts of Reeds, and had War
' with his Brother OUSOUS[b] *Lightening,* who
' first made a Covering of a wild Beast's Skin.
' Storms of Wind and Rain having broke
' down the Trees about *Tyre,* they took fire
' and burnt the adjacent Wood. OUSOUS
' taking a Trunk, and lopping off the Branches,
' first adventured upon it to go to Sea, and
' erected two Pillars to WIND and FIRE.—
' Many Ages thereafter, of MEMROUM's Race
' were born *Hunter* and *Fisher,* Inventers of
' *Hunting* and *Fishing* ; and after whom *Hun-*
' *ters*

of Fire like Whirlwinds, frequently burst through the Ground.
' Here the *Giants,* they say, fought with the Gods ; and here,
' *for that Reason,* they do Sacrifice to the THUNDER, to the
' LIGHTNING, and to the STORM.' PAUSAN. *Arcadic.*

[z] Τείνατο δ' Ουρεα μακρὰ, Θεῶν χαρίεντας ἐναύλες. ΗΣΙΟΔ.

[a] Had not *Philo* explained this ὑψυράνο, *Heaven-high,* I
should have translated it the *Waters above,* from מַיִם *Waters,* and
רום *High.* The Ancients imagined there was a Store of Water
above, as well as in the Abyss below, as their Word in the *dual*
Number seems to imply : But now I suppose the first Letter of
שׁמַיִם the *Heaven* has been lost.[*]

[b] From the *Chaldee* חשׁמל *Fulgura* ; which, because of its
Affinity to חזה *Vidit,* signifies likewise *Vifunes.*[*]

' *ters* and *Fishers* were so denominated.
' these again sprang two *Brothers*, Inventers
' of *Iron*, and *Iron-work*. One of the Bro-
' thers, *Gold-Sword*, studied *Eloquence*, and
' *Charms*, and *Prophecy*. He found out a
' Hook and Bait, Line and Rod; and first of
' all Mankind sailed the Sea; wherefore they
' adored him as a God after Death, and called
' him DIAMICHIUS ᵇ, *the Bewailed*. His
' Brother first invented *Brick-walls*. After-
' wards arose two Youths of his Race, called
' the one ARTIST, the other EARTHMAN:
' They contrived to mix Stubble with Brick-
' Clay, to dry it in the Sun, and make Roofs.
' From these came other two, named the one
' CORN-LAND, the other LABOURER or PEA-
' SANT, whose Statue and portable Shrine was
' held in high Veneration in *Phœnicia*. The
' *Byblians* distinguish him with the Appella-
' tion of *the greatest of the Gods* ᶜ. They ad-
' ded *Courts* and *Yards* to Buildings, and con-
' trived *Enclosures* and *Grottoes*; of them are
' all *Peasants* and *Hunters*, who were called
' *Claymen* and *Wanderers*. They begot AMY-

Y 3   NOS

ᵇ From the *Syriac* דִּמְעָא *Démeha* Lacryma.•

ᶜ While the *Jews* and *Phenicians* were speaking nearly the
Dialect of *Canaan*, the Epithet שַׁדַּי *Shaddai*, the powerful,
seems to have been equivocal to three; שָׁדַי *Vastator potens*, omnipotens; שָׂדַי *Agricola*, and שֵׁאר *Genius, Dæmon*. It appears
that *Philo* has blended the two first.•

Let.18. ' NOS[d], *Truth* and *Wealth*; and MAGOS[e],
' *Forefight* or *Knowledge*, who taught Men to
' live together in Villages, and tend their
' Flocks. From thefe again came MISOR[f]
' and SYDIC[g], *Liberty* and *Juftice*, Inventers
' of *Salt*[h]. Of *Myfor*, *Liberty*, came TAAUT[i],
' *Letters*, (the Invention of the finer Arts)
' and of *Sydic* came the DIOSCURI[k], mighty
' *Sons* of *Jove*, whofe Priefts were Sacrificers[l],
' fkilled in the Myfteries of Nature[m], and who
' firft invented a *Ship*, (Authors of Commerce).
                                                    ' To

[d] Fom אֱמוּנָה *Emunah*, Nom. Fem. *Veritas*; or the *Chaldee* מָאמוֹנָה *Mammonah*, Wealth.*

[e] So I fuppofe *Philo* has rendered חַרְטֹם, *Chartam*, one
skilled in NATURE, ΦΥΣΙΚΟΣ, a *Chaldean Magus*; or perhaps
חֹתֶה *Chofeh*, *Videns*, a *Seer*; a Prophet who, like the *Chaldeans*, fees Futurities in the Stars.* See *Efaiah*, Ch. xlvii. Ver.
13. addreffing the בַּת כַּשְׂדִּים *Daughter of the Chaldeans*.

[f] PHILO explains it "Αλυτ-, *loofe*, *difentangled*. The *Syrians*
fay שְׁרִי *Séri-folutus*, and with the Servile מָשְׁרָיָ D. *Meóri*.

[g] צַדִּיק, *Tzadic*, *Juftus*: one of the triteft Words in all the
Eaftern Tongues.

[h] All is tafielefs without them: an Allegory, I fuppofe, added
by *Sanchuniathon*.

[i] I am inclined to think that *Taaut* is pure *Egyptian* for
LETTERS, from תָּו *Taau*, *Signum Nota*, fuch as the *Egyptian*
Letters efpecially were: thence אוֹתֹת *Ottoth*, *Signa Literæ*, and
with the ת tranfpofed from the Middle, or the *Coptic* Article
T. put before it *Taaut*.*

[k] Kings and Judges were *Jupiter*'s Sons:—'Εκ δὲ ΔΙΟΣ βασι-
λῆες.   HΣIOΔ.

[l] CORYBANTES, *Sacrificers*, is a plain Tranfpofition of the
Chaldee קוּרְבַּן *Coureban*, a Victim, or any Oblation to a God.
The *Phenician* Priefts perpetually calling for *Courebans*, the
Greeks called them *Corybantes*. The fame Word fignifies
Fighters: thence the *armed Priefts* of the *Syrian Goddefs*. From
the firft Acceptation is the *Corban* mentioned in the Gofpel.*

[m] SAMOTHRACIANS, *fkilled in Myfteries*: All the Explication of SYDIC's Genealogy is an Addition by PHILO. See p.

'To these succeeded the Inventers of *Botany*, of Cures for *Bites*, and of *Charms* or *Spells*[n]. Let. 18.

'At the same time was ELIOUN[o], *the Most High*, and a Female BEEROUTH[p], *Springs* or *Moisture*; of whom came TERRESTRIAL, or *Earthman*, called also HEAVEN; and his Sister, of the same Parents, called EARTH. HEAVEN, succeeding to his Father's Kingdom, took his Sister *EARTH* in Marriage, and had by her four Children, ILUS (*THE GOD*[q]) or SATURN, *Time*; BETYLA[r], *the Virgin*; DAGON[s], *Corn*; and ATLAS[t], *Knowledge of the Seasons*. HEAVEN had likewise much Offspring by *other* Wives; which made EARTH jealous, and rail at him, until they parted asunder: But HEAVEN, tho' separated from her, came back when he pleased, and having by Force approached her, again retired; attempting likewise to destroy the

[n] Such the TELCHINES are described.

[o] It is just עֶלְיוֹן *Elion* sublimis; whence ΗΛΙΟΣ ELIOS, the *Sun*: *Elion* and *Beeroth*, the Parents of Heaven and Earth, are without Father and Mother themselves.

[p] בְּאֵרוֹת BEEROTH, *Springs*: The MOST HIGH operating upon Moisture, produced *Heaven* and formed the *Earth*, according to the Ancients.*

[q] אֵל EL, or EIL, GOD, the *Strong*: χρόνος γὰρ οὐκ ἦν πρὸ κόσμου. ΦΙΛΩΝ. ΙΟΥΔ.

[r] בְּתוּלָה BETULA, the *Virgin*, meaning VESTA. See Page 58, 61, 62, and 86.*

[s] דָּגָן, DAGAN, Corn, meaning CERES.

[t] Page 52 (n) r. Among the *Phenicians* he seems to have corresponded with the JANUS and VERTUMNUS of the *Latins*. The *Pole* or Axis of Heaven *turned* on his Shoulders; and the *Arabs* call a *Lever* عتلة ATALO to this Day.*

Let. 18. ' the Children he had by her [u] : But EARTH
' having gathered Affiftance, ftood on the De-
' fenfive ; and TIME come to Maturity, with
' the Advice and Aid of thrice mighty MER-
' CURY [w] his Scribe (*Invention* and *Records*)
' took part with his Mother, and repulfed the
' Attempts of HEAVEN.

' SATURN, or TIME, was the Parent of
' *Pallas* and *Proferpine* [x] ; the latter dying a
' Virgin, by Advice of the former and of
' *Mercury*, he made a Scythe and Spear of
' Iron. Then *Mercury* having faid Spells over
' TIME's *Allies*, infpired them with Ardor to
' fight for EARTH againft HEAVEN ; and by
' this means TIME engaging with HEAVEN,
' drove him from the Kingdom, and reigned in
' his ftead. In the Battle a fav'rite Miftrefs of
' HEAVEN was taken big with Child. TIME
' gave her to DAGON in Marriage, in whofe
' Poffeffion fhe was delivered of the Burthen
' of her Belly begot by HEAVEN, which was
' called DEMAROUS, *Lord of Plenty* [y]. Then
' fufpecting his Brother ATLAS, at the Sug-
' geftion of *Mercury*, he buried him under
' Ground.

[u] HESIOD, Theogon. Ver. 156.

[w] Page 175.

[x] PROSERPINE is פְּרִי־סְבוּנָה *Peri-fephuna*, Περςςφωνὴ, Hidden Fruit, Covered Seed ; who generally dies a Virgin, if her
Head be not cut off every Year by TIME.*

[y] From דַאי DAï, *Copia*, *Poffeffio*, and מָרָן MARAN Dominus. Of the firft is the Arabic داو DAU, Habens, Poffef-
for ; and the *Syriac* נ of the laft, is in the *Greek* Genitive Δημα-
ςωϊπο.*

" Ground [z]. His other Auxiliaries were called Let.18.
' ELOEIM [a], *the Gods.*

' TIME having had a Son SADID [b], *Effer-*
' *vefcence,* he difpatched him through Sufpi-
' cion with his own Sword, and in the fame
' manner cut off his *Daughter's* [c] Head; fo
' that all the Gods trembled at the Defigns of
' TIME. But HEAVEN then in Exile, fent
' his eldeft Daughter ASTARTE [d], a Virgin,
' with two other Sifters RHEA and DIONE [e],
' to deftroy TIME privily. Thefe his Sifters
' TIME took and made them his *young Brides.*
' His Father informed of this, fent other
' Forces againft him, the SEASONS and FATE,
' with other Allies, whom TIME likewife con-
' ciliated to himfelf, and kept in his own
' Power. Then the God HEAVEN invented
' BAI-

[z] The GREEKS faid it was his Children, not his Brother, he hid under Ground. See Page 85.

[a] אֱלֹהִים ELOHIM; the Plural of the Word ufed by the *Affyrians, Syrians, Phenicians, Hebrews,* and *Arabs,* for GOD; and which being moft ufed in that Number, has given Scope to *Criticifm.*

[b] אֲזִיד *AZID,* or *ADSID,* Chald. *Efferbuit, Ebulliit:* ܣܕܝܕܘܢ SADIDON, or SADID, Arabic, *Sanies, Putrefaĉtio,* the Effeĉt of Fermentation. It is remarkable, that an analogous Word ܣܝܕܬܘܢ *Saïdaton,* or *Saïdat,* fignifies a *Holocauft,* or *whole Burnt-Offering,* and is fo ufed GENES. xxii. [e]

[c] PROSERPINE'S. See above, Note ([z]).

[d] The elder VENUS. Τὴν δὲ ΑΣΤΑΡΤΗΝ Φοίνικες τὴν ΑΦΡΟ-ΔΙΤΗΝ εἶναι λέγουσι. She had her *Phenician* Name from the Fecundity of Flocks, עַשְׁתָּרֹת ASHTOROTH. *Greges.* See Page 91, Note [e].

[e] Ibid. Note [d].

Let.18. ' BAITYLIAS [f], having produced *animated*
〰〰 ' *Stones.*

' TIME had by *Aſtarte*, the genial Power,
' ſeven Daughters, the *Titaneſſes* [g] or *Artemi-*
' *deſſes*, and as many Sons by *Rhea*; the
' youngeſt of whom JUPITER was deified
' from his very Birth [h]. Then *Dione* brought
' him two Females, and *Aſtarte* gave him
' likewiſe two Males more, DESIRE and
' LOVE.——*Sydic*, Juſtice, married to a *Tita-*
' *neſs* [i], produced *Eſculapius*, *Health*; and to
' TIME were further born in *Peraia* [k], a *Land*
' *of Fruit*, younger *Time* [l], of his own Name,
' *Jupiter Belus*, or the LORD, who is *Apollo* [m].
Along

[f] See Note [e] immediately preceding, compared with Page 58.
Τὰ παλαιότερα, κ̀ πᾶσι τοῖς Ἕλλησι, τιμὰς θεῶν ἀντὶ ἀγαλμάτων
εἶχον ἀργοὶ λίθοι. ΠΑΥΣΑΝ. Ἀχαικ.

[g] Page 49, 51, 85.

[♓] Page 86, 137, 140, 143.

[i] Juſtice and good Order, joined to a ſound Conſtitution,
produce قلب - عز *Aaz-kélpho*, Ἀισ-κλησιϴ, *The Power of the
Heart*; or, *The Virtue of Converting*, from Sickneſs to Health.
As theſe Words ſound nearly like אִישׁ כָּלֶב *Iſh-Keleb.* Some
will have *Eſculapius* to mean the Dog-man, a Dog being often
among his Symbols. *

[k] פְּרִי PERI, *Fruit*; פְּרִיא PIRAIA, *Fruitful*, to wit, *Country.* *

[l] TIME diſtinguiſhed and divided into Seaſons; or *Time* mea-
ſured by the Courſe of *Jupiter Belu*, the Sun, and other heavenly Bodies, whom *Proclus* therefore calls Ὄργανα τῶ χρόνε, *the
Tools of* TIME.

[m] I am apt to be'ieve that *Philo* has writ ὁ κ̀ Ἀπόλλων. EM-
PEDOCLES ſaid there were two Suns. δυὸ Ἡλίως, τὸν μὲν ἀρχέτυ-
πον, τὸν δὲ φαινομένον, one viſibie in the Heavens; the other his
Archetype and Original; and all the Ancients agree in calling the
SUN but the *Child* of ETHER, as being only δόχημα κ̀ ὄχημα
τῶ πυρὸς, the *Receptacle* and *Vehicle* of FIRE. It is the *Egyptian*
and *Phenician* VULCAN, who is אֲבִי אֵשָׁא, FATHER-FIRE;
the Sun is only his Child. See Page 89. *

‘ Along with them were produced PONTUS,
‘ *the Sea*, and TYPHO, *fubterraneous Fires*,
‘ and NEREUS, *Fluidity*, the Father of the
‘ *Ocean.* Of *Pontus*, the SEA, came SIDON,
‘ the *Fifh-town*ⁿ, and NEPTUNE, *failing.*
‘ SIDON's Sweetnefs of Voice firft found out
‘ the Melody of a Song°; and to DEMAROUS,
‘ Lord of Plenty, was born MELICARTHUSᵖ,
‘ or *Hercules, Prince of the Town.*

‘ After thefe Things there was again War
‘ between HEAVEN and SEA. He retiring,
‘ joined DEMAROUS, *Lord of Plenty.* This
‘ Lord attacked OCEAN, was put to Flight, and
‘ vowed a Sacrifice. But in the thirtieth and
‘ fecond Year of his Reign and Power, THE
‘ GOD, or TIME, lay in Ambufh for his
‘ Father in a certain Place in the Middle of
‘ the Earth, and having got him in his Power,
‘ caftrated him near Springs and Rivers. There
‘ HEAVEN was confecrated, his (creative)
‘ Breath ftopp'd, his Blood dropped into the
‘ *Springs* and *Rivers*ᵖ, and that Place is fhewn
unto this Day. AND

ⁿ Sea-faring People are idle in fine Weather, and apt to fing.
The ancient Mariners had no fooner fixed their Sails, than they
fet a Bowl upon the Table, and began to pour out Libations and
to fing : ‘ The Ships of *Tarfhifh* did *fing* of *Tyre* in the Market :
‘ She was replenifhed and made very glorious in the Midft of the
‘ Sea. *Ezek.* Ch. xxvii. Ver. 25.

° Compounded of מֶלֶךְ, *Melec*, Prince or Lord ; and קַרְתָּא,
Kartha, Town : The Epithet of *Phenician Hercules*—Whence
the *Greek* Fable of *Leucothoe* and *Melicerthus.* *Sp Melius*, who
was thrown from the *Tarpeian* Rock, endeavoured to become
King of *Rome* by Diftributions of *Corn* among the Populace.

ᵖ They retain fome of the genial procreative Power of recent
Heaven. See Page 97, 100, 106, 107.

Let.18.　' AND *now* ASTARTE the mightieſt, *JU-*
　　　　' PITER, *Lord of Plenty,*＊ and ADOD Prince
　　　　' of the Gods, the *firſt or ſole* (alſo a *Torch)*
　　　　' governed the World with Conſent of TIME⁹.
　　　　' *Aſtarte* adorned her own Head with the
　　　　' Horns of a Bull, Emblems of Royalty (of
　　　　' *Fecundity* and *Power)* and thus going round
　　　　' the World, ſhe found a Star dropp'd from
　　　　' the Sky, took it up, and conſecrated it in
　　　　' the holy Iſle of TYRE'. TIME likewiſe go-
　　　　' ing round the Globe, gave the Government
　　　　' of *Attica* to his Daughter *Minerva*; and in
　　　　' a Peſtilence and vaſt Mortality, he offered
　　　　' his own only begotten Son in a Burnt-offering
　　　　' to his Father HEAVEN, and was circumci-
　　　　　　　　　　　　　　　　　　　　　　　' ſed

＊ ΖΕΥΣ ΔΗΜΑΡΟΥΣ.

⁹ Here is the grand Revolution, and final Settlement of the
Univerſe after the Creation was compleated. TIME having
exhauſted the productive Virtue of HEAVEN, makes a kind of
Ceſſion of the Government to the *firſt Cauſe of Generation,* (P.
91, Note ᵈ) to the *Lord of Plenty,* and to the *one Sole* GOD.
ASSYRII Deo quem ſummum maximumque venerantur *Adad*
nomen dederunt: (it ſhould be *Ahad*) ejus nominis Interpretatio
ſignificat UNUS. *Macrob. Saturn. Lib.* I. § 23. It is from
אחד AHAD, *unus,* according to *Macrobius.* I have ſometimes
thought it was האחד HAOD (with the emphatic ה) THE PRIN-
CIPLE, THE CAUSE, whence אוד OUD, a Burning Torch.＊

ʳ LUCIFER; the *Morning-Star* ſacred to *Aſtarte* or *Venus,*
and peculiarly adored in *Tyre:* the ſame painted by HOMER, as,

　　The Star benign, that faireſt in the Sky,
　　Proclaims th' Approach of roſy-fingered Morn. ΟΔΥΣ. N.

But I have not met with the *Tradition* that ſhould explain that
Circumſtance *of its being fallen from Heaven*; unleſs we under-
ſtand it according to the *Sabian* Doctrine, that the Power of
Generation formerly reſiding in *Heaven,* fell from it in proceſs
of *Time* to the *Earth,* and was now transferred to the MORN-
ING-STAR worſhipped in TYRE.

☞ The *Notes* marked with an Aſteriſm, explain ſuch of the
Phenician Names mentioned by SANCHUNIATHON, as are nei-
ther paraphraſed by *Philo,* nor truly deduced by ſubſequent
Commentators.

' fed himfelf with all his Allies. Not long
' after he deified his Son MUTH, *Death*, born
' of *Rhea*, whom the *Phenicians* call PLUTO.
' Then he gave *Byblos* to the Goddefs BAAL-
' TIS (the LADY) called *Dione*; and *Bery-*
' *tus* (the *Fountains*) to NEPTUNE, and to
' the other great Gods of Land and Water,
' who alfo confecrated the Relicks of PONTUS,
' the SEA in *Berytus*, the City of Wells.

' BEFORE this, the God TAAUT had, in
' Imitation of HEAVEN, expreffed the Ap-
' pearances (Afpects) of the Gods TIME and
' DAGON, and the other Deities in the facred
' Engravures of Letters——To him (TAAUT)
' TIME, going afterwards to the Land of the
' South, gave all the Kingdom of *Egypt* to
' be his Royal Seat."

HAD *Sanchuniathon's* great Work reached us entire, it would have been a valuable
Curiofity. This Specimen of the Tranflation,
lame and maimed as it is, fhews the irreparable Lofs we have fuftained in the perifhed Records kept by the Priefts in the chief Cities in
Egypt, and all over the *Eaft*; but efpecially
in the grand Temples of *Thebes*, *Memphis*,
Babylon and *Tyre*. Thofe kept by the *Jewifh*
Priefts under divine Direction, in the Temple
of *Jerufalem*, make a confiderable Part of
holy Writ; and tho' they be Chronicles of no
learned nor mighty Nation, tho' they be generally

Let.18. nerally confined to their own little State, and it be a nice Point to adjuft their Chronology, yet their meer *hiftorical* Ufe (fetting afide higher Confiderations) makes us juftly regret the Originals of which they are but Abridgements, and to which they fo often refer.

If we review the ancient *Cofmogonies* that have reached us, *Hefiod*'s Birth of the Gods, *Ovid*'s Transformations, *Silenus*'s Song in *Virgil*, and the *Phenician* Theology, we fhall not find them precifely reftricted to a Hiftory of the Creation, or Production of the Univerfe; they take generally a Step further; they proceed to the Hiftory of the firft Ages, interweave the Inventions of Arts, and as it were *account* for the prefent Face the World wears; the *Origins* of Nations, *Appellations* of Places, and *Manners* of Men. The Works of the primitive Bards already mentioned, that were collected into one Body, and made the old *theological Syftem*, deduced their allegorical Tale, not quite fo far as *Nafo* prays the Gods to do his Verfe :

> ———*ipfoque ab origine Mundi*
> *ad mea perpetuum deducite tempora Carmen,*

' from the very Origin of the World to his ' *own Times* ;" but down to the Commencement of the *hiftorical* Period; that is, to the *Trojan War*.

SAN-

SANCHUNIATHON's Work, as it now ftands, feems to have been a Compofition extracted from *two* Cofmogonies by the Author, and interfperfed with a *third* in the Paraphrafe.' It contains therefore, I. The pure *Egyptian Doctrine*, written by TAAUT in Marks and facred Sculptures; being, I fuppofe, no more than a *fimple Genealogy*; that is, the *Sign* of the God, with a Mark for Marriage, and *a* Symbol of Parentage or Iffue. II. The *Phenician Theology* compiled by the *Priefts*, intermixed with Traditions about the Invention of Arts, and with *Sanchuniathon*'s own Allegories. III. Shreds and Similitudes of the *Greek Mythology*, fo interwove by *Philo*, that though I have omitted many, feveral yet remain not eafily untwifted from the Thread of the Narration. We may accordingly perceive a threefold Doctrine, difcovering itfelf in different Strains throughout the Fragment; a *natural*, a *moral*, and a *political Mythology*. The firft, written by *Taaut*, comprehends the Rife of Things, and the chief Tranfactions until the Dethronement of *Heaven*. The fecond lies principally in the *moral* and *hiftorical* Epifodes of *Phenician* Extract; fuch as the Defcent of *Demarous* and *Sidon*, the Progeny of *Mifor* and *Sydic*, and the Invention of Arts *inferted before* the Hiftory of *Elioun* the Moft High. The *political* Part, and all the

Illuftra-

Let.18.Illuſtrations, ſeem to be Trappings added by the Tranſlator to *Sanchuniathon*'s Allegories. According to him, *Egypt* the Land of Learning and Parent of Writing, is given to *Taaut*, LETTERS; and *Attica*, the Country of Science, early famous for military Skill, is aſſigned to *Pallas*, CONDUCT and KNOWLEDGE. He even condeſcends to explain to his *Grecian* Readers the Eyes and Wings with which the Eaſterns accoutred the Image of TIME, and the other Gods, with many minute Circumſtances, which I have waved in the Tranſlation.

THIS Remain of Antiquity is too curious not to have raiſed Diſputes, and treats of too great and intereſting Subjeɥts not to have afforded abundance of Play to Fancy, and room for Conjeɥture. It has been condemned as wholly ſpurious[s], it has been defended as perfeɥtly genuine[t]; it has been applied as a Prop of a new Syſtem in *biſtoric* Fable[u], (that the old *Saci*, or *Celtes*, were the true *Titans* and Gods of Antiquity) and has been treated as an unintelligible Rhapſody from beginning to end. But the greateſt Pains, and moſt exquiſite Learning, have been employed in finding out the Similitude or *Sameneſs* of this *Phenician*,

or

---

[s] M. *Dodwell*. Father *Simon*, *Monfaucon*, *Stillingfleet*.

[t] *Voſſius*, *Bochart*; but eſpecially Dr. *Cumberland* and M *Fourmont*.

[u] Pere PEZRON, Antiquité des *Celtes*.

or rather *Egyptian* Tradition of the Hiftory of the Creation, with that delivered by the *Jewifh* Lawgiver. The Parents of Eaftern Criticifm [a] were contented to find in it, 'Some ' Sparks of Truth concerning the *Creation of* ' *the World, the Origin of Idolatry, and the* ' *Abufe of the Names of God* intermix'd with ' Fables:' But fome of their learned Succeffors, particularly a knowing Prelate of our own Country [b], and a Profeffor of uncommon Erudition in *France* [c], have attempted to demonftrate a marvellous Harmony between *Sanchuniathon* and *Mofes.*

As I make not the leaft doubt, of the good Intentions of thefe eminent Authors, in taking fuch indefatigable Pains, they have in fo far the faireft Claim to Thanks and Commendation : But whether thefe Pains were at the fame time *wifely* beftowed ; or whether, (fuppofing they had as fully agreed in proving their Point, as they have widely differ'd) it were truly calculated for promoting their pious Purpofe, is ftill, methinks, a Queftion.

I⊤ has been thought by Men of the trueft Judgment [d], to be a fufpicious Symptom of any Rite or Ceremony in Religion, if it refembled a known Practice in the Heathen Superftition.

Z

[a] *Scaliger, Selden, Bochart, Marfham, Kircher,* &c.
[b] Dr. *Cumberland,* Bifhop of *Peterborough.*
[c] M. *Fourmont,* Profeffor of Arabic in the Royal College of *France,* &c.
[d] Dr. CONYERS MIDDLETON's Parallel of the Roman and Heathen Rites.

Let.18. Superſtition. And juſt on the contrary, many more have thought it no ſmall Confirmation of the Truth and Antiquity of our Worſhip, that Traces of it were to be found in moſt Parts of the old Idolatry. ' It ' is, ſurely, ſays the contemplative Phyſician, ' already quoted, a blamable Curioſity to try ' the Tiuth of the *ſacred Scriptures* by their ' Agreement with *human Writings* ; to prove ' the Book of *Eſther* to be genuine, becauſe it ' agrees with *Megaſthenes,* or is confirmed by ' *Herodotus.* As for my own part, I cannot ' deny my ſuperfluous and unſucceſsful Curio- ' ſity in this Matter, until that ſilly Story of ' *Juſtin's* about the *Jews* let me ſee my ' Folly ; *that they were driven out of* Egypt, ' *becauſe of ſome Plague or Leproſy*[e].' But, in direct Contradiction to this, ſays a learned *Gleaner* in Antiquity, ' When I read theſe ' Propheſies (of *Eſaiah* and *Jeremiah*) and ' ſuch other Pieces of Scripture, and compare ' them with the ancient Authors, *Herodotus* ' and *Xenophon,* it is impoſſible to deſcribe the ' Joy, — the Rapture — that inſtantly diffuſes ' thro' my Heart.'[f] This puts me in mind of the different Judgments paſſed upon the famous *Orphic Hymns,* which you have ſo often heard mentioned as the moſt curious Syſtem of *Grecian*

---

[e] Sir Thomas Brown. See a different Opinion in Characterist. Vol. III. Miſcell. 2. § 1.

[f] Exprimi nequit quanta voluptate, quanto gaudio illico perfundar. G. Jameson *Spicilegia Antiquit.* Egypt. Cap. V. § 13.

cian Divinity. A keen Critic never took them up, but he thought he was perufing the De-vil's *Prayer-Book* ; or, to fpeak more proper-ly, *Satan's genuine Liturgy* : [g] And the Won-der of his Age for Learning, JOHN PICO, Earl of *Mirandola*, thought them a *Treafure of fublime and myfterious Theology* [h]; as did another Man of immenfe Reading, *Kircher* ; who even undertook to demonftrate their perfect Con-formity with the *Hebrew Siphri*, and *Hie-roglyphics* of *Egypt* [i]. Amid fuch Diverfity of Sentiments, you fee, however eafy it may be to agree in an authentic Original, it is vaftly difficult to fix upon a proper **Commentary**; which, after all, every Man chufes according to his *Reach*, and *peculiar Propenfities*.

How various, for Example, are the De-cifions; how much of the Hiftory of *Pa-radice* and *Fall* of the firft mortal Pair is *allegorical* *, and how much is to be un-derftood ftrictly according to the *Letter*? Many have believed the miraculous Trees of

Z 2 *Life*

---

[g] DAN. HEINSIUS. Arifarch.

[h] Io. PICI Com. Mirand. CONCLUSIONES.

[i] OEDIP. T. II. P. I.

* In veteri Inftrumento, fi præter *Hiftoriam* nihil fpectes, et audias, ' ADAM è limo conditum, Uxorculam e dormientis latere ' furtim fubtractam, Serpentem illecebrâ Pomi follicitantem mu-' lierculam, Deum ad auram inambulantem, Romphæam foribus ' præfidentem'— nonne putes ex HOMERI officinâ profectam Fabulam ?—At fub his Involucris quam fplendida latet Sapientia DES. ERASMI CHILIAD. III. ΣΕΙΛΗΝΟΙ ΛΛΚΙΒ.

Let.18. *Life* and of *Knowledge* *, to point to the former : But PHILO, a fanciful Platonic *Jew* [k],
and ORIGEN, a fanciful Platonic *Christian*,
incline to think the whole Transaction, from
Beginning to End, the Trees, the Rivers, the
Cherubs, even to the *Coats of Skins* [l], made
for the recent Exiles from *Eden*, to be a perfect *Allegory.* St. AUSTIN seems very willing
to accept of the *Allegory*, if, at the same time,
you will believe the Relation to have been
real Fact [m]: But another learned Father, more
strictly orthodox, ties it rigidly down, in every
Circumstance, to the literal Meaning, and
confutes the *Jew* and the *Christian*, as equally
heretical

---

* Voyez LETTRES FANATIQUES. Lettre septieme.

k Καλὰ τὸν θεῖον ΠΑΡΑΔΕΙΣΟΝ ἔμψυχα κ᾽ λογικὰ τὰ φύτα
παῖι᾽ εἶναι συμβέβηκε, καρπὸν φέροιια τὰς ἀρέιας.— ταῦτα δὲ μοὶ
δοκεῖ συμβολικῶς μᾶλλον ἢ κυρίως φιλοσοφεῖσθαι·— ἐςὶ γὰρ διεῖσμα-
Ία τύπων ἐπ᾽ ἀλληίορίαν καλῦῖιων. ΦΙΛΩΝ ΙΟΥΔ. περὶ Κοσμοω.
Μὴ γὰρ τοσαύτη καλάςχοι τὸν ἡμῖέρον λογισμὸν ἀσιβἰια ὡς·ὑπο-
λαβεῖν ὅτι ὁ θεὸς γεωπονεῖ κ᾽ φυιεύει παραδεισον·
Τῦ αὐτῦ Νομῶι ἱερῶν ΑΛΛΗΓΟΡΙΑΙ.

l ΩΡΙΓΕΝΗΣ καῖ᾽ εἰκόνα φησὶν ἀπολωλεκέναι τὸν ΑΔΑΜ· ἰνίευθεν
φησὶ κ᾽ τὰς χιῶνας τὰς δερμαῖινας ἐπισημήνασθαι τὴ γραφὴν, ὅτι
(ὁ θεὸς) ἐποίησεν αὐλοῖς χιῶνας δερμαῖινας, κ᾽ ἰνέδυσεν αὐῖὰς, τὸ
σῶμα, φησὶν, ἐςί.— ἀλληἰορεῖ δὲ λοιπὸν ὡσαπερ διναῖαι τὸ τι Πα-
ράδεισοι, τά τι τῆῖε ὑδαῖα, κ᾽ τὰ ἐπάνω τῶι οὐρανῶι, κ᾽ τὸ ὕδωρ τὸ
ὑποκατω τῆς γῆς.   ΕΠΙΦΑΝΙΟΥ καῖα Αἱρησ. βιϐ. β.

m Τὰ περὶ τὸν Ὄφιν, ὡς ἀιἱπράσσοιΙα τοῖς τῦ θιῦ παραῖγίλμασιν—
ὅτι Παραδεισος, ὃν πεφυΙευκέιναι λέγεῖαιὁ θιος ἐν Ἐδὶμ καῖ᾽ ἀιαΙολάς ;
κ᾽ μῖιὰ τῦτο ἐξαιατῖαλκέιναι ἐκ τῆς γῆς πᾶι ξύλον ὡραῖον ἰις ὅρα-
σιν, κ᾽ καλὸν ἰις βρῶσιν, κ᾽ τὸ ξύλον τῆς ζωῆς ἰν μέσῳ τῦ παραδίσου,
κ᾽ τὸ γνωςὸν καλῶ κ᾽ ποιηρῦ ξύλὸν, πάια ταῦτα ὐκ ἀΖέρμως τροπο-
λογεῖται.— κ᾽ ὁ ἐκϐαλλόμενος ἐκ τῦ παραδεισῳ ἄνθρωπος, μῖια τῆς
γυναικὸς, τὰς δερμαῖινας ἠμφιεσμένος χιῶνας, ὡς διὰ τὴν παραϐασιν
τῶν ἀνθρώπων ἐποίησεν τοῖς ἀμαρίησασι ὁ θεὸς, ἀποϐρηΙόν τινα κ᾽ μυ-
ςικὸν ἔχει λόγον.   ΩΡΙΓ. καῖα Κιλσ. βιϐ. δ.

m Commentaria in GENESIN.

heretical upon that Point [n]. ' I have avoided,
' says a great Modern, to mention MOSES's
' *Cosmopoïa*, because I think it is delivered by
' him, rather as a *Lawgiver* than a *Philoso-*
' *pher*, which I intend to shew at large in
' another Treatise, as not thinking that Dis-
' cussion proper for the vulgar Tongue.——His
' Account of the Creation consists of two
' Parts; the first of which describes the great
' general Masses of Matter, and the disorder'd
' State of Things; and proceeds upon- the
' same Principles, and observes the same Or-
' der which the ANCIENTS have constantly
' observed :—— And in this almost all the Chri-
' stian Interpreters agree with us, that the
' *Mosaïc* TOHU BOHU, is the same thing as
' the CHAOS of the *Ancients*; that the Dark-
' ness, described by *Moses*, is their TARTA-
' RUS, and EREBUS, and NIGHT; that his
' *Incubation of the Spirit, or Breath of GOD,*
' is collusive with the Birth of PHANES,
' EROS, or LOVE. So far *Moses*, and the *old*
' Philosophers agree : But *here* he breaks off
' his philosophic Strain, and takes up another
' Method; a *human*, or, if you like it better,
' a *theological* Strain; in which, having en-
' tirely neglected the various *Motions* of the

Z 3 ' CHAOS,

[n] Φάσκεις, ὦ οὗτος, ἐπισκομμαλίζων, ὅτι μὴ ἄρα βυρσοδέψης ἦ ὁ
ΘΕΟΣ ἵνα χιλίας δερμαλίνας τοῖς περὶ τὸν Ἀδὰμ ποιήσῃ. μηδέπω ζώων
τεθυμένων εἰ δὲ κỳ ἐτύθη ζῶα, οὐκ ἦσαν, φησὶ χιλίας δερμαλίνες,
ἀλλὰ τὸ γήινον ὃ περικείμεθα σῶμα. — ὁ Θεὸς. ὦ ἄπιϛε, δερμαλίνας
φύσει χιλίας, ἄνευ ζώων, ἄνευ τέχνης τινὸς ἀνθρωπίνης κỳ πολυμόρφω
ἐργασίας ἠθέλησε γίνεσθαι· κỳ ἅμα θέλων ἐποίησε τοῖς περὶ τὸν ΑΔΑΜ
ΕΠΙΦΑΝΙΟΥ κατὰ Αἵρες. βιϐ. β.

Let. 18. 'CHAOS, according to the Laws of Nature, 'and overlooked the *Action* of divine LOVE 'upon it, and its consequent successive Changes, into various *Strata*, *Regions*, and *Elements*; having, I say, superseded all these, 'he has framed a *popular* Relation of the Rise 'of Things, in the manner we all know [o].

THE Description of the *Elysian* Fields by the ancient Poets, Philosophers, and Divines, is thought to have been originally borrowed from *Moses*'s Draught of Paradise [p]. 'If we 'compare, they say, the Ease, the Pleasure, 'the Delicacies of the Place; the Mildness of 'the Climate, the Fruitfulness of the Soil, 'and constant Serenity of the Sky, we will 'find the Terms differ in the different De'scriptions, but the *Subject* and *Sentiments* 'exactly the same.' From *Moses*' EDEN, said the Fathers, *Plato* took his Idea of the Garden of the Gods, in which *Porus* and *Penia* (Plenty and Want) begot *Cupid*, or Desire [q]; nay, all the Heathen Mythology, according to others, took its Rise from the Truth of the Scriptures misunderstood; insomuch, that there is no one Fable which is not founded in Fact, and all of them bear the same Resemblance to some part or other of the sacred Canon, as *Deucalion*'s Deluge does to *Noah*'s Flood [r].

A

[o] Dr. BURNET's Theory of the EARTH.

[p] Ἐν φαντασίᾳ τοῦ καθ' ἡμᾶς παραδείσου. Γ. NAZIANZ. Λογ. κ.

[q] EUSEBIUS, ORIGEN, CLEMENS.

[r] HORAT. TURSELLINI Histor. Epitom.

A pious Prelate, ſays he could very eaſily Let. 18.
demonſtrate, ' that no ſmall Part of the *Hea-*
' *theniſh* Mythology and Divinity, was fetch-
' ed from *Hebrew* Stories and Practices; —
' and that when they invented their poetical
' Deities, their Dreams were the Offspring of
' ſome *real Things* which they had ſeen, or
' heard out of the Book of GOD '. This, in
the Opinion of another great Scholar, already
mentioned, does no ſmall Honour to holy
Writ. Full of *French* Vivacity, after unrid-
dling, as *he* imagines, the Names of *Cœlus*,
Saturn, and *Jupiter*, which, to his Aſtoniſhment, no Mythologiſt had ever dared to ex-
Z 4   plain ;

* Dr. S. PATRICK, Biſhop of *Ely*, in his *Menſa Myſtica*, In-
troduct. The four Inſtances he gives of this, are very curious.
I. CASSANDRA, in her prophetic Fury, calls *Hercules* τριάσαι-
ρ•ο λίων, *the three-night Lion, whom the ſharp-tooth'd Dog of*
Neptune *took within his Jaws.* This the good Biſhop, after
Iſ. Tzetzes, takes to be originally from the Prophet JONAH'S
having been ſo long in the Belly of the Whale. *Lycophron* ſeems
to have alluded to the three Nights in which *Hercules* was begot,
and to his Combat with *Cerberus.* II. The Stories of *Iphige-*
genia and *Julia Luperca*'s being to be ſacrificed, and a Hind and
Panther offered in their Stead, are founded on the real Hiſtories
of *Iſaak* and *Jeptha*'s Daughter. Human Sacrifice, and Perſons
devoted to Death, was an ancient wide-ſpread Rite. III. The
wondrous Cave of the *Nymphs*, deſcribed by *Homer*, Odyſ.
XIII. and ingeniouſly commented by *Porphyry*, is an Allegory
of Man's *Conception in the Womb*, and is ſtole from *Pſa.* cxxxix.
§. 15. *I am fearfully and wonderfully made.* IV. The *Lydian*
Prieſts, mentioned by *Pauſanias* (Ηλιαχῶν a.) who laid unkindled
Wood on their Altar, invoked an unknown God (I ſuppoſe to
the *Greeks*) and immediately and infallibly (πᾶσα ἀναλκη) the
Wood took Fire, is a Perverſion of the Hiſtory of *Elias*'s Mi-
racle in calling for Fire from Heaven, to confound the Prieſts of
Baal. Theſe *Lydians* have been *Zabians*, Prieſts of *Baal.* See
Page 90 in the Notes.

Let. 18. plain [t]; that is, having made *Terah* the HEA-
VEN, *Abraham* TIME, *Isaak* ETHER, and
Jacob TYPHON, he immediately subjoins, ' that
' the *Scripture* appears now, as it were, in a
' new *Majesty*; which, for certain, very few
' People would have thought it could have
' ever acquired [u].'   And in consequence of this
Way of Thinking, an Author of the same
Nation has composed an entire Treatise, *Of
the Conformity of ancient Fables with the sacred
Remains of* Jewish *Writings* [w].

   COULD *Numbers* ascertain Truth, there
would be no Difference of Sentiment on the
Subject; the far greater Part of Authors having
ranged themselves on *this* Side the Question.
But others, no less Masters of Reason, are
of a different Opinion: One of these has endeavoured to prove, ' that *Idolatry* is worse
' than *Atheism*;' or, in other Words, ' that
' unworthy affronting Worship, with respect
                                          ' to

---

   [t] Une chose étonnante : jamais aucun Mythologiste a-t-il
osé dire, qu'il savoit la cause des noms de *Jupiter, Cronos, Ou-
ranos*, &c.—Je dis moi, que les voici decouverts—Voila donc
ce que l'on cherche depuis trois mille Ans, la Raison du Nom
d'*Uranus* :—Quiconque ne sent pas cela, ne sent rien.
           M. FOURMONT *Reflex. Crit.* Liv. II. Sect. III. Ch. 2.

   [u] Tranchons le mot : un Lecteur, homme d'esprit, aimant la
verité (Je le suppose degagé de tous Prejugez) sera ravi non seu-
lement d'appercevoir ici ce que l'on cherche depuis 3000 Ans,
la Naissance du Paganisme, & l'Origine de ses Dieux, mais aussi
de remarquer (Assertion qui frappe à present les Yeux comme
l'Eclair qui passe de l'Orient à l'Occident) de remarquer, dis-je,
' Que l'ECRITURE paroit dans une *Majesté* comme NOUVELLE,
' à laquelle certainement peu de gens se seroient attendûs.'
                                 Ibid. Sect. IV. Ch. 17.

   [w] Conference de la *Fable*, avec *l'Histoire Sainte*.   Par M. de
LAVAUR.

‘ to the Object to which it is addreſſed, is
‘ worſe than no Worſhip at all :’ Which, if
true, muſt it not neceſſarily follow, ‘ That
‘ any Connexions, Similitudes, or Alluſions,
‘ between the idolatrous Rites of the *Egyp-*
‘ *tians*, *Phenicians*, or other Heathens, and our
‘ *ſpiritual* Devotion, are rather diſadvantage-
‘ ous ; and, inſtead of illuſtrating, ſeem to
‘ *cloud* the Purity of our Religion?’ So that,
rather than ſearch for new Reſemblances,
ought not we, in good Conduct, to aim at
diſproving the old ? Thus far ſeems to be certain, that any Doctrine, carrying its own Evidence, ſtands in no need of weak collateral
Proofs to ſupport it; ſince the greateſt Diſſer-
vice that can be done to *Truth*, is to tack
Falſehood to it, as if it were of the ſame Quality.   The Patch raiſes Suſpicion of the Sound-
neſs of the Piece ; as an unſkilful Pleader ruins
a good Cauſe, by reſting it on an inconcluſive
Argument.   The trueſt Service therefore, that
can be done to any reaſonable Doctrine, is to
repreſent it in its own genuine Simplicity ; to
ſtrip it of the old uſeleſs Accoutrements,
with which it had been equipped by, perhaps,
very well-meaning Men, and remove the rot-
ten Props that portend imminent Ruin.   The
fair Pillar of TRUTH totters when officiouſly
ſhored up, and threatens Subverſion : It can
only ſtand poiſed by its *own* native Weight,
and reſt upon its *own* immediate Foundation.

The

Let.18   The *Mofaic* Accounts of the Creation, and
Genealogy of Mankind, need no ftrained unnatural Applications from mythological Writers, to fupport their received Authority: 'Tis
quite enough, if, by comparing the *Egyptian*
Traditions of the Rife of Things from *Sanchun-*
iathon or *Taaut*, we find fome Traces of the
Origin of that Affertion, ' *That the Hebrew*
' *Lawgiver was inftruƈted in all the Wifdom*
' *of the* EGYPTIANS [z].'

I am, &c.

[z] 'Επαιδεύθη ΜΩΣΗΣ πάσῃ σοφίᾳ· ΑΙΓΥΠΤΙΩΝ.
Πραξ. τῶν ΑΠΟΣΤ. Κεφ. ζ.

L E T T E R

LETTER XIX.

THERE is an Obſervation which, tho' it lie not within every one's Compaſs, is very entertaining to thoſe who can ground it upon a wide Knowledge of the Fates of Nations, and upon juſt Views of human Nature. From a Survey of *theſe*, it would ſeem, ' that ' among the People called *Heathen*, there has ' happened, as of Policy and Power, ſo like- ' wiſe a ſort of CIRCLE, *or Succeſſion of* RE- ' LIGION.' I do not mean, that the ſeveral religious Rites were propagated by Conqueſt or Commerce, along with the other Arts of Life, from one Country to another; *that* we find in every Hiſtory: But that in Religion itſelf, as conſidered among the *Heathen* Nations (that is, all Mankind excepting the *Jews*) we may obſerve *a certain Progreſſion from Purity to Star-Worſhip, from Star-Worſhip to Polytheiſm, and thence to the groſſeſt Idolatry: That in ſome Ages a Diſtaſte of Superſtition returns, in conſequence of which Reforms are ſet on foot ; Purity is retrieved, and zealouſly affected: But new adopted Deities from ſome Out-ſkirts of the Scheme, make way for a Multiplication of Myſteries, and that for a Relapſe into Ignorance and Credulity.*

A

Let.19.   A DEDUCTION of every Step of this Obſervation, and Inſtances adduced to verify it,
would be no eaſy Undertaking.   It might
regulate the Plan of ſo vaſt and various a Work
as that of the laborious *John-Gerard Voſſius,*
OF THE ORIGIN AND PROGRESS OF IDO-
LATRY: For had there been leſs Detail in
that immenſe Collection, and more Connection of the Changes in Religion, with the
Changes in Government and Manners, it
would have been much more inſtructive. His
vaſt Learning wanted but ſuch a Clew to prevent his being loſt in the Labyrinth, and as it
were o'erwhelmed with the inexhauſtible Subject.   My Views are confined to the two re-
moteſt Steps of the Revolution; which will
yet require all our Attention, as the tracing
them leads through ſome of the moſt untrod-
den Paths in Hiſtory and Literature.

As far as we can penetrate into the dark
Receſſes of ANTIQUITY, the moſt ancient
Worſhip upon Record in the World, ſeems
to have been that of ONE ALMIGHTY GOD,
Governor of all Things: A Worſhip that does
not appear to have been confined to any one
Nation or Tribe, but to have prevailed all
over the EAST, and principally in *Chaldea,*
its perpetual Seat.   This is that Religion
which is ſtill known under the Name of *Za-*
biiſm among the Eaſtern Writers, whoſe early
6   Profeſſors

Profeffors worfhipped neither in Temples, nor
by Images, but offered Prayer with Odours
immediately under Heaven, the Habitation of
the Moft High, the Patriarch, or Head of the
Tribe, being commonly both *Prieft* and *King*.

WHEN the Prophet, whofe Doctrines now
fill the fineft Countries of the Globe, firft
afferted his divine Miffion, his Countrymen,
the *Arabs*, were immerfed in grofs Ignorance,
and as tenacious of their Pagan Superftitions,
as they are now of *Iflamifm*; for it is rare
that Religion wholly changes the Character
of a Nation, unlefs it have firft altered the
Conftitution of their civil Government. To
the North and Weft of them dwelt *Jews* and
Chriftians, a large Mixture of both having
likewife fettled in *Arabia* itfelf; but to the
Eaft lay the People long famous under the
Name of CHALDEANS, zealous Teachers of
a refined fort of Idolatry. Now the *Arabs*,
new Converts to the Belief of *one* God (the
firft Article of *their* Apoftle's Creed) were to
be diftinguifhed from all the reft, and warned
againft the Infection of the furrounding Sects,
of whom he commonly claffes four together;
Jews, *Zabians*, *Chriftians*, and *Magians* [a].
He calls the firft three frequently *Scripturals*,
People who found their Faith upon a Book,
and arms his Followers with Anfwers to their
Objections, as many of them were apoftati-
zing

[a] Al CORAN. Suras II. V. XXII.

Let.19. zing to the ZABIANS, *Eafterns* [b]; by whom he
no doubt means the Inhabitants of *Chaldæa.*

MAHOMET was himfelf illitterate: He frequently glories in it, and makes it a Proof of
his Miffion from Heaven; fince it was impoffible a Book of fuch divine Eloquence as
the CORAN, fhould be the Compofure of an
ignorant Prophet [c]. The *Moflems* accordingly
admire and adore it: They make it not only
the Rule of their Life, but the Standard of
their Style, and Model of their Language:
They borrow every Term ufed in it, and are
perpetually alluding to it in their Writings.
Among the other Sects, finding the *Chaldeans*
mentioned by their Prophet under the Appellation of *Zabiin, Eafterns,* they retained the
Term; and by tranflating many of their Books,
have made a Name unknown to the *Greek*
and *Roman* Writers famous thro' the World.

FOR fome Generations the *Khalifs, Maho-*
met's Succeffors [*], were barbarous bloody Enthu-
fiafts. They declared War againft the Learning, as well as the Religion of other Nations,
and burnt all the Books they could lay Hands
on.

[b] صبح fignifies the *Morning*; and thence, by a Metaphor, common to moft Languages, the *Eaft*. An Adjective
formed from that, is, صابيون Orientales, *Eafterns*; and,
by an eafy Tranfition, *Apoftates*, who change their Religion,
and particularly who turn *Zabians.*

[c] نبي الامي *Nabi al emeion.* The untaught Prophet, ignorant as he came from his *Mother.* CORAN, Sura VII.

[*] خليفة Khalifaton (vu go *Califa*) Succeffor, Vicarius. The
four acknowledged by the orthodox *Sunnites,* were *Ababecr,*
Omar, Ofman, and *Hali.*

on. The Deftruction in particular of the ce-
lebrated *Alexandrian* Library, was the greateft
Wound ever received by Literature. But about
the Beginning of the third Century of the
Hejira, the Conqueft of rich and polite Na-
tions, having by Degrees divefted the *Arabs*
of their former Fiercenefs, they turned this
Contempt of Knowledge, and Hatred of the
Means of it, into the moft ardent Purfuit of
Science that ever poffeffed a People.

Mutavit mentem Populus levis, & calet uno
Scribendi ftudio——

For not contented with the infinite Productions
of their own fruitful and fiery Genius, with
indefatigable Pains they fet themfelves to tranflate, into their wondrous Tongue, all the
principal Authors in Hiftory, Poetry, Philofophy, Medicine and Mathematics, that were
in greateft Vogue among the conquered Nations. Thus they have *Plato* and *Ariftotle*,
Euclid and *Archimedes*, *Hippocrates* and *Ga-*
len, and even *Homer* and *Livy*, fpeaking the
Language of the victorious *Moflems* *.

In the Beginnings of this happy Difpofition, the Books of the *Zabians* could not
efcape their Curiofity. They were writ in a
Dialect of their own Speech, and contained
both the Philofophy and Religion that had
been

* While Europe was immerfed in Barbarity and Mona-
chifm, all polite Learning paffed under the Defignation of *Studia*
Arabum.   6

Let. 19. been long prevalent over the *East.* The great
Hiſtorian, ABUL-FARAGI, ſays, ' That the
' Religion and Rites of the *Zabians*, in the
' current Opinion of the *Arabian* Doctors,
' were the very ſame with thoſe of the ancient
' *Chaldeans* ; that their chief Seat was in *Ha-*
' *ran*, on the *Chaldean* Border, where they
' had their grand Temple on the Top of a
' Hill[d] : ' It was called the City of the *Za-*
bians, and was ſo famous as the prime Reſi-
dence of the Sect, that a *Haranite* and a *Za-*
bian were equivalent Terms[e]. The chief Points
of their Doctrine are theſe :

' THEY believe the World to be eternal;
' governed by a co-eternal MIND, whom they
' worſhip under the Symbol of *Fire*; they
' pay a proportioned Reverence to the *Sun,*
' its apparent Source, and to the *Moon* and
' *Stars* participating of the ſame celeſtial Na-
' ture.   In conſequence of theſe Principles,
' they invented ſignificant Rites, and pious
' Practices, expreſſive of their Veneration, and
' -calculated, as they thought, to obtain the
' Favour of theſe inferior Rulers of the Uni-
' verſe.' This is preciſely the Religion of the
old Chaldeans; and this the eaſtern Sages call
                                          the

[d] HISTORIA DYNAST. Dynaſt. IX.

[e] Gentile nomen حرلني Harani Haranita, ſæpe uſurpari
ſolet pro صابي Sabi Sabita, qui eſt Cultor Stellarum. The *Sa-*
bians go in Pilgrimage to *Haran*, in the ſame Manner as the
Mahometans go to *Mecca*, and *We* were wont to go to *Jeru-*
ſalem.   GOLII Not. ad *Alfragan.*

the *primary and moſt ancient Religion in the* *World.* In this, ſays the moſt learned of the Rabbins [*], was *Abraham* educated among the *Chaldees* his Countrymen ; and this was the Foundation of the Religion practiſed by the *Magi*, or Prieſts of the *Aſſyrian, Median,* and *Perſian* Empires.

HERE then we find the firſt Point of our Circle, *early Purity in Principle and Practice.* For the learned and candid *Shahreſtan* aſſures us, that the *Zabians* continued firm in the Belief of one ſupreme God themſelves ; and that the Arguments brought by them to convince others of the Unity of his Godhead, were unanſwerable [f]. Now that this *Zabian* Principle of the Worſhip of one God by Prayer and Incenſe, was not confined to any one Tribe or Nation, appears evident from the Authority of our holy Scriptures: There we find a *Canaanitiſh* Prince, MELCHIZEDEC, King of *Salem,* the Prieſt of *the moſt high God* [s].

　　—*Chi con una ſola Verga*
　　Reggea l'humane e le divine coſe [h].

We find another of the petty Princes of *Paleſtine,* ABIMELECH King of *Gerar,* ſo little ſurprized with a heavenly Viſion, as to expoſtulate freely with God nimſelf [i]. *Laban*

　　　　　A a　　　　　　　　the

---

[*] R. MOSES Ben Maimon.
[f] Apud POCOCK.
[s] GENES. xiv. § 18.
[i] GENES. xx. § 4, 5.

[h] *Battiſta Guarini.*

the *Syrian*, and *Bethuel* the *Chaldean*, may be
perhaps fuppofed, as *Abraham*'s Relations, to
have received fome traditional Knowledge of
one God, handed down from him, tho' mixed
with *Teraphim* [k], or Image-Worfhip : But patient and righteous Jοв, tho' an *Arab*, and
abfolute Stranger to the *Jews* and their Law,
and living in the fame unfettled paftoral Way
as fome of the *Arabian Shieks* do now, is a
fhining Inftance of the fame Belief; a Belief
not peculiar to that good Man, but common
to all his Friends, who, tho' born of different
Tribes, and dwelling in diftant Lands, zea-
loufly maintain the fovereign Sway of one fupreme Ruler of the World.

In later Times, we find JETHRO, *Mofes'*
Father-in-law, a Prieft in the Land of *Mi-
dian* [l], of no Idol, we may fuppofe, nor falfe
God (elfe fuch honourable mention had never
been made of him, nor Affinity contracted
with him by the great Enemy of Idolatry)
but blefling the true God for his Goodnefs to
the heaven-guided Lawgiver, and offering a
Sacrifice, of which *Mofes* and *Aaron*, and all
the Elders of *Ifrael*, were Partakers [m]. *Balac*,
King of *Moab*, as a Defcendant from *Lot*,
may have been led to acquiefce in the Power
of God, to blefs and to curfe whom he pleafes:
But

[k] GENES. xxxi. § 31.
[l] The Province of *Hijaz* in *Arabia*, upon the Eaft Coaft of
the *Red-Sea*. The Town, near the Head of the Gulph called
Madion, now demolifhed, is the *Modiana* of *Ptolemy*.
[m] GENES. xviii.

But BALAAM the Son *Beor*, tho' dwelling Let. 19. in *Aram* (*Syria*) *in the Mountains of the Eaſt*, takes up his Parable under the uncontroulable Direction of divine Inſpiration [n].

IF we take a wider Circle, and look farther around us among other Nations, we will learn from *Herodotus*, the Father of Hiſtory, ' That ' the EGYPTIANS gloried in being the *firſt* of ' Mankind who built Temples, reared Altars, ' and erected Statues to the Gods.' They had then none before ; and even the *firſt* Temples of the *Egyptians* themſelves, according to another Author, ἀξόανοι ἦσαν, *had no Statue in them* [o].

THEIR Rivals in Antiquity and Religion, the old CHALDEANS, had, in Proceſs of Time, built a Temple at *Babylon*, the Wonder of the World for Magnificence and Grandeur : But ſo late as the Days of *Herodotus*, ' there was ' no Statue in that Temple ; nor did any mor- ' tal Creature (as was ſuppoſed) paſs the Night ' in it, excepting one Lady at a time, a Na- ' tive of the Country, whom the GOD fa- ' voured, ſaid the *Chaldean* Prieſts, and was ' pleaſed to call to his Couch by Name [p].'

THAT the PERSIANS of moſt early Time were no Idolaters, but worſhipped one God, the Creator of the World, under the Symbol

A a 2 of

---

[n] NUMB. xxiv. § 12, 13.

[o] ΛΟΥΚΙΑΝ. περὶ Θίας Συρ.

[p] ΑΓΑΛΜΑ δὲ οὐκ ἐν ἐϝδὲν αὐτοθὶ ἐνιδρυμένον, &c.
HΡΟΔΟΤ. ΚΛΕΙΩ.

Let.19. of *Fire*, is acknowledged by all their Historians, and has been set in the clearest Light
by our excellent Mr. *Hyde*[q].   Their Zeal for
this Principle, seems to have carried them to
great Extremes, and made them tolerate no
Way of Worship but their own.   A Strain of
it may have possibly mixed with *Cambyses'*
Madness, in the Havoc he made of the *Egyptian* Divinities[r]—and influenced the Conduct
of *Xerxes* in demolishing the *Grecian* Temples, and defacing their Statues wherever he
passed.   As this was the constant Practice of
the *Persians*, the apocryphal Author of the
Book of *Judith*, seems to have stretched it to
the portentuous Reason given for the King of
Nineve's Expedition against the whole Earth,
' That all Nations, Tongues, and Tribes,
' might worship *Nebuchadnezar*[s], and call
' upon him as their only God.'

THE GREEKS and ROMANS had their Religion at second hand from powerful and knowing Nations, but who had departed from their
first Establishment, before their Intercourse
with European People[t].   It is not therefore to
be expected, that *these* should be wiser than
their Masters, and exercise a Purity they had
never received.   Yet there are many Traces of
noble

---

[q] De Religione veterum PERSARUM.   [r] See above, p. 280.
[s] Not the *Babylonish* Conqueror; but a King, whose Name or
Expedition is no where else recorded in History.
[t] See above, p. 177.

noble Simplicity, fhall I fay, or, in more fa-
fhionable Stile, of a ruftic Plainnefs to be feen
in the Rites of both Nations.

'For the firft hundred and feventy Years,
' fays M. *Varro*, after *Romulus*, there was not
' a Statue in any Temple at ROME[u]:' And,
in exact Conformity with that learned *Roman*,
Plutarch affures us, ' that anciently there was
' no Image of a God, either painted or car-
' ved, to be feen among that People; that
' for the firft hundred and feventy Years of
' their State, they built Temples indeed, and
' offered Sacrifices, but there was no Statue
' placed in the Shrine, nor Likenefs contrived
' for the Divinity[w].' Even the rude illiterate
GERMANS, fo late as the Age of *Tacitus*, retained thus much of the ancient Opinion,
' that it was foolifh to endeavour to coop up
' the Gods within Walls, and impious to
' frame any Image of them in the Similitude
' of the human Countenance[x]:' And, to fay
the Truth, the firft Statues erected for them,
hardly deferved the Name, being only *great
Stones fet on End*[y], generally *fquare*[z], fome-

A 3

times

[u] The firft Statue that was caft at *Rome*, was much later.
ROMÆ *fimulacrum ex aere factum* CERERI *primum reperio, ex
peculio* Sp. Caffii, *quem regnum affectantem pater ipfius intereme-
rat.* PLIN.
[w] See p. 247. [x] Cohibere parietibus Deos, atque in ullam
humani oris fpeciem affimilare nefas exiftimant.
De Moribus GERMANORUM.
[y] The Word מַצֵּבָה, which the *Jews* are prohibited to erect,
does not ftrictly mean a *Statue* or *Image*, but what the *Greeks*
called ΣΤΗΛΗ (Cippus, Titulus) a *Pillar*, or *Column*; a *Stone*
fet

Let.19.times *conical* [a], fometimes *pyramidal*, or *ſe-micircular* [b], and frequently quite *rough* and *unhewn* [c], without Touch of a Tool.

BUT

ſet on End as a Monument or Memorial, fuch as that which *Jacob* erected between him and *Laban*. *And* Jacob *took a Stone, and ſet it up.* מַצֵּבָה A STATUE. GENES. xxxi. §. 45.

[a] The Statues of the oldeſt *Mercury* (fee Page 175) were originally long *ſquare* Stones : The *Athenians* firſt put an old Man's Head on them, and afterwards, taught by the *Pelaſgi*, added the *Symbol* of Generation. MACROBIUS. The Statue of the Mo-THER of the GODS, brought to *Rome* from *Phrygia*, was a great black *ſquare* Stone. *Feſtus Pompey* fays, fhe is called KYBHAH and KYBHBH, from KYBOΣ a CUBE, to fhew that fhe was the *Foundation* and *Baſis* of the UNIVERSE.

[a] The ancient PHENICIANS had an Image of the SUN, which they believed not to have been formed by human Art, but to have fallen immediately down from Heaven. It was a large black Stone, round and broad at the Bottom, but diminiſhing by degrees, and terminating in a ſlender Point. HEROD. *Simulacrum Deae* (VENERIS) *non effigie humana : continuus Orbis, latiore initio tenuem in ambitum, Metae modo, exurgens.* TACIT. I remember a pleaſant Reaſon aſſigned by a learned Antiquary for this Figure of the Goddeſs ; *Pur Io mi ricordo di haver letto che queſta Figura rappreſenta l'*OMBILICO *del Corpo humano ; ed è dato a* Venere *perche ſi crede che la Libidine alle Donne ſtia e comminci in queſta parte.* VINCENZO CARTARI. The SUN's being the Center of our *Planetary Syſtem*, is the real Reaſon both of the umbilical Figure of theſe Statues, and of the conſtant Tradition, that DELPHI was the NAVEL of the Earth : in Sign whereof, they kept in the Temple a Stone of white Marble cut in that Shape, and religiouſly wrapp'd up in Swaddling-cloaths.

[b] The MEGAREANS worſhipped a great Stone in the Form of a *Pyramid*, under the Name of *Apollo*. Their more elegant Neighbours, the ATHENIANS, had him in human Shape, but with a Head long and ſharp, in the Form of a *Pyramid*. PAU-SAN. A ſmall Globe ſplit in two, and one of the Halves ſet on the Top of a Pole, was the Object, or rather Symbol, adored by the ancient PEONIANS. MAX. TYR.

[c] The oldeſt Idol of the *Arabs*, was مَنَاة MANAH, a Goddeſs, like VENUS and FATE, worſhipped under the Form of a great unhewn Stone. SHAHRESTAN. The Statue of the *Theſpian* CUPID, was a rough Stone untouch'd by a Tool. PAUSAN. And fee Page 346, Note [f].

BUT as the EAST feems always to have led
in Matters of Religion, and that Purity remained longer untainted in that devout Climate, than in moft Parts of the Earth, let us
take a nearer Survey of its early Eftablifh-
ment.

AND firft, let us remember that ORIENTAL
Wifdom was always in the higheft Reputation;
fo high, that the *Jewifh* Prince, celebrated as
the wifeft of Mankind, is magnified by the
Comparifon: ' His Wifdom, we are told,
' was greater than the Wifdom of all the *Sons*
' *of the* EAST, than all the Wifdom of the
' *Egyptians* ᵈ.' And that we may not hefitate
about the Preference, the Wife-men of EGYPT
itfelf, the Privy-Counfellors of the Nation,
that boafted the fublimeft Science, and looked
on the Sages of all other People, as little better than *Children*; thefe very Men are introduced by the moft knowing of the Prophets,
as founding their Claim to Knowledge upon
their EASTERN Defcent, and thereby fairly
allowing the Superiority of their *Chaldean
Mafters* ᵉ.

NOR was this a fhort-lived Reputation, that
flourifhed for an Age, and then evanifhed: It
furmounted even their national Calamities;

A a 4 and,

ᵈ III. KINGS IV. §. 30.

ᵉ אֵיךְ תֹּאמְרוּ אֶל־פַּרְעֹה בֶּן־חֲכָמִים אָנִי בֶּן־מַלְכֵי־קֶדֶם
How will ye fay unto PHARAOH, *I am a Son of the* WISE, *a
Son of the Kings of the* EAST: So קֶדֶם ought to be tranflated,
ISAIAH XIX. §. 11.

Let. 19. and, like the *Grecians* [f] of old, and the *Chinese* [g] of late, enabled the Vanquished to give Law to the Victors. These knowing and polite Nations civilized the rude *Roman* and rugged *Tartar*, their Conquerors; and, in the same manner, the haughty *Mede* and hardy *Perſian*, submitted to the Leſſons of their *Chaldean Subjects*, both in Religion and Policy. They are particularly celebrated for their Skill in *Aſtronomy*, which a part of them afterwards abuſed, by applying it to *Horoſcopes* and *Divination* [h]: But the Hiſtory of the *Wiſemen*, as our Tranſlation renders the ΜΑΓΟΙ, (MAGI) of the Original [i], guided by a *Star*, portending, or rather announcing, the Birth of a King to the *Jews*, does great Honour to

the

---

[f] GRAECIA capta *ferum* victorem cepit, et artes
Intulit *agreſti* LATIO.   HORAT.

[g] Of the two and twenty Families that have reigned in CHINA, three were *Tartars*, who quickly adopted the *Chineſe* Manners and Literature. See *Viaggi di M. Marco Polo Gentilhuomo Ve\
netiaro*, Anno 1297. *Abdalla* BEIDAWI. Edit. *Muller*. ANNALES SINICAE, &c.

[h] Tu ne quæſieris ſcire, nefas, quem mihi quem tibi
Finem Di dederint *Leuconoë*: neu BABYLONIOS
Tentaris numeros.   HORAT.
CHALDAEIS ſed major erit fiducia : quicquid
Dixerit *Aſtrologus* credent à fronte relatum
HAMMONIS.   JUVENAL.
Annum diemque ultimum vitæ jampridem ſuſpectum habebat
(*Domitianus*) Horam etiam ; nec non et genus mortis. Adoleſcentulo CHALDAEI cuncta prædixerant.   SUETON.

[i] Ἰδὺ ΜΑΓΟΙ ἀπὸ ἀνατολῶν παρεγίνοντο. ΜΑΤΘ. B. α. St. IGNATIUS ſays the Splendor of the Star was ineffable, and ſtruck all who beheld it with Amazement; for all the other Stars, together with the SUN and MOON, attended it in a Chorus, while in Luſtre it outſhone them all. XIV. *Epiſt. ad Epheſ.*

the Science of thefe *eaftern Sages*, and wonderfully quadrates with their conftant Contemplation of the Hoft of Heaven.

DISTANCE of *Time*, and Want of *Records*,
permit us not to determine the precife Period
when the *Chaldeans* departed from the Purity
of their primitive Syftem. But as in all human Societies, there is a Mixture of good and
bad, of noble and bafe, it would feem that a
meaner Set of them had early proftituted their
Science to Incantation and Magic[k]; while the
founder and fuperior Part renounced them for
fo doing, and acquired fuch Reputation by
their upright Conduct and celeftial Science,
as, like other divine Lawgivers, to be thought
worthy of Empire[l]. It is paft doubt, that
before they were known to the *Arabs*, under
the Name of *Zabians*, they had fuperadded to
their firft Principle of *one fupreme GOD* (to
which they inviolably adhered) a fecond Principle, of the *heavenly Bodies* béing, as it were,
his *Minifters*, and *Mediators* between him and
finful Men. Upon this they built fuch a Train
of

---

[k] See ISAIAH xlvii. § 12 and 13, where by the הֹבְרֵי שָׁמַיִם
the *Society of the Heavens*, or *Heaven-Companions*, which we
have tranflated *Aftrologers*, feems to be meant the feparated, or,
if you pleafe, the confecrated Body of the *Chaldean Aftronomers* ;
and by the *Star-gazers* and *monthly Prognofticators*, the Fortune-
tellers and Genethliacs. They ftill fwarm in the EAST.

[l] Ἀφῄρισο δ' ἐν τῇ βαβυλωνίᾳ καλοικία τοῖς ἐπιχωρίοις φιλοσό-
φοις τοῖς ΧΑΛΔΑΙΟΙΣ προσαγορευομένοις, οἳ περὶ ἀστρονομίαν εἰσὶ
τὸ πλέον· προσποιοῦνται δέ τινες κ' γενεθλιαλογεῖν ὥς ὂν καταδέχον-
ται οἱ ἕτεροι. ΣΤΡΑΒ. ΒΙΒ. ιϛ. See alfo his Account of *Mofes*,
in the XVI Book, under the Article of SYRIA:

Let.19. of fuperftitious Practices, performed in Honour of the brighteft Stars, as made fome fancy them to be denominated [m] from thefe Objects of their Worfhip, which favoured ftrongly of Idolatry. High Devotion, like other Paffions, when divorced from Underftanding, ftands on the Brink of a Precipice, with a Defcent fo flippery, that, without fome Counter-Paffion to keep the Poife, down it hurls into Super-ftition and Folly [a].

'THESE vifible *Planets*, faid they, thefe
'glorious incorruptible Orbs, are the eternal
'Habitations of GENII, or Vehicles of pure
'fpiritual Subftances, which animate them as
'the human Soul does the Body, and by
'whofe Miniftry and Interpofition, the fu-
'preme Being (whom they call the God of
'Gods, and Lord of Lords) governs the
'World, and difpofes of the Fates of Men.
'It is *they* that reveal his fovereign Will to
'Mortals, and by *their* Means his Bene-
'fits are conveyed to the Inhabitants of the
'Earth.' At firft therefore, continues my
Author, they offered up their Prayers to thefe
Minifters

---

[m] From צְבָא־שָׁמַיִם Tzaba-Shamaim, the *Hoft of Hea-ven.*

[a]   Diverfe Bande
Diverfi han Riti, et Habiti, e Favelle.
Altri adora le Belve ; altri la grande
Commune Madre ; il Sole altri e le Stelle :
V' è chi d' abominevoli Vivande
Le Menfe ingombra, fcelerate e felle.
E'n fomma, ogn'un che'n quà da *Calpa* fede
Barbaro è di coftumi, empio di fede.   TASSO.

4

Minifters of the divine Will; then they proceeded to burn Incenfe and make Oblations,
fuch as they thought moft agreeable to their
fuppofed Natures.   They accurately obferved
their Rifing and Setting, their Conjunctions
and Afpects, their *Houfes,* as they are called,
or Manfions among the Conftellations, dividing the World among them, and affigning
fuch and fuch a Species of Being to each particular Planet's Adminiftration.   According to
their Number, they made a fucceffive Revolution of Time in feven Days, which we call
a *Week,* and confecrated each Day to its *Guardian Planet;* a Cuftom that, from them, has
fpread thro' moft Nations, and feems to favour the Affertion of the *Jewifh* and *Arabic*
Authors, that their Religion, as it is among
the oldeft in the World, has likewife fpread
itfelf over the Face of the whole Earth.

BUT in procefs of Time their Rites mul-
tiplied, and their Worfhip grew more fenfual.
Their mediatory *Planet,* they obferved, frequently withdrew from their Sight, while
they ftood in conftant Need of his Interceffion
and Influence.   They therefore formed to
themfelves *Figures* or *Schemes,* myftically reprefenting the Powers and Properties, not only
of each Planet, but of the *Lord of all,* and
his chief *Attributes.*   Thefe were put in a
fort of *Shrine* of a proportionable Form, to
which they paid a pious Reverence.

THUS

Let. 19. ' THUS the Shrine of the FIRST CAUSE was
' fet over all the reft, and received their prime
' Devotions. Under it was the Shrine of
' MIND, or *Underftanding*; then the Shrine
' of PROVIDENCE, or *Forefight*; then of
' SPIRIT; and, laft of all, the Shrine of
' NECESSITY—all of a perfect *fpherical* Fi-
' gure, denoting *Eternity* °. After thefe, ftood
' the Shrine of *Saturn*, an Hexagon, or Fi-
' gure of fix Angles; then the Shrine of *Ju-*
' *piter*, a Triangle; of *Mars*, an oblong
' Square; of the *Sun*, a perfect Square; and
' fo of the other Planets.' Now, from the
Worfhip paid to thefe myftic *Shrines*, and
fymbolical Reprefentations, intelligible to few
but their Priefts, it was natural for a new Sect
to form itfelf, fond of a *real Image*, or rather
a *fancied Likenefs* of the favorite Planet ᴾ.
This they made of fuch Metal as they imagined was moft confonant to its Nature; of
Gold, to the Sun; of *Silver*, to the Moon;
of *Iron*, to *Mars*;—and thereby fixed the Tradition of the Names given to Metals by the
Chymifts, which is equally received over the
World, as their Doctrine of the *Days* of the
Week.

° PHILOLAUS, the eminent *Pythagorean*, fays the *Circle* was
confecrated as the Symbol of the GODS, ϻϵϱωϲ θϵωϲ ἢ ϧοϵϱοὶ, as
they were *Intelligences*. Action within the Agent, which the
Schoolmen call *Actus immanens*, is the Action of MIND : Such,
they fay, is a Circle put in Motion.   DAMASCIUS.

ᴾ There are two Sects of ZABIANS, fays *Shabreftan* الريباطل
الاتخاص احباب and, *Shrine-Worfhippers*, احباب *Image-Wer-*
fhippers.

Week. Then offering, at the proper Hour and precife Minute of the Day confecrated to the Planet, the moft grateful Perfumes and Sacrifices, which they always burnt entire, they believed that the pure fpiritual Intelligence, defcending from its Orb at their Prayer, alighted on its *myftic Symbol,* faid the better fort; on its *real Image,* faid the more fenfual, which it animated, and made fometimes to fpeak, and at other Times appear in Dreams and Vifions, to reveal the Will of the moft High God, and direct its pious Votaries to their own Advantage [1].

HERE we find the *fecond* Step of our Progreffion, the Introduction of *Star-Worfhip* among a People who formerly adored *one only* GOD, and who ftill pretended to implore his Bleffing thro' the Mediation of thefe his fuppofed Minifters. In order to defcribe the *third,* we muft fhift the Scene, and take leave of the *Zabians;* for we never read of their falling into grofs *Polytheifm,* and deifying every thing around them. But the Tafk would be now equally fuperfluous as endlefs. Let us content ourfelves with this general melancholy Truth, ' That there is no Nation known in ' Hiftory, which in fome Period or other of ' its Duration, has not been addicted to ab- ' furd Ceremonies, and plunged in fome Spe- ' cies of Idolatry.' Could any Nation have hoped

[1] POCOCK. Specimen Hift. ARABUM.

Let. 19. hoped for Exemption, it muſt have been a *choſen* People, ſelected from all the Tribes and Families of the Earth, to be holy Patterns of a pure Worſhip, and, as it were, Guardians of a divine Diſpenſation ʳ. And yet we are aſſured, by the moſt unſuſpicious Authority, that it was quite otherwiſe; no Race or Society of Men having more quickly ˢ or groſly abandoned the noble Simplicity of their primitive Inſtitution, tho' viſibly revealed from Heaven, and ſupported by a Succeſſion of the moſt ſtriking Miracles. Their *Zabian* Neighbours continued much longer untainted, nor did they ever arrive at· ſuch a Pitch of Stupidity and Corruption, as the ſtubborn *Hebrews* ᵗ. But if your Curioſity ſhould lead you

---

ʳ Baſtame por Prueva de la Excelencia del *Pueblo* de *Yſrael* el haverlos Dios eſcogido por Pueblo *Suyo* de entre las Naciones del Mundo, y poſar el *Caſo divino* ſobre ſu Moltitud, haſta que llegaron todos ellos al grado de la *Prophecia*, y paſſò la coſa a ſus Mugeres.—(Los Patriarcas) fueron el *Coraçon* del genero humano, y ſu *Teſoro*—y los demas fueron como *Corteſas.* CUZARI. Diſcorſ. I.

ˢ EXOD. xxxii. §. 8.

ᵗ It does not appear, that ever there was a People ſo prone to Idolatry as the *Jews*, before they were carried Captives to BABYLON. *The Number of thy Gods are according to the Number of thy Cities,* O JUDAH! ſays one of their Prophets (1); who likewiſe affirms, that, to the Aſtoniſhment of Heaven and Earth, no Nation had ſuch Proneneſs to change their *falſe* Gods as the *Jews* to abandon the *true* (2) He paints this in the ſtrongeſt Metaphors that human Language or human MANNERS can afford (3). But thro' all their Hiſtory, they are chiefly reproached with *two* Sorts of Idolatry; firſt, the Worſhip of BAAL, and ſecondly, of ASHTEROTH. Sometimes theſe are joined, as Gods worſhipped by *one* People, and ſometimes diſtinguiſhed

---

(1) JEREM. ii. § 28.   (2) Ibid. § 10, 11, 12.·   (3) JERIM. iii. § 1, 2. compared with EZECH. xvi. § 25, 26.

you to inquire into the Degeneracy of this
very *Chaldean* Tribe, so pure at the beginning,
and so long uninfected, you will find it painted
in strong Colours by a very learned *Jew* [n],
who yet does them not the Justice they have
met with, both from *Christian* and *Mahometan* Writers [w].

THEIR Doctrine is nearly the same with
that delivered by PLATO, in the Person of
the celebrated DIOTIMA, a learned Lady,
whom *Socrates* owned as his *Mistress:* Not
in

tinguished as GODS of *different* Nations. The first is *frequently*
used in the plural Number, BAALIM; and the last is *always*
so. The *Jews* were originally CHALDEANS (4) or, as we are
elsewhere told, their Father was an *Amorite*, and their Mother
a *Hittite* (5); and from a small Tribe grew, in 430 Years, to be
a numerous People in EGYPT. Now the *Chaldeans*, their
Forefathers, besides *the most High God*, worshipped the HOST of
HEAVEN, the BAALIM (see Page 89, Note [a]) and the *Egyptians*, their Masters, for whose Country and Customs they retained
such Fondness, worshipped the *Ox*, the *Heifer*, the *Calf*, the
Goat, the *Ram*, in short שִׂירוֹת THE FLOCKS. No wonder
if a superstitious Nation, sprung from *one* Country, and *modelled*
in another, followed the Worship of their *Progenitors* and *Lords*.
That this was their Practice, appears plain from the *Golden
Calf*, compared with the Speech of one of their greatest Cap-
tains: ' *Now therefore put away the* GODS *which your Fathers
* served on the other Side of the* RIVER (*Euphrates*; that is, the
' CHALDEANS) *and in* EGYPT; *and serve ye* JEHOVAH. *And
* if it seem evil to you to serve* JEHOVAH, *choose you this Day
* whom you will serve; whether the* GODS *which your Fathers
* served on the other Side of the* RIVER, *or the* GODS *of the
* Amorites in whose Land ye dwell?* ' The *Chaldeans*, on the
other Side the *River*, worshipped the BAALIM, and the *Egyptians*, and their Neighbours the *Amorites*, the ASHTEROTH.
But this must not be confounded either with אֲשֵׁרוֹת GROVES, the
Place of Worship; nor with אֲשִׁירִים pl. masc. signifying a collateral Object, STATUES.

(4) GENES. xi. § 28, 31.   (5) EZECH. xvi. § 3.

[n] MOREH NEVO. Lib. III. Cap. 29.

[w] GREGOR. ABUL. FARAGI. Dr. POCOCK.

Let.19. in the Senfe that Term is ufed in Town, but meaning a holy Prophetefs, from whom he profeffed to have learned abundance of fine Things upon the moft important Subjects, and which neither he, nor his illuftrious Pupil, durft venture to publifh as their *own*. From her he learned, as his Scholar makes him fay, ' that the *Species* of GENII is *a mid-* ' *dle Nature,*—fomething between *Gods* and ' *Men.* As fuch, its chief Employment is to ' ferve as the Organ of Communication be- ' twixt them, to convey the Tranfactions on ' Earth to the Gods, and explain to Mortals ' the good Pleafure of Heaven : For this great ' Purpofe, it is placed in the *Middle* between ' both, filling the apparent empty Space, and ' connecting the mighty Extremes of the ' WHOLE. Thro' this *middle Species* of Be- ' ing, *Prophecy*, in all its different Shapes, ' and all the Science of the Priefts about fa- ' cred Matters, is conveyed to Men ; fuch as ' *Sacrifices, Ceremonies, Prayers,* and *Charms*; ' and, in a word, every fort of *Divination* and ' *Jugglery* : For the *divine* Nature never im- ' mediately mixes, nor communicates with ' the *mortal* ; but, thro' the Canal of this ' *Species of Genii*, all Communion and Inter- ' courfe between Gods and Men, is carried on, ' whether awake or afleep [x].

IT

---

[x] Διὰ τούτου καὶ ἡ μαντικὴ πᾶσα χωρεῖ, καὶ ἡ τῶν ἱερέων τέχνη τῶν τε περὶ τὰς θυσίας καὶ τὰς τελετάς καὶ τὰς ἐπῳδὰς, καὶ τὴν μαντείαν πᾶσαν καὶ ΓΟΗΤΕΙΑΝ. ΠΛΑΤΩΝ. ΣΥΜΠΟΣ.

I⊤ is not at all improbable, that the learned
Philofopher may have drawn this Doctrine
from the fame Source, whence it was generally believ'd he had his Knowledge of the
Soul's Immortality [y]. However that may be,
it is certain, that a *Subordination of Deities*, or
different *Orders* of celeftial Powers, is a very
ancient, and efpecially an eaftern Tenet. We
find Traces of it in moft of their religious
Syftems; nay, and fometimes their Divinities
not only *fubordinate*, but even *oppofite* to one
another. Thus the CHALDEANS, immovea-
ble in the Belief of one *fupreme* Being, yet laid
it down as a fundamental Principle, ' that his
' Will and Benefits were conveyed to Mortals
' by the fole Miniftry of *fpiritual Subftances*,
' in the fame Manner, fays *Shahreftan*, as the
' Orthodox of other Religions, Jewifh, Chri-
' ftian, and Mahometan, believe he employs
' *Men* like themfelves.' Thus the ancient
MAGI built their Belief and Practice upon
two Principles, L I G H T and D A R K N E S S.
They called the firft KADIMAN [z], the *Ancient*
or *Eternal*; and the fecond AHRAMAN [a], the

B b   Latter

---

[y] I know, fays *Paufanias*, that the CHALDEANS of *Affyria*,
and the *Indian* MAGI, were the firft Afferters of the Immortality of the Soul of Man; an Opinion that has been fince adop.ed
by PLATO the Son of *Arifto*, and fome others of the *Grecian*
Philofophers.   MESSENIAC.

[z] From the *Chaldée* קדם *Prioritas. Primordium temporis*,
comes the numeral in the fame Dialect קדמאי *Primus, Princi-
pium*.

[a] It is plainly from אחרין Auchêran, Chald. *Pofterior, Ul-
timus.*

Let.19. *Latter* or *Created.*   Some faid thefe Principles
were oppofite and *coeval*; others, that they
were oppofite but *fucceffive*; and thefe Sects
continued difputing, until their great Reform-
er ZARADUSHT, or *Zoroafter*, taught them
that neither *Kádiman*, nor *Abraman*, were
eternal; but both created by the *one eternal*
GOD, who had no Companion nor Equal,
and of whom he forbid to frame any Statue
or Likenefs, but only to worfhip him under
the Symbol of *Fire* [b].

THESE various Creeds and Inftitutions will
appear lefs ftrange, if we caft an Eye back-
ward upon the many monftrous Herefies that
fprang early up in the primitive Church [c]; and
if we recollect that fome very learned Men of
late, have intermix'd Opinions not unlike
Plato's and the *Zabians*, with the Doctrines
of Chriftianity.   It is the famous POSTEL
that I have chiefly in my Eye, who in the
former Part of his Life was the Wonder of
France, and indeed of all the Republic of
Letters.   His Reputation was fuch, that many
Princes had Recourfe to him in Queftions of
Literature; nor did he lofe it but by an Attempt to become a *Catholic Apoftle*, and to
convert by his *fuperior Reafon* all the Nations
of

---

[b] See Exop. iii. § 2. xxiv. § 17. xl. § 34, 38.   LEVIT-
ix. § 23, 24.

[c] See *Epiphanius* and *Irenæus*, chiefly on the MANICHEES
and GNOSTICS.

of the Earth to Chriſtianity. For this Purpoſe he wrote under a very appoſite Name,
(*Elias Pandochæus,* or *Receiver General*) his
PANTHENOSIA ; *five Tubæ penultimæ Clan-
gor :* That is *Univerſal Unity,* or *the Sound
of the laſt Trumpet ſave one.* There he pretends to demonſtrate the Conſiſtency of all
Sects, *Jews, Mahometans, Heretics, Pagans,*
with the *Chriſtian* Doctrines. He maintains,
that *all* Nations knew from the Beginning,
and practiſed the ſelf-ſame Religion in Subſtance, tho' under different Symbols : He even
enters into a Detail, and affirms that the Books
of *Zohar, Rabboth,* and the *Medraſhim* (Col-
lections of *Jewiſh* Comments and Traditions)
proceed from the very ſame Spirit that dictated the *Goſpel ;* and in ſhort, that the *Cha-
lani,* the *Magi,* the *Gymnoſophiſts,* the *Chaldean, Egyptian,* and *Jewiſh* Prophets, are all
of one and the ſame Original [d].

THE beſt Key to this Conduct, is to tell
you, that this great Man was, at times, a little crazy, though with ſome lucid Intervals.
The *Converſion of all Nations,* was the tick-
liſh String of his happy Enthuſiaſm, which
at illumined Hours, made him drive an
Idea entertained by many in a leſſer Degree,
to the Pitch of Extravagance I have repreſented. Among many great Names I could

B b 2   men-

---

[d] G. POSTELLI de Origin. Cap. xvii.

Let. 19. mention, the ingenious Abbé *Pluche*, who
has transformed the *Egyptian* Deities into
Puppets dreſſed up for public Signals, allows
the *primitive Religion* to have been *pure*; and
the Worſhip of *one* God to have been ſettled
as the traditional Practice *all over the Eaſt*:
And another Author, of fluent Expreſſion and
good Intentions, ſeems to have writ a long
learned Romance *, only to ſhew that all the
Heathen Nations, not only held the Principle
of Unity in the Godhead, but had Notions
of the moſt myſterious Points of our Belief
concerning his Being and Providence.

THO' theſe Views of the Conſent of Nations be perhaps ſtretched full as far as they
will bear, yet their humane Tendency, *to
make all Mankind happy*, ſurely pleads for
ſome Grains of Allowance. Who can doubt
but the good *Poſtel's* Heart was overflowing
with Charity, when his Head was warm with
a fancied Reſemblance or Identity of all the
Religions in the World; and feeding his Hopes
of being the glorious Inſtrument of a total
Coalition? Let us therefore, in conſideration
of ſo beneficent a Temper, ſmile at his Sallies, and ceaſe to wonder, if finding every
where Traces of ſpiritual Intelligences, Mini-
ſters to *the Moſt High*, he adopted the *Zabian* or *Platonic* Principle into *his* apoſtolical
Theory,

* Voyages de CYRUS.

Theory[e]; and now purſue the next Step of Let. 19. our *own*.

  ‘ Time was, ſays a ſagacious *Rabbi*, when
‘ the whole Earth was covered with Blindneſs
‘ and Error, ſome few of the *Patriarchs* only
‘ excepted. One Nation ſaid there was no
‘ *firſt* Cause, nor any Part of the Univerſe
‘ that cou’d with greater Propriety call itſelf
‘ a Creature than a Creator, ſince the Whole
‘ was *eternal*. Another ſaid the *Empyreum*,
‘ or celeſtial Sphere, was eternal, the Author
‘ of all Things, and adored it accordingly.
‘ A third believed that *Fire* was the Sub-
‘ ſtance and Cauſe of Light, and of the ſtu-
‘ pendous Productions we ſee in the World,
‘ for which they adored it; and ſaid the *Soul*
‘ too was *Fire*. Others, and the greater Part,
‘ worſhipped the *Sun*, the *Moon*, the *Planets*,
‘ and the Figures of *Animals* formed in Like-
‘ neſs to thoſe in the *Zodiac*. Others wor-
‘ ſhipped their *Princes* or their *Wiſe-men*;
‘ and all agreed, that it was impoſſible for
‘ any thing in the World to ſwerve from the
‘ Courſe of Nature.

B b 3   ‘ Things

[e] Je montre par mes Ecrits qu’au deſſous de la Trinité il y a neceſſairement *une premiere Intelligence*, qui contient toutes les Intelligences du monde, tant humaines comme angeliques, qui de leur Naturel toutes ſont bonnes ;—de laquelle *premiere Intelligence*, qui eſt premierement émanée comme la Lumiere du *Soleil trinum*, ou comme l’odeur du corps odorant, et en après eſt creée formée et faite, et unie principalement à la ſeconde Perſonne qui eſt paſſive—&c.

Apologie de Guilleaume Postel, M. S. de la Biblioteque du Roi.

Let.19. ‘ THINGS *continued in this State*, proceeds
‘ the Rabbi, *until the* PHILOSOPHERS, *Men of*
‘ *a fine fubtile Wit and profound Meditation,*
‘ *difcovered and confeffed that there muft be a*
‘ FIRST CAUSE, *almighty and fupreme, whom*
‘ *no created Being can refemble.* But they
‘ erred in the Progrefs of their Reafoning ;
‘ faying, that tho’ GOD created, he does not
‘ now operate in the World in general, much
‘ lefs in Individuals, nor direct particular Events;
‘ which they thought too mean to fall under
‘ the Cognizance of fo exalted a Being, efpe-
‘ cially as he never innovates nor alters their
‘ original Nature.’

AND *now, My Friend!* we have reached
the grand revolving Point of our *Circle :*

Magnus ab integro Seclorum nafcitur Ordo
Pollio ! et incipient magni procedere Menfes :

The *Point* when found PHILOSOPHY brought
Men back to ancient Simplicity in Belief and
Worfhip, in Times of the greateft Superfti-
tion and Fondnefs of fplendid Ceremonies.
To fhew this in its genuine Light, I have
chofe the Teftimony of a ftaunch *Jew*[f], as
the plaineft and leaft liable to Exception :
But either he confines the latter Part of his
Obfervation folely to the *Epicureans,* who de-
nied

[f] Rabbi JUDA the *Levite,* Author of the excellent *Dialogue* infcribed CUZARY.

nied the *Providence* of GOD[g], and whom, for that Reaſon, all his Nation cordially hate, or he is highly unjuſt to the other pious Philoſophers; for even thoſe who by their deepeſt Reſearches cou'd not find out the Almighty to Perfection, who were perſuaded that in *him* we live, and move, and have our Being, but cou'd not decide whether he were a Principle ſeparate from the Univerſe, or the vital Source of Life and Exiſtence diffuſed thro' the Whole, even *thoſe* aſſerted and admired his *Providence.*

A GREAT Aſtronomer and Mathematician concludes his Conſtruction of *Aratus'* Sphere with this remarkable Doubt, and its Solution. ' There is a Queſtion put, ſays he, whe-
' ther JUPITER (the ſupreme God) be *ma-*
terial, or an *active* Principle; whether he
' be a *Living Soul* animating the World, or
' a *pure Intelligence*, or ſome *ſuperior Power*
' far exalted above the Heavens, and by Na-
' ture *immoveable?*' As for *Aratus* he has mentioned the Name of *Jupiter* in the common Acceptation, as the *Baſis of Being*, and *Foundation of the Univerſe* : But one of two is certain, ' That either the all-diſpoſing *Pro-*
' *vidence* of the Deity reaches and acts thro'
B b 4 ' the

Let.19.' the Whole, and that his Essence, extend-
' ing throughout, is the *Bond* of its Union;
' or, that he is *a separate Being* acting accord-
' ing to the *Names* given him by the Anci-
' ents, (who ascribed the Good of every Event
' to God) to point out his Perfections: They
' call him *generative* and *parental* Jove, *so-*
' *cial, supplicative, regal, governing, friendly,*
' and *hospitable,* the *Counsellor,* the *Thunderer,*
' the *Deliverer,* and such like: Or, in more
' intelligible Terms, Jupiter, the Source of
' Being, the Bond of Relations, and Director
' of Birth; the Author of Society, the Hearer
' of Prayer, the Governor of Kings and Na-
' tions, the President of Friendship, the Pro-
' tector of the Stranger, the Inspirer of Coun-
' sel, and first Cause of whatever happens in
' the natural or moral World [h].' His almighty Hand holds the unerring Ballance that
weighs the Fates; and hard by his Throne,
on Right and Left, stand the two inexhaust-
ed Urns, the one filled with Good Fortune
and Happiness, the other with Misfortune and
Misery. Out of these, this Father of Gods
and Men, mixes to every Mortal his Dose of
Life; and as he tempers the destined Draught,
so are their Days embittered with Disasters, or
flow serene in Ease and Prosperity [i]. From
its Pedestal hangs the wond'rous Chain of Gold,

that

[h] ΛΕΟΝΤΙΟΥ ΜΗΧΑΝΙΚΟΥ Διαίρεσις Σφαίρας.
ΟΜΗΡΟΣ ΙΛΙΑΔ. Ω.

that binds the Planets to their Spheres, and
fufpends the Sea, and Earth, and Air, and
all they contain, infeparably linked to his eternal Throne [k].

THESE Pictures, drawn by the Ancients,
of the *divine Providence*, are too lively and
ftriking to need any Explication: But it is
with Diffidence that I enter upon the Sequel
of my Enterprize, to tranfmit the Conceptions, or copy the Stile of the Language
judged worthy to be fpoken by the Gods,
efpecially on fuch a Subject as the *Creation* and
Government of the World: Let me attempt
it, upon two equitable Conditions: Firft, that
you remember where it was the great Philofopher lived and wrote— among a giddy People, nurfed in Ignorance, drunk with Power,
and jealous of their national Superftitions—:
Next, that you make a large Allowance to
me, beyond what *Timæus* afks, before he enter upon his exalted Theme.

SPEECH, fays he, fhould bear fome Proportion to the *Subjects:* But as no Words can
fully exprefs their Effence, or reach their Subftance and internal Nature, we muft be content if we can deliver fome Likenefs or Image,
fuch as may convey a Shadow or Semblance
of the Truth. ' If therefore, my Friend! of
' the numberlefs Doctrines which many have
advanced

[k] ΣΕΙΡΗΝ χρυσίαν ἐξ οὐρανόθεν κρεμάσαντες
Πάντες δ' ἐξάπτεσθε θεοὶ, πᾶσαί τε θέαιναι. ΙΛΙΑΔ. Θ.

Let.19. ' advanced concerning the *Nature of the*
         ' Gods, and *Creation* of the *World*, we are
         ' not able to make out an *exact* and *confiftent*
         ' *Scheme*, you muft not be furprized, but be
         ' pleafed if we can reach a *probable one*; re-
         ' membering, that both I who fpeak, and you
         ' who hear and judge, have no *divine*, bu
         ' an imperfect *human* Nature; whom it there-
         ' fore becomes, upon fuch *high* Subjects, to
         ' reft fatisfied with *probable* Accounts, without
         ' morofe Enquiry into the Matter.

LET US THEN DECLARE, for what Rea-
fon the Author of Being and Creator of the
World, at firft compofed the wond'rou
Frame?

HE IS GOOD:——But ENVY or ILL-WILL
is in no refpect incident to the GOOD: Exempt
from *thefe* it was his Will, that all Things
fhould be made as like to *Himfelf* as poffible.
With *this* Intention, finding all vifible MAT-
TER, not in a State of Reft, but toffed to and
fro, in a wild irregular Motion, *He* firft
brought Order out of Confufion, as the preferable State. For it was and is utterly impoffible, that the *beft of Beings* fhould produce
that Thing which is not the *beft* and *faireft*
the *Materials* admit of. Wherefore contem-
plating, he faw, that even among material
Objects, nothing void of *Thought* could, in
whole or in part, ever compare for Excellency
                                    with

with what was poffeffed of *Intelligence* ; and
then, that it was impoffible *Thought* fhould
refide in any Subftance but in *Mind* or *Spirit*.
HE therefore endow'd a MIND with Intelligence, and conjoining that Mind to the immenfe material Frame, he finifhed the mighty
Work, the Fabric of the World, with the
higheft Beauty and Perfection of which its
Nature was capable.

THUS, in a *probable* way of Reafoning, we
muft needs conclude, that the Univerfe is,
in truth, an *animated thinking Subftance*, fo
formed by the Fore-knowledge of GOD."
Then the Philofopher proceeds to give an Account of the Compofition of the Elements,
of the Formation of the Heavens, of the fpherical Figure of the Univerfe, and of the harmonic Proportions concurring in the Production of the immaterial thinking Subftance
which animates the WHOLE. *This, as its*
Father who begot it, perceived to be felf-
moved and felf-fubfiftent, and the Image of
the eternal *Gods*, he approved and was glad,
and went on to liken it ftill more to the original *Model.* Wherefore as it is an eternal
animated Subftance, he refolved to render the
whole Creation, as far as poffible, *the fame.*
But fince the Nature of an immortal Subftance cannot be perfectly adapted to *gene-*
rated Matter, the great Architect contrived a

certain

Let.19. certain moving Semblance of *endlefs Duration.*
Having therefore put the Heavens in order
(*Duration* or *Eternity* continuing ftill the felf-
fame individual Thing) he framed a progreffive Imitation of it, perpetually encreafing by
Number and Quantity, which we call TIME[1].
For *Days*, and *Nights*, and *Months*, and *Years*,
(all Parts of *Time)* did not exift until the
Heavens were made, and were by him ordained to co-exift along with the *Heavens*
how foon they were fet a going.   It is true
that *Men*, when they fpeak of *Paft* and *Future*, improperly and inadvertently apply thefe
Parts of *created Time* to *eternal Duration:*
But in found Reafon, we can with Propriety
only fay, of the latter, that IT IS; while *it
was,*

---

[1] So our *plaintive* POET :
――――― The long deftined Hour
From everlafting Ages growing ripe,
That memorable Hour of wond'rous Birth,
When the dread Sire on Emanation bent
And big with Nature, rifing in his Might
Called forth *Creation.*――――Then TIME firft was *born*,
By Godhead ftreaming thro' a thoufand Worlds.

   And with ftill greater Maftery and higher Colouring,
――――― From the great Days of Heaven,
From old *Eternity*'s myfterious Orb
Was TIME cut off, and caft beneath the Skies;
The Skies which watch him in his new Abode,
Meafuring his Motions by revolving Spheres,
That horologe Machinery divine :
Hours, *Days*, and *Months*, and *Years*, his Children, play
Like numerous Wings around him as he flies;
Or rather as unequal Plumes, they fhape
His ample Pinions, fwift as darted Flame
To gain his Goal, to reach his ancient Neft,
And join a new ETERNITY, his Sire,
In his *Immutability* to reft.
                              THE COMPLAINT. Night II.

was, and *it will be*, fhould be folely applied
to progreffive Exiftence, proceeding Step by
Step *in Time.* For thefe Expreffions (*it was*,
and *it will be*) denote fucceffive Movements;
But the other (Eternal Duration or Exiftence)
is for ever the fame, indivifible, immoveable,
without poffibility of its becoming elder or
younger, or that it fhould be faid to be *now
paft*, or that it is yet *to come.* In a word,
nothing can be applied to it, which *Generation*, or the receiving a *Beginning* of Exiftence, makes us apply to fenfible Objects;
thefe laft being all Portions of *Time*, which
revolves in fucceffive Periods, and only *imi-
tates* ETERNITY.——

T I M E therefore began with the *Heavens*,
that as they took Rife together, they may be
together *diffolved*, if fuch Diffolution fhall ever
happen. It was formed upon the *Model* of
the ETERNAL NATURE, and made as like to
it as poffible; the *Model* having exifted for
all *Eternity*, and the *Copy* being to exift for
all *Time*, of which alone it can be faid, *it
was, it is*, and *it will be* hereafter. Such then
being the Decree and Purpofe of GOD concerning the Formation of *Time*, the SUN was
produced, and the MOON, and the other *five
Stars* commonly called *Planets* (Wanderers)
in order to generate TIME, and to divide and
preferve its Numbers. Their feveral *Bodies*
were

Let.19. were firſt formed by *God*, and then placed in the Orbits which they were ſeverally to deſcribe, ſeven in Number as they are ſeven; the *Moon* in the Orbit nearest the Earth; the *Sun* in that next above it; the *Morning Star*, and that conſecrated to *Mercury*, he ordained to circumvolve with equal Velocity as the *Sun*, but with a contrary Tendency; whence it comes to paſs, that they frequently overtake, and are overtaken in the ſame Place by one another, both the *Sun*, and *Mercury*, and the *Morning Star*. As for the other *Planets*, if one were to treat of them all, and account for their Movements, it would exceed the Bounds for which they are here mentioned.

THEN the *Pythagorean* proceeds to rehearſe ſome of the Cauſes and Conſequences of their Motions—and particularly their being animated with living Souls[m], capable of receiving and executing their Creator's Command: He mentions the Production of Light in the *ſecond* Orbit; the Generation of *Day* and *Night*, of *Months* and *Years*; and the *grand Period* of the Revolution, when all the heavenly Bodies return to their firſt Starting-place, and in the ſame Order they were at firſt whirled off, begin their Circumvolutions anew. After that he deſcribes the Creation of the remaining animated

---

[m] Δεσμοῖς ἐμψύχοις σώματα δεθέντα ζῶα ἐγεννήθη, τότε προσά-
γων ὅμαθι.   ΤΙΜΑΙΟΣ.

animated Parts of the Univerſe. They were
to be of four Sorts. Firſt, the celeſtial Race
of the *Gods*; next, the pinioned Inhabitants
of the Sky; then the watery Shoals in the liquid Element; and, laſtly, the Animals of
the dry Land. After explaining the igneous
Compoſition of the firſt, whom he calls *viſible* and begotten Gods[n], he ſubjoins the celebrated Paſſage already mentioned[o], ' That
' as for the *other Deities* (beſides theſe hea-
' venly Bodies) it was above his Capacity
' to deſcribe their Natures, or comprehend
' their Generation : But that we muſt believe
' thoſe inſpired Perſons, who, as they them-
' ſelves ſay, are Deſcendants of the Gods, and
' who, ſome way or other, have come at a
' clear Knowledge of their Progenitors. No
' matter tho' what they ſay be deſtitute of
' probable or neceſſary Proofs : We cannot re-
' fuſe our Aſſent to theſe Children of the
' Gods, both as they profeſs to relate their
' Family Concerns, and likewiſe in due Obe-
' dience to the Laws.'—But the great CREA-
TOR having finiſhed the Production of his celeſtial Progeny, called them all together, and
ſpoke in this Manner :

" GODS of the *Gods !* whoſe Maker I am,
" and Author of your Powers, which pro-
" ceeding from Me, if I ſo will, ſhall never
" be

---

[n] Τὰ περὶ θιῶν ὁρατῶν κ̧ γεντῶν φύσεως ἰχίτο τίλΘ. 'ΑυτοΘ.
[o] Page 275.

Let.19. " be diſſolved! Whatever hath been tyed, can
        " be unloofed; but to undo what has been
        " well done, or deſtroy an harmonious Frame,
        " is malicious and evil. Wherefore, as you
        " have once received a Being, immortal in-
        " deed, or indiſſolvable, you are not; yet
        " ſhall you never be diſſolved, nor taſte the
        " Deſtiny of Death; my unchangeable Will
        " being a greater and more authentic Security
        " than the Bonds of Life, in which you were
        " bound at your Creation.   Now then at-
        " tend and learn what I appoint and enjoin.
        " Three Species of mortal Creatures are yet
        " to be made: While theſe are wanting, the
        " *Heaven* will be imperfect, which would not
        " contain every Kind of living Creature, as it
        " muſt do to be entirely compleat.   But were
        " they to be generated by me, and receive
        " under my Hand the Sources of Life, they
        " muſt likewiſe prove immortal, and be on
        " a Level with the *Gods*.   In order therefore
        " that they may both be *mortal*, and that the
        " WHOLE may indeed be compleat, do you,
        " according to your Natures, undertake the
        " Work, and imitating my Power in the
        " Production of *yourſelves*, finiſh the Ani-
        " mal Creation.   As for that Part which
        " is to be ſtiled *immortal* and *divine*, and
        " which will be the *leading Principle* in ſuch
        " of them as always wiſh to follow RIGHT
        " and Us, *that* I myſelf will create, and de-
                                    " liver

" liver over to you : Then, for what remains, Let. 19.
" do you, interweaving the *Mortal* with *Im-*
" *mortality*, form and generate Animals, nou-
" rifh them with Food, and receive them to
" your Bofom when fallen to Decay."

THUS HE SPOKE : — and turning again to
the *eternal CRATER*, in which he had mixed and tempered the *Soul of the Univerfe*, he
poured on the Remains of the celeftial Creation, and mixing them together nearly after
the fame manner, but not now fo pure and
genuine as before; nor all equally fo, but of a
firft, fecond, and third Alloy, he compounded
the mighty Mafs, and diftributed *Minds* equal
in number to the Stars —— a Mind to every
Star ; in which having placed them as it were
in a Chariot, he fhewed them the *Nature* of
the WHOLE OF THINGS, and fixed their *irrevocable* Laws. ' Firft, that *one common Ori-*
' *gin* fhould be allotted to all, that no one
' might have lefs than another at the Hands
' of his *Maker*; but that when they were
' diffeminated each into the *Organ of Time*
' (heavenly Body) proper to them, they fhould
' produce the moft religious and God-like of
' mortal Creatures, MAN. But as the *human*
' *Nature* was to be twofold, the better Sex was
' to be called the *Male*. And fince they were
' of courfe to be tranfplanted into *Bodies*, now
' in Contact, and now at a diftance from fur-

C c   ' rounding

Let.19. ' rounding Objects, in the firſt place *one ge-*
' *neral Senſe* muſt be natural to all, eſpecially
' a Perception of external Violence: Next,
' mutual LOVE, but mixed with *Pleaſure* and
' *Pain*; and along with theſe *Fear* and *An-*
' *ger*, with all their Conſequences, and all their
' Contraries. *Theſe Paſſions*, if they can *com-*
' *mand*, they ſhall live in Juſtice and Felicity;
' but if *commanded* by them, in Wrong and
' Miſery: And whoſoever lives well his allot-
' ted Time, ſhall after Death return to the
' Habitation of his congenial Star, and there
' lead a bleſſed Life; but failing, he muſt at
' next Birth aſſume the *Female* Nature. Both
' Male and Female, after a thouſand Years,
' ſhall by Lot enter upon a *ſecond* State, and
' chuſe what kind of Life each pleaſes to lead;
' when it ſhall ſometimes happen, that a
' human Soul ſhall come to animate a wild
' Beaſt; and if even there it do not refrain
' from its wonted Wickedneſs, it ſhall, at the
' various Turns of Birth, always change to
' that Species of a Brute, whoſe Manners it
' laſt copied: Nor ſhall it ever be diſintang-
' led, and arrive at the End of its Sufferings,
' until it hath performed an equal Period to
' that in which it contracted its Droſs and
' Dregs, the Cauſe of its Deformity; and
' then having maſtered by Reaſon the irra-
' tional tumultuous Appetites ariſing from
' Fire

' Fire and Water, Earth and Air, it re-attain
' the purer Species of its *firſt* and *beſt* Exi-
' ſtence.'

THE eternal Laws of *Being* and *Happineſs*
thus eſtabliſhed, that the Creator might be free
of the Evil incident to the Creature, he diſſemi-
nated the MINDS he had made, ſome into the
Sun, ſome into the *Moon,* ſome into the other
Members of TIME: And after their Diſſemina-
tion, he empowered the recent Deities to form
mortal Bodies, and whatever was to be joined
with the human Soul. This, and all that enſues
upon their Conjunction, *they* are to frame and
govern in the beſt and moſt excellent manner
poſſible, that the mortal Creature may not
prove the Source of Evil to itſelf. And now
the CREATOR, having thus ordained all Things,
remained in his *firſt* Eſtate, worthy of his
Nature; while his *Sons* obſerving their Parent's Command, and receiving at his Hand
an *immortal Principle* of a *mortal Creature,*
imitated their Maker; and borrowing a Par-
ticle from each of the four Elements, Fire,
Water, Earth and Air, which they were again
to repay, they fitted them together, and created MAN.

WHETHER *PLATO* drew his Doctrine
concerning theſe *inferior* Gods, *Intelligences*
animating the Sun, Moon, and Planets, im-

mediately

Let. 19. mediately from CHALDEA (where they had
them ranged into

Thrones, Dominions, Princedoms, Virtues, Powers,

and confidered them as Attributes and Emana-
tions of the *fupreme* Being[a]) or whether it was
traced back from the firft Ideas of his national
Religion to their *eaftern* Source, is at prefent of
little Importance. The Queftion that calls
our Attention, and arifes from the Subject, is,
How natural it muft be in confequence of
fuch Doctrine, for blind Devotion to lead
Men into *Star-Worfhip*, even while the Unity
of the *Moft High* GOD was demonftrated by
the *Zabians*, and the Eternity and unchangeable Godhead of the great CREATOR, was
afferted by *Pythagoras* and *Plato?* So true it
‘ is, that new adopted Deities, from fome Out-
‘ fkirts of the Scheme, make way for a Mul-
‘ tiplication of Myfteries, and that for a Re-
‘ lapfe into Ignorance and Credulity.’ This
affects not only the bewildered Bulk of Mankind, but even thofe who profefs to follow a
more refined Plan, and to practife the fublimeft Piety. For many Ages after *Plato*,
his

[a] אוריאל *Uriël*, the FIRE or LIGHT of GOD. גַּבְרִיאֵל
Gabriel, the STRENGTH of GOD. עַבְדִיאֵל *Abdiël*, the SER-
VANT of GOD. מִיכָאֵל *Michaïl*, who is LIKE GOD? And in
the Book afcribed to *Enoch* (which feems to have been a *Chaldean Allegory* of the World, as *Sanchuniathon's* is a *Phenician*)
the chief Angel is SEMEXAS, the prime *Servant* of GOD שמש
the SUN. AMARIEL, the WORD of GOD. ARAKIEL, the
MARSHAL of GOD. RAMIEL, the ARCHER of GOD, the
EKHBOΛOΣ of the *Greeks*, &c. The *Jews* make frequent mention of Angels after the *Babylonifh* Captivity.

his Followers continued to teach nearly the same Doctrine concerning the Deity: But in later Times some great Proficients in his Philosophy, seem, I say *seem*, to have substituted the Power of the Sun to that of a supreme Mind and eternal Providence [b].

This is that alluring Worship of the grand *Luminary*, the Source of Light and Life in the material World, which I observed was the widest spread and of the longest Continuance. It is not confined to our Hemisphere; it reaches round the Globe, and co-extends with the human Race; there being hardly a People who, at some Time or other, have not paid Homage to his all-chearing Ray. Take one curious Instance of a great Nation, who are at this Day *solar* Idolaters.

In *North America* there is a fine Country, lying between thirty-three and thirty-seven Degrees of North Latitude. It is a vast Valley, bounded on the East and North by a Chain of high Mountains called the *Apalates;* by the barbarous Province of *Tagouësta,* or *Tegesta,* on the South; and on the West by the *Rio del Spirito santo* (which they call *Hitanachi*) and some little Hills that lie between it and the *Cofakites.* The present Inhabitants of this Country, have no Records but Tradition: They have the *Complexion, Features, Hair,* and particularly the *Eyes of*

the

[b] ΙΟΥΛΙΑΝ. ΥΜΝ. ἰ; ΒΑΣΙΛΕΑ ΗΛΙΟΝ. Macrobius.

Let.19. the moſt northern *Tartars* ; as alſo a great
Reſemblance of their Manners, Language,
and Government. Two Tribes, the *Houſta-
mins* and *Elamins*, wander yet through the
Wilds of *Florida*, in the *Tartar*-Faſhion. The
reſt were perſuaded by their *Paracouſſe* (Prince)
MAYRDOC to ſettle in *Apalachia*, about nine
or ten Days Journey from the Sea, with which
they communicate by means of the *Hitanachi*,
which diſcharges itſelf into the Gulph of
Mexico.

THE APALAKITES, planted in a happy
Soil, ſoon taſted the Sweets of good Order
and Policy. They turned populous, ſent Colonies ſouthward, and were, in their Turn,
attacked by the northern *Coſakites*. Part of
theſe coaleſced with the *Apalakites*, and Part
having been expelled, wandered down to the
Sea-Coaſt, paſſed over into the *Antilles*, and
were termed *Caraïbes*, that is, *Strangers*, or
Warriors added to the Nation. As for their
Religion, the *Apalakites*, and moſt Part of the
Americans, *worſhip the* S U N, whoſe Beams
they believe to be of ſuch Virtue, as to give
Life and Motion to every living Thing :
From *him*, they ſay, the various Species of
Animals draw Vigour and Health, the Hills
and Vales their Fruitfulneſs, and the World
itſelf its Stability and Duration.. Their daily
Worſhip is ſimple and pure ; they ſtand in
the

the Door of their Houfe; they falute him at Let.19.
his Rifing, and fing Hymns to his Praife.
On folemn Days, inftead of putting Beafts to
Death in Honour of the Source of Life, they
burn Perfumes, and celebrate in Songs his
Glory and Beneficence. This is accompanied
with Alms to the Poor, and fuch Prefents to
their *Jaouäs* (Priefts) who are likewife their
Phyficians, as are neceffary for their Subfift-
ence. Their grand Temple is a fpacious
CAVE of wond'rous Form and Extent, on
the Top of Mount *Olaïmi*, about three Miles
diftant from MELILOT, the Capital of the
Province of *Bemarin*, and the royal Seat.

NOR was the Doctrine of MAN's Creation
by the GODS, confined to *Afia* or *Greece*; it
came northward with the Defcendants of
the *Tartar* Tribes that over-ran *Europe*, the
Goths and *Vandals*[c]. ' The GODS, faid thefe
' Northerns, made the firft MAN of an *Aſh-*
' *Tree*, and called him Aʃkur (*Æſc*) and his
' Wife Embla (*Embla*). They were at firft
' lifelefs Lumps, without Speech or Motion;
' until three of the celeftial Race, mighty
' and mild Aeʃars (*Aſers*) coming to a cer-
' tain Place, found the wretched *Æſk* and
' *Embla* lying helplefs on the Beach. *Breath*
' they had not, nor *Blood*—neither had they
' *Reafon*, nor a *beautiful Face*. ODIN gave
' them

C c 4

' Page 278. Note [1]

Let. 19. ' them Breath, HENER Reafon, and LODUR
' gave Blood, and a beautiful Face d.'

IT muft be allow'd that *Philofophy* and *Religion* make not always a good Affociation;
yet I cannot recollect any one Inftance of
Learning's having flourifhed in a Nation, without introducing the Belief of *one fupreme Being* among its prime Favorites.   Keep the
Reftriction fteadily in View, that it is of the
Heathen Nations I fpeak, and you may confider them as moft *religious,* or rather as moft
fincere in their Religion, when they are moft
fimple and virtuous in their Manners;—not in
the higheft Meaning of the Expreffion, but
leaning to that Part of Virtue we call So-
briety and Innocence : But they are *pureft* in
their Belief at the Period of their greateft
Knowlege; which however belongs only to
a chofen *Few,* and can never extend to the
Generality of an idolatrous People.   *Plutarch,*
in one of his Treatifes, fpeaking of a future
State, tells, That when Philofophy was at its
Height in *Athens,* a comic Writer, the celebrated *Menander,* with two or three Lines of a
Play, had filled all *Greece* with Terror and
Superftition.   Great muft his Character have
been, and no lefs their Credulity ! *Human
Life* is the verieft *Proteus* in the World.
The Manners of Men and Nations are in a
perpetual Flux; their Laws, Cuftoms, and
                                   Religion,

* EDDA SÆMUND. ex Cluf·pa. Apud Hickes.

Religion, like their Habits, are ever ſhifting
Modes ; and, as the humorous Poet ſays,

―――*Now natural, now ſtrange* ;
Subject to Time, and Whim, and ſlippery Change.

But, with his Permiſſion, that Inſtability is
not wholly owing to *Caprice* : Could we trace
their Hiſtory, unravel their Politics, and compare Circumſtances and Conjunctures, we
would find that the *Neceſſity of their Affairs,*
in the various Turns of their Fortune, produced the Variation.

THE *CIRCLE, My Friend!* is drawn ;
my Promiſe is fulfilled ; the Opinions of the
ANCIENTS concerning the Riſe and Government of the World, are faithfully ſet before
you. You have, in the general Plan of
Mythology, firſt the *grand Key,* ' That the
' Powers producing, and Parts compoſing
' the Univerſe, were their greateſt GODS ;'
and then the *Out-Lines* directing to the peculiar Nature of their ſeveral Deities. Shou'd
we deſcend lower, and enquire into all their
Attributes, Rites, and Operations, the Detail
would be endleſs, and not very ſatisfactory.
Who can pretend to aſcertain the particular
Aſpect of Things, that *pleaſing Proportion,*
or *faſcinating Species,* that every ſpeculative
Man, of a different Country and Character,
took for a *View* of the Divinity ? Leſs ſtill
can

Let. 19. can we be abſolutely ſure of their Symbols and Ceremonies, depending upon the deep-laid Deſigns of a Prieſt, or the heated Imagination of a Poet. The minute Application muſt be therefore left, as *Religion* was, of old, to every one's own particular Turn and Extent of Capacity.

NATURE IS FULL OF WONDERS;—Her Operations are marvellous; her Proportions divine; their Effects are ſtriking and powerful; and the finer the Genius, — the wider the Underſtanding, the more lively are the Senſations of her ſilent Beauties. But according to the infinite Varieties of the human Mind, both as different in itſelf, and more diverſified by the various Modes of *Education, Climate, Accidents,* and *Train of Life,* ſo different are our Conceptions of *Nature,* and of the Powers and Connexions that influence Mankind.

Now, Time was when each of theſe Powers, and every Type and Reſemblance of them, was *deïfied;* when their mutual Dependencies, Sympathies, Antipathies, and chief Operations, figured either as Steps of a *Pedigree* in the Genealogy of the GODS; or as *War in Heaven,*—Plots and Counter-plots among the jarring Deities, which were ſometimes amicably adjuſted, and ſometimes ended in ſuch fatal Cataſtrophies as Caſtrations,

Uſur-

Ufurpations, and Imprifonment; — not told
alike in every Nation; — but *differently*, as
the Caufes above-mentioned made them ftrike
differently upon the Mind of the *Patriarch*,
Prieft, or *Lawgiver*, that modelled the Infant-State: — While above them all,

The P O E T's Eye, in a fine Frenzy rolling,
Did glance from Heaven to Earth, from
Earth to Heaven ;
And as Imagination bodied forth
The Forms of Things unknown, the Poet's Pen
Turn'd them to Shape, and gave to airy Nothing
A local Habitation and a Name.

F I N I S.

INDEX.

LETTER

INDEX.

10

INDEX.

INDEX.

INDEX.

rather

INDEX.

D d

INDEX.

pure

and

INDEX.

INDEX.

INDEX.

INDEX.

INDEX.

INDEX.

E e

INDEX.

F I N I S.

The two following Books by the AUTHOR *of the* LETTERS *concerning* MYTHOLOGY.

I. A N Enquiry *into the* LIFE *and* WRITINGS *of HOMER.* In 12 Sections. The Book is properly an Anfwer to this Queftion : " By what Fate, or Difpofition of Things it has " happened, that no Poet has equalled him for 2700 Years, nor " any, that we know, ever furpaffed him before ?" Sect. I. An Enquiry into *Homer*'s Country and Climate. II. Into the public Manners of his Nation. III. Into his Language : Origin of Language. IV. Into his Religion : Origin of the *Grecian* Rites. V. Into the Manners of the Times : ancient and modern Manners compared. VI. Into the Influence of fuch a Conjecture. VII. Into *Homer*'s Education and Learning : Hiftory of Learning, and preceding Writers. VIII. Into his Character, Employment, and Manner of Life. IX. His Journey to *Egypt :* His Allegories. X. His vifiting *Delphi :* Rife of Oracles and Theology. XI. His Converfe with the *Phenicians :* His Miracles. XII. His Subject : The *Trojan* War, and Wanderings of *Ulyffes.* With a new Head of *Homer,* and 16 Copper Plates done by the greateft Mafters : As alfo a new Map of *Greece,* and of the Countries known to the ancient *Greeks* about the Time of the *Trojan* War ; their ancient Names, and firft Inhabitants, with a Draught of the Voyages of *Menelaus* and *Ulyffes. The Second Edition.* Price bound 6 *s.*

II. PROOFS of the Enquiry into *HOMER*'s LIFE and WRITINGS, tranflated into *Englifh :* Being a Key to the ENQUIRY; with a curious Frontifpiece. Price ftitch'd 2 *s.*

N. B. *A fmall Number of the above two Books are printed on large Paper.*